CONTENTS

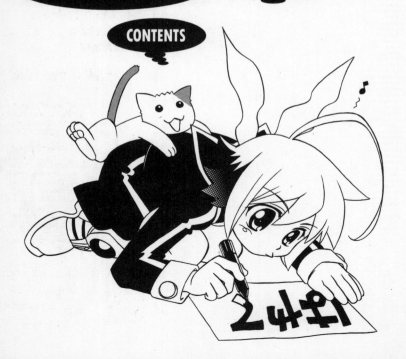

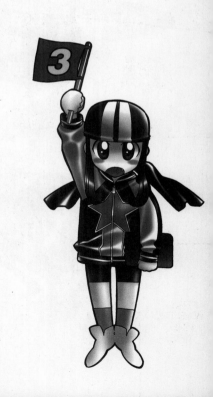

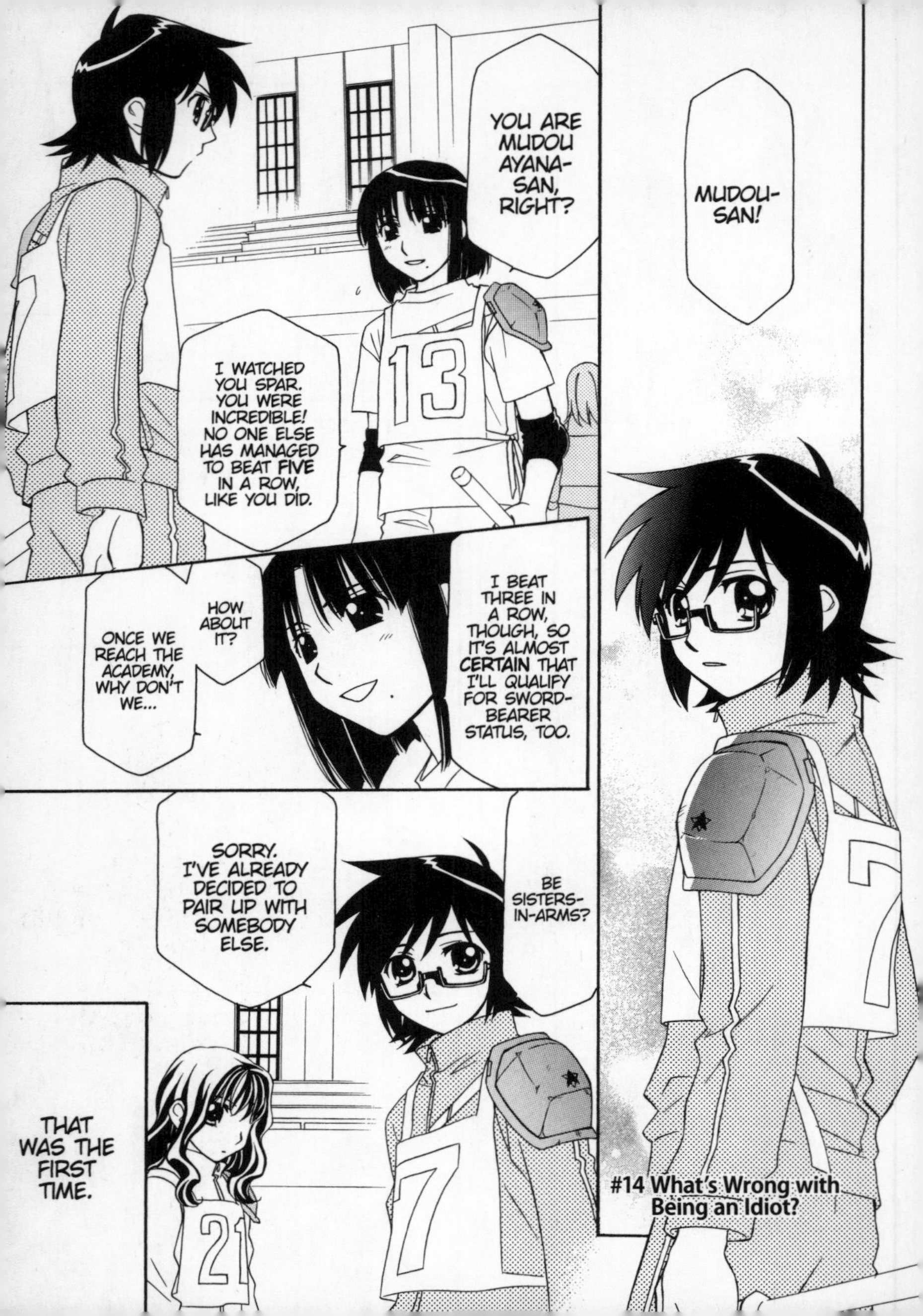
MUDOU-SAN!
#14 What's Wrong with Being an Idiot?
YOU ARE MUDOU AYANA-SAN, RIGHT?
I WATCHED YOU SPAR. YOU WERE INCREDIBLE! NO ONE ELSE HAS MANAGED TO BEAT FIVE IN A ROW, LIKE YOU DID.
I BEAT THREE IN A ROW, THOUGH, SO IT'S ALMOST CERTAIN THAT I'LL QUALIFY FOR SWORD-BEARER STATUS, TOO.
HOW ABOUT IT?
ONCE WE REACH THE ACADEMY, WHY DON'T WE...
BE SISTERS-IN-ARMS?
SORRY. I'VE ALREADY DECIDED TO PAIR UP WITH SOMEBODY ELSE.
THAT WAS THE FIRST TIME.

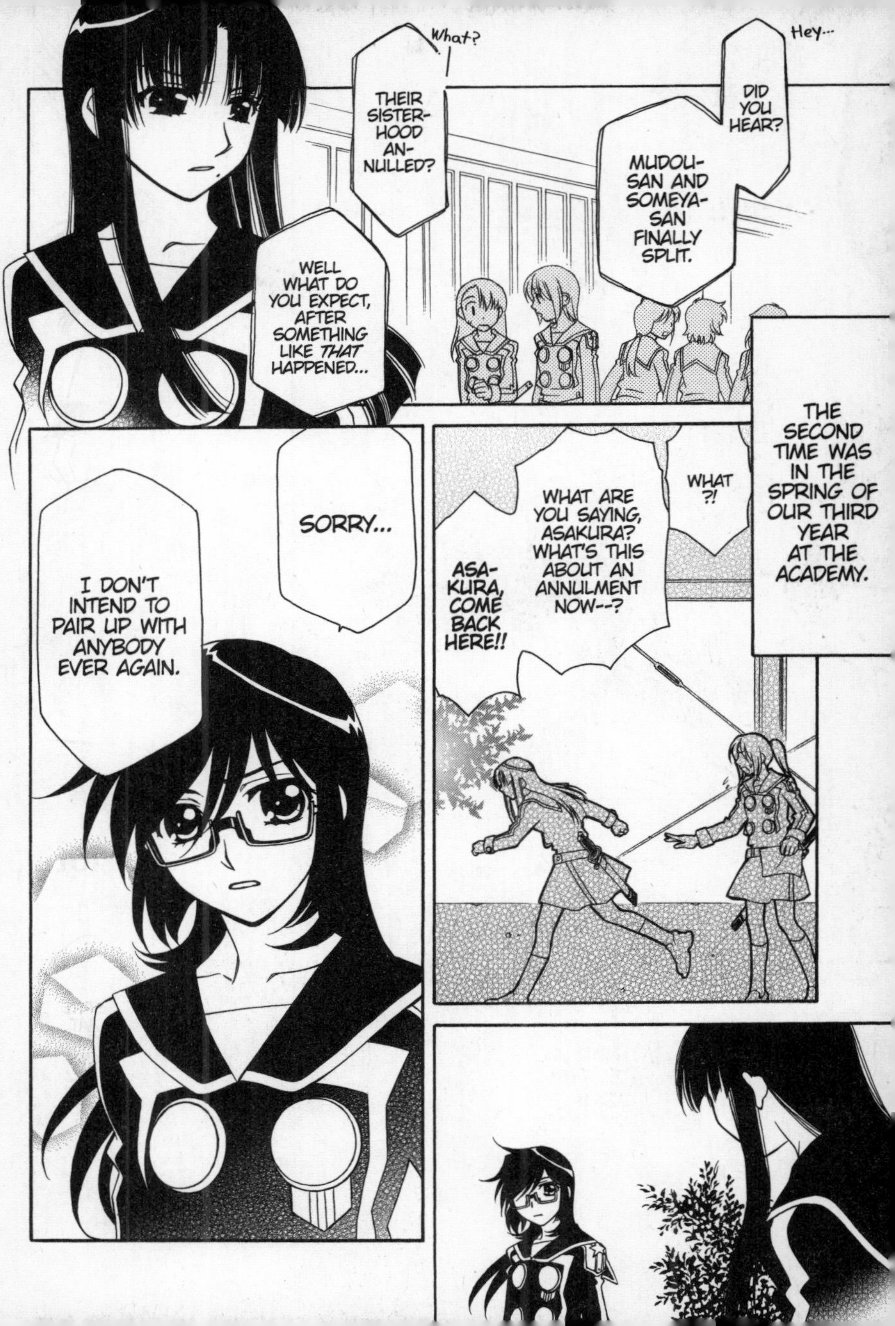
Hey...
DID YOU HEAR?
MUDOU-SAN AND SOMEYA-SAN FINALLY SPLIT.
What?
THEIR SISTER-HOOD AN-NULLED?
WELL WHAT DO YOU EXPECT, AFTER SOMETHING LIKE *THAT* HAPPENED...
THE SECOND TIME WAS IN THE SPRING OF OUR THIRD YEAR AT THE ACADEMY.
WHAT ?!
WHAT ARE YOU SAYING, ASAKURA? WHAT'S THIS ABOUT AN ANNULMENT NOW--?
ASA-KURA, COME BACK HERE!!
SORRY...
I DON'T INTEND TO PAIR UP WITH ANYBODY EVER AGAIN.

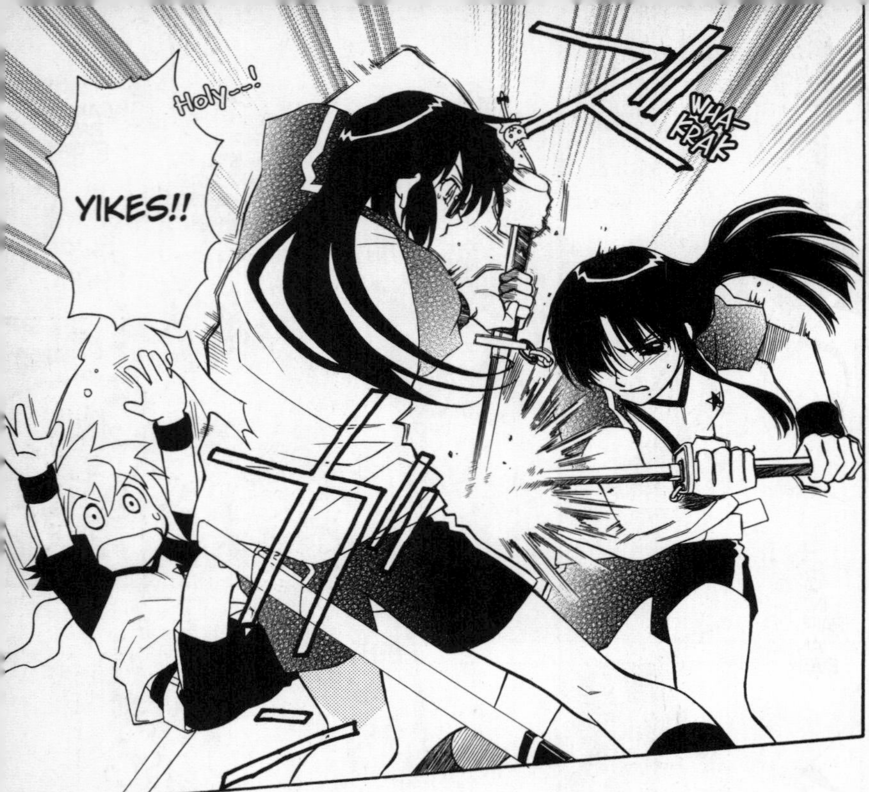
WHA-KRAK
Holy--!
YIKES!!

#14 What's Wrong with Being an Idiot?

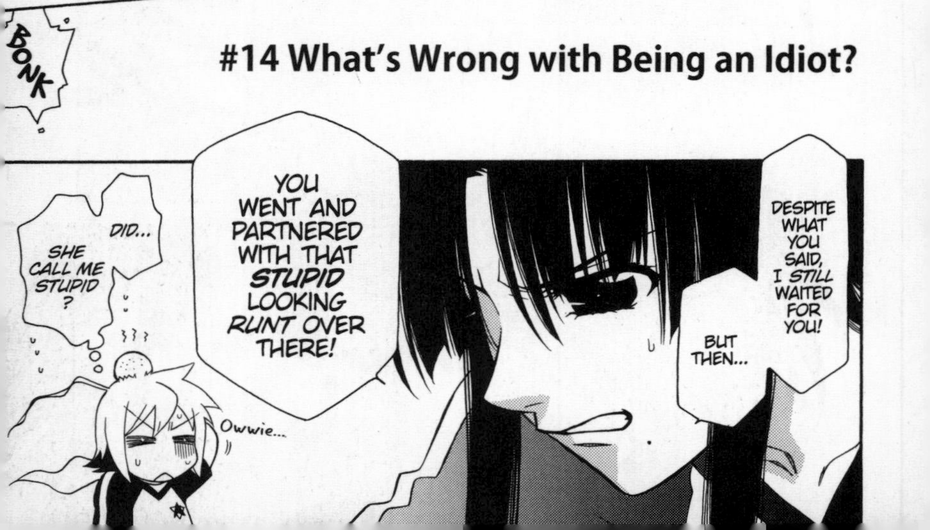
BONK
DESPITE WHAT YOU SAID, I *STILL* WAITED FOR YOU!
BUT THEN...
YOU WENT AND PARTNERED WITH THAT ***STUPID*** LOOKING *RUNT* OVER THERE!
DID... SHE CALL ME STUPID?
Owwie...

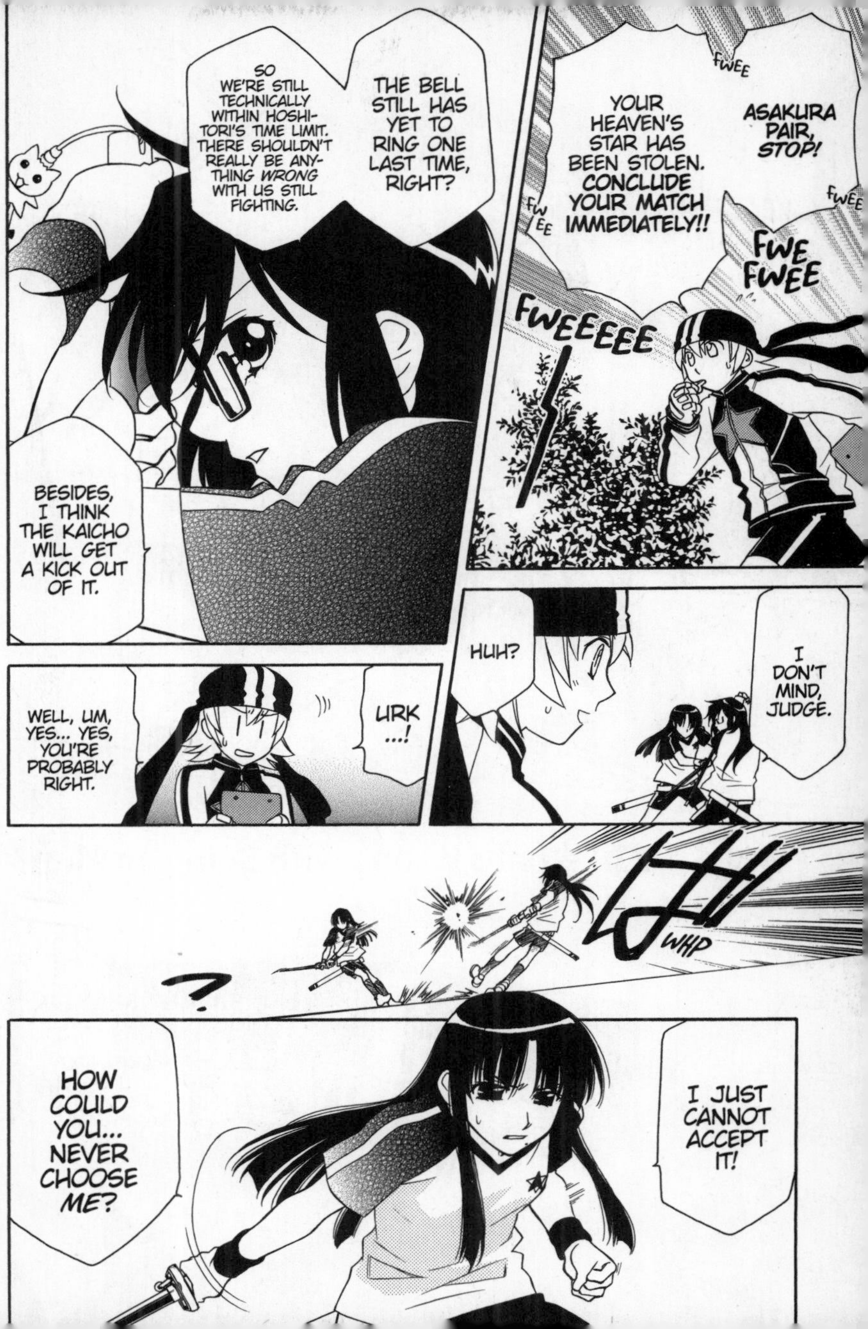
FWEE
ASAKURA PAIR, *STOP!*
YOUR HEAVEN'S STAR HAS BEEN STOLEN. CONCLUDE YOUR MATCH IMMEDIATELY!!
FWEE
FWEE
FWE FWEE
FWEEEEEE
THE BELL STILL HAS YET TO RING ONE LAST TIME, RIGHT?
SO WE'RE STILL TECHNICALLY WITHIN HOSHITORI'S TIME LIMIT. THERE SHOULDN'T REALLY BE ANYTHING *WRONG* WITH US STILL FIGHTING.
BESIDES, I THINK THE KAICHO WILL GET A KICK OUT OF IT.
I DON'T MIND, JUDGE.
HUH?
URK ...!
WELL, UM, YES... YES, YOU'RE PROBABLY RIGHT.
WHP
I JUST CANNOT ACCEPT IT!
HOW COULD YOU... NEVER CHOOSE *ME?*

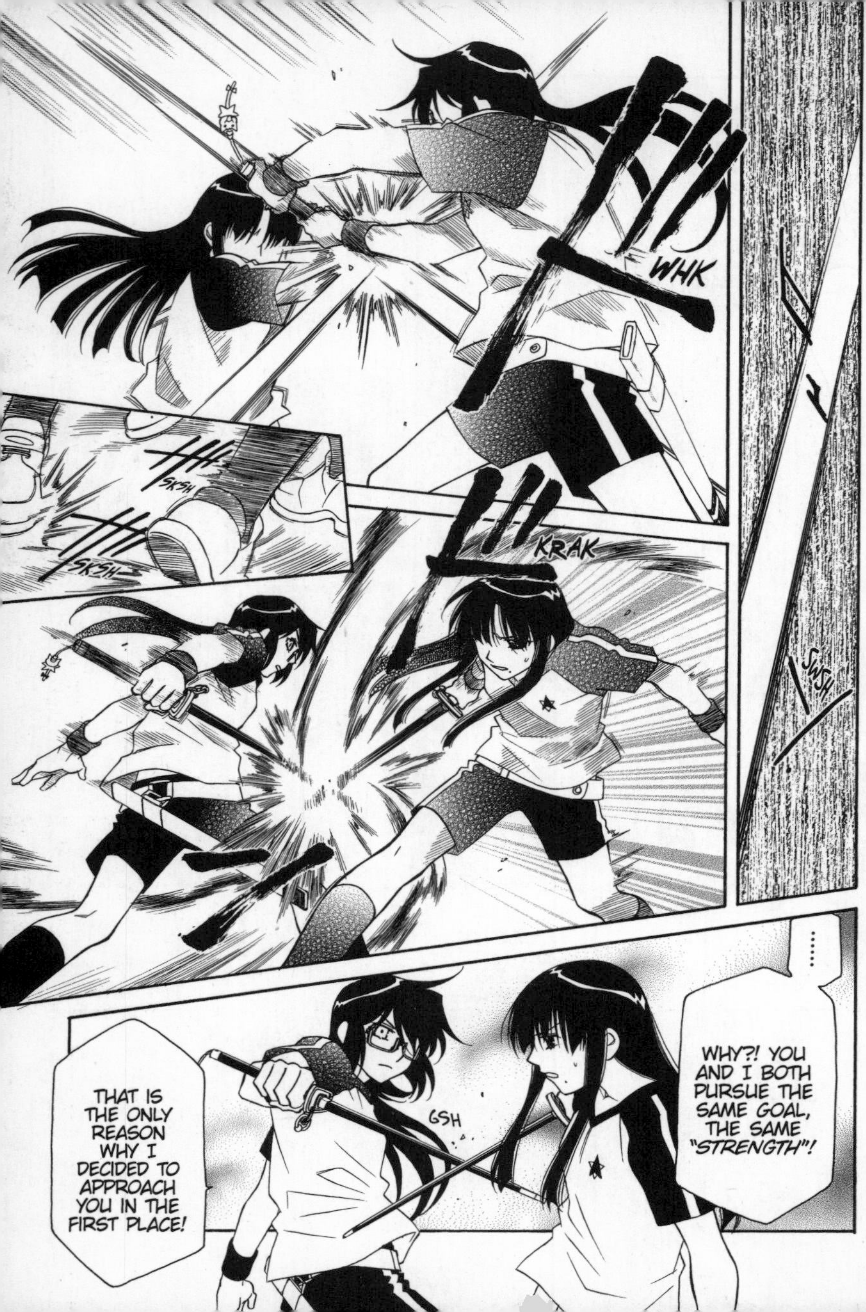
SWSH
WHK
SKSH
SKSH
KRAK
......
WHY?! YOU AND I BOTH PURSUE THE SAME GOAL, THE SAME "STRENGTH"!
GSH
THAT IS THE ONLY REASON WHY I DECIDED TO APPROACH YOU IN THE FIRST PLACE!

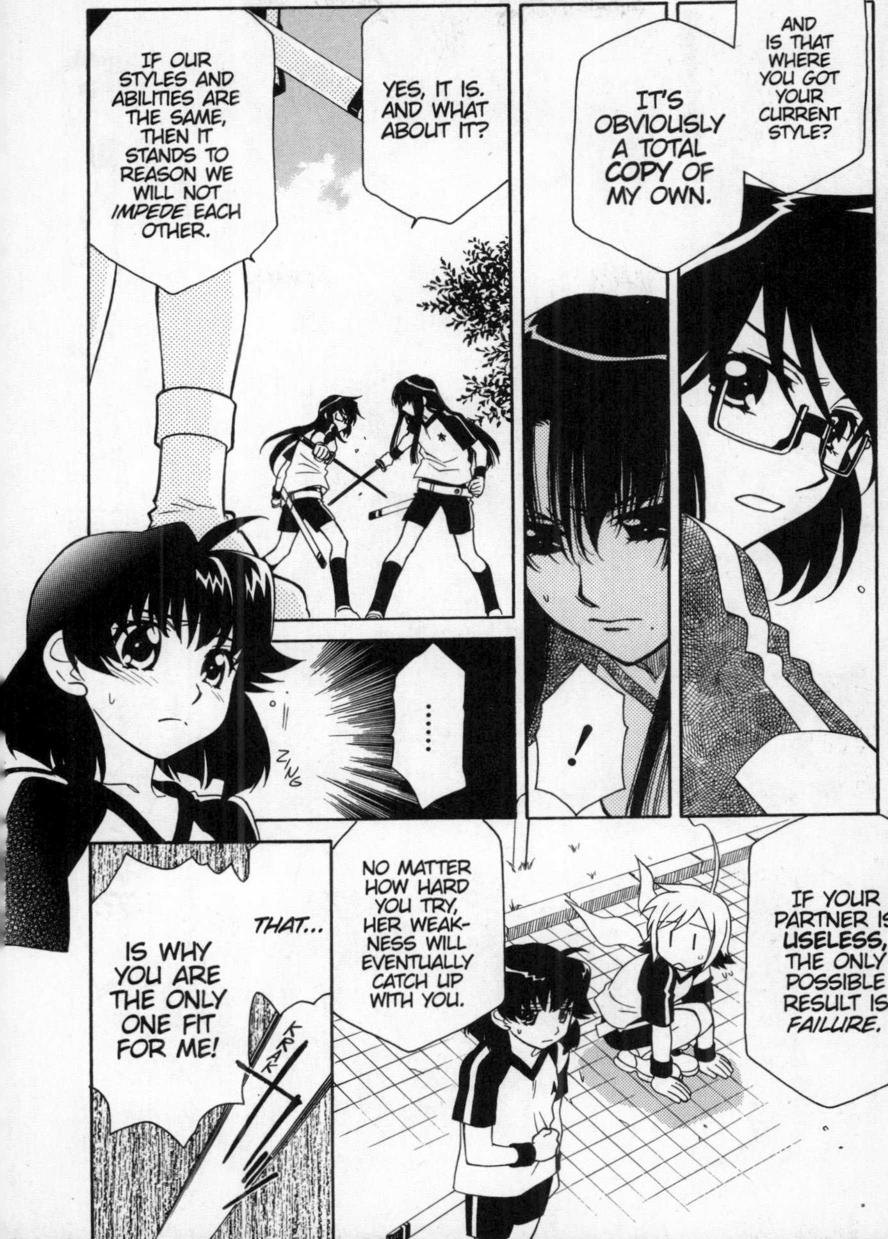
AND IS THAT WHERE YOU GOT YOUR CURRENT STYLE?
IT'S OBVIOUSLY A TOTAL COPY OF MY OWN.
!
YES, IT IS. AND WHAT ABOUT IT?
IF OUR STYLES AND ABILITIES ARE THE SAME, THEN IT STANDS TO REASON WE WILL NOT IMPEDE EACH OTHER.
......
ZING
IF YOUR PARTNER IS USELESS, THE ONLY POSSIBLE RESULT IS FAILURE.
NO MATTER HOW HARD YOU TRY, HER WEAK-NESS WILL EVENTUALLY CATCH UP WITH YOU.
THAT...
IS WHY YOU ARE THE ONLY ONE FIT FOR ME!
KRAK

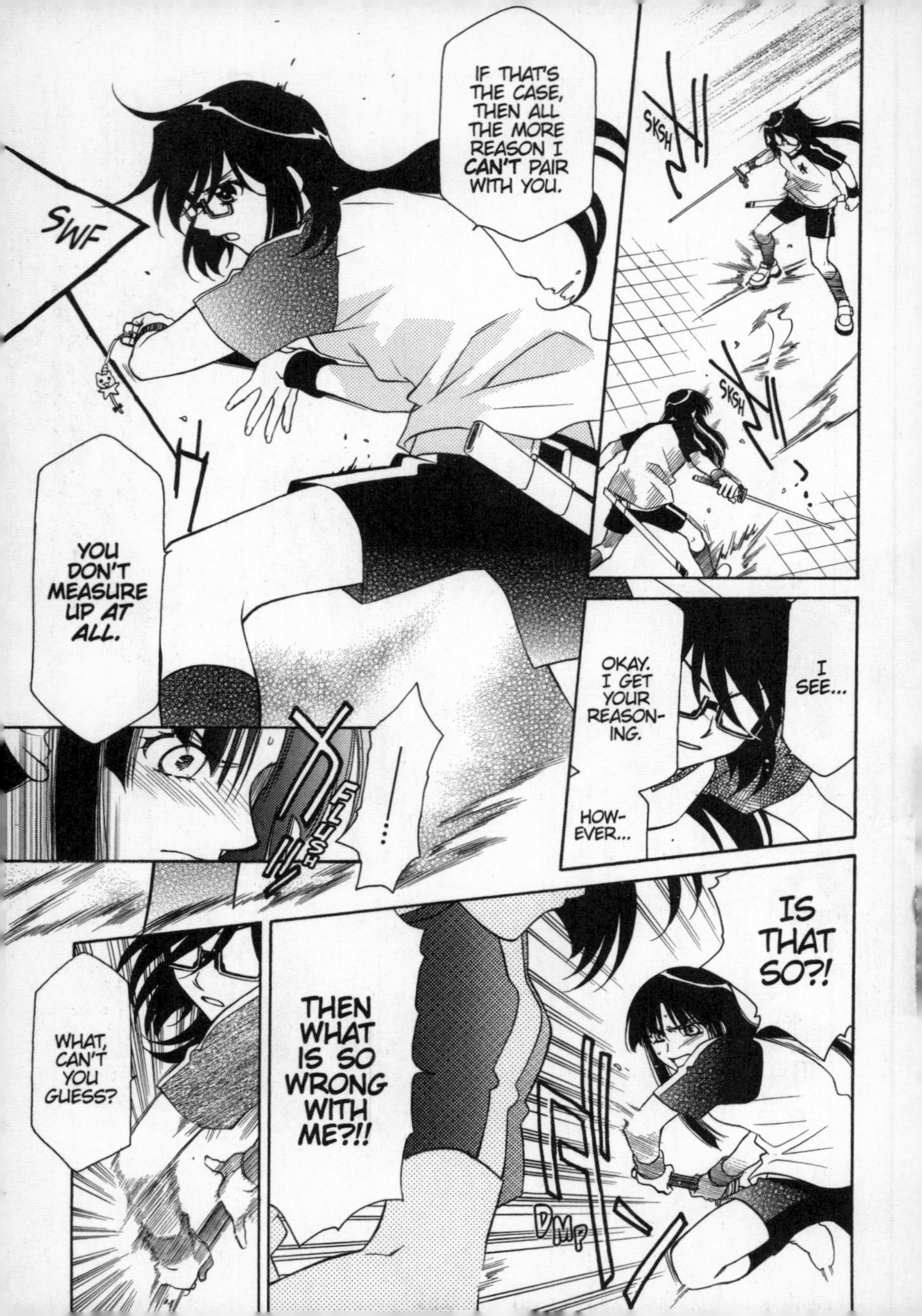
SKSH
SKSH
I SEE...
OKAY. I GET YOUR REASONING.
HOWEVER...
SWF
IF THAT'S THE CASE, THEN ALL THE MORE REASON I CAN'T PAIR WITH YOU.
YOU DON'T MEASURE UP AT ALL.
FLUSH
...
IS THAT SO?!
THEN WHAT IS SO WRONG WITH ME?!!
DMP
WHAT, CAN'T YOU GUESS?

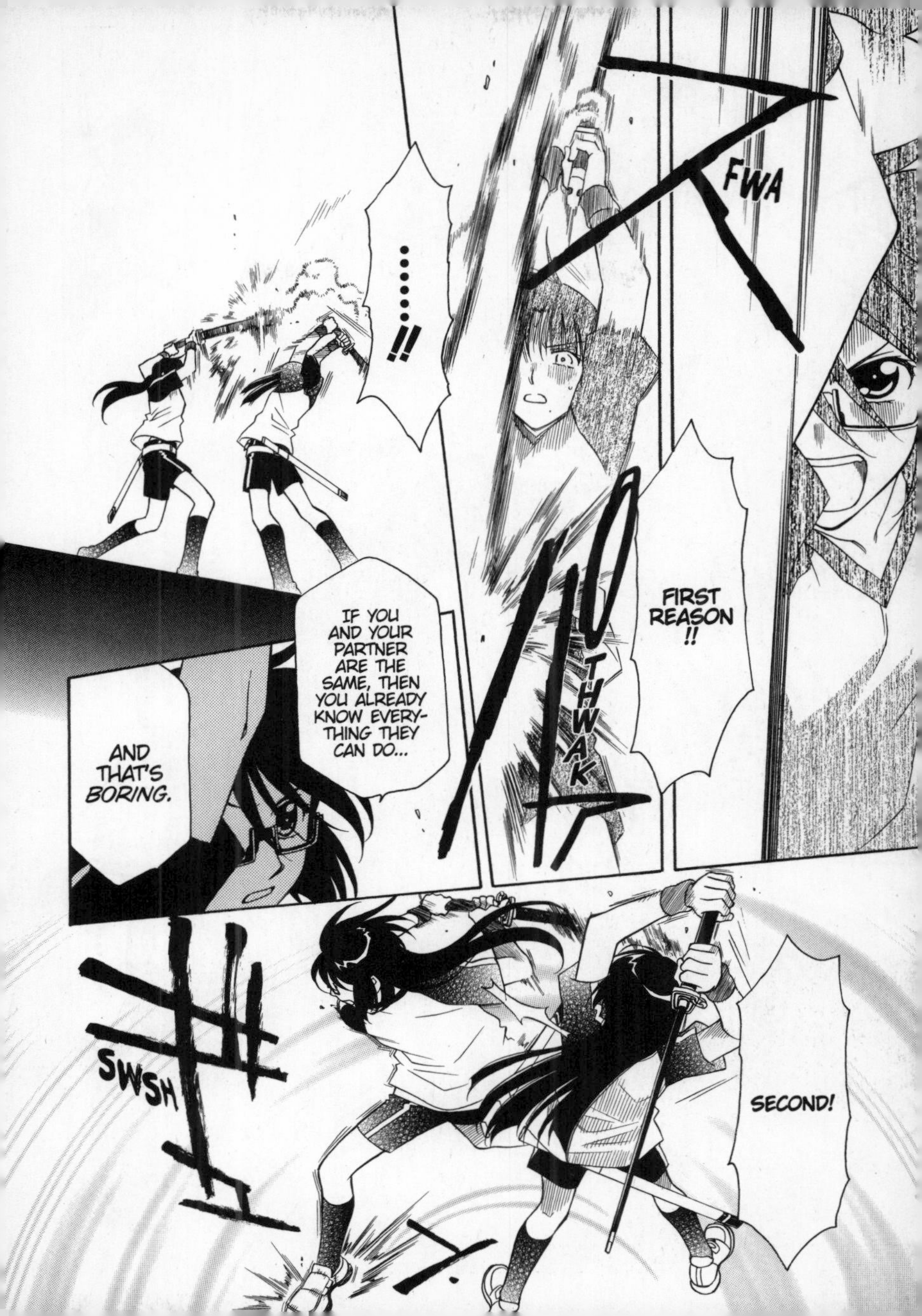
FWA
FIRST REASON !!
THWAK
......!!
IF YOU AND YOUR PARTNER ARE THE SAME, THEN YOU ALREADY KNOW EVERY-THING THEY CAN DO...
AND THAT'S BORING.
SECOND!
SWSH

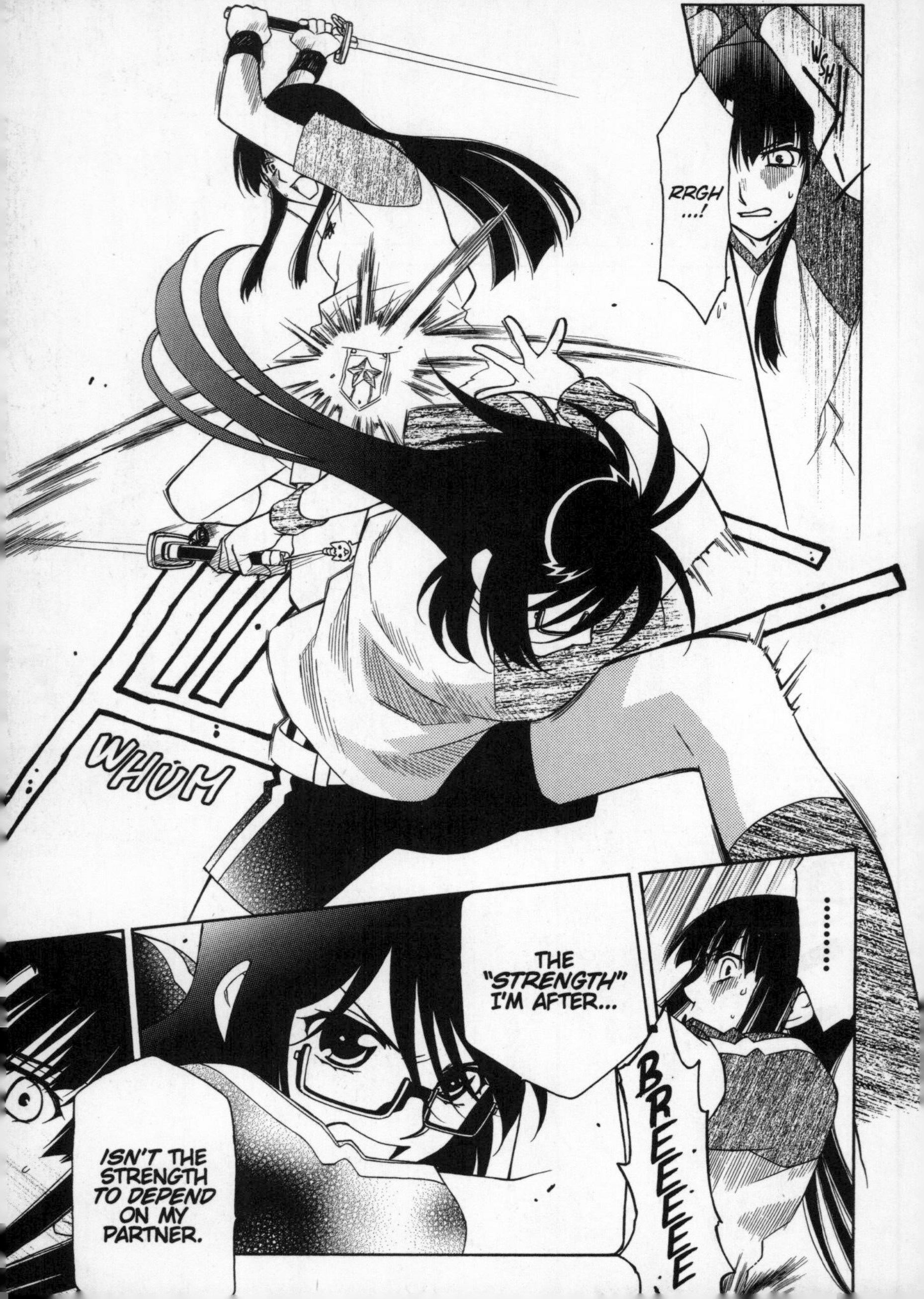
WSH
RRGH ...!
WHUM
......
THE "STRENGTH" I'M AFTER...
BREEEEEE
ISN'T THE STRENGTH TO DEPEND ON MY PARTNER.

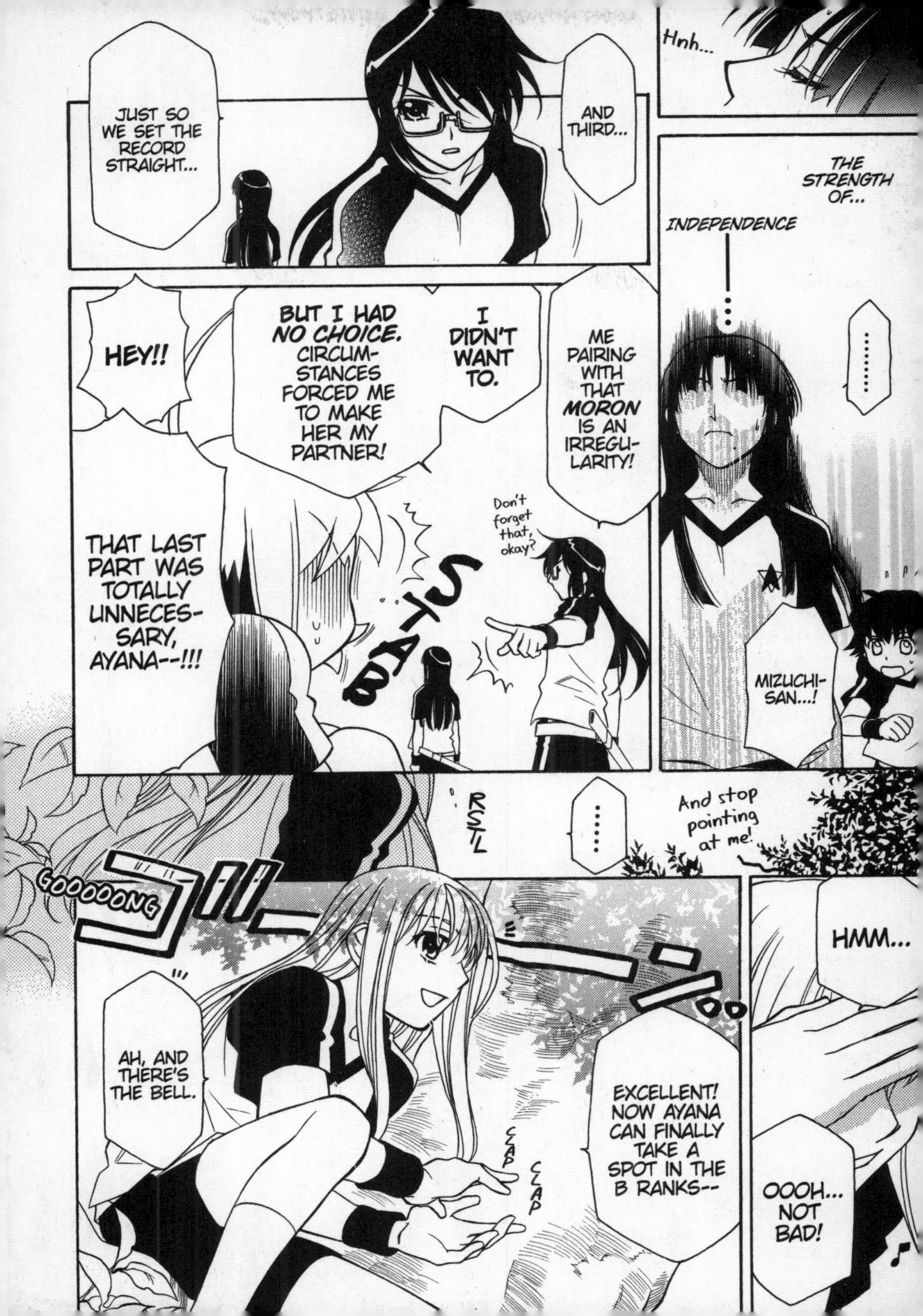

Hnh...
THE STRENGTH OF...
INDEPENDENCE
......
......
MIZUCHI-SAN...!
AND THIRD...
JUST SO WE SET THE RECORD STRAIGHT...
ME PAIRING WITH THAT *MORON* IS AN IRREGULARITY!
I DIDN'T WANT TO.
BUT I HAD *NO CHOICE.* CIRCUMSTANCES FORCED ME TO MAKE HER MY PARTNER!
HEY!!
Don't forget that, okay?
STAB
THAT LAST PART WAS TOTALLY UNNECESSARY, AYANA--!!!
And stop pointing at me!
......
RSTL
HMM...
OOOH... NOT BAD!
GOOOOONG
EXCELLENT! NOW AYANA CAN FINALLY TAKE A SPOT IN THE B RANKS--
AH, AND THERE'S THE BELL.
CLAP CLAP

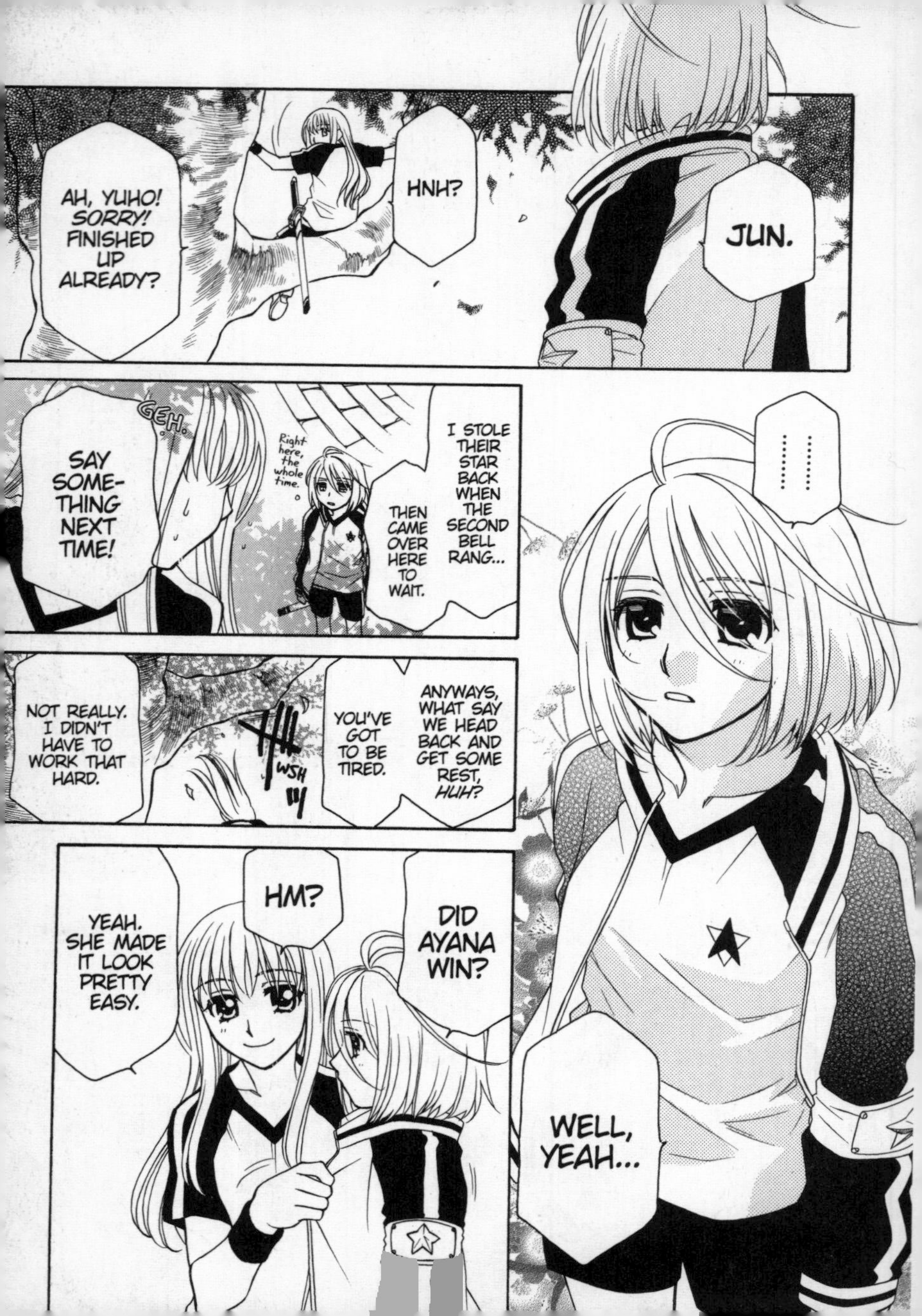
JUN.
HNH?
AH, YUHO! SORRY! FINISHED UP ALREADY?
......
WELL, YEAH...
I STOLE THEIR STAR BACK WHEN THE SECOND BELL RANG...
THEN CAME OVER HERE TO WAIT.
Right here, the whole time.
GEH.
SAY SOME-THING NEXT TIME!
ANYWAYS, WHAT SAY WE HEAD BACK AND GET SOME REST, HUH?
YOU'VE GOT TO BE TIRED.
WSH
NOT REALLY. I DIDN'T HAVE TO WORK THAT HARD.
DID AYANA WIN?
HM?
YEAH. SHE MADE IT LOOK PRETTY EASY.

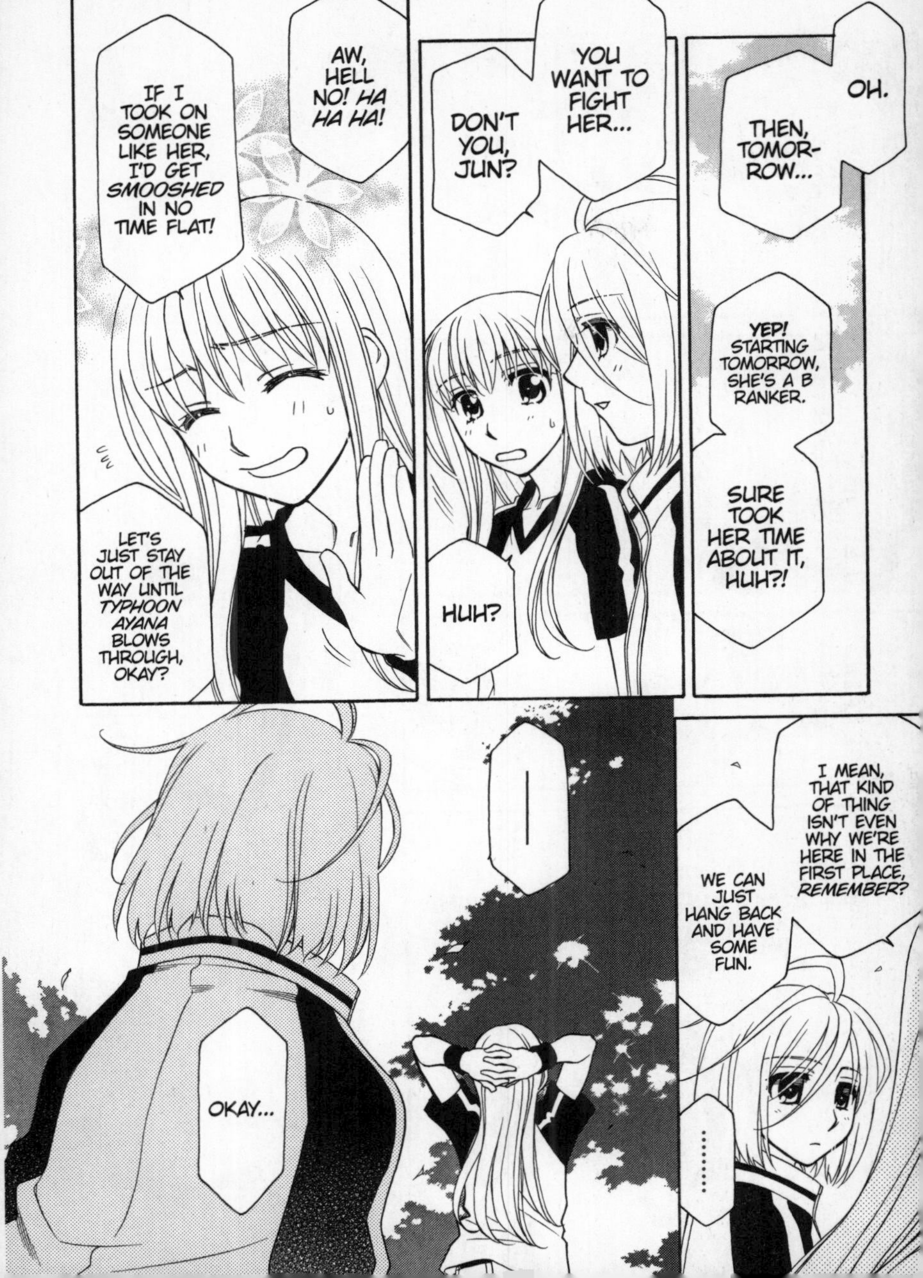
OH.
THEN, TOMORROW...
YEP! STARTING TOMORROW, SHE'S A B RANKER.
SURE TOOK HER TIME ABOUT IT, HUH?!
YOU WANT TO FIGHT HER...
DON'T YOU, JUN?
HUH?
AW, HELL NO! *HA HA HA!*
IF I TOOK ON SOMEONE LIKE HER, I'D GET *SMOOSHED* IN NO TIME FLAT!
LET'S JUST STAY OUT OF THE WAY UNTIL *TYPHOON AYANA* BLOWS THROUGH, OKAY?
I MEAN, THAT KIND OF THING ISN'T EVEN WHY WE'RE HERE IN THE FIRST PLACE, *REMEMBER?*
WE CAN JUST HANG BACK AND HAVE SOME FUN.
......
OKAY...

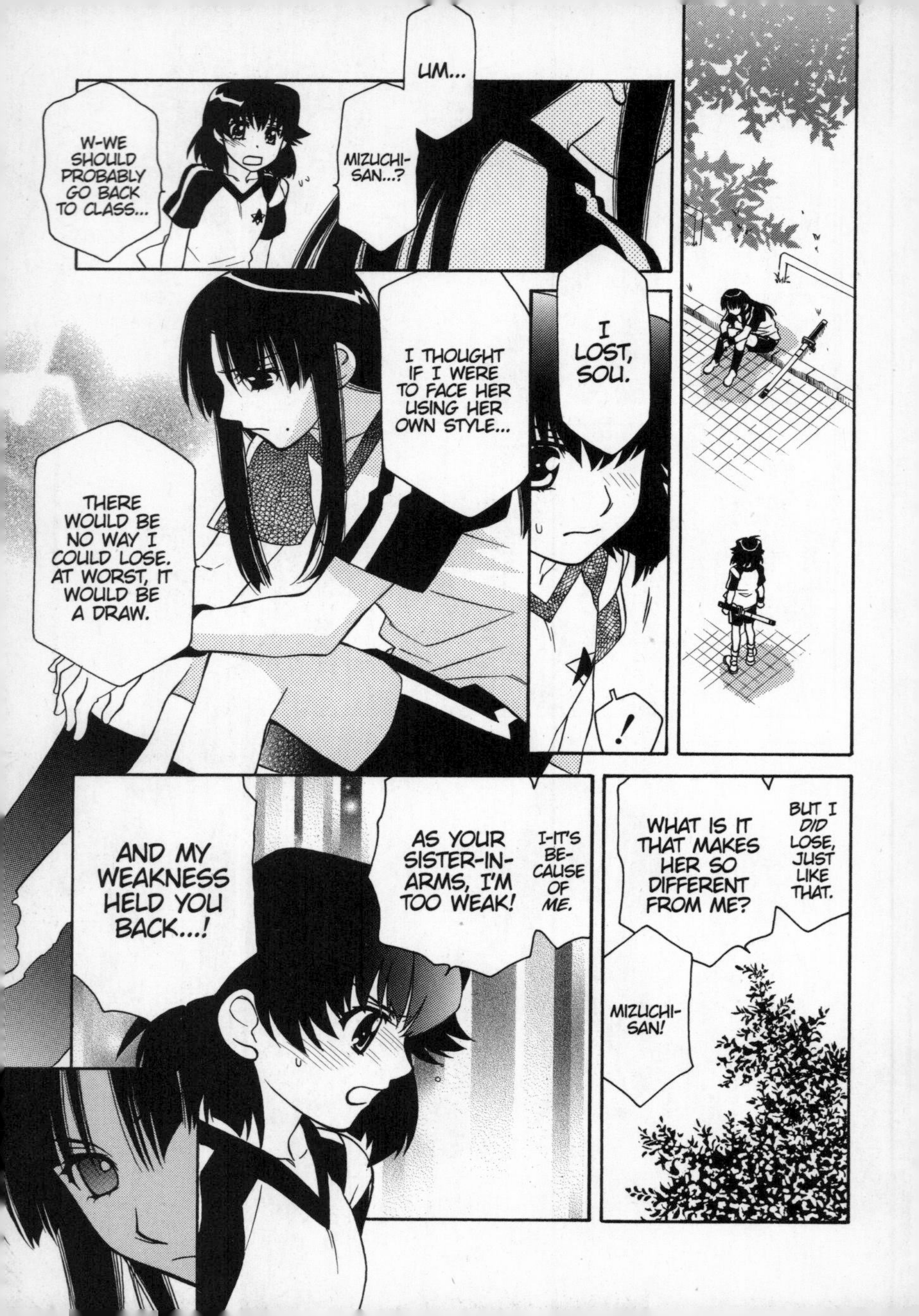
UM...
MIZUCHI-SAN...?
W-WE SHOULD PROBABLY GO BACK TO CLASS...
I LOST, SOU.
!
I THOUGHT IF I WERE TO FACE HER USING HER OWN STYLE...
THERE WOULD BE NO WAY I COULD LOSE. AT WORST, IT WOULD BE A DRAW.
BUT I *DID* LOSE, JUST LIKE THAT.
WHAT IS IT THAT MAKES HER SO DIFFERENT FROM ME?
MIZUCHI-SAN!
I-IT'S BE-CAUSE OF *ME.*
AS YOUR SISTER-IN-ARMS, I'M TOO WEAK!
AND MY WEAKNESS HELD YOU BACK...!

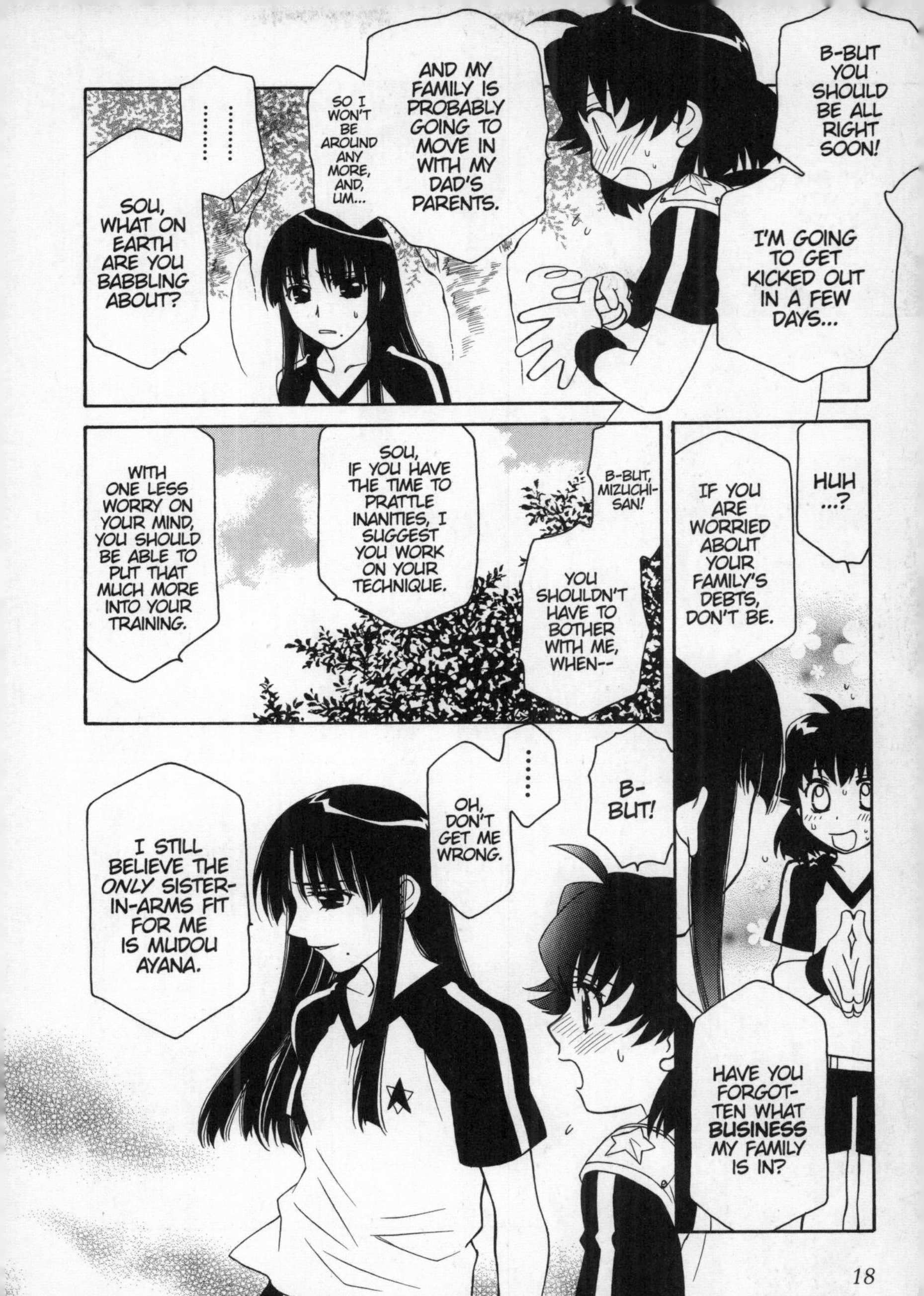
B-BUT YOU SHOULD BE ALL RIGHT SOON!
I'M GOING TO GET KICKED OUT IN A FEW DAYS...
AND MY FAMILY IS PROBABLY GOING TO MOVE IN WITH MY DAD'S PARENTS.
SO I WON'T BE AROUND ANY MORE, AND, UM...
......
SOU, WHAT ON EARTH ARE YOU BABBLING ABOUT?
HUH ...?
IF YOU ARE WORRIED ABOUT YOUR FAMILY'S DEBTS, DON'T BE.
HAVE YOU FORGOTTEN WHAT **BUSINESS** MY FAMILY IS IN?
B-BUT, MIZUCHI-SAN!
YOU SHOULDN'T HAVE TO BOTHER WITH ME, WHEN--
SOU, IF YOU HAVE THE TIME TO PRATTLE INANITIES, I SUGGEST YOU WORK ON YOUR TECHNIQUE.
WITH ONE LESS WORRY ON YOUR MIND, YOU SHOULD BE ABLE TO PUT THAT MUCH MORE INTO YOUR TRAINING.
B- BUT!
......
OH, DON'T GET ME WRONG.
I STILL BELIEVE THE *ONLY* SISTER-IN-ARMS FIT FOR ME IS MUDOU AYANA.

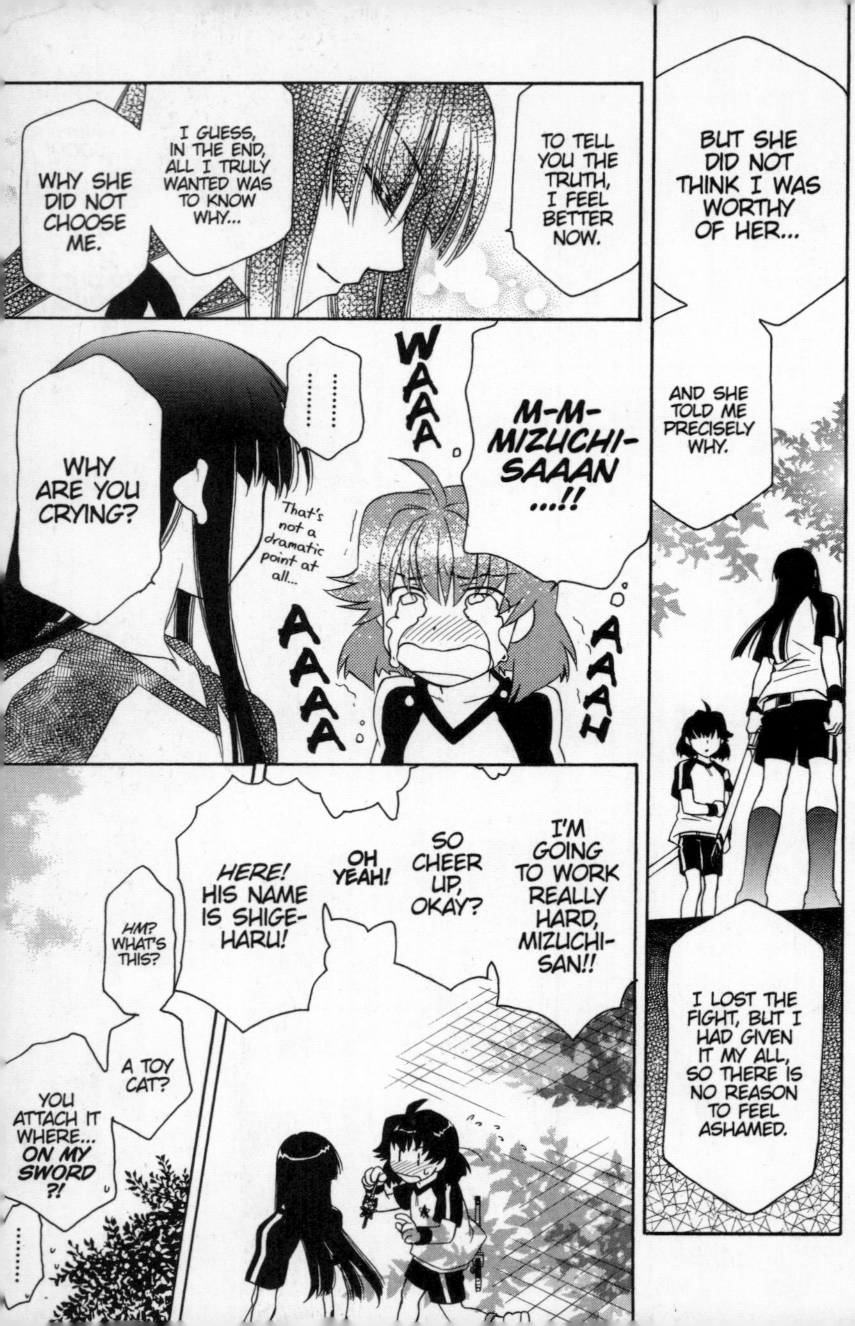
BUT SHE DID NOT THINK I WAS WORTHY OF HER...
AND SHE TOLD ME PRECISELY WHY.
I LOST THE FIGHT, BUT I HAD GIVEN IT MY ALL, SO THERE IS NO REASON TO FEEL ASHAMED.
TO TELL YOU THE TRUTH, I FEEL BETTER NOW.
I GUESS, IN THE END, ALL I TRULY WANTED WAS TO KNOW WHY...
WHY SHE DID NOT CHOOSE ME.
M-M-MIZUCHI-SAAAN ...!!
WAAA
AAAH
AAAA
......
That's not a dramatic point at all...
WHY ARE YOU CRYING?
I'M GOING TO WORK REALLY HARD, MIZUCHI-SAN!!
SO CHEER UP, OKAY?
OH YEAH!
HERE! HIS NAME IS SHIGE-HARU!
HM? WHAT'S THIS?
A TOY CAT?
YOU ATTACH IT WHERE... ON MY SWORD?!
......

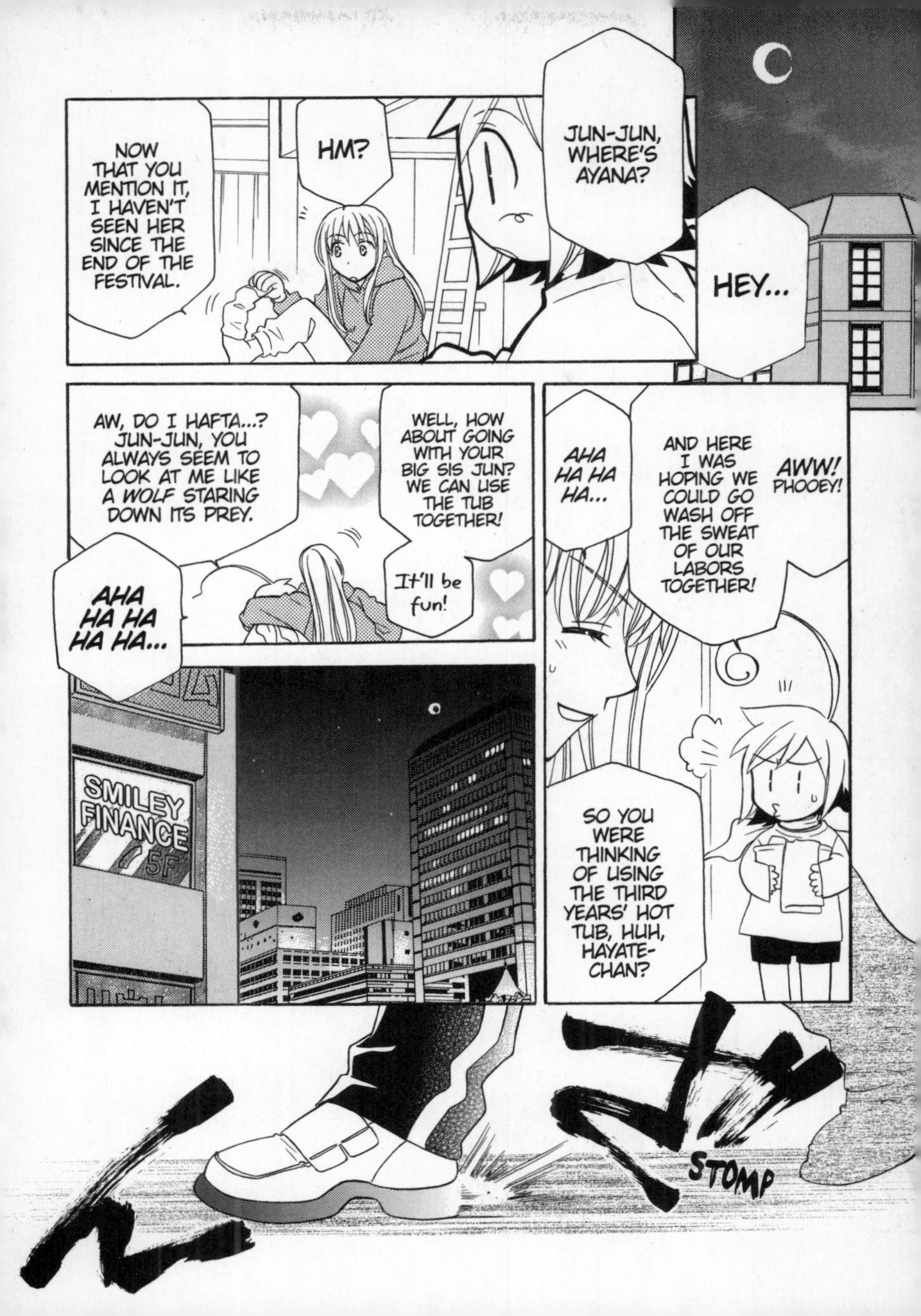
HEY...
JUN-JUN, WHERE'S AYANA?
HM?
NOW THAT YOU MENTION IT, I HAVEN'T SEEN HER SINCE THE END OF THE FESTIVAL.
AWW! PHOOEY!
AND HERE I WAS HOPING WE COULD GO WASH OFF THE SWEAT OF OUR LABORS TOGETHER!
AHA HA HA HA...
WELL, HOW ABOUT GOING WITH YOUR BIG SIS JUN? WE CAN USE THE TUB TOGETHER!
It'll be fun!
AW, DO I HAFTA...? JUN-JUN, YOU ALWAYS SEEM TO LOOK AT ME LIKE A *WOLF* STARING DOWN ITS PREY.
AHA HA HA HA HA...
SO YOU WERE THINKING OF USING THE THIRD YEARS' HOT TUB, HUH, HAYATE-CHAN?
SMILEY FINANCE
5F
STOMP

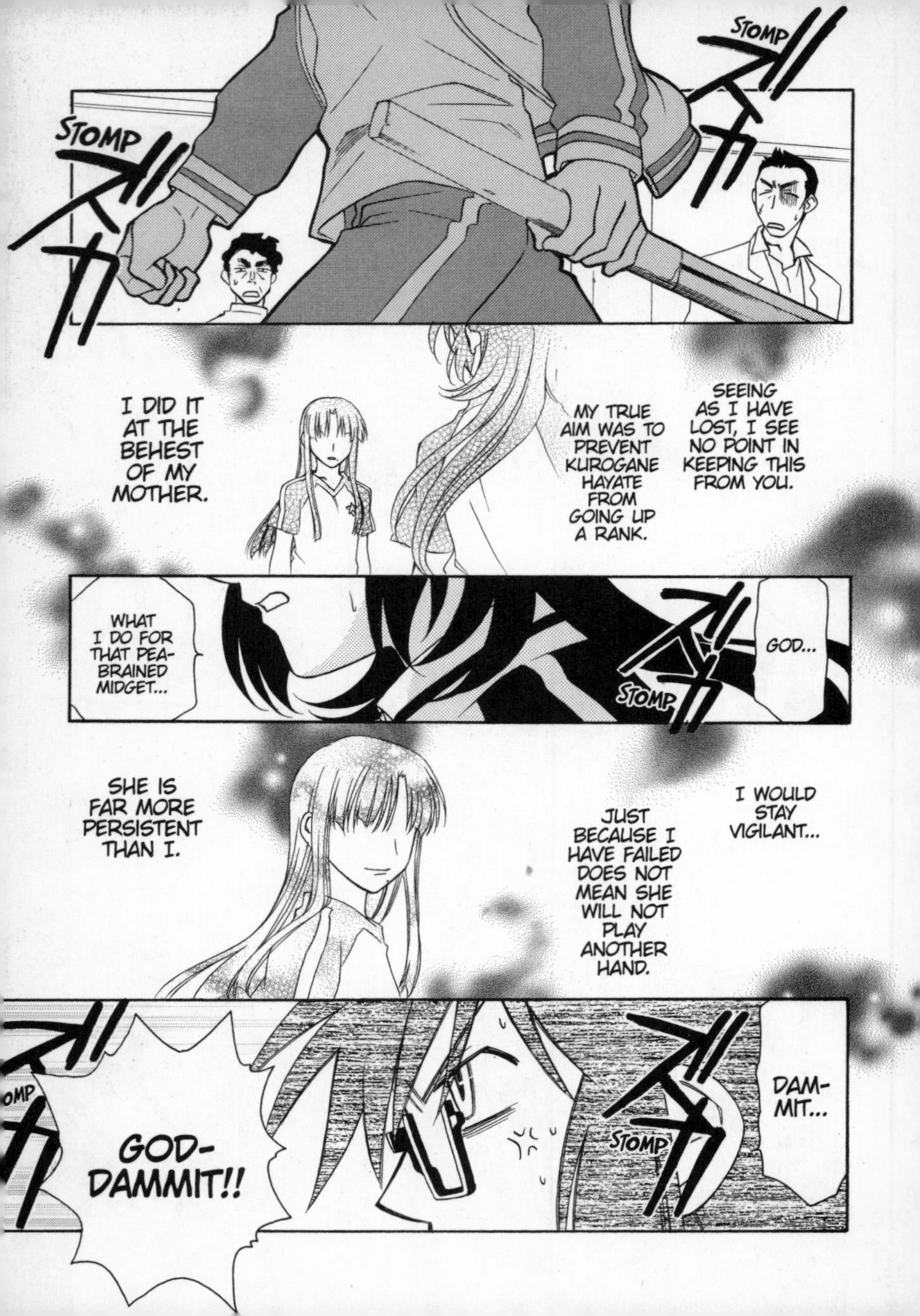
STOMP
STOMP
SEEING AS I HAVE LOST, I SEE NO POINT IN KEEPING THIS FROM YOU.
MY TRUE AIM WAS TO PREVENT KUROGANE HAYATE FROM GOING UP A RANK.
I DID IT AT THE BEHEST OF MY MOTHER.
GOD...
STOMP
WHAT I DO FOR THAT PEA-BRAINED MIDGET...
I WOULD STAY VIGILANT...
JUST BECAUSE I HAVE FAILED DOES NOT MEAN SHE WILL NOT PLAY ANOTHER HAND.
SHE IS FAR MORE PERSISTENT THAN I.
DAM-MIT...
STOMP
GOD-DAMMIT!!

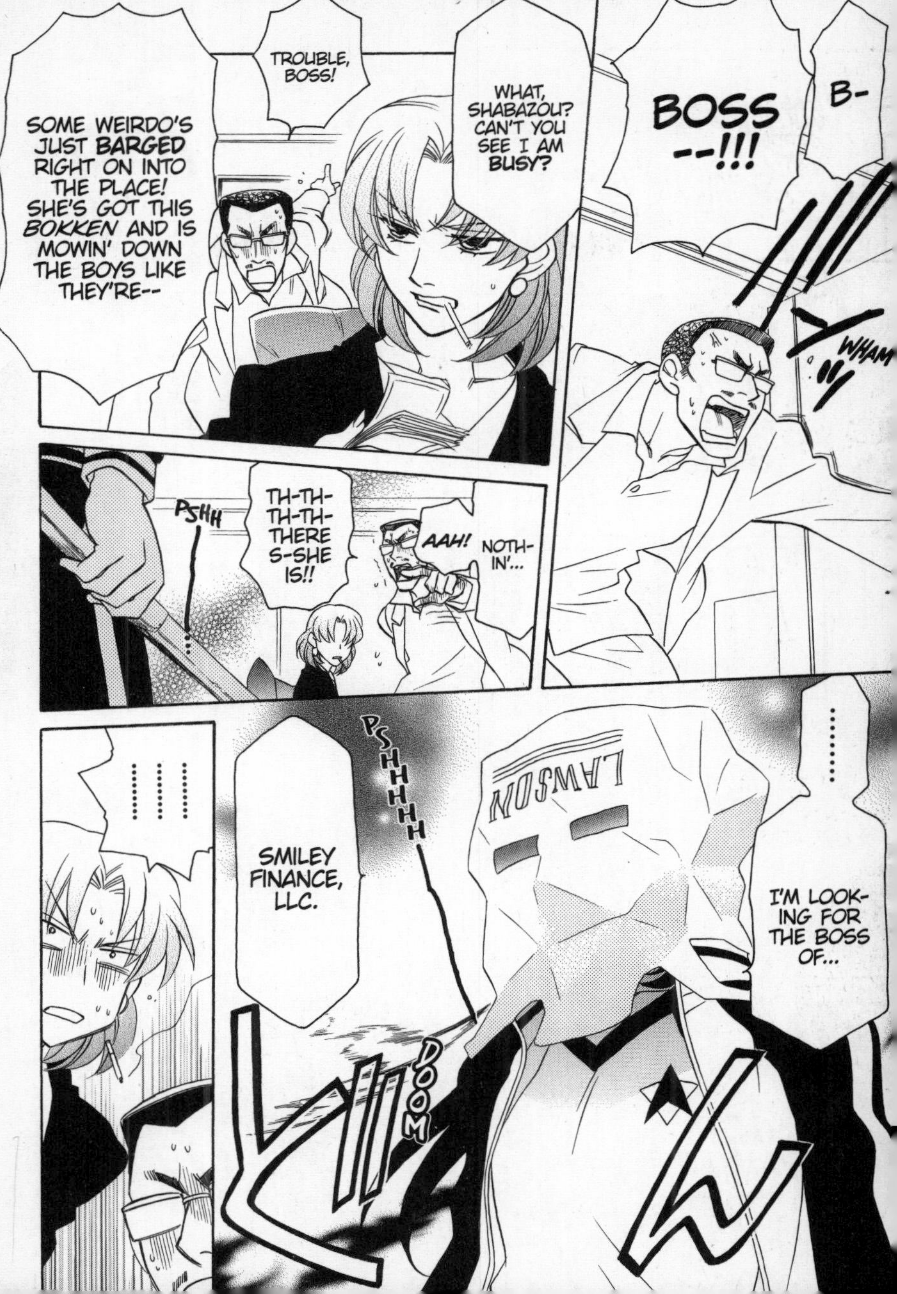
B-
BOSS --!!!
WHAM
WHAT, SHABAZOU? CAN'T YOU SEE I AM BUSY?
TROUBLE, BOSS!
SOME WEIRDO'S JUST BARGED RIGHT ON INTO THE PLACE! SHE'S GOT THIS *BOKKEN* AND IS MOWIN' DOWN THE BOYS LIKE THEY'RE--
NOTH-IN'...
AAH!
TH-TH-TH-TH-THERE S-SHE IS!!
PSHH
......
I'M LOOK-ING FOR THE BOSS OF...
LAWSON
SMILEY FINANCE, LLC.
PSHHHHHH
DOOM
....

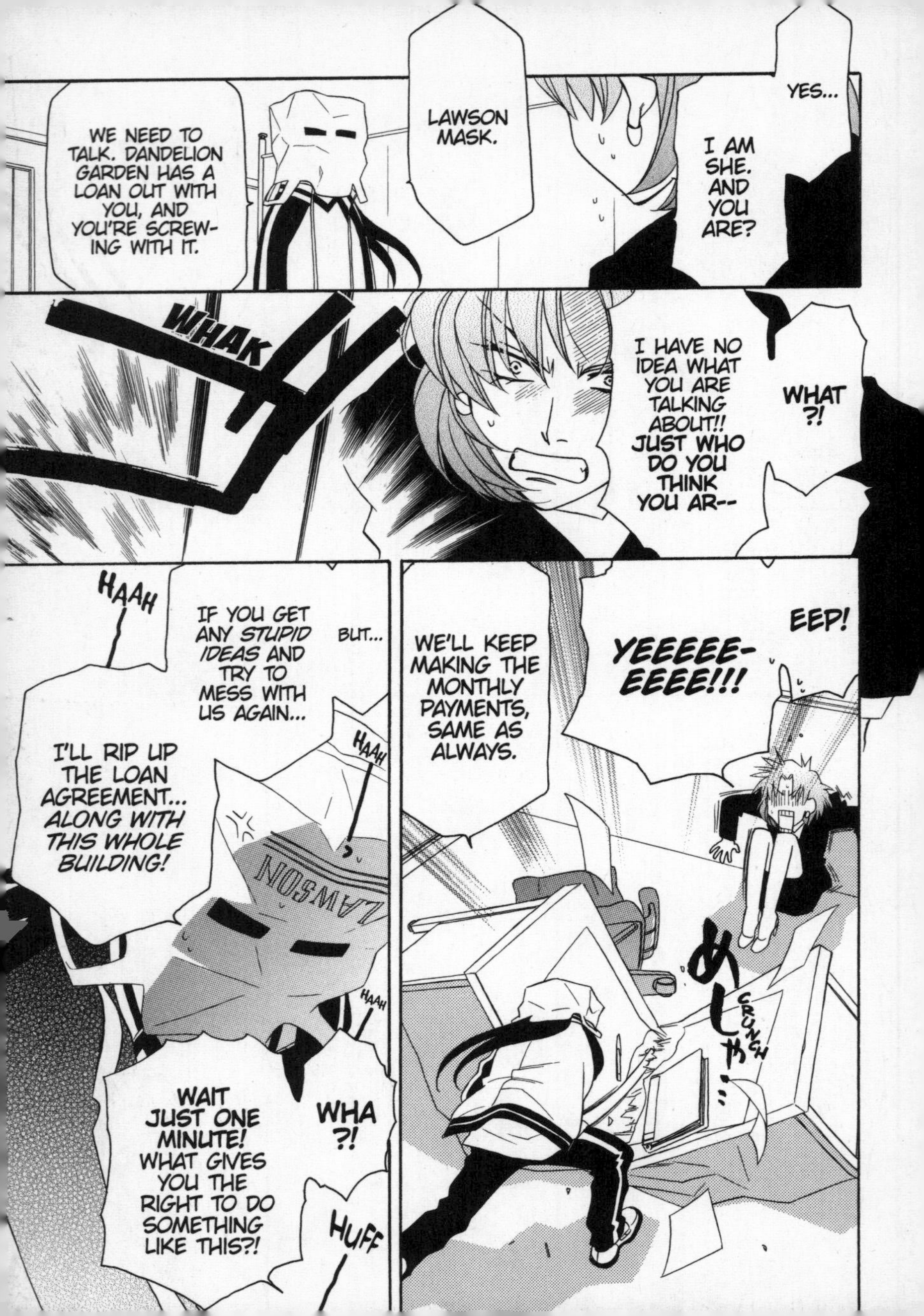
YES...
I AM SHE. AND YOU ARE?
LAWSON MASK.
WE NEED TO TALK. DANDELION GARDEN HAS A LOAN OUT WITH YOU, AND YOU'RE SCREW-ING WITH IT.
WHAT ?!
I HAVE NO IDEA WHAT YOU ARE TALKING ABOUT!! JUST WHO DO YOU THINK YOU AR--
WHAK
EEP!
YEEEEE-EEEE!!!
めしゃ…
CRUNCH
WE'LL KEEP MAKING THE MONTHLY PAYMENTS, SAME AS ALWAYS.
BUT...
IF YOU GET ANY *STUPID IDEAS* AND TRY TO MESS WITH US AGAIN...
HAAAH
I'LL RIP UP THE LOAN AGREEMENT... *ALONG WITH THIS WHOLE BUILDING!*
HAAH
HAAH
WHA ?!
WAIT JUST ONE MINUTE! WHAT GIVES YOU THE RIGHT TO DO SOMETHING LIKE THIS?!
HUFF

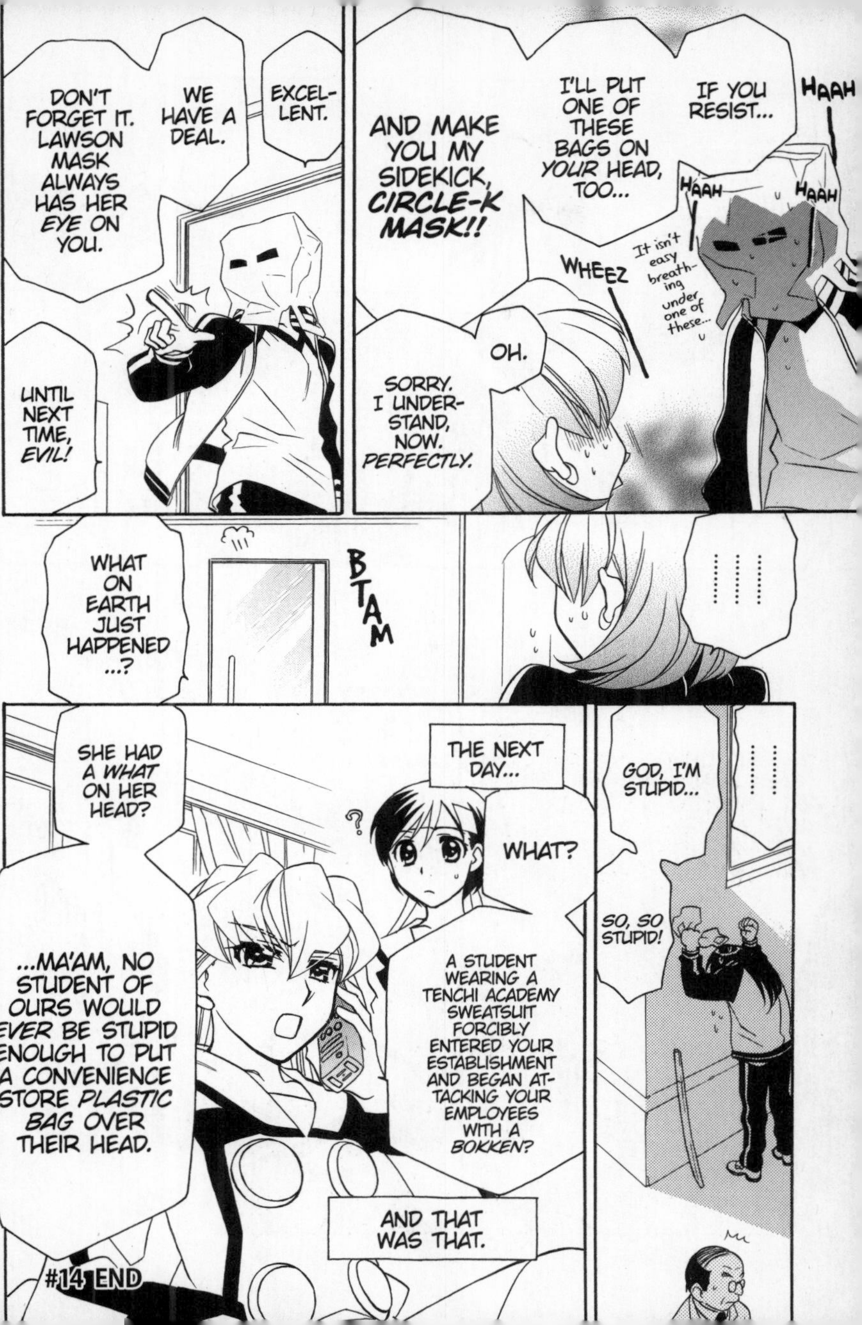
IF YOU RESIST...
I'LL PUT ONE OF THESE BAGS ON YOUR HEAD, TOO...
AND MAKE YOU MY SIDEKICK, CIRCLE-K MASK!!
HAAH
HAAH
HAAH
It isn't easy breathing under one of these...
WHEEZ
OH.
SORRY. I UNDERSTAND, NOW. PERFECTLY.
EXCEL-LENT.
WE HAVE A DEAL.
DON'T FORGET IT. LAWSON MASK ALWAYS HAS HER EYE ON YOU.
UNTIL NEXT TIME, EVIL!
......
BTAM
WHAT ON EARTH JUST HAPPENED...?
......
GOD, I'M STUPID...
SO, SO STUPID!
THE NEXT DAY...
WHAT?
SHE HAD A WHAT ON HER HEAD?
A STUDENT WEARING A TENCHI ACADEMY SWEATSUIT FORCIBLY ENTERED YOUR ESTABLISHMENT AND BEGAN AT-TACKING YOUR EMPLOYEES WITH A BOKKEN?
...MA'AM, NO STUDENT OF OURS WOULD EVER BE STUPID ENOUGH TO PUT A CONVENIENCE STORE PLASTIC BAG OVER THEIR HEAD.
AND THAT WAS THAT.
#14 END

HAYATE
HAYATE CROSS BLADE
BLADE

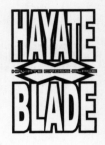

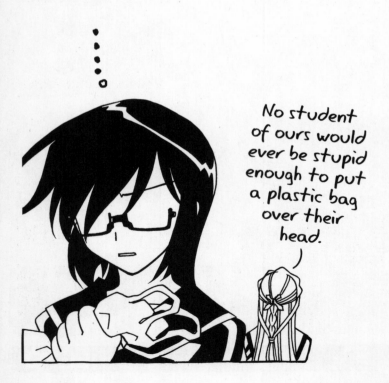

.....
No student of ours would ever be stupid enough to put a plastic bag over their head.

TENCHI ACADEMY STAFF LIST

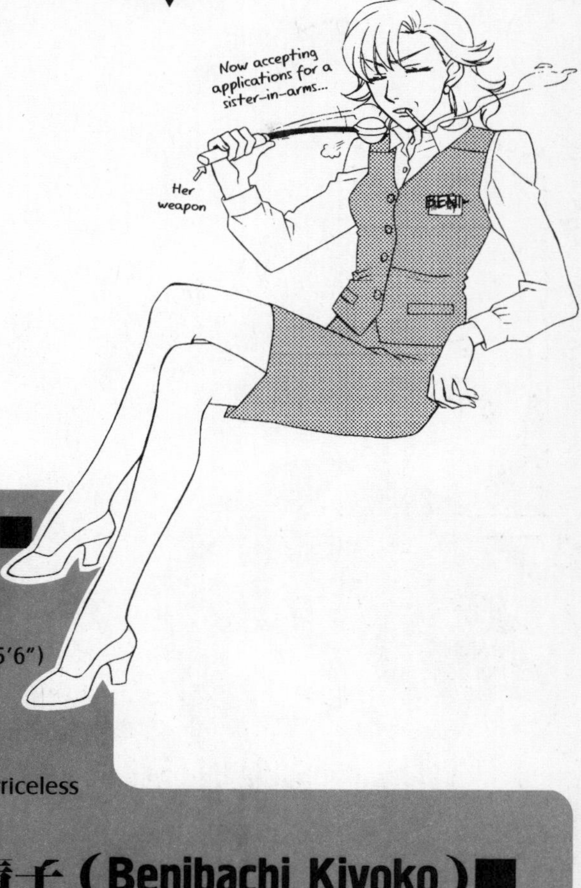
Now accepting applications for a sister-in-arms...
Her weapon

■DATA■

Office Clerk

Height: 167cm (5′6″)

Age: 46
(now & forever)

Blood Type: A

Favorite Word: Priceless

■紅蜂清子 (Benibachi Kiyoko)■

#15 She Who Rings the Bell is an Idiot

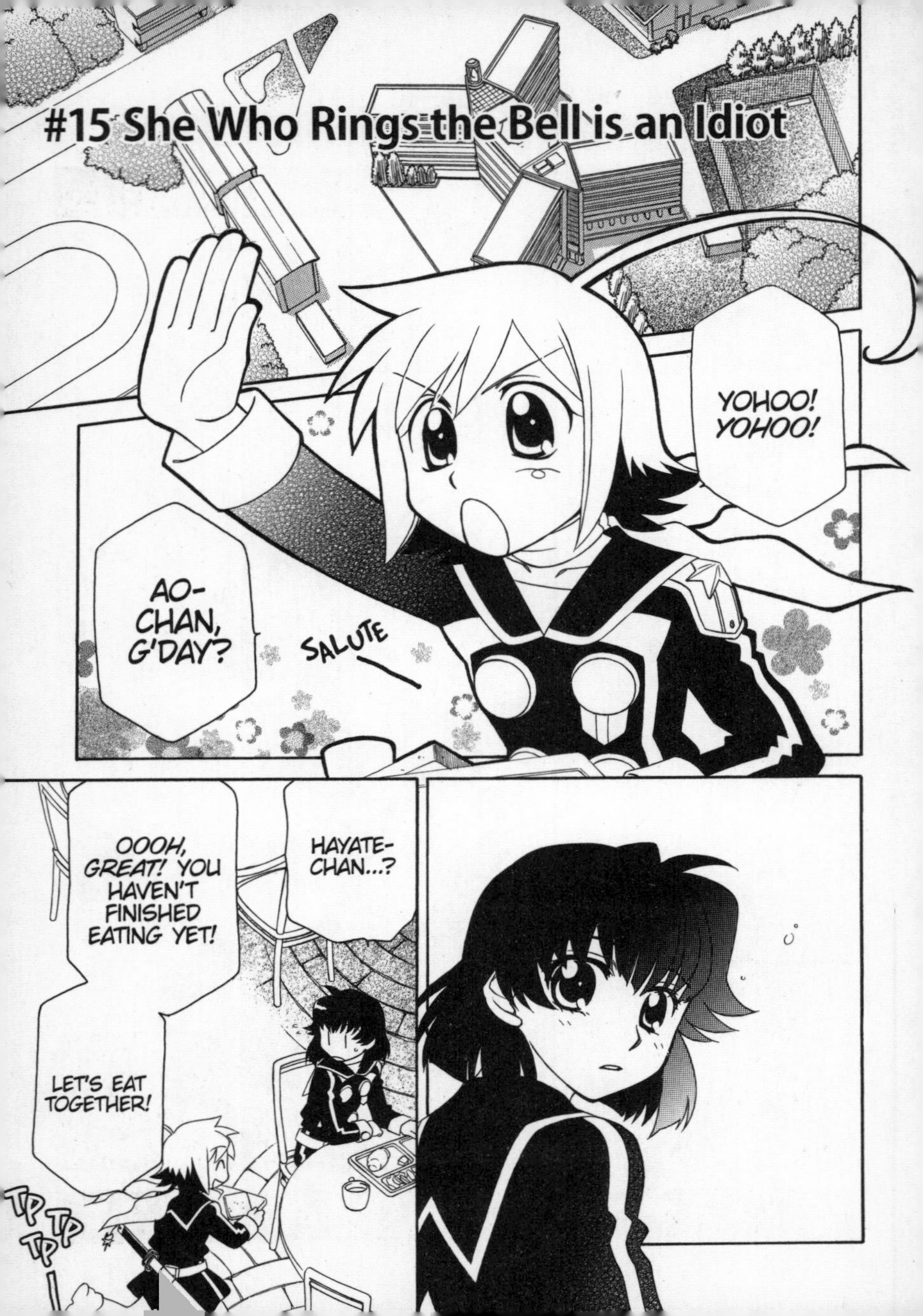
YOHOO! YOHOO!
SALUTE
AO-CHAN, G'DAY?
HAYATE-CHAN...?
OOOH, GREAT! YOU HAVEN'T FINISHED EATING YET!
LET'S EAT TOGETHER!
TP TP TP TP

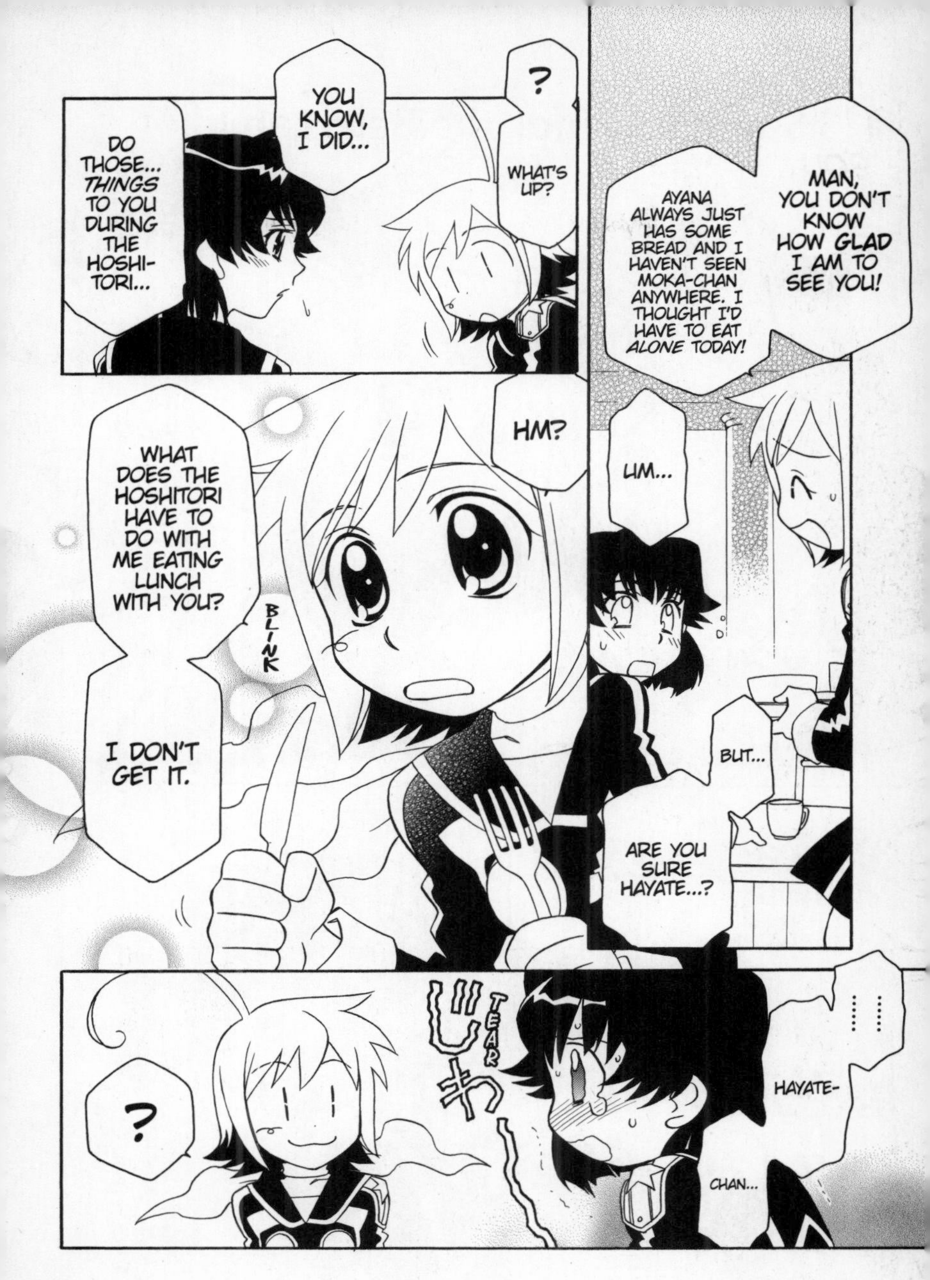
MAN, YOU DON'T KNOW HOW GLAD I AM TO SEE YOU!
AYANA ALWAYS JUST HAS SOME BREAD AND I HAVEN'T SEEN MOKA-CHAN ANYWHERE. I THOUGHT I'D HAVE TO EAT *ALONE* TODAY!
UM...
BUT...
ARE YOU SURE HAYATE...?
?
WHAT'S UP?
YOU KNOW, I DID...
DO THOSE... *THINGS* TO YOU DURING THE HOSHI-TORI...
HM?
WHAT DOES THE HOSHITORI HAVE TO DO WITH ME EATING LUNCH WITH YOU?
BLINK
I DON'T GET IT.
......
HAYATE-
CHAN...
TEAR
?

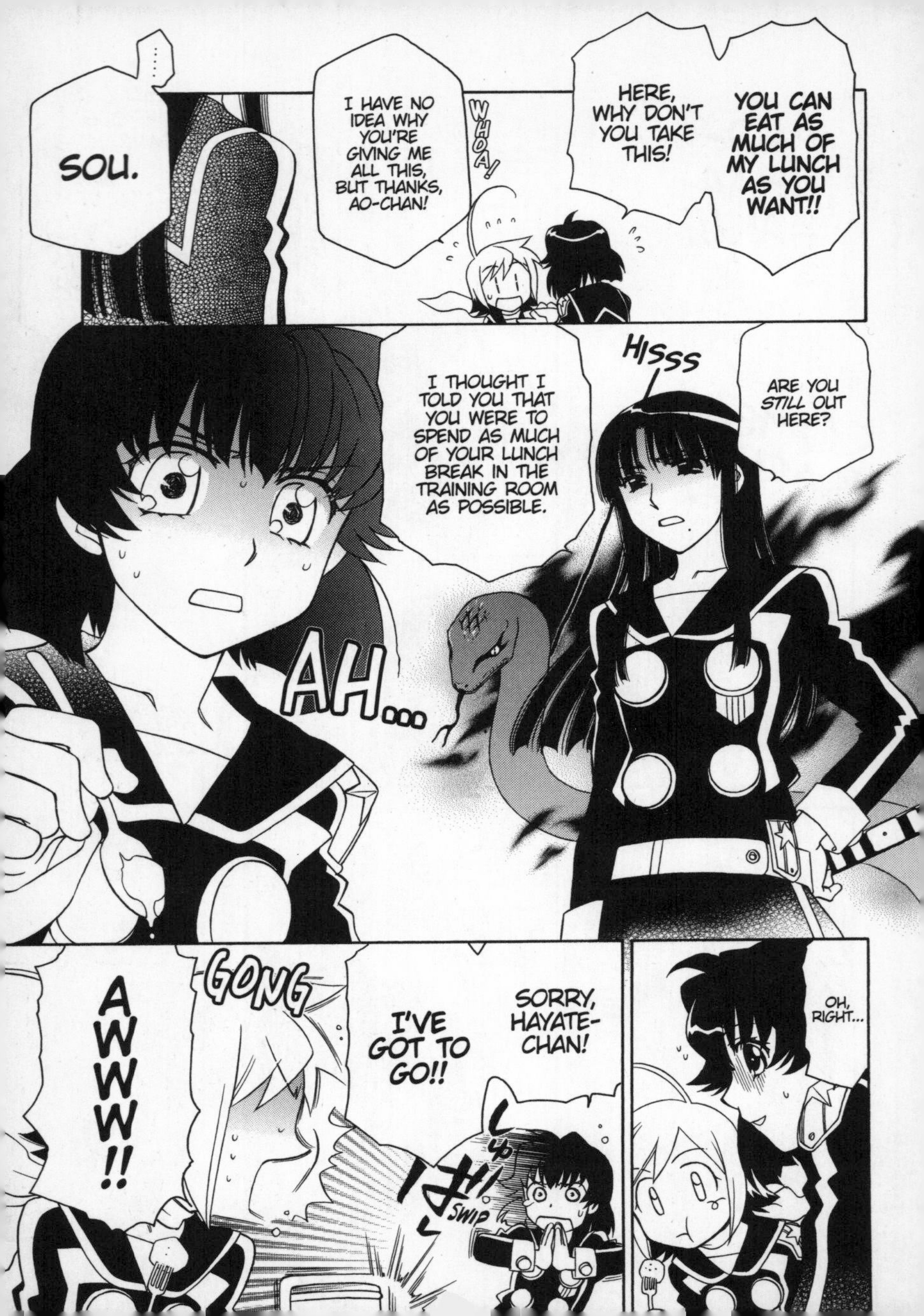
HERE, WHY DON'T YOU TAKE THIS!
YOU CAN EAT AS MUCH OF MY LUNCH AS YOU WANT!!
WHOA!
I HAVE NO IDEA WHY YOU'RE GIVING ME ALL THIS, BUT THANKS, AO-CHAN!
...
SOU.
ARE YOU STILL OUT HERE?
HISSS
I THOUGHT I TOLD YOU THAT YOU WERE TO SPEND AS MUCH OF YOUR LUNCH BREAK IN THE TRAINING ROOM AS POSSIBLE.
AH...
OH, RIGHT...
SORRY, HAYATE-CHAN!
I'VE GOT TO GO!!
SWIP
GONG
AWWW!!

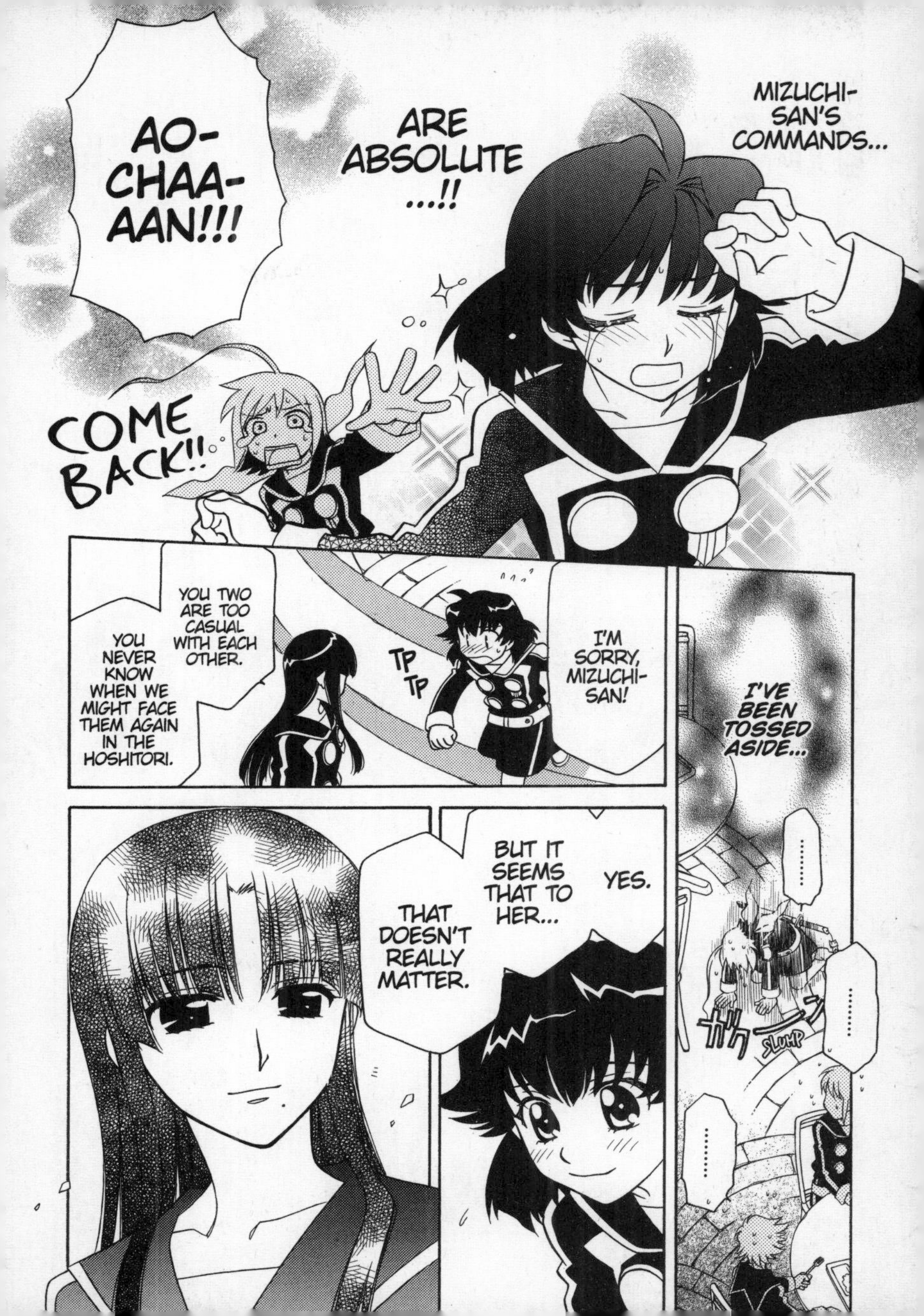
MIZUCHI-SAN'S COMMANDS...
ARE ABSOLUTE...!!
AO-CHAAA-AAN!!!
COME BACK!!
I'VE BEEN TOSSED ASIDE...
......
......
SLUMP
......
I'M SORRY, MIZUCHI-SAN!
TP TP
YOU TWO ARE TOO CASUAL WITH EACH OTHER.
YOU NEVER KNOW WHEN WE MIGHT FACE THEM AGAIN IN THE HOSHITORI.
YES.
BUT IT SEEMS THAT TO HER...
THAT DOESN'T REALLY MATTER.

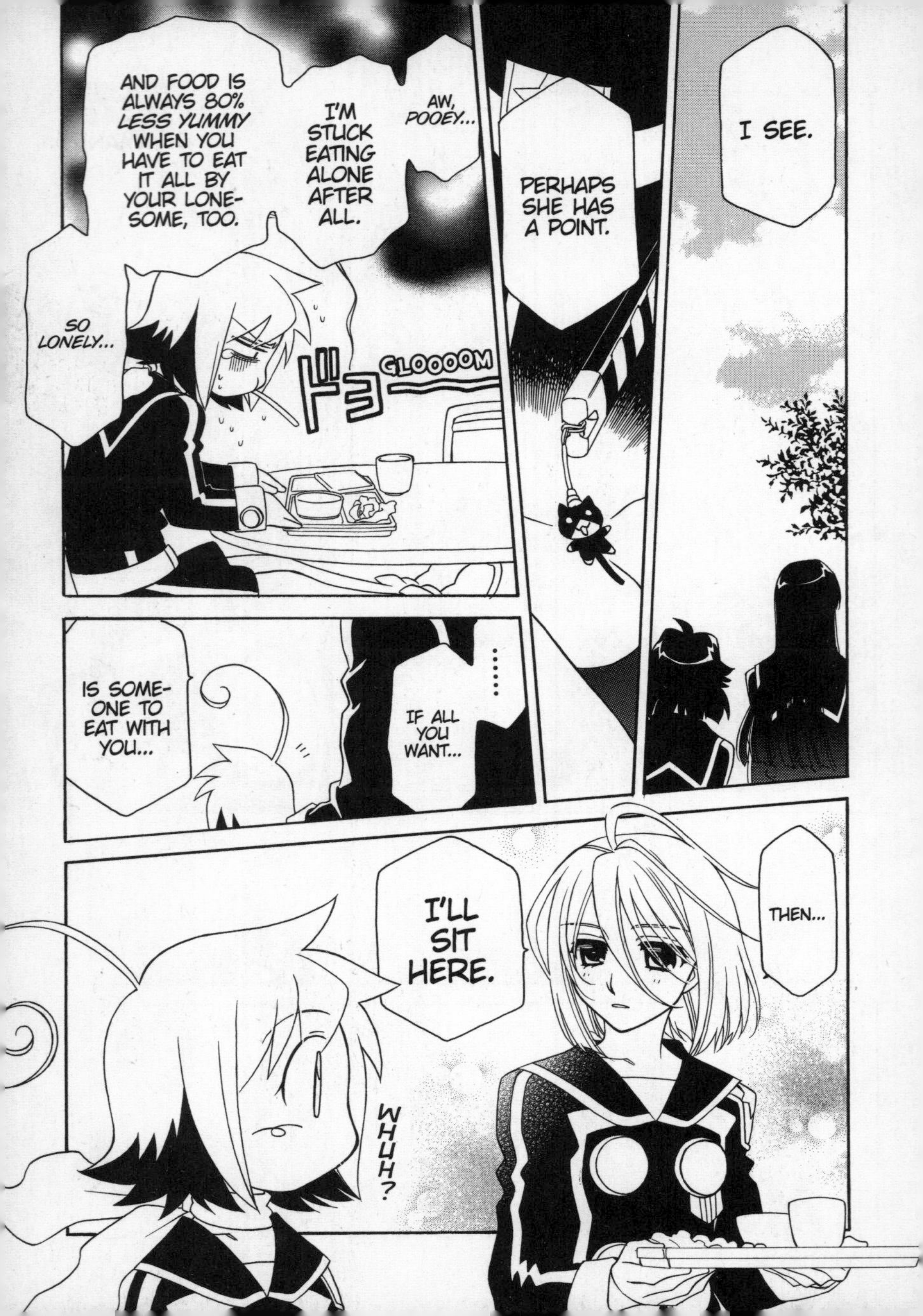

I SEE.
PERHAPS SHE HAS A POINT.
AW, POOEY...
I'M STUCK EATING ALONE AFTER ALL.
AND FOOD IS ALWAYS 80% LESS YUMMY WHEN YOU HAVE TO EAT IT ALL BY YOUR LONESOME, TOO.
SO LONELY...
ドヨ GLOOOOM
......
IF ALL YOU WANT...
IS SOMEONE TO EAT WITH YOU...
THEN...
I'LL SIT HERE.
WHUH?

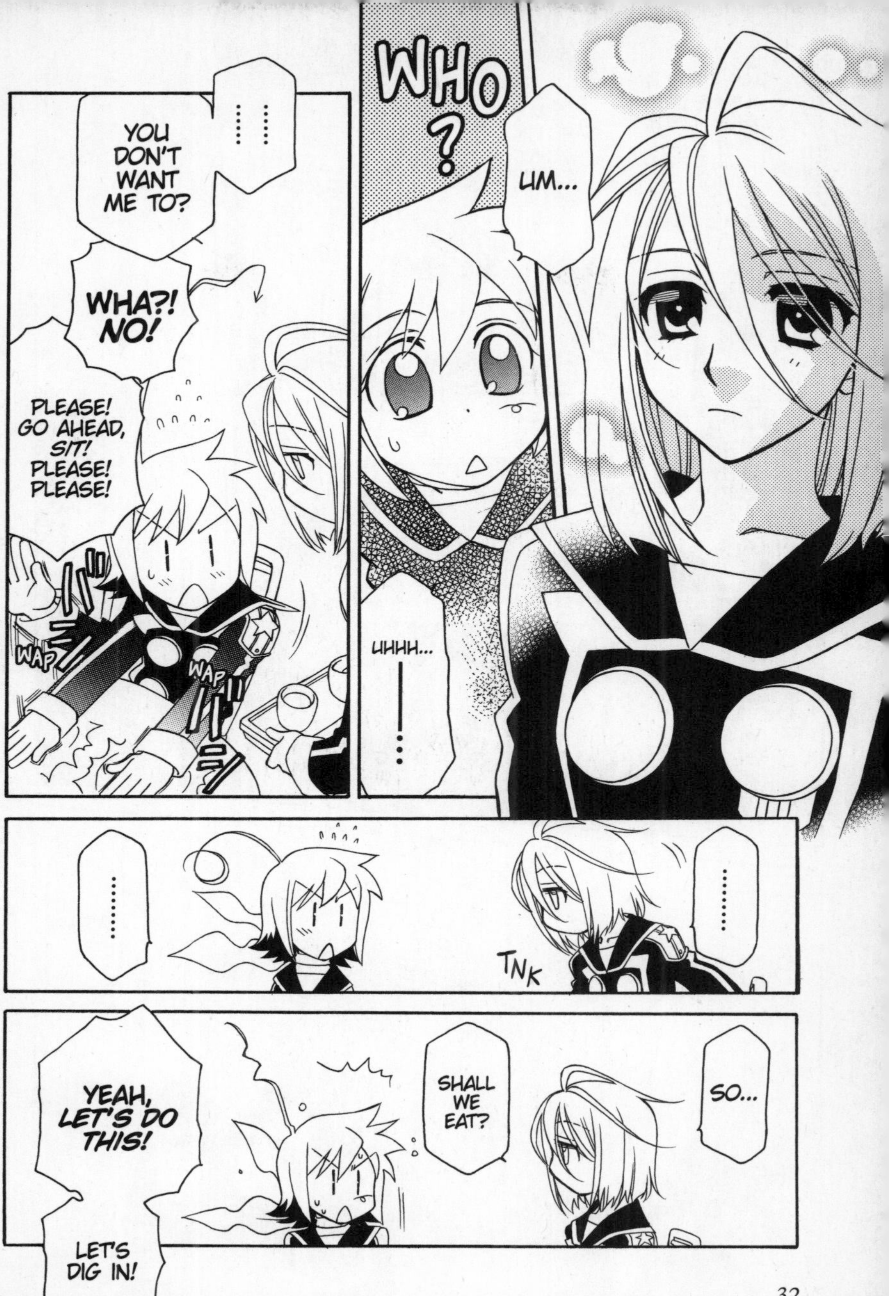

UM...
WHO?
UHHH......
......
YOU DON'T WANT ME TO?
WHA?! NO!
PLEASE! GO AHEAD, SIT! PLEASE! PLEASE!
WAP
WAP
......
TNK
......
SO...
SHALL WE EAT?
YEAH, LET'S DO THIS!
LET'S DIG IN!

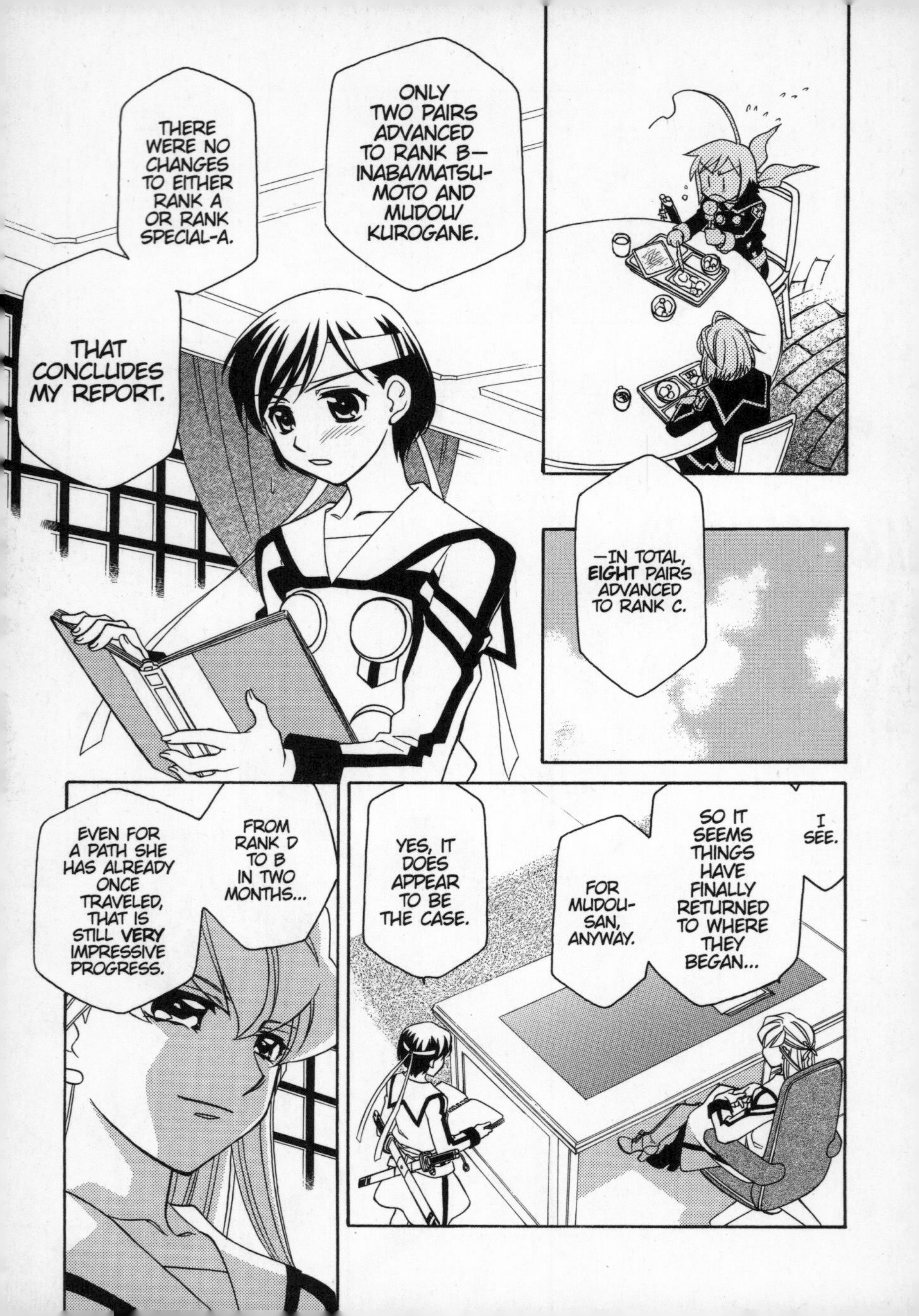
—IN TOTAL, **EIGHT** PAIRS ADVANCED TO RANK C.
ONLY TWO PAIRS ADVANCED TO RANK B— INABA/MATSUMOTO AND MUDOU/ KUROGANE.
THERE WERE NO CHANGES TO EITHER RANK A OR RANK SPECIAL-A.
THAT CONCLUDES MY REPORT.
I SEE.
SO IT SEEMS THINGS HAVE FINALLY RETURNED TO WHERE THEY BEGAN...
FOR MUDOU-SAN, ANYWAY.
YES, IT DOES APPEAR TO BE THE CASE.
FROM RANK D TO B IN TWO MONTHS...
EVEN FOR A PATH SHE HAS ALREADY ONCE TRAVELED, THAT IS STILL **VERY** IMPRESSIVE PROGRESS.

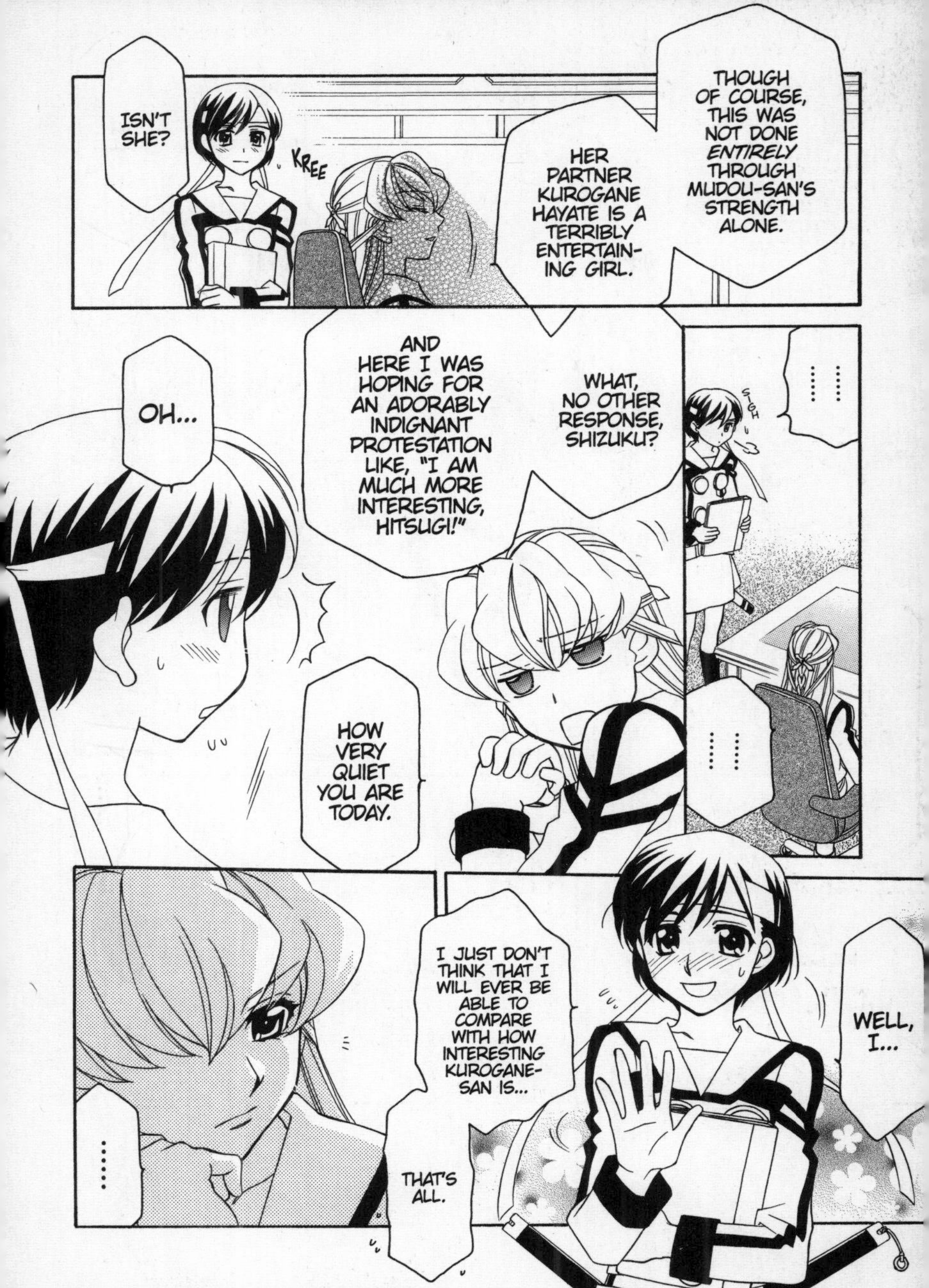
THOUGH OF COURSE, THIS WAS NOT DONE *ENTIRELY* THROUGH MUDOU-SAN'S STRENGTH ALONE.
HER PARTNER KUROGANE HAYATE IS A TERRIBLY ENTERTAINING GIRL.
KREE
ISN'T SHE?
......
SIGH
......
WHAT, NO OTHER RESPONSE, SHIZUKU?
AND HERE I WAS HOPING FOR AN ADORABLY INDIGNANT PROTESTATION LIKE, "I AM MUCH MORE INTERESTING, HITSUGI!"
HOW VERY QUIET YOU ARE TODAY.
OH...
WELL, I...
I JUST DON'T THINK THAT I WILL EVER BE ABLE TO COMPARE WITH HOW INTERESTING KUROGANE-SAN IS...
THAT'S ALL.
......

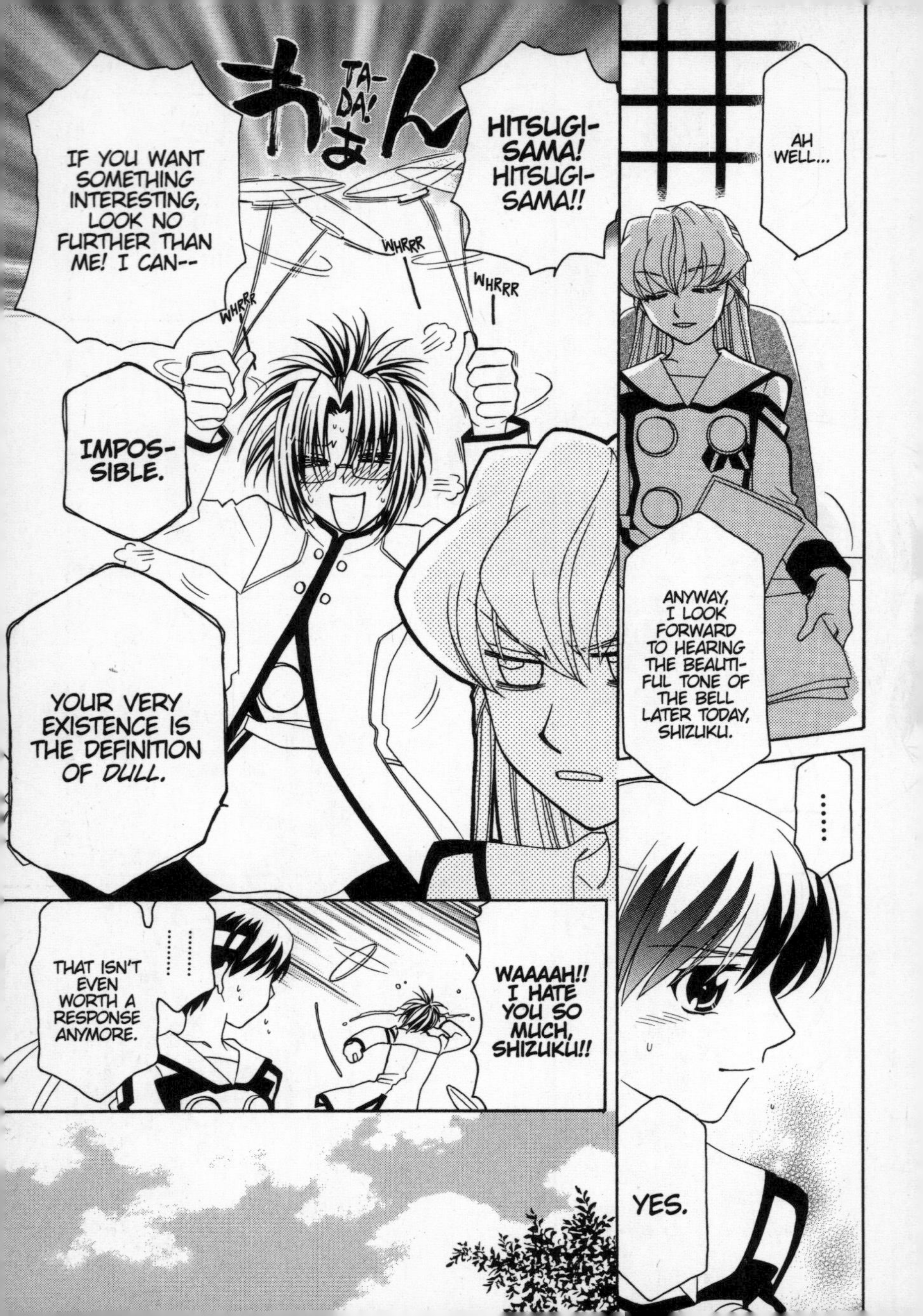
AH WELL...
ANYWAY, I LOOK FORWARD TO HEARING THE BEAUTIFUL TONE OF THE BELL LATER TODAY, SHIZUKU.
TA-DA!
HITSUGI-SAMA! HITSUGI-SAMA!!
IF YOU WANT SOMETHING INTERESTING, LOOK NO FURTHER THAN ME! I CAN--
WHRRR
WHRRR
WHRRR
IMPOSSIBLE.
YOUR VERY EXISTENCE IS THE DEFINITION OF DULL.
......
YES.
WAAAAH!! I HATE YOU SO MUCH, SHIZUKU!!
......
THAT ISN'T EVEN WORTH A RESPONSE ANYMORE.

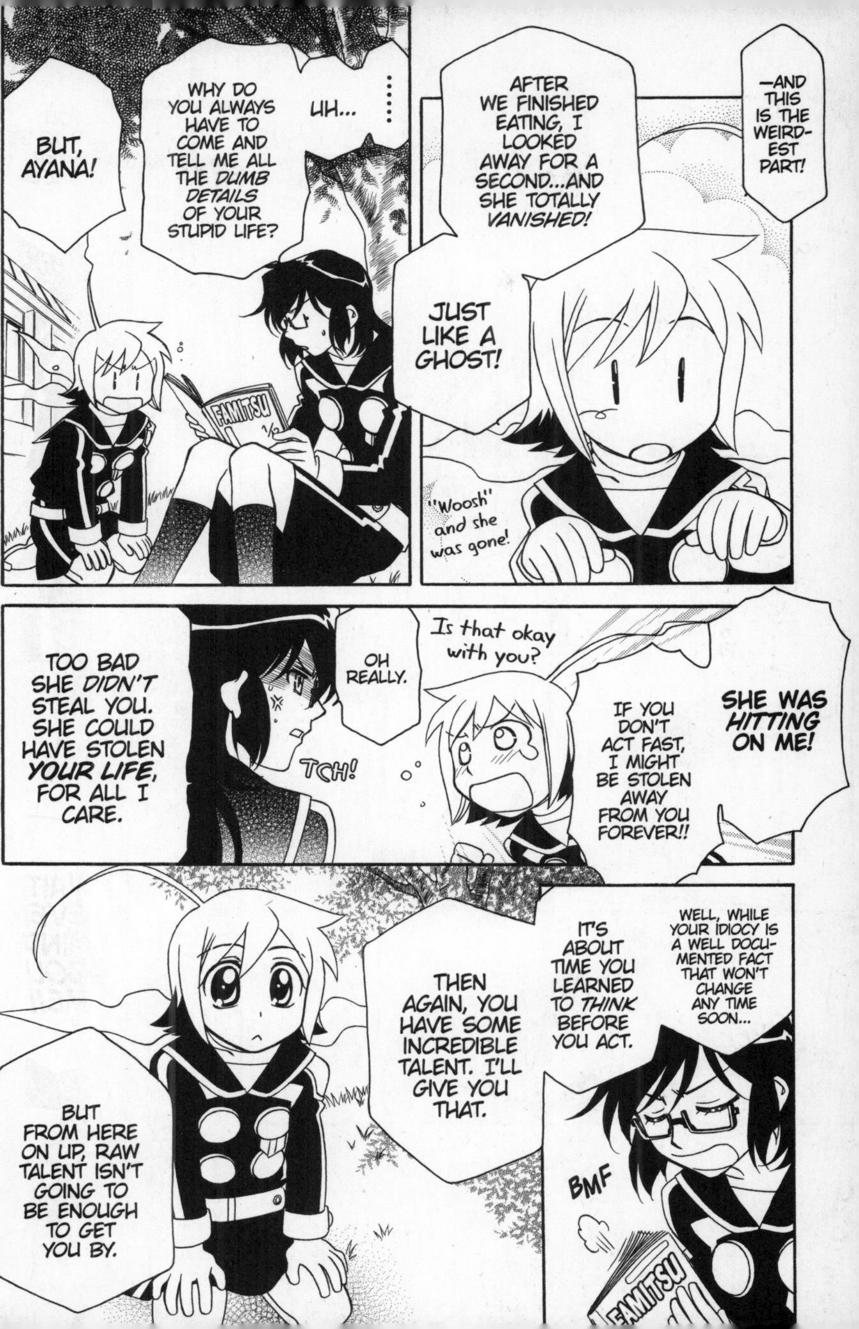
—AND THIS IS THE WEIRDEST PART!
AFTER WE FINISHED EATING, I LOOKED AWAY FOR A SECOND...AND SHE TOTALLY VANISHED!
JUST LIKE A GHOST!
"Woosh" and she was gone!
......
UH...
WHY DO YOU ALWAYS HAVE TO COME AND TELL ME ALL THE DUMB DETAILS OF YOUR STUPID LIFE?
BUT, AYANA!
FAMITSU
SHE WAS HITTING ON ME!
IF YOU DON'T ACT FAST, I MIGHT BE STOLEN AWAY FROM YOU FOREVER!!
Is that okay with you?
OH REALLY.
TCH!
TOO BAD SHE DIDN'T STEAL YOU. SHE COULD HAVE STOLEN YOUR LIFE, FOR ALL I CARE.
WELL, WHILE YOUR IDIOCY IS A WELL DOCUMENTED FACT THAT WON'T CHANGE ANY TIME SOON...
IT'S ABOUT TIME YOU LEARNED TO THINK BEFORE YOU ACT.
THEN AGAIN, YOU HAVE SOME INCREDIBLE TALENT. I'LL GIVE YOU THAT.
BMF
FAMITSU
BUT FROM HERE ON UP, RAW TALENT ISN'T GOING TO BE ENOUGH TO GET YOU BY.

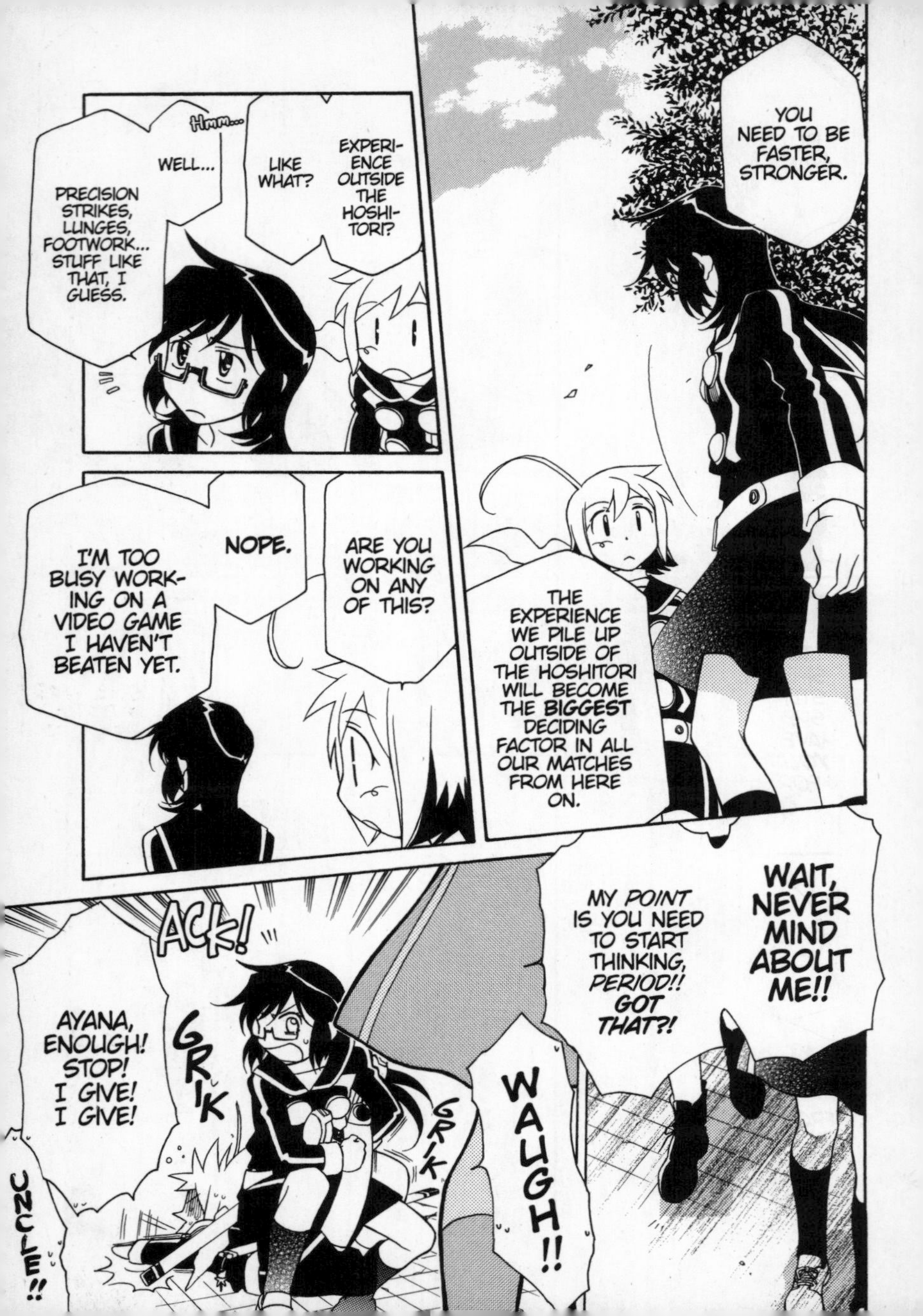
YOU NEED TO BE FASTER, STRONGER.
THE EXPERIENCE WE PILE UP OUTSIDE OF THE HOSHITORI WILL BECOME THE BIGGEST DECIDING FACTOR IN ALL OUR MATCHES FROM HERE ON.
EXPERIENCE OUTSIDE THE HOSHITORI?
LIKE WHAT?
Hmm...
WELL...
PRECISION STRIKES, LUNGES, FOOTWORK... STUFF LIKE THAT, I GUESS.
ARE YOU WORKING ON ANY OF THIS?
NOPE.
I'M TOO BUSY WORKING ON A VIDEO GAME I HAVEN'T BEATEN YET.
WAIT, NEVER MIND ABOUT ME!!
MY POINT IS YOU NEED TO START THINKING, PERIOD!! GOT THAT?!
WAUGH!!
GRIK
ACK!
GRIK
AYANA, ENOUGH! STOP! I GIVE! I GIVE!
UNCLE!!

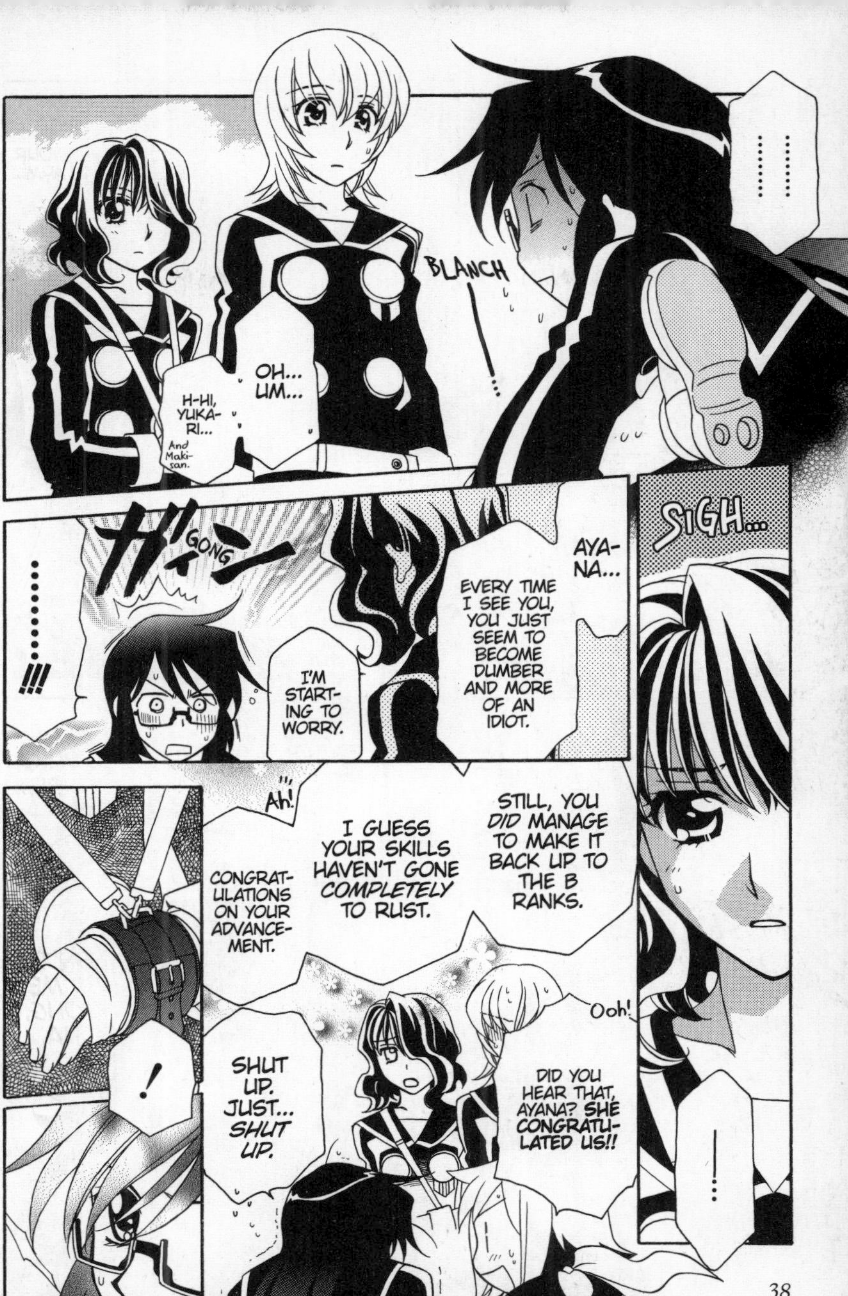

......
BLANCH
...!
OH... UM...
H-HI, YUKARI...
And Maki-san.
SIGH...
AYANA... EVERY TIME I SEE YOU, YOU JUST SEEM TO BECOME DUMBER AND MORE OF AN IDIOT.
I'M STARTING TO WORRY.
GONG
......!!!
...!
STILL, YOU DID MANAGE TO MAKE IT BACK UP TO THE B RANKS.
I GUESS YOUR SKILLS HAVEN'T GONE COMPLETELY TO RUST.
CONGRATULATIONS ON YOUR ADVANCEMENT.
Ah!
Ooh!
DID YOU HEAR THAT, AYANA? SHE CONGRATULATED US!!
SHUT UP. JUST... SHUT UP.
!

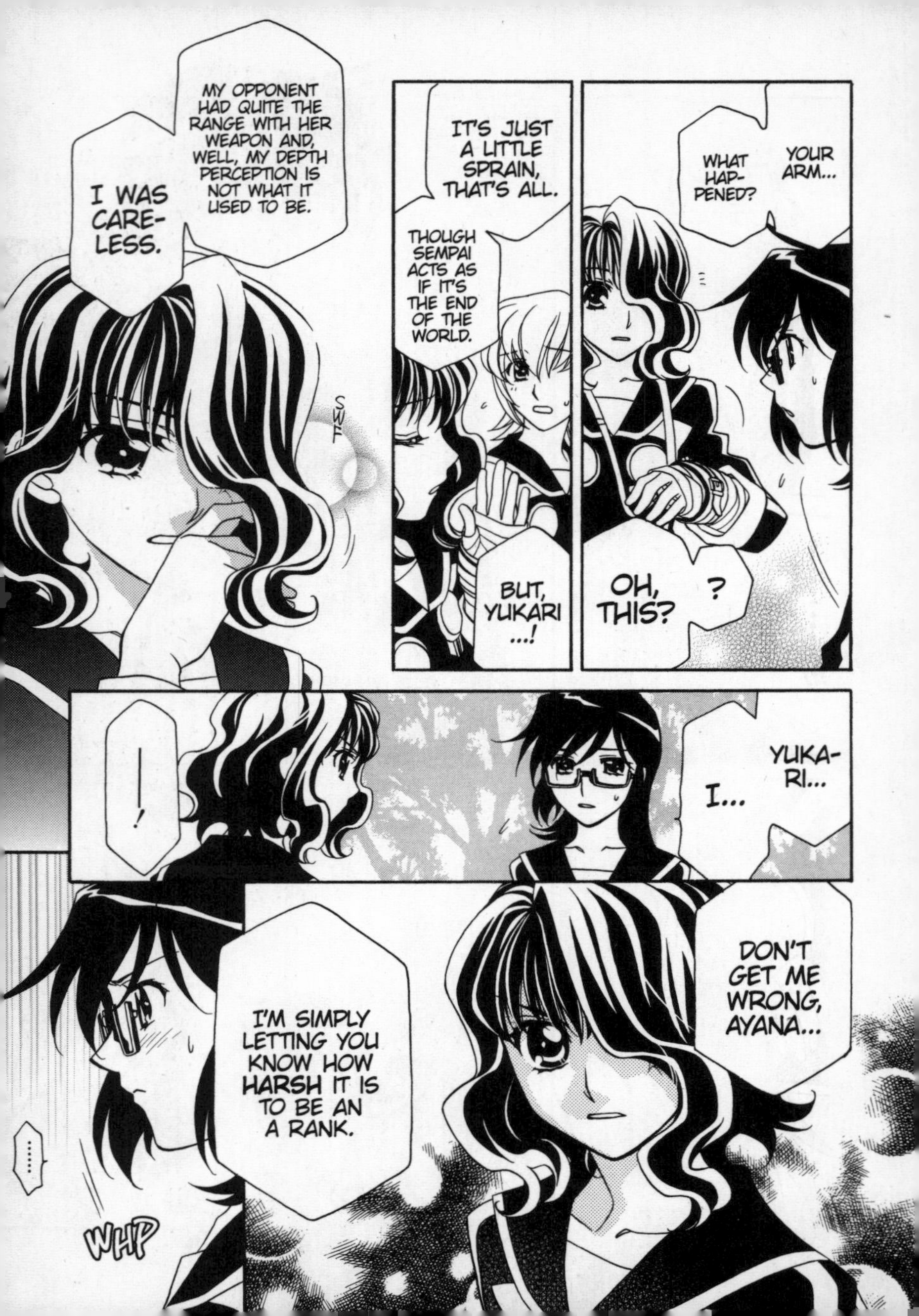

YOUR ARM...
WHAT HAP-PENED?
?
OH, THIS?
IT'S JUST A LITTLE SPRAIN, THAT'S ALL.
THOUGH SEMPAI ACTS AS IF IT'S THE END OF THE WORLD.
BUT, YUKARI ...!
MY OPPONENT HAD QUITE THE RANGE WITH HER WEAPON AND, WELL, MY DEPTH PERCEPTION IS NOT WHAT IT USED TO BE.
I WAS CARE-LESS.
SWF
YUKA-RI...
I...
!
DON'T GET ME WRONG, AYANA...
I'M SIMPLY LETTING YOU KNOW HOW HARSH IT IS TO BE AN A RANK.
......
WHP

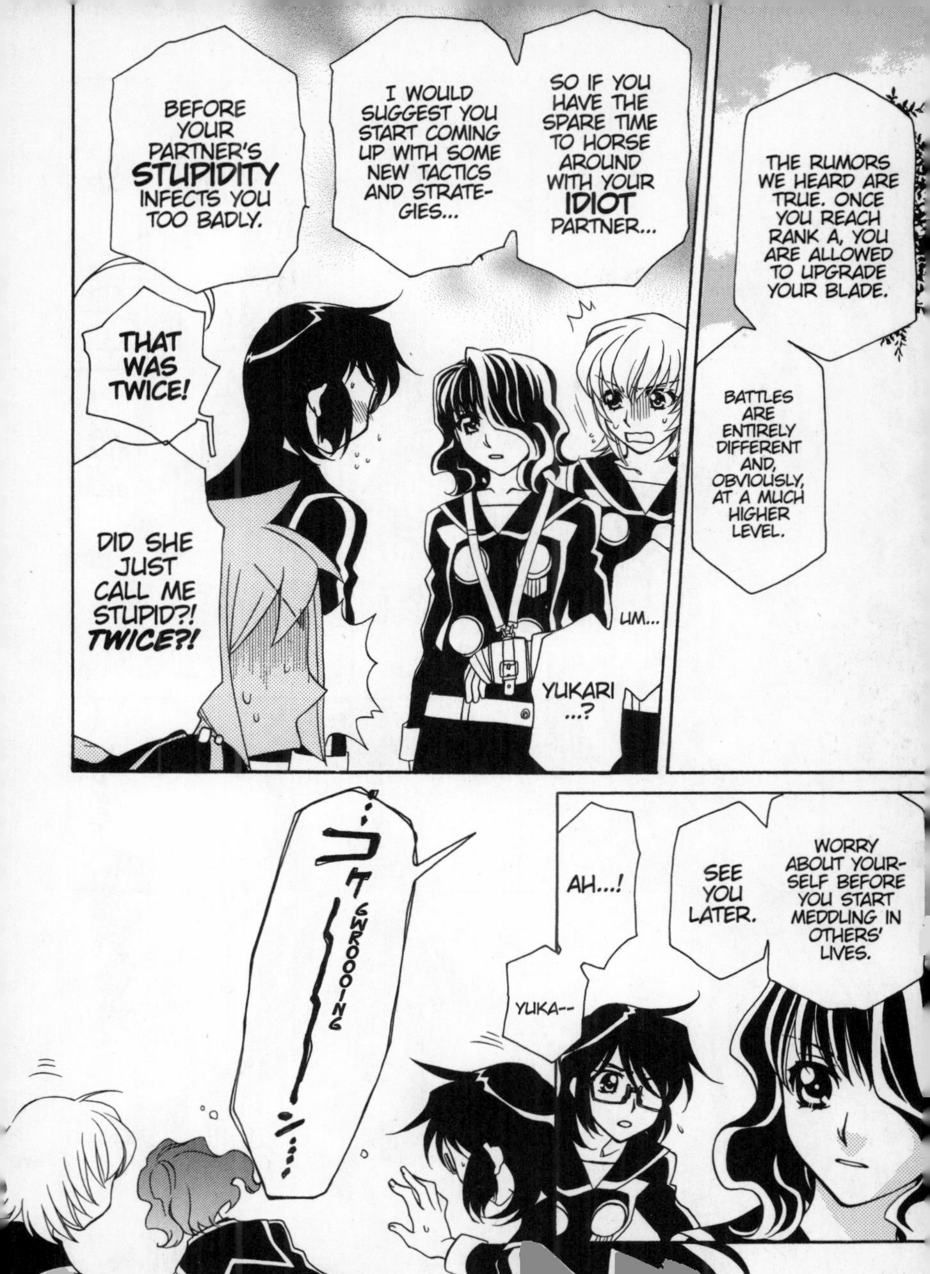
THE RUMORS WE HEARD ARE TRUE. ONCE YOU REACH RANK A, YOU ARE ALLOWED TO UPGRADE YOUR BLADE.
BATTLES ARE ENTIRELY DIFFERENT AND, OBVIOUSLY, AT A MUCH HIGHER LEVEL.
SO IF YOU HAVE THE SPARE TIME TO HORSE AROUND WITH YOUR **IDIOT** PARTNER...
I WOULD SUGGEST YOU START COMING UP WITH SOME NEW TACTICS AND STRATE- GIES...
BEFORE YOUR PARTNER'S **STUPIDITY** INFECTS YOU TOO BADLY.
UM...
YUKARI ...?
THAT WAS TWICE!
DID SHE JUST CALL ME STUPID?! ***TWICE?!***
WORRY ABOUT YOUR- SELF BEFORE YOU START MEDDLING IN OTHERS' LIVES.
SEE YOU LATER.
AH...!
YUKA--
GWROOOOING

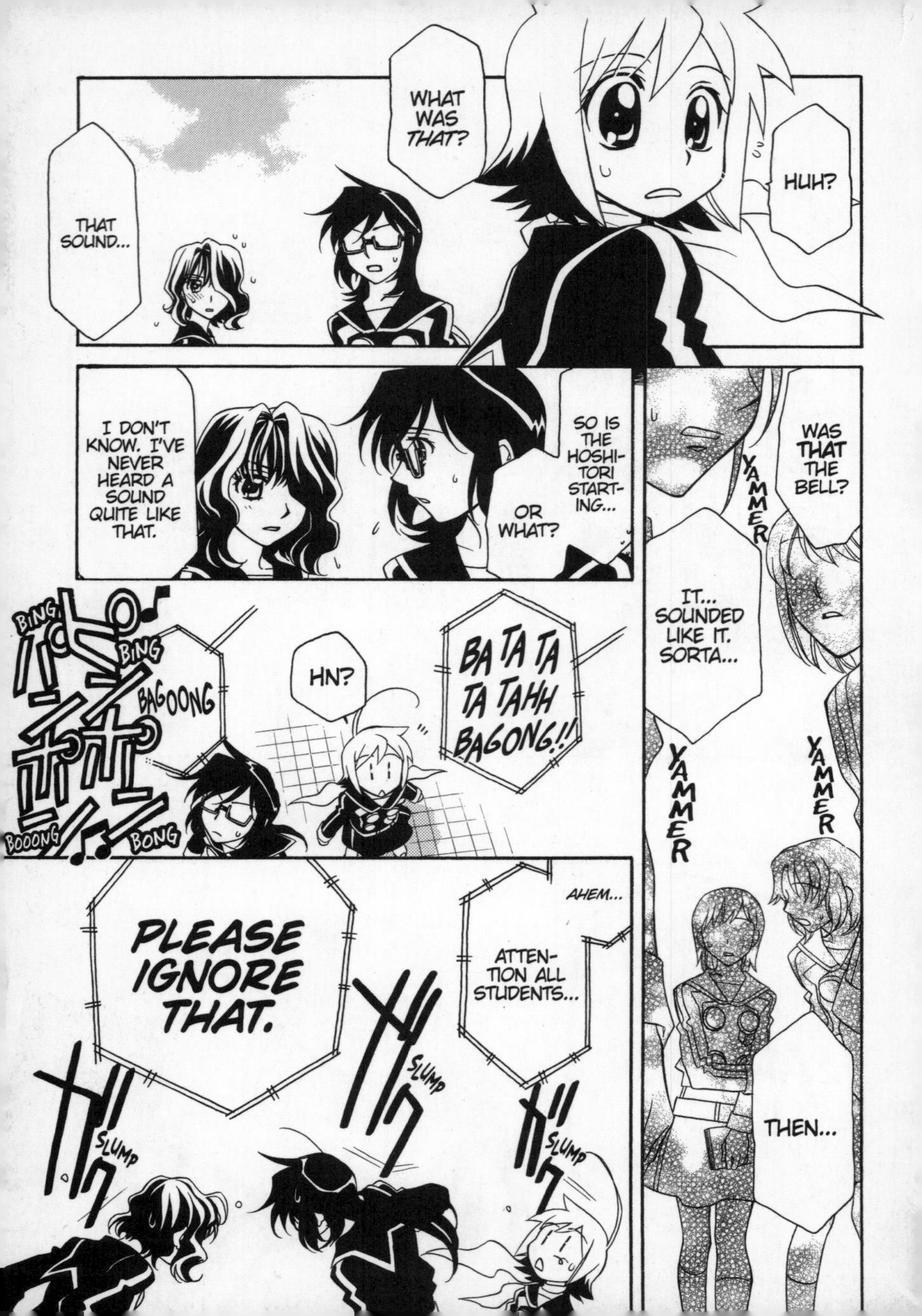
HUH?
WHAT WAS THAT?
THAT SOUND...
WAS THAT THE BELL?
YAMMER
IT... SOUNDED LIKE IT. SORTA...
YAMMER
YAMMER
THEN...
SO IS THE HOSHI-TORI START-ING...
OR WHAT?
I DON'T KNOW. I'VE NEVER HEARD A SOUND QUITE LIKE THAT.
BA TA TA TA TAHH BAGONG!!
HN?
BING
BING
BAGOONG
BONG
BOOONG
AHEM...
ATTEN-TION ALL STUDENTS...
PLEASE IGNORE THAT.
SLUMP
SLUMP
SLUMP

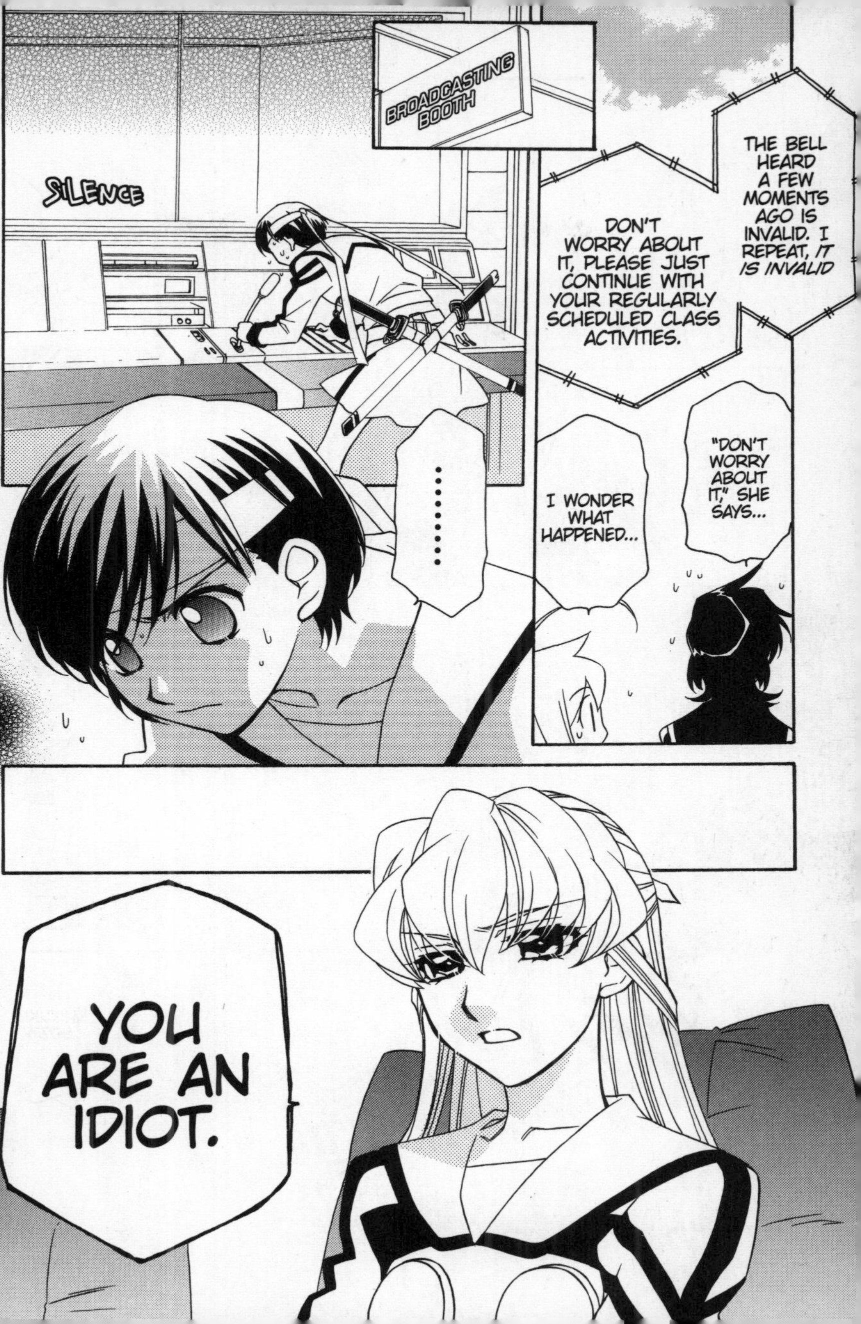
THE BELL HEARD A FEW MOMENTS AGO IS INVALID. I REPEAT, *IT IS INVALID*
DON'T WORRY ABOUT IT, PLEASE JUST CONTINUE WITH YOUR REGULARLY SCHEDULED CLASS ACTIVITIES.
BROADCASTING BOOTH
SILENCE
"DON'T WORRY ABOUT IT," SHE SAYS...
I WONDER WHAT HAPPENED...
....
YOU ARE AN IDIOT.

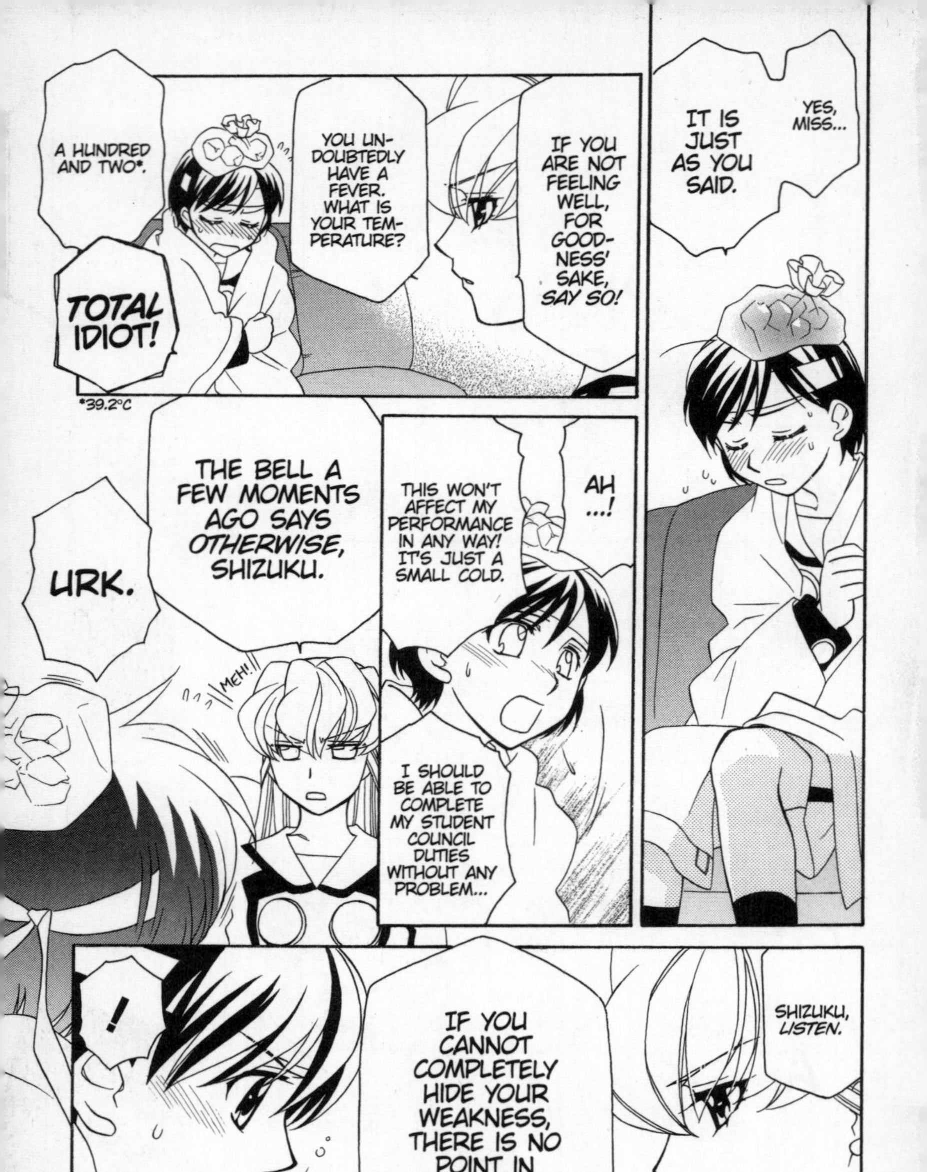
YES, MISS...
IT IS JUST AS YOU SAID.
IF YOU ARE NOT FEELING WELL, FOR GOODNESS' SAKE, SAY SO!
YOU UNDOUBTEDLY HAVE A FEVER. WHAT IS YOUR TEMPERATURE?
A HUNDRED AND TWO*.
TOTAL IDIOT!
*39.2°C
AH ...!
THIS WON'T AFFECT MY PERFORMANCE IN ANY WAY! IT'S JUST A SMALL COLD.
I SHOULD BE ABLE TO COMPLETE MY STUDENT COUNCIL DUTIES WITHOUT ANY PROBLEM...
THE BELL A FEW MOMENTS AGO SAYS OTHERWISE, SHIZUKU.
MEH!
URK.
SHIZUKU, LISTEN.
IF YOU CANNOT COMPLETELY HIDE YOUR WEAKNESS, THERE IS NO POINT IN REMAINING STANDING.
!

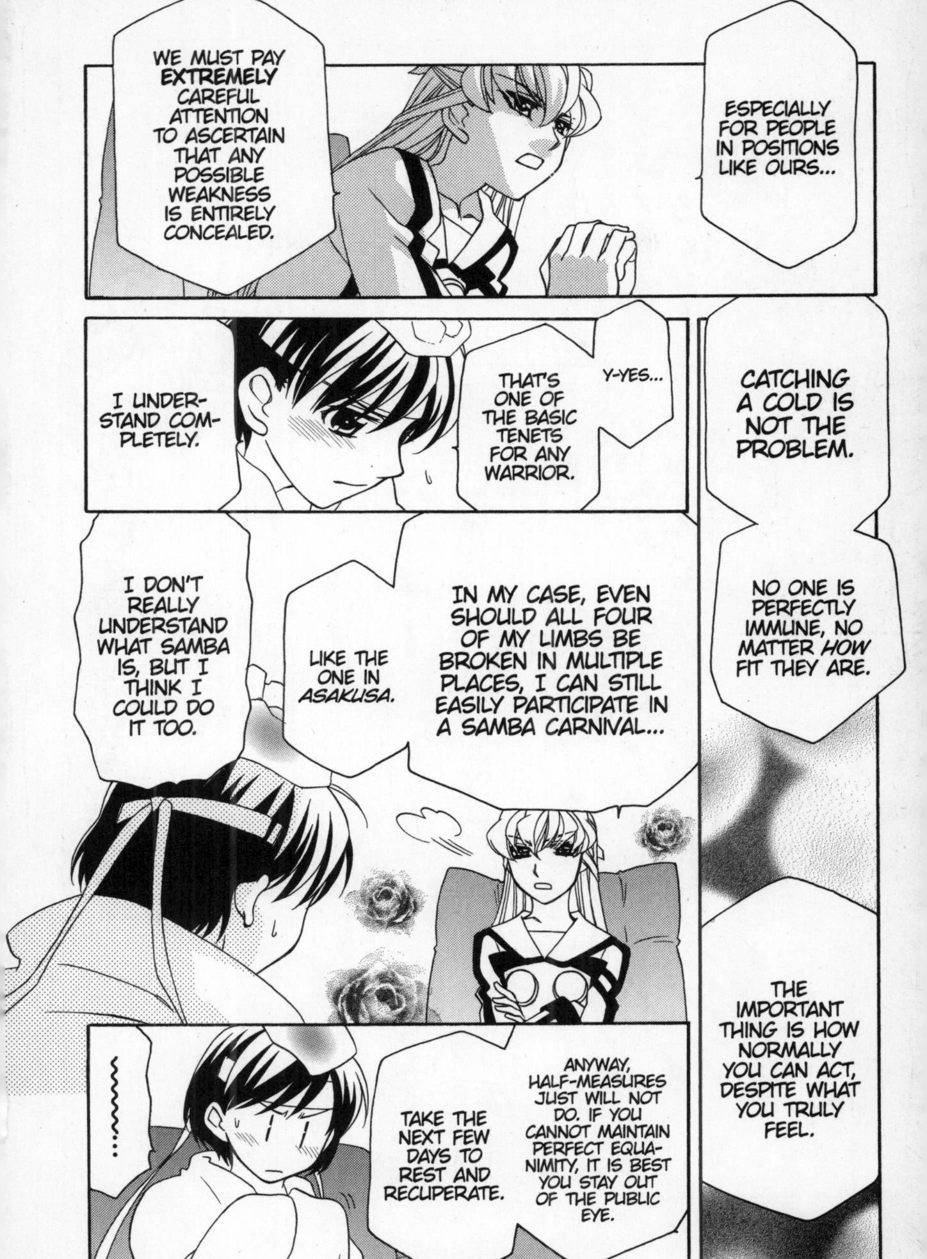
ESPECIALLY FOR PEOPLE IN POSITIONS LIKE OURS...
WE MUST PAY **EXTREMELY** CAREFUL ATTENTION TO ASCERTAIN THAT ANY POSSIBLE WEAKNESS IS ENTIRELY CONCEALED.
CATCHING A COLD IS NOT THE PROBLEM.
NO ONE IS PERFECTLY IMMUNE, NO MATTER *HOW* FIT THEY ARE.
THE IMPORTANT THING IS HOW NORMALLY YOU CAN ACT, DESPITE WHAT YOU TRULY FEEL.
Y-YES...
THAT'S ONE OF THE BASIC TENETS FOR ANY WARRIOR.
I UNDER-STAND COM-PLETELY.
IN MY CASE, EVEN SHOULD ALL FOUR OF MY LIMBS BE BROKEN IN MULTIPLE PLACES, I CAN STILL EASILY PARTICIPATE IN A SAMBA CARNIVAL...
LIKE THE ONE IN *ASAKUSA.*
I DON'T REALLY UNDERSTAND WHAT SAMBA IS, BUT I THINK I COULD DO IT TOO.
ANYWAY, HALF-MEASURES JUST WILL NOT DO. IF YOU CANNOT MAINTAIN PERFECT EQUA-NIMITY, IT IS BEST YOU STAY OUT OF THE PUBLIC EYE.
TAKE THE NEXT FEW DAYS TO REST AND RECUPERATE.
......

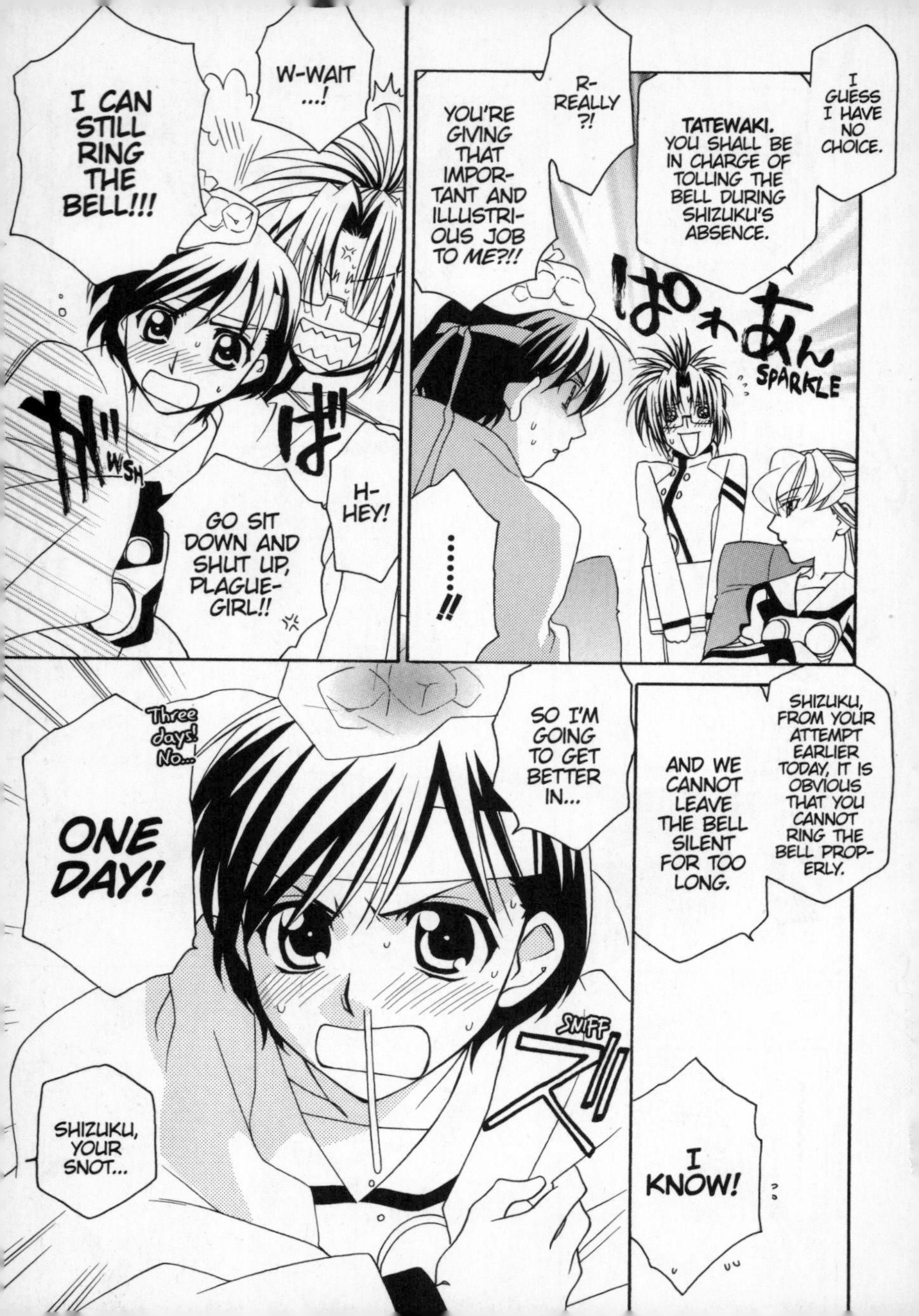
I GUESS I HAVE NO CHOICE.
TATEWAKI. YOU SHALL BE IN CHARGE OF TOLLING THE BELL DURING SHIZUKU'S ABSENCE.
R-REALLY?!
YOU'RE GIVING THAT IMPORTANT AND ILLUSTRIOUS JOB TO ME?!!
SPARKLE
......!!
W-WAIT ...!
I CAN STILL RING THE BELL!!!
H-HEY!
GO SIT DOWN AND SHUT UP, PLAGUE-GIRL!!
WSH
SHIZUKU, FROM YOUR ATTEMPT EARLIER TODAY, IT IS OBVIOUS THAT YOU CANNOT RING THE BELL PROPERLY.
AND WE CANNOT LEAVE THE BELL SILENT FOR TOO LONG.
I KNOW!
SO I'M GOING TO GET BETTER IN...
Three days! No...
ONE DAY!
SNIFF
SHIZUKU, YOUR SNOT...

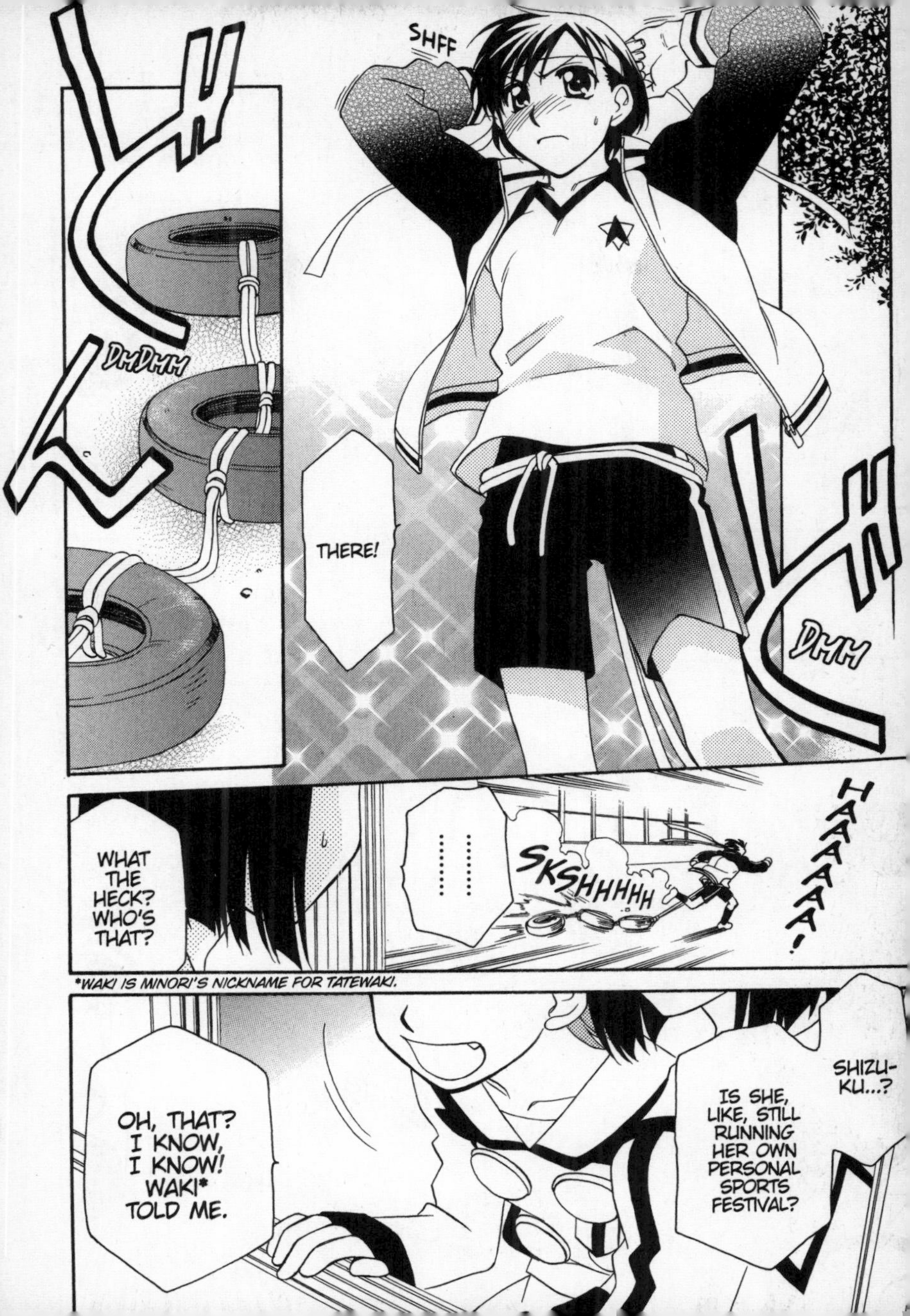
SHFF
THERE!
DMDMM
DMM
HAAAAAA!
SKSHHHHH
......
WHAT THE HECK? WHO'S THAT?
*WAKI IS MINORI'S NICKNAME FOR TATEWAKI.
SHIZU-KU...?
IS SHE, LIKE, STILL RUNNING HER OWN PERSONAL SPORTS FESTIVAL?
OH, THAT? I KNOW, I KNOW! WAKI* TOLD ME.

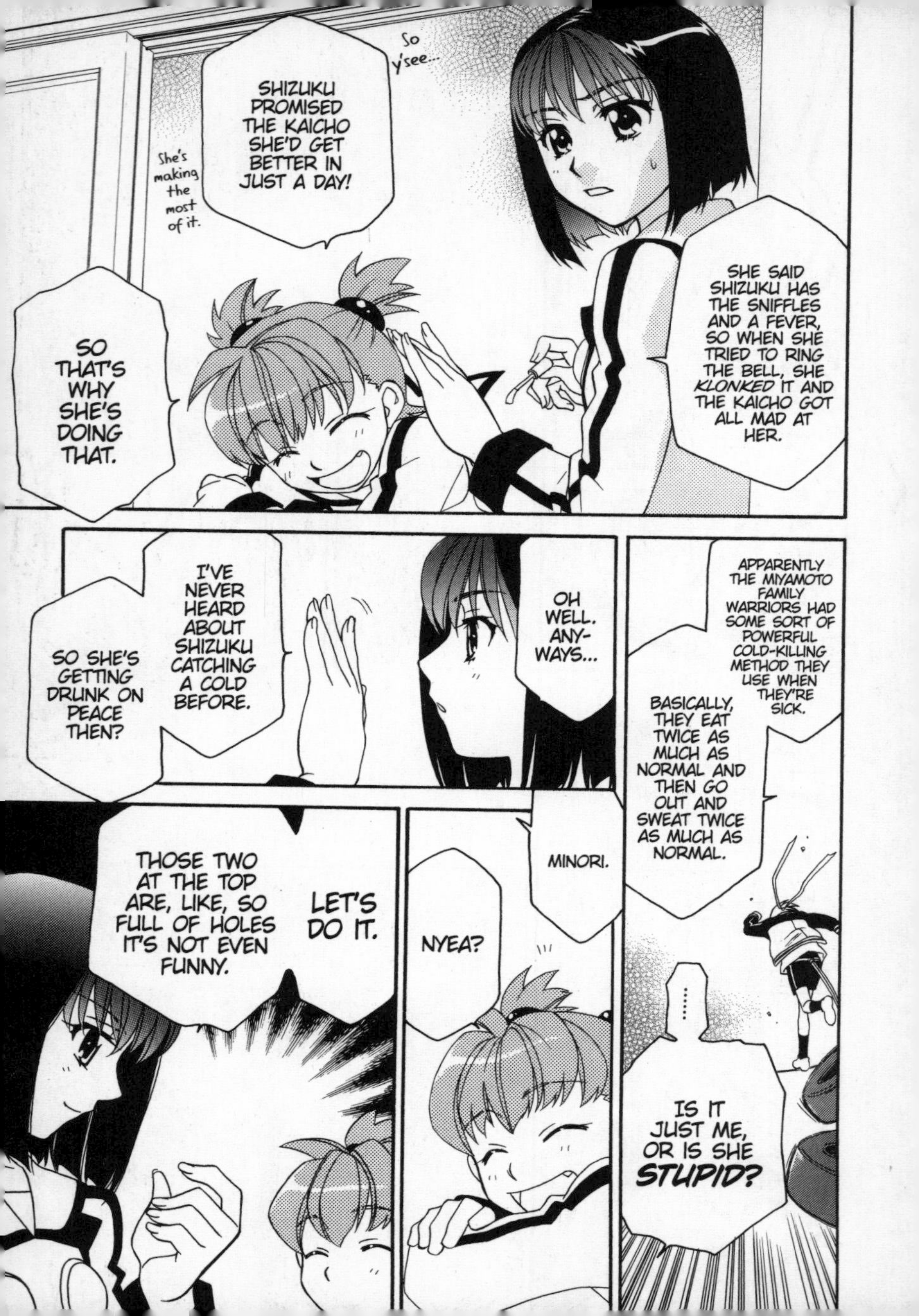
So y'see...
SHE SAID SHIZUKU HAS THE SNIFFLES AND A FEVER, SO WHEN SHE TRIED TO RING THE BELL, SHE *KLONKED* IT AND THE KAICHO GOT ALL MAD AT HER.
SHIZUKU PROMISED THE KAICHO SHE'D GET BETTER IN JUST A DAY!
She's making the most of it.
SO THAT'S WHY SHE'S DOING THAT.
APPARENTLY THE MIYAMOTO FAMILY WARRIORS HAD SOME SORT OF POWERFUL COLD-KILLING METHOD THEY USE WHEN THEY'RE SICK.
BASICALLY, THEY EAT TWICE AS MUCH AS NORMAL AND THEN GO OUT AND SWEAT TWICE AS MUCH AS NORMAL.
I'VE NEVER HEARD ABOUT SHIZUKU CATCHING A COLD BEFORE.
SO SHE'S GETTING DRUNK ON PEACE THEN?
OH WELL. ANY-WAYS...
......
IS IT JUST ME, OR IS SHE **STUPID?**
MINORI.
NYEA?
THOSE TWO AT THE TOP ARE, LIKE, SO FULL OF HOLES IT'S NOT EVEN FUNNY.
LET'S DO IT.

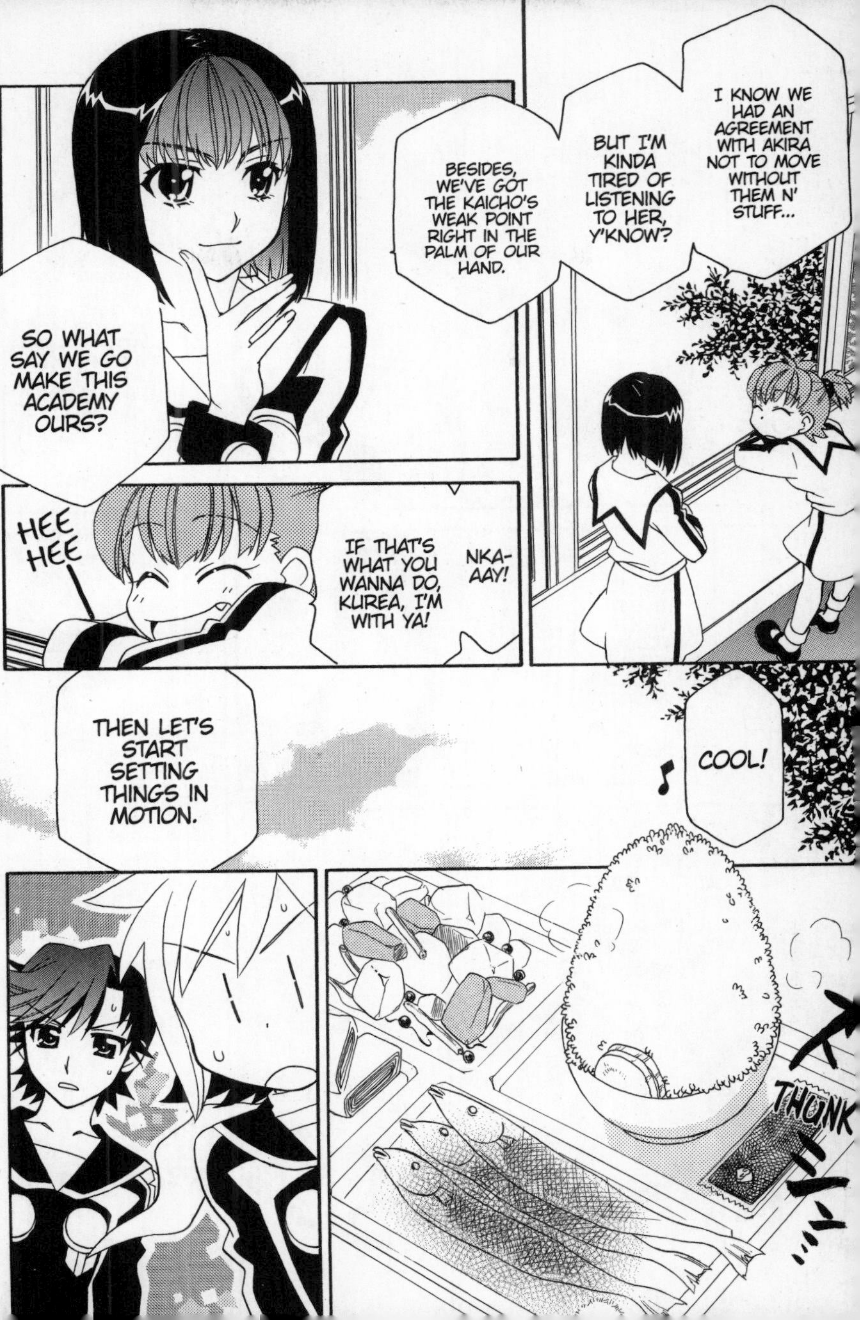
I KNOW WE HAD AN AGREEMENT WITH AKIRA NOT TO MOVE WITHOUT THEM N' STUFF...
BUT I'M KINDA TIRED OF LISTENING TO HER, Y'KNOW?
BESIDES, WE'VE GOT THE KAICHO'S WEAK POINT RIGHT IN THE PALM OF OUR HAND.
SO WHAT SAY WE GO MAKE THIS ACADEMY OURS?
NKA-AAY!
IF THAT'S WHAT YOU WANNA DO, KUREA, I'M WITH YA!
HEE HEE
COOL!
THEN LET'S START SETTING THINGS IN MOTION.
THUNK

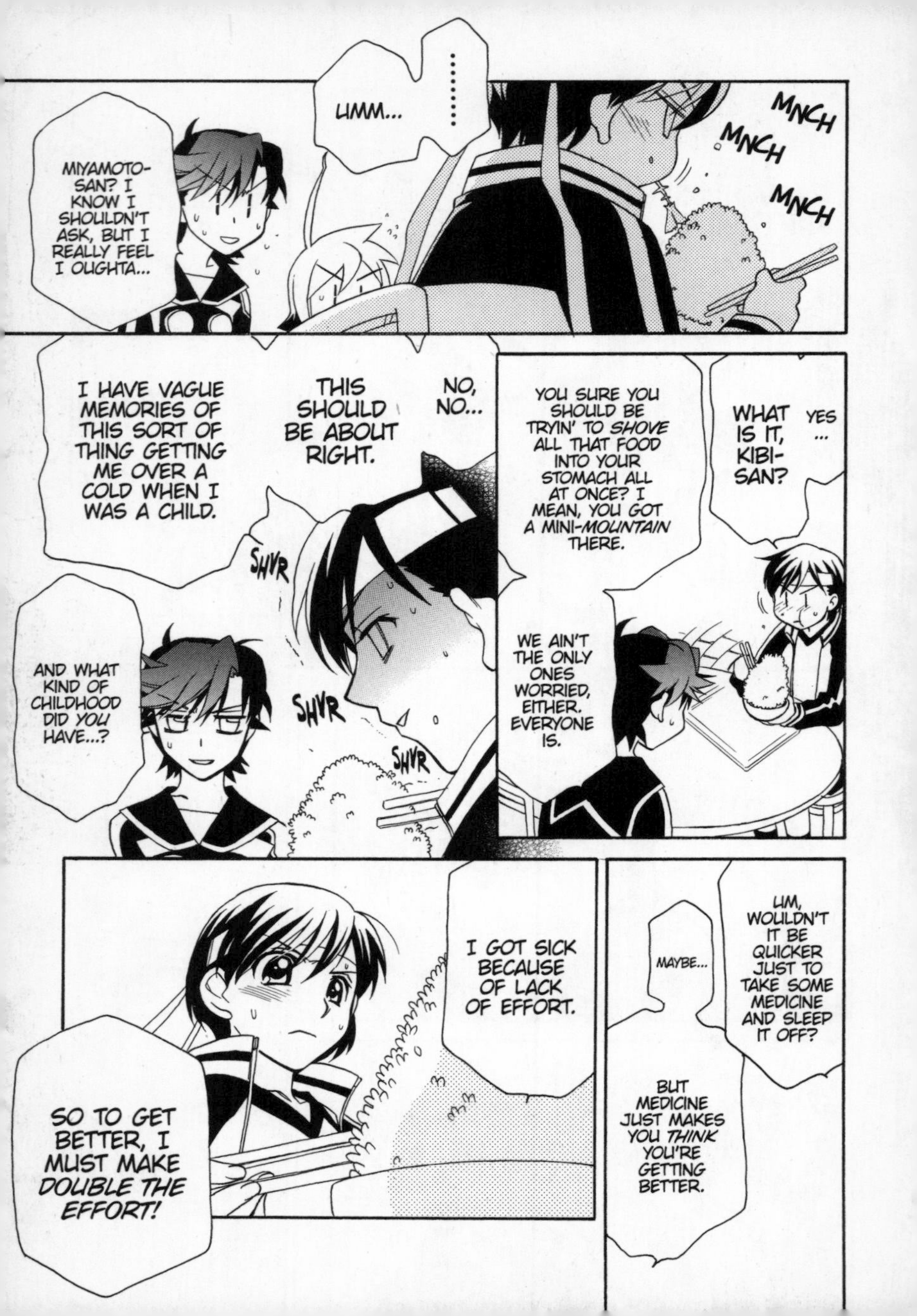
MNCH
MNCH
MNCH
......
UMM...
MIYAMOTO-SAN? I KNOW I SHOULDN'T ASK, BUT I REALLY FEEL I OUGHTA...
YES ...
WHAT IS IT, KIBI-SAN?
YOU SURE YOU SHOULD BE TRYIN' TO *SHOVE* ALL THAT FOOD INTO YOUR STOMACH ALL AT ONCE? I MEAN, YOU GOT A MINI-*MOUNTAIN* THERE.
WE AIN'T THE ONLY ONES WORRIED, EITHER. EVERYONE IS.
NO, NO...
THIS SHOULD BE ABOUT RIGHT.
I HAVE VAGUE MEMORIES OF THIS SORT OF THING GETTING ME OVER A COLD WHEN I WAS A CHILD.
SHVR
SHVR
SHVR
AND WHAT KIND OF CHILDHOOD DID *YOU* HAVE...?
UM, WOULDN'T IT BE QUICKER JUST TO TAKE SOME MEDICINE AND SLEEP IT OFF?
MAYBE...
BUT MEDICINE JUST MAKES YOU *THINK* YOU'RE GETTING BETTER.
I GOT SICK BECAUSE OF LACK OF EFFORT.
SO TO GET BETTER, I MUST MAKE *DOUBLE THE EFFORT!*

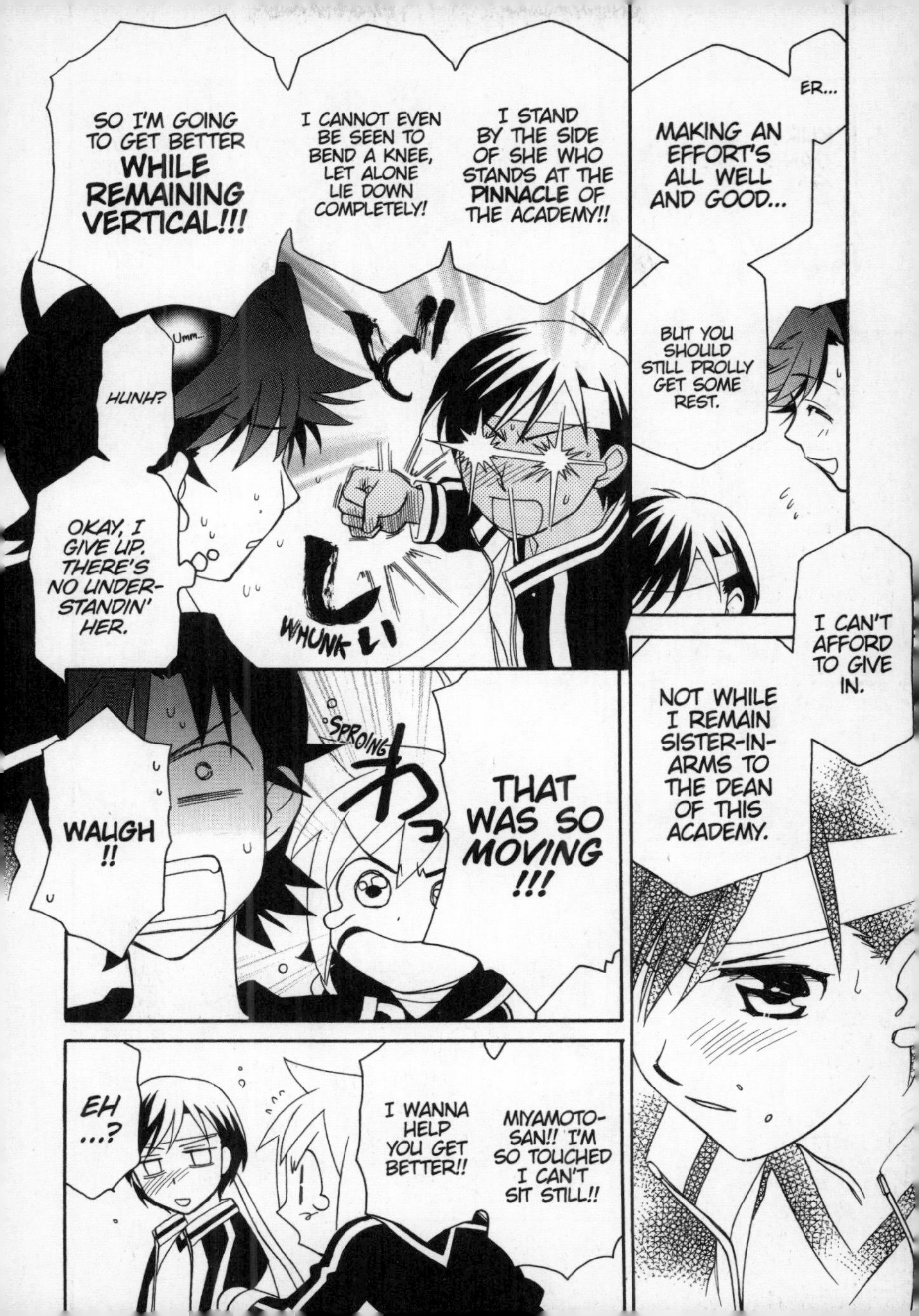
ER...
MAKING AN EFFORT'S ALL WELL AND GOOD...
BUT YOU SHOULD STILL PROLLY GET SOME REST.
I STAND BY THE SIDE OF SHE WHO STANDS AT THE PINNACLE OF THE ACADEMY!!
I CANNOT EVEN BE SEEN TO BEND A KNEE, LET ALONE LIE DOWN COMPLETELY!
SO I'M GOING TO GET BETTER **WHILE REMAINING VERTICAL!!!**
Umm...
HUNH?
WHUNK
OKAY, I GIVE UP. THERE'S NO UNDER-STANDIN' HER.
I CAN'T AFFORD TO GIVE IN.
NOT WHILE I REMAIN SISTER-IN-ARMS TO THE DEAN OF THIS ACADEMY.
SPROING
THAT WAS SO MOVING!!!
WAUGH!!
MIYAMOTO-SAN!! I'M SO TOUCHED I CAN'T SIT STILL!!
I WANNA HELP YOU GET BETTER!!
EH...?

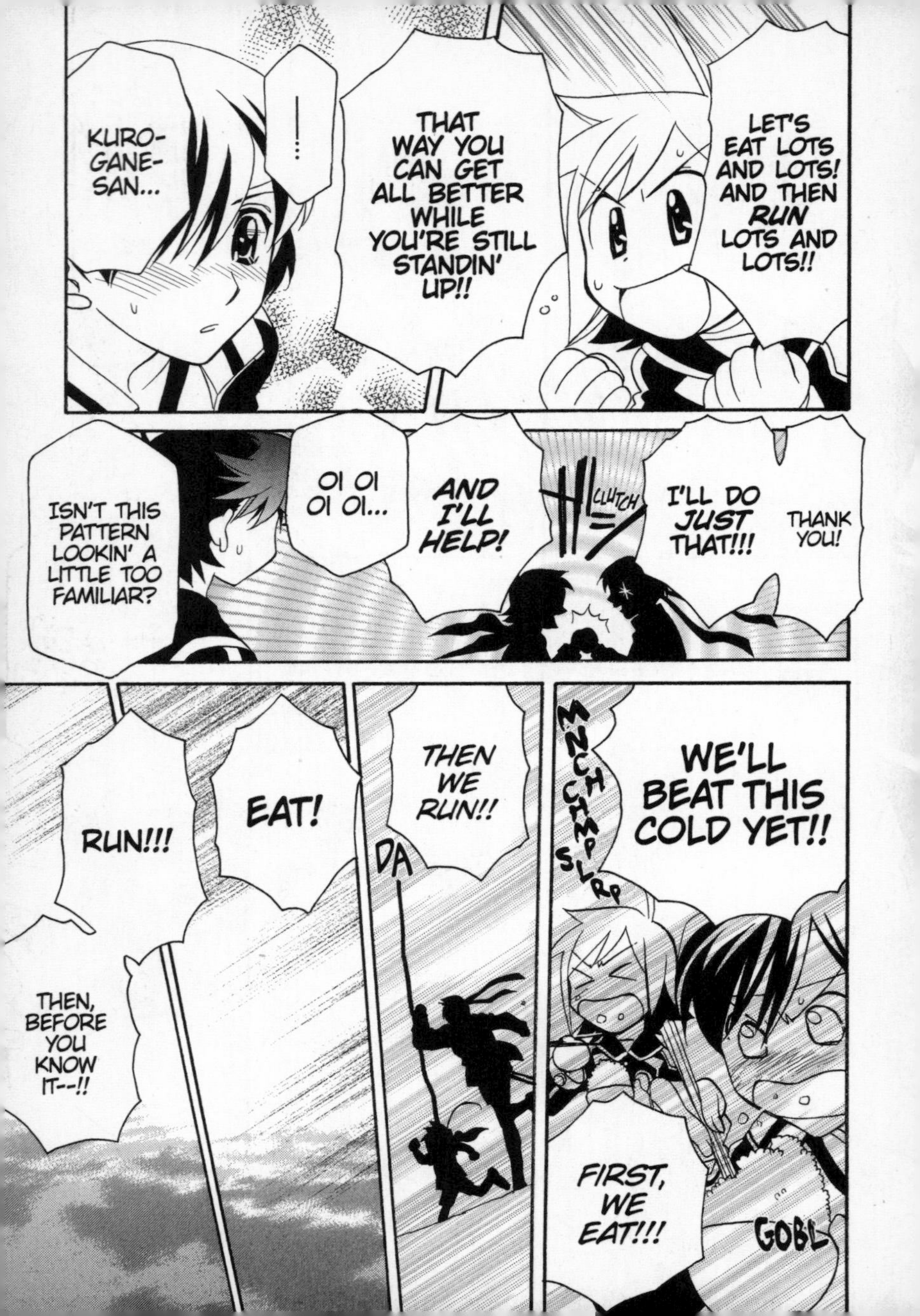
LET'S EAT LOTS AND LOTS! AND THEN *RUN* LOTS AND LOTS!!
THAT WAY YOU CAN GET ALL BETTER WHILE YOU'RE STILL STANDIN' UP!!
......!
KURO-GANE-SAN...
THANK YOU!
I'LL DO *JUST* THAT!!!
CLUTCH
AND I'LL HELP!
OI OI OI OI...
ISN'T THIS PATTERN LOOKIN' A LITTLE TOO FAMILIAR?
WE'LL BEAT THIS COLD YET!!
MNCH CHMP SLRP
FIRST, WE EAT!!!
GOBL
THEN WE RUN!!
DA
EAT!
RUN!!!
THEN, BEFORE YOU KNOW IT--!!

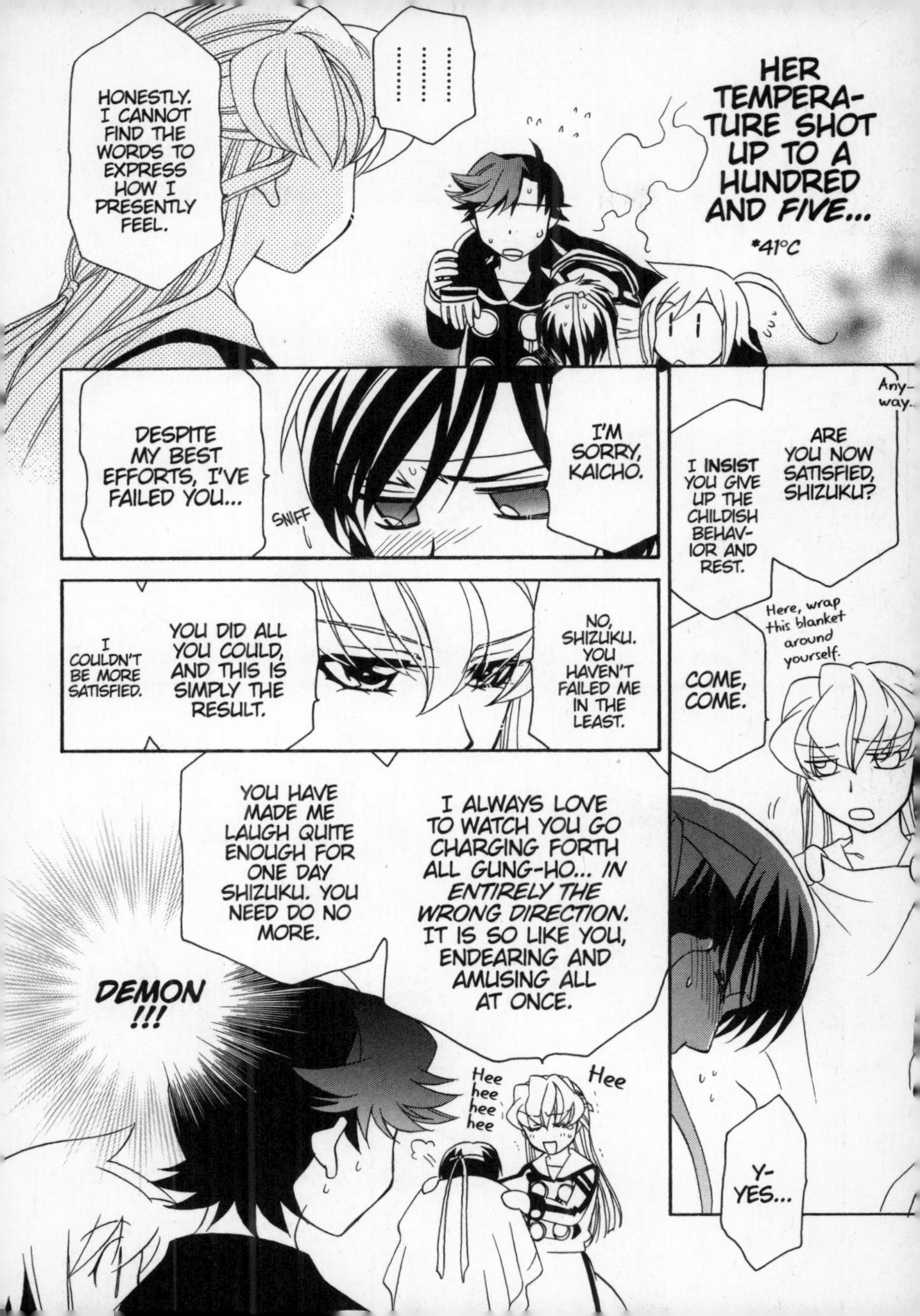
HER TEMPERATURE SHOT UP TO A HUNDRED AND *FIVE...*
*41°C
......
HONESTLY. I CANNOT FIND THE WORDS TO EXPRESS HOW I PRESENTLY FEEL.
Any-way..
ARE YOU NOW SATISFIED, SHIZUKU?
I **INSIST** YOU GIVE UP THE CHILDISH BEHAVIOR AND REST.
Here, wrap this blanket around yourself.
COME, COME.
Y-YES...
I'M SORRY, KAICHO.
DESPITE MY BEST EFFORTS, I'VE FAILED YOU...
SNIFF
NO, SHIZUKU. YOU HAVEN'T FAILED ME IN THE LEAST.
YOU DID ALL YOU COULD, AND THIS IS SIMPLY THE RESULT.
I COULDN'T BE MORE SATISFIED.
I ALWAYS LOVE TO WATCH YOU GO CHARGING FORTH ALL GUNG-HO... *IN ENTIRELY THE WRONG DIRECTION.* IT IS SO LIKE YOU, ENDEARING AND AMUSING ALL AT ONCE.
YOU HAVE MADE ME LAUGH QUITE ENOUGH FOR ONE DAY SHIZUKU. YOU NEED DO NO MORE.
Hee
Hee hee hee hee
DEMON !!!

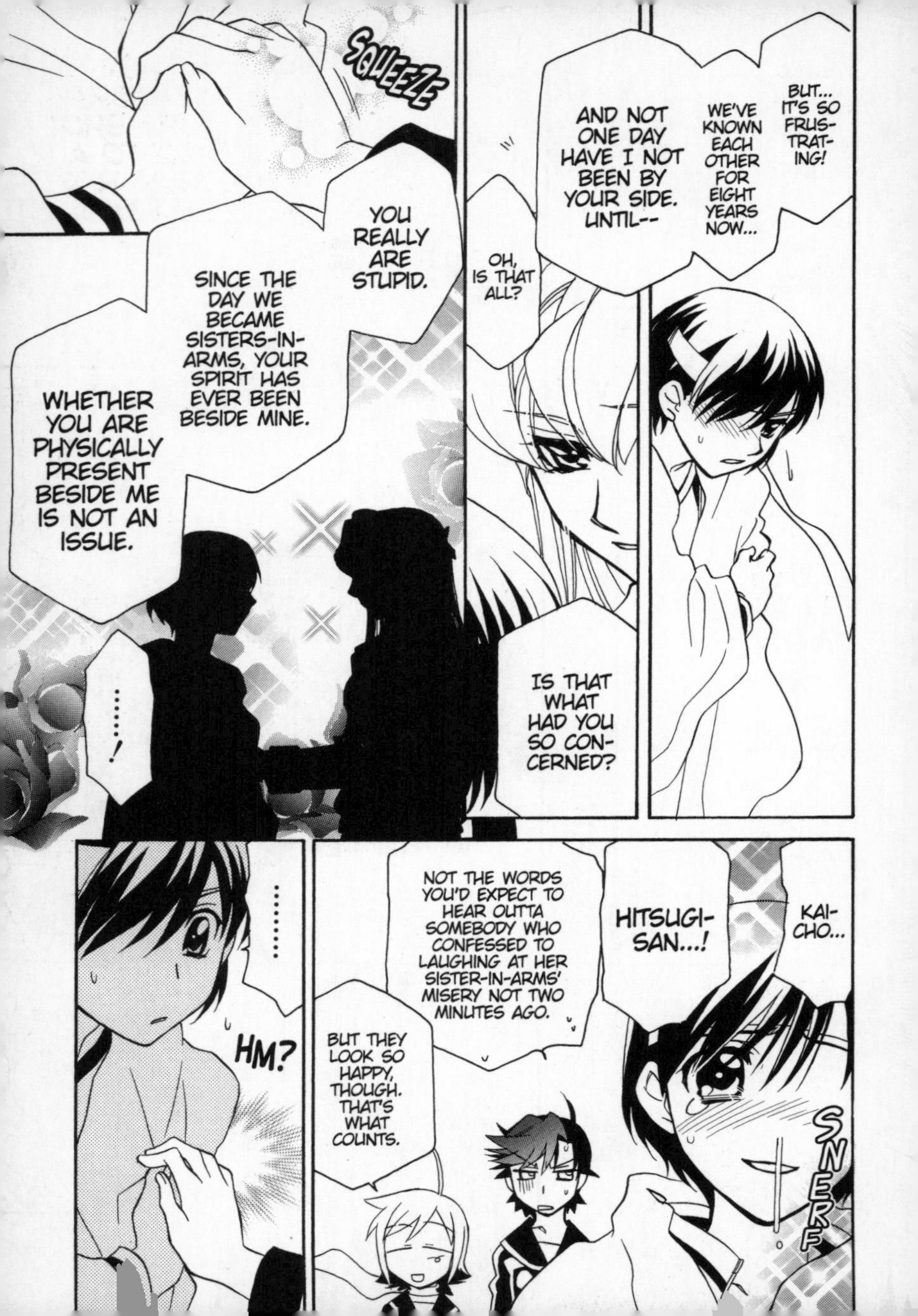
BUT... IT'S SO FRUS-TRAT-ING!
WE'VE KNOWN EACH OTHER FOR EIGHT YEARS NOW...
AND NOT ONE DAY HAVE I NOT BEEN BY YOUR SIDE. UNTIL--
SQUEEZE
OH, IS THAT ALL?
IS THAT WHAT HAD YOU SO CON-CERNED?
YOU REALLY ARE STUPID.
SINCE THE DAY WE BECAME SISTERS-IN-ARMS, YOUR SPIRIT HAS EVER BEEN BESIDE MINE.
WHETHER YOU ARE PHYSICALLY PRESENT BESIDE ME IS NOT AN ISSUE.
......!
KAI-CHO...
HITSUGI-SAN...!
NOT THE WORDS YOU'D EXPECT TO HEAR OUTTA SOMEBODY WHO CONFESSED TO LAUGHING AT HER SISTER-IN-ARMS' MISERY NOT TWO MINUTES AGO.
BUT THEY LOOK SO HAPPY, THOUGH. THAT'S WHAT COUNTS.
SNERF
......
HM?

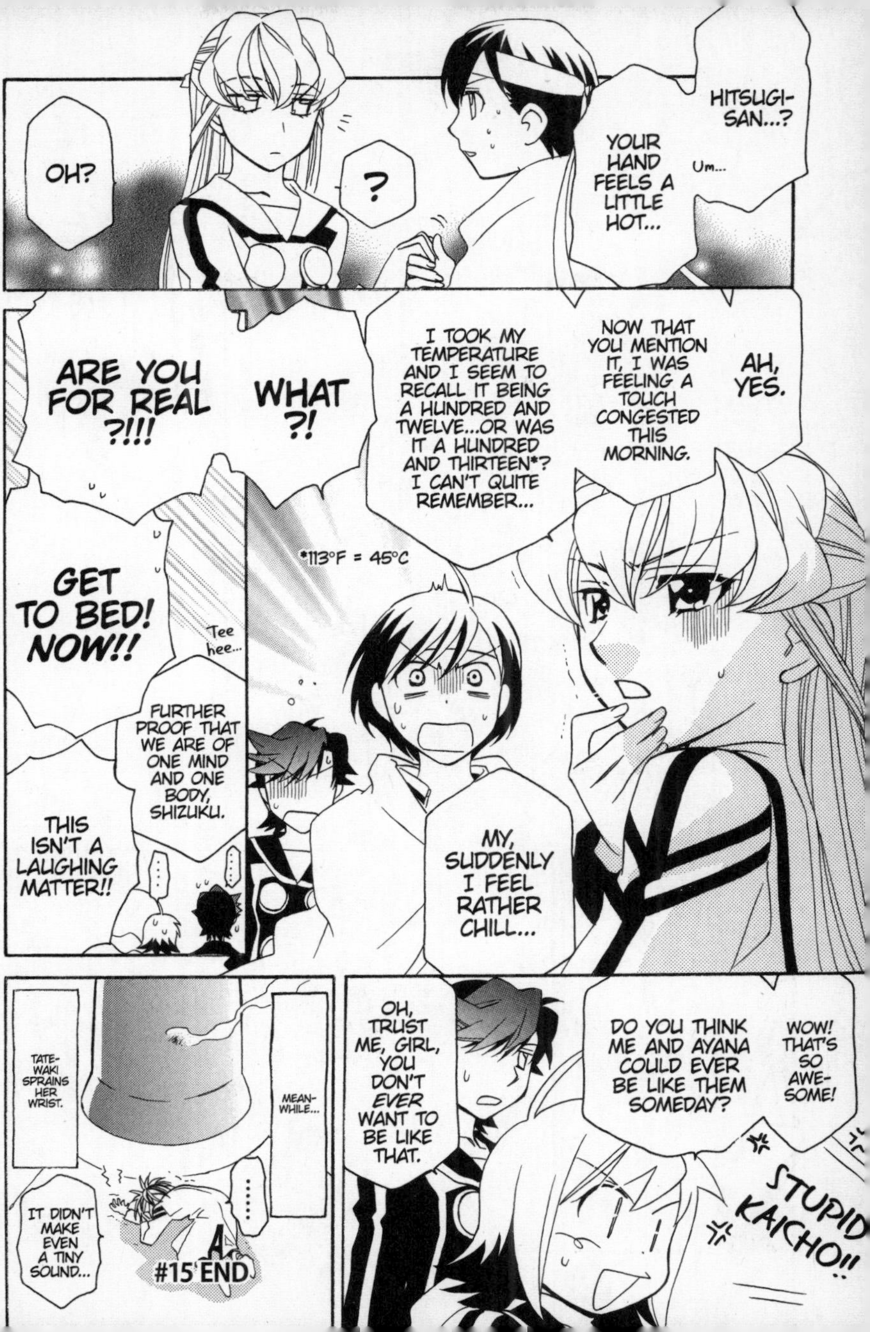
HITSUGI-SAN...?
YOUR HAND FEELS A LITTLE HOT...
Um...
?
OH?
AH, YES.
NOW THAT YOU MENTION IT, I WAS FEELING A TOUCH CONGESTED THIS MORNING.
I TOOK MY TEMPERATURE AND I SEEM TO RECALL IT BEING A HUNDRED AND TWELVE...OR WAS IT A HUNDRED AND THIRTEEN*? I CAN'T QUITE REMEMBER...
*113°F = 45°C
MY, SUDDENLY I FEEL RATHER CHILL...
WHAT?!
ARE YOU FOR REAL?!!!
GET TO BED! NOW!!
Tee hee...
FURTHER PROOF THAT WE ARE OF ONE MIND AND ONE BODY, SHIZUKU.
THIS ISN'T A LAUGHING MATTER!!
....
....
WOW! THAT'S SO AWE-SOME!
DO YOU THINK ME AND AYANA COULD EVER BE LIKE THEM SOMEDAY?
OH, TRUST ME, GIRL, YOU DON'T EVER WANT TO BE LIKE THAT.
STUPID KAICHO!!
MEAN-WHILE...
TATE-WAKI SPRAINS HER WRIST.
......
IT DIDN'T MAKE EVEN A TINY SOUND...
#15' END

HAYATE × BLADE

HAYATE CROSS BLADE

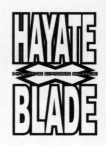

And that was the last time the wretch known as Tatewaki was ever seen.
Stop that. Coming from you, it sounds like it might come true...

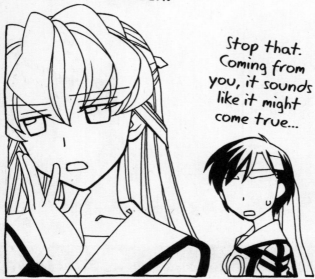

TENCHI ACADEMY SWORD-BEARER LIST

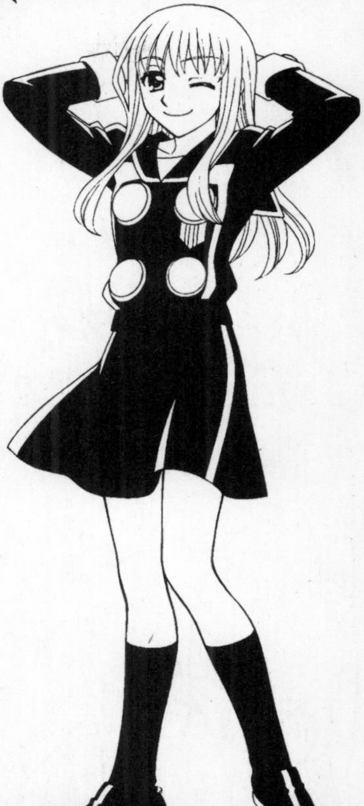

■ DATA ■

Middle School, Class 3-G

Height: 160cm (5′3″)

Weight: 48kg (105lbs.)

Birth Date: June 20

Zodiac: Gemini

Blood Type: B

Favorite Word:
Yuusuu (Morning Star)

■久我順(Kuga Jun)■

●FILE11●

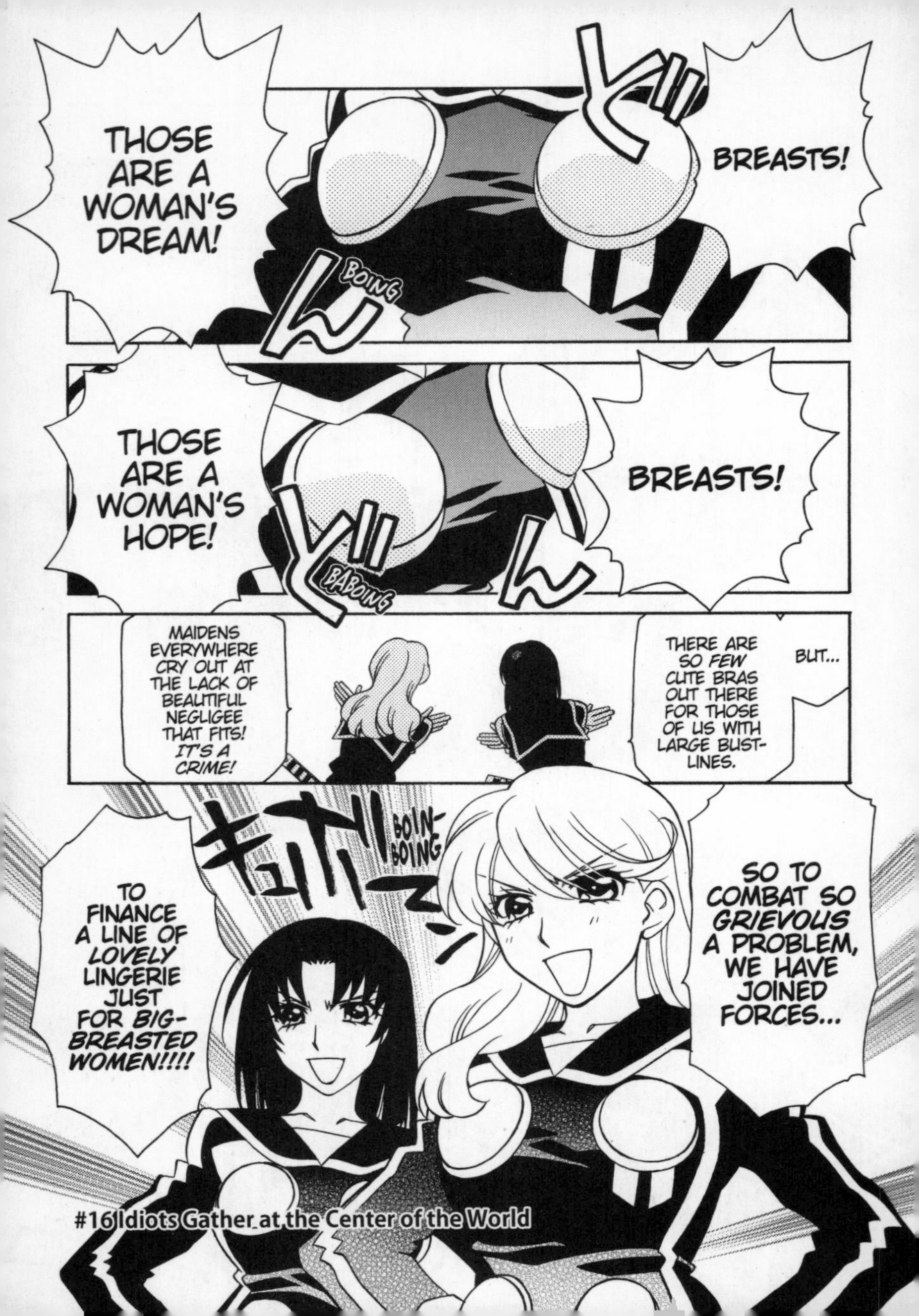
BREASTS!
THOSE ARE A WOMAN'S DREAM!
BOING
BREASTS!
THOSE ARE A WOMAN'S HOPE!
BABOING
BUT...
THERE ARE SO FEW CUTE BRAS OUT THERE FOR THOSE OF US WITH LARGE BUST-LINES.
MAIDENS EVERYWHERE CRY OUT AT THE LACK OF BEAUTIFUL NEGLIGEE THAT FITS! IT'S A CRIME!
SO TO COMBAT SO GRIEVOUS A PROBLEM, WE HAVE JOINED FORCES...
BOIN-BOING
TO FINANCE A LINE OF LOVELY LINGERIE JUST FOR BIG-BREASTED WOMEN!!!!

#16 Idiots Gather at the Center of the World

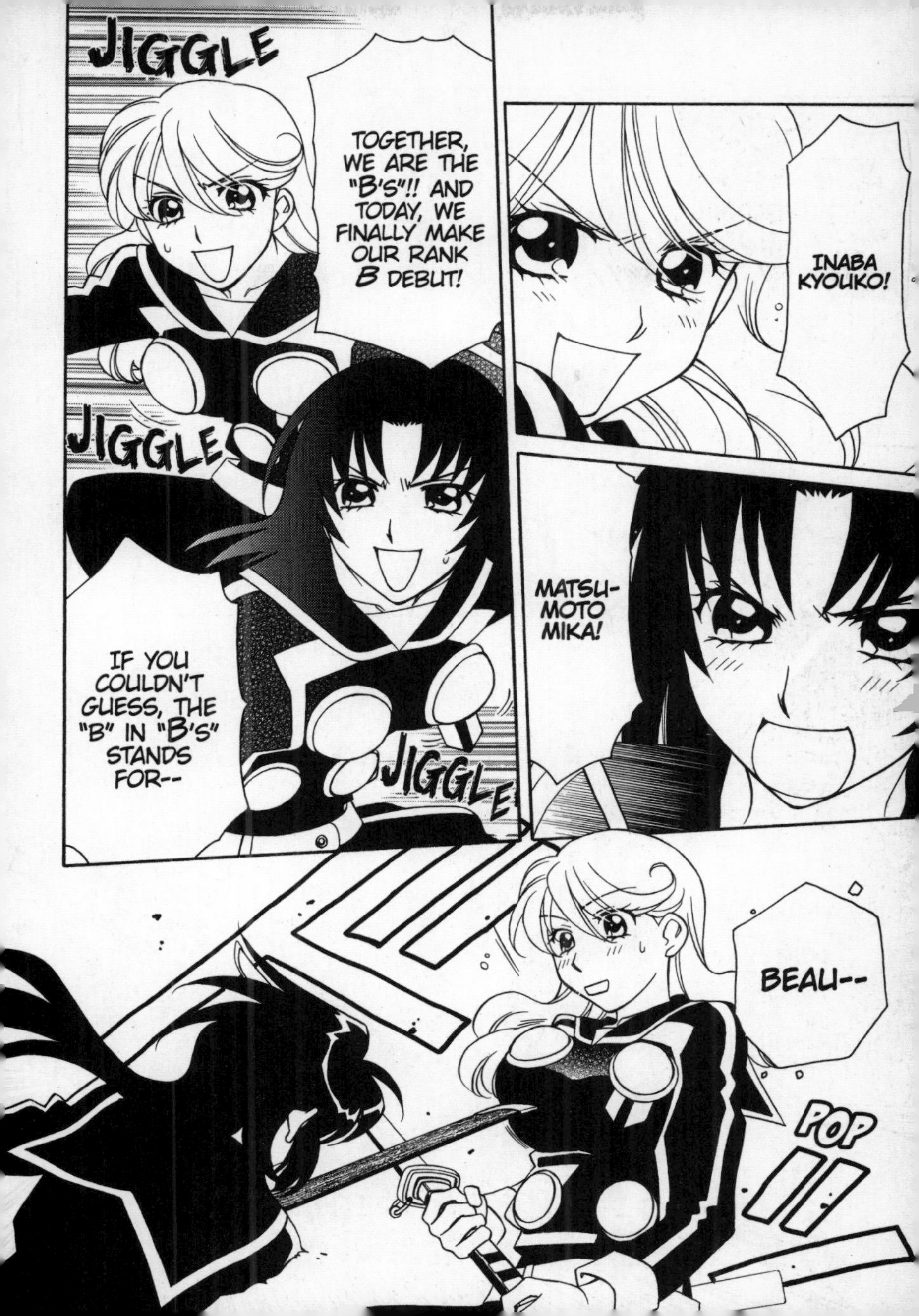
INABA KYOUKO!
MATSU-MOTO MIKA!
TOGETHER, WE ARE THE "B'S"!! AND TODAY, WE FINALLY MAKE OUR RANK B DEBUT!
JIGGLE
JIGGLE
IF YOU COULDN'T GUESS, THE "B" IN "B'S" STANDS FOR--
JIGGLE
BEAU--
POP

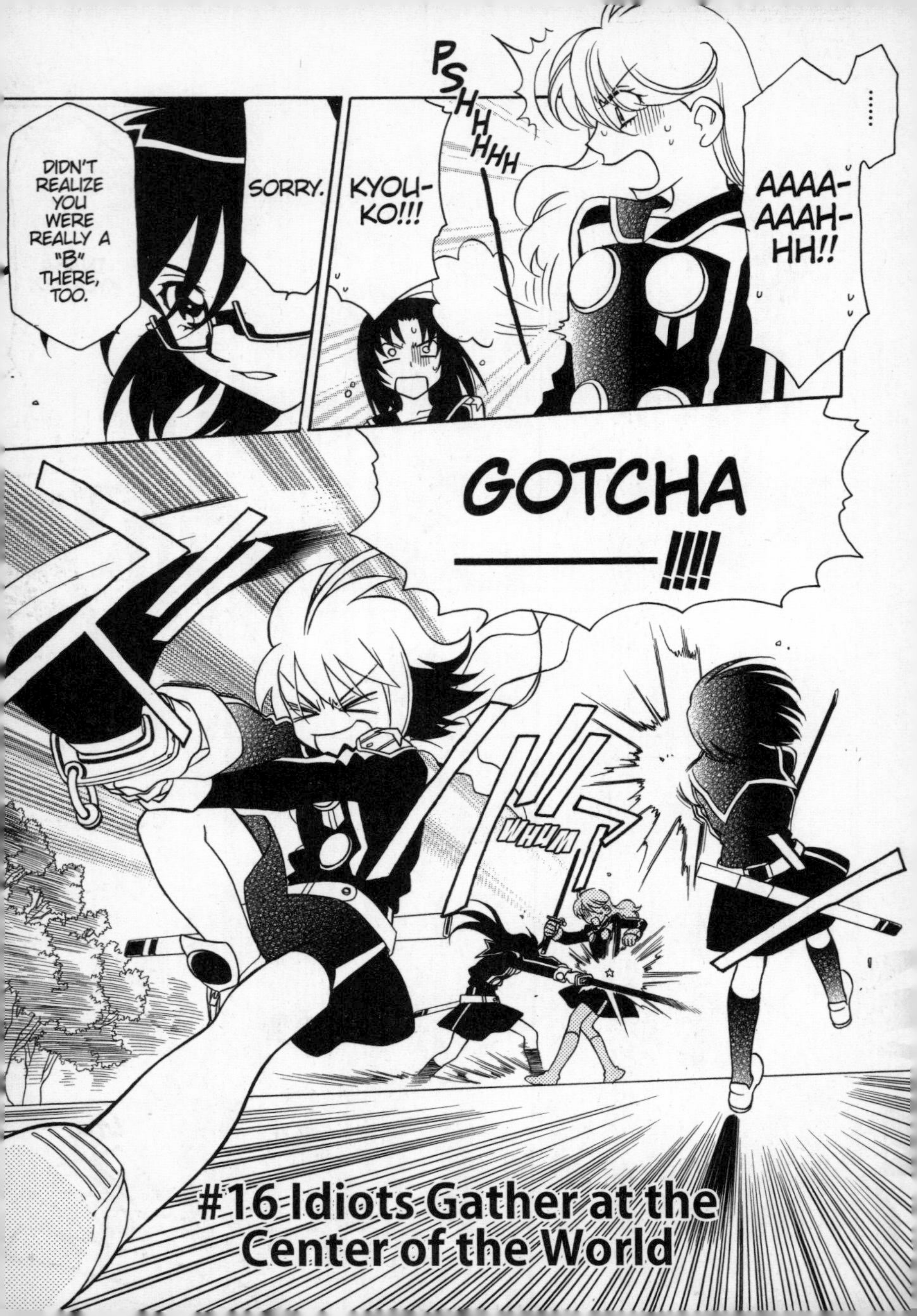
......
AAAA-AAAH-HH!!
PSHHHHHH
KYOU-KO!!!
SORRY.
DIDN'T REALIZE YOU WERE REALLY A "B" THERE, TOO.
GOTCHA ——!!!!
WHUM

#16 Idiots Gather at the Center of the World

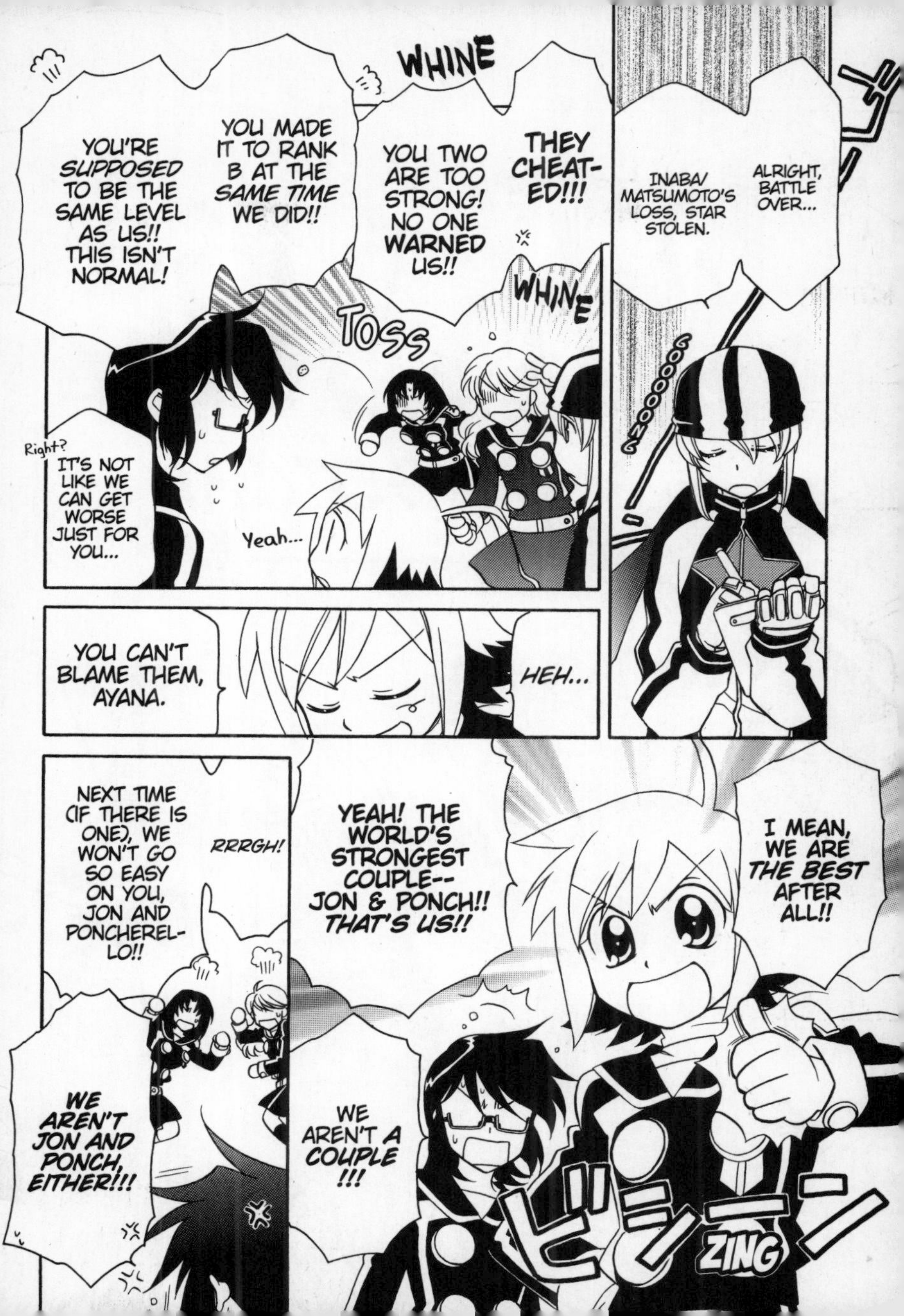
ALRIGHT, BATTLE OVER...
INABA/ MATSUMOTO'S LOSS, STAR STOLEN.
GOOOOONG
THEY CHEAT-ED!!!
WHINE
YOU TWO ARE TOO STRONG! NO ONE WARNED US!!
YOU MADE IT TO RANK B AT THE SAME TIME WE DID!!
YOU'RE SUPPOSED TO BE THE SAME LEVEL AS US!! THIS ISN'T NORMAL!
WHINE
TOSS
Yeah...
Right? IT'S NOT LIKE WE CAN GET WORSE JUST FOR YOU...
HEH...
YOU CAN'T BLAME THEM, AYANA.
I MEAN, WE ARE THE BEST AFTER ALL!!
YEAH! THE WORLD'S STRONGEST COUPLE-- JON & PONCH!! THAT'S US!!
RRRGH!
NEXT TIME (IF THERE IS ONE), WE WON'T GO SO EASY ON YOU, JON AND PONCHEREL-LO!!
WE AREN'T A COUPLE !!!
WE AREN'T JON AND PONCH, EITHER!!!
ZING

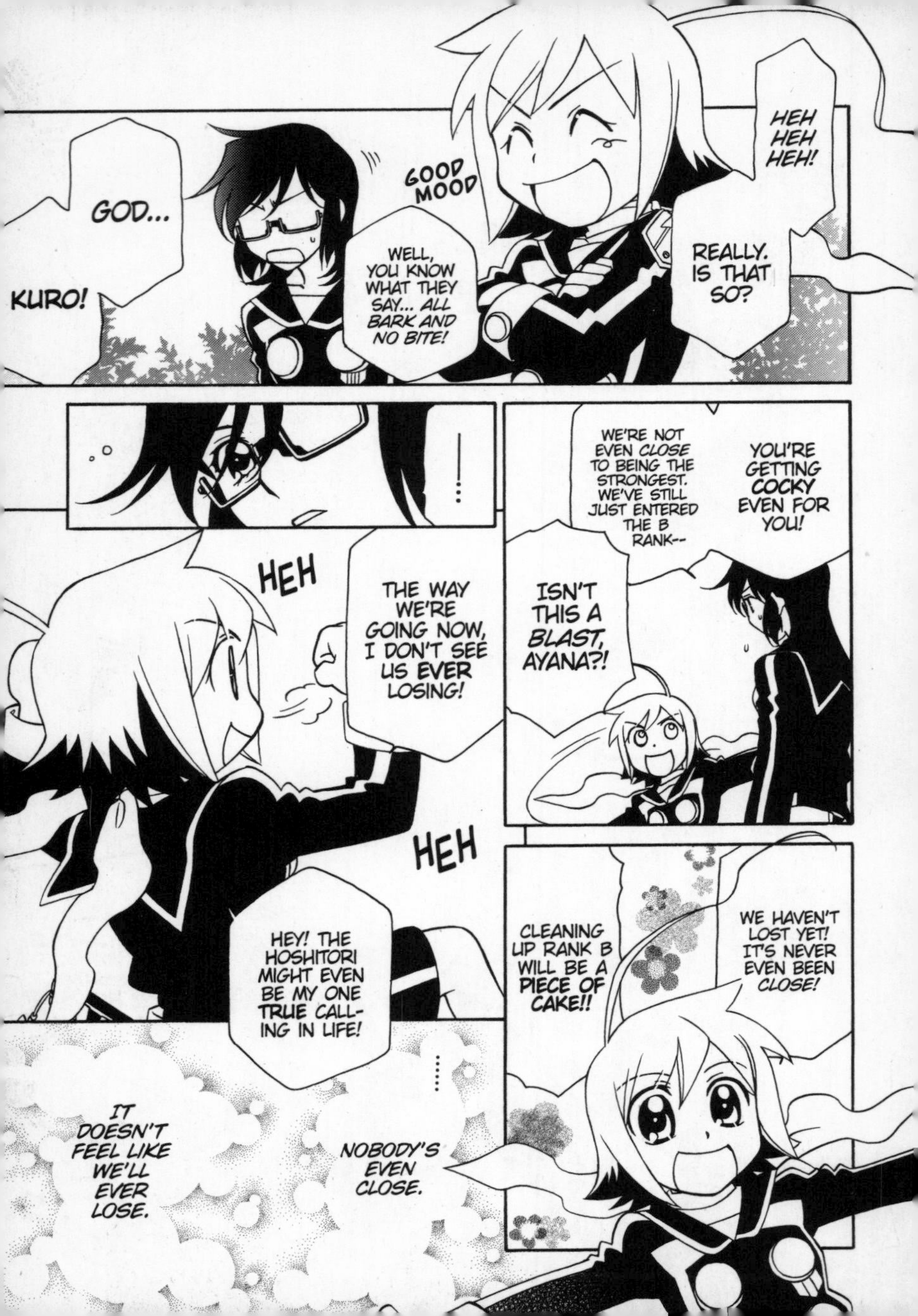
HEH HEH HEH!
REALLY. IS THAT SO?
GOOD MOOD
WELL, YOU KNOW WHAT THEY SAY... *ALL BARK AND NO BITE!*
GOD...
KURO!
YOU'RE GETTING **COCKY** EVEN FOR YOU!
WE'RE NOT EVEN *CLOSE* TO BEING THE STRONGEST. WE'VE STILL JUST ENTERED THE B RANK--
ISN'T THIS A *BLAST*, AYANA?!
......
HEH
THE WAY WE'RE GOING NOW, I DON'T SEE US **EVER** LOSING!
HEH
HEY! THE HOSHITORI MIGHT EVEN BE MY ONE **TRUE** CALL-ING IN LIFE!
WE HAVEN'T LOST YET! IT'S NEVER EVEN BEEN *CLOSE!*
CLEANING UP RANK B WILL BE A **PIECE OF CAKE!!**
......
NOBODY'S EVEN CLOSE.
IT DOESN'T FEEL LIKE WE'LL EVER LOSE.

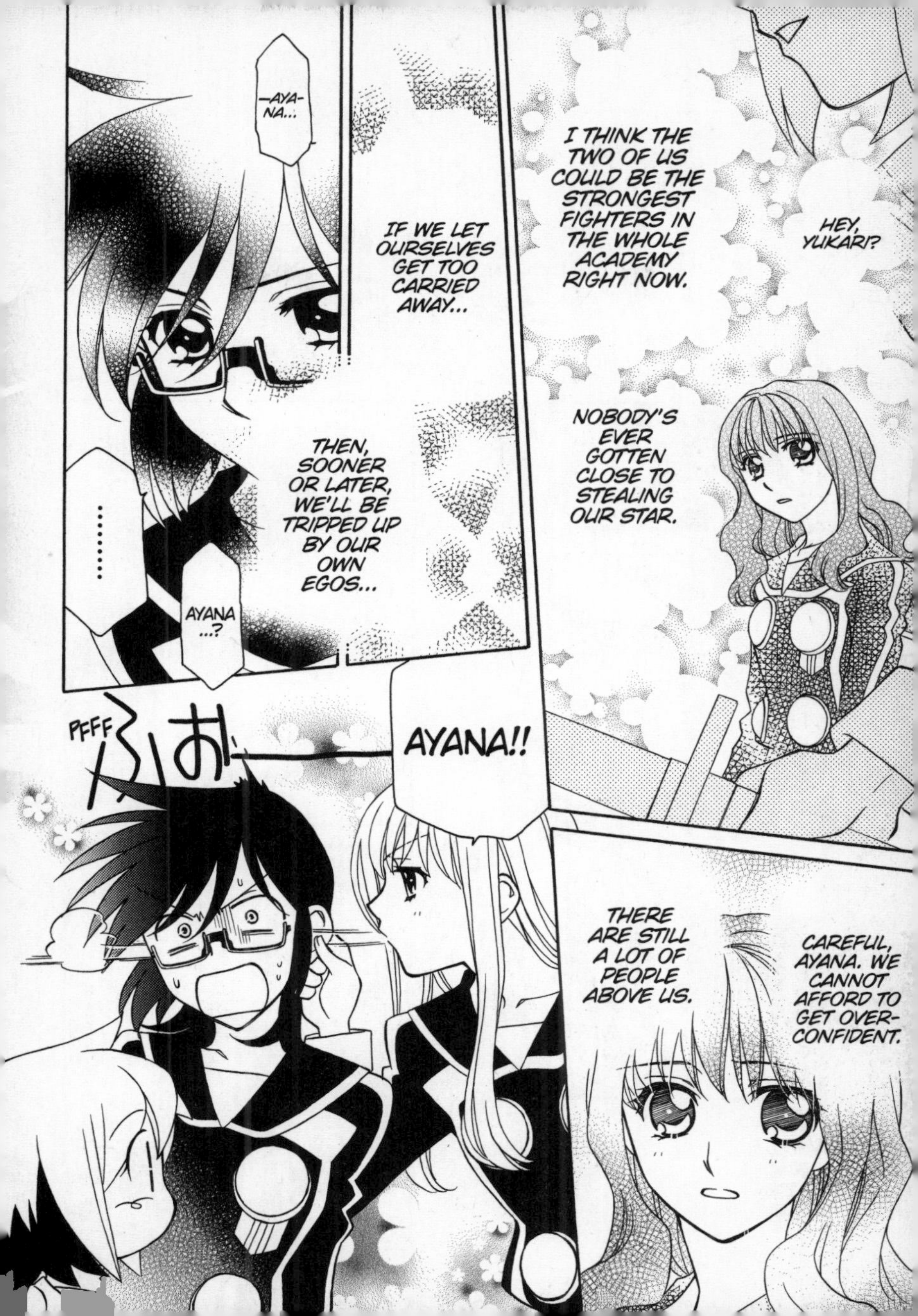
HEY, YUKARI?
I THINK THE TWO OF US COULD BE THE STRONGEST FIGHTERS IN THE WHOLE ACADEMY RIGHT NOW.
NOBODY'S EVER GOTTEN CLOSE TO STEALING OUR STAR.
IF WE LET OURSELVES GET TOO CARRIED AWAY...
THEN, SOONER OR LATER, WE'LL BE TRIPPED UP BY OUR OWN EGOS...
—AYA-NA...
....
AYANA ...?
CAREFUL, AYANA. WE CANNOT AFFORD TO GET OVER-CONFIDENT.
THERE ARE STILL A LOT OF PEOPLE ABOVE US.
AYANA!!
PFFF
ふぉ!

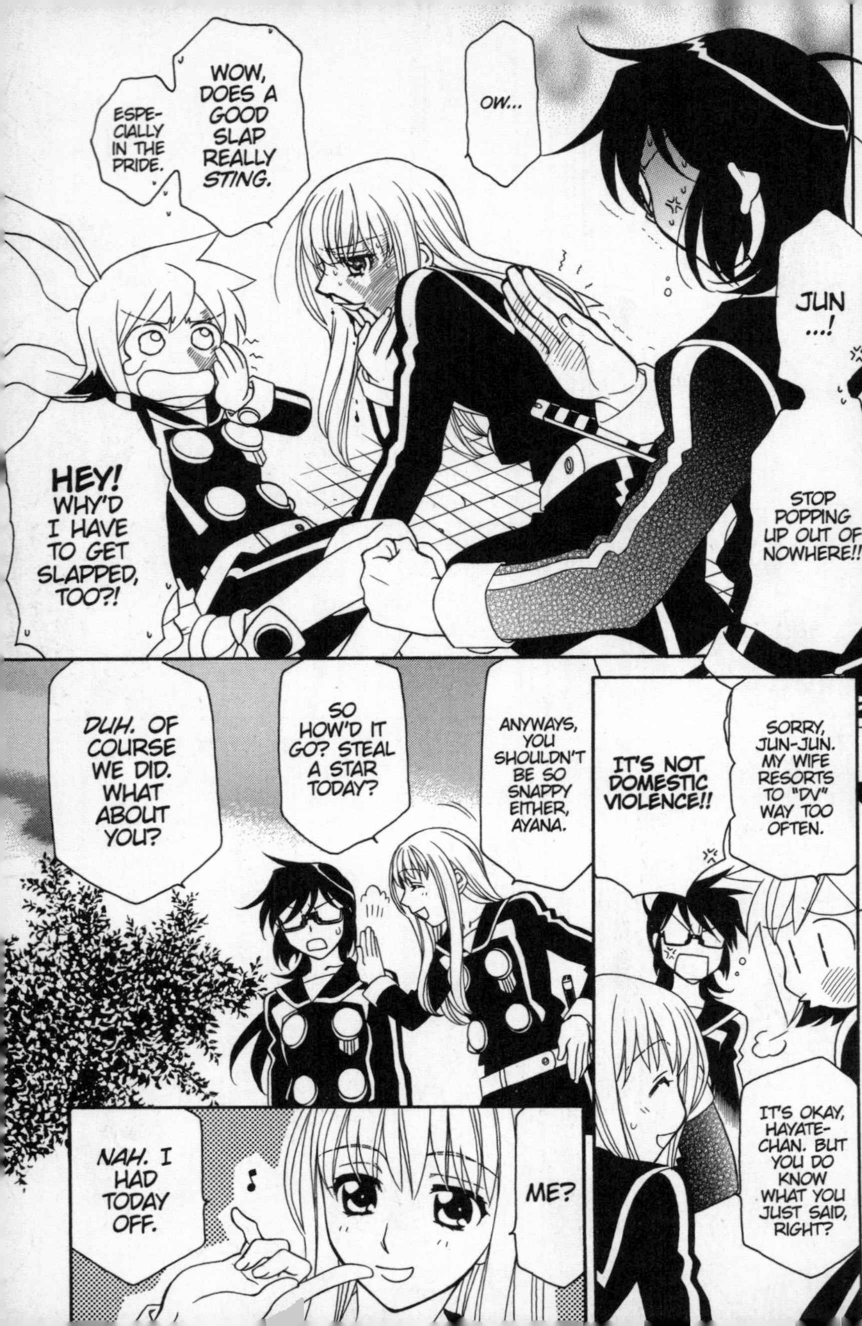
OW...
WOW, DOES A GOOD SLAP REALLY STING.
ESPECIALLY IN THE PRIDE.
JUN ...!
STOP POPPING UP OUT OF NOWHERE!!
HEY! WHY'D I HAVE TO GET SLAPPED, TOO?!
SORRY, JUN-JUN. MY WIFE RESORTS TO "DV" WAY TOO OFTEN.
IT'S NOT DOMESTIC VIOLENCE!!
IT'S OKAY, HAYATE-CHAN. BUT YOU DO KNOW WHAT YOU JUST SAID, RIGHT?
ANYWAYS, YOU SHOULDN'T BE SO SNAPPY EITHER, AYANA.
SO HOW'D IT GO? STEAL A STAR TODAY?
DUH. OF COURSE WE DID. WHAT ABOUT YOU?
ME?
NAH. I HAD TODAY OFF.

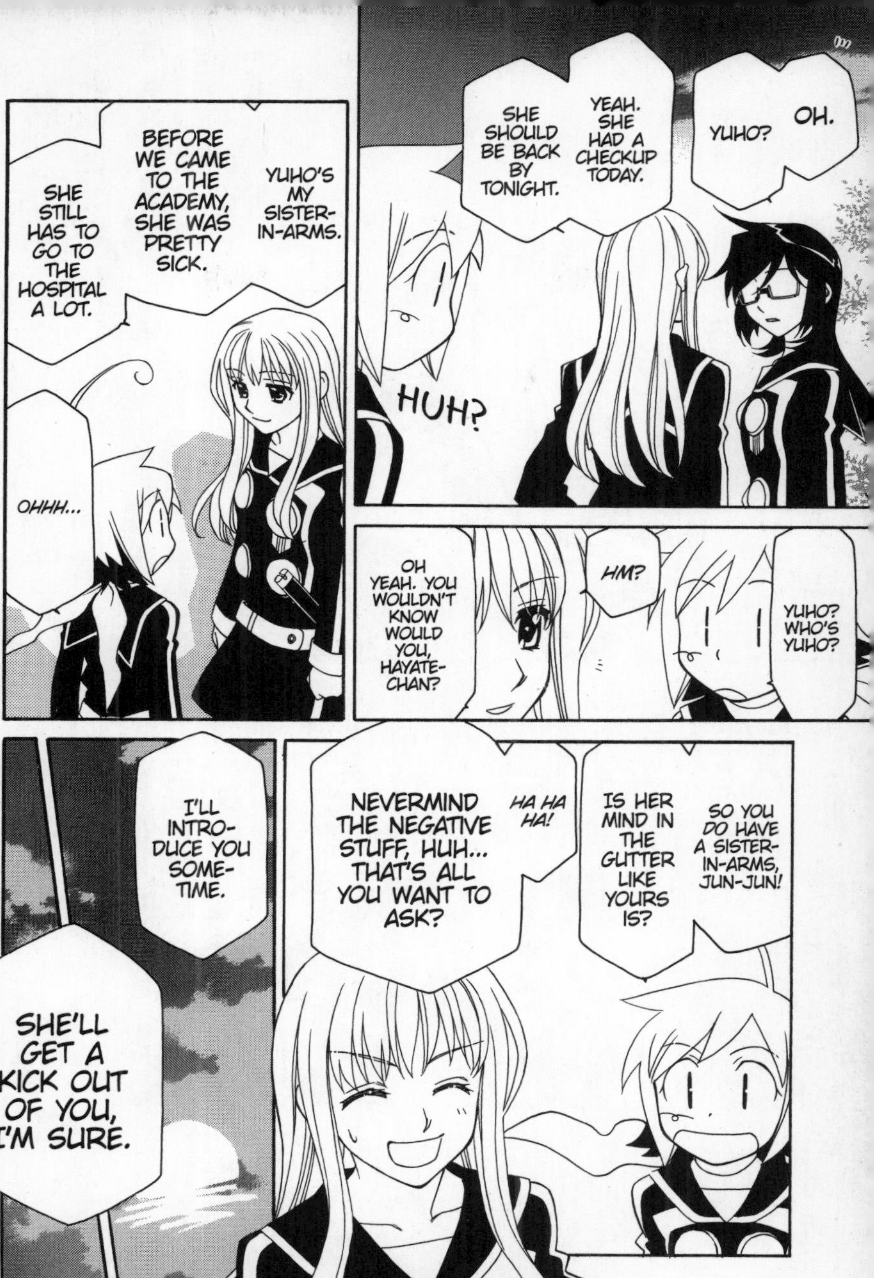
OH.
YUHO?
YEAH. SHE HAD A CHECKUP TODAY.
SHE SHOULD BE BACK BY TONIGHT.
HUH?
YUHO? WHO'S YUHO?
HM?
OH YEAH. YOU WOULDN'T KNOW WOULD YOU, HAYATE-CHAN?
YUHO'S MY SISTER-IN-ARMS.
BEFORE WE CAME TO THE ACADEMY, SHE WAS PRETTY SICK.
SHE STILL HAS TO GO TO THE HOSPITAL A LOT.
OHHH...
SO YOU DO HAVE A SISTER-IN-ARMS, JUN-JUN!
IS HER MIND IN THE GUTTER LIKE YOURS IS?
HA HA HA!
NEVERMIND THE NEGATIVE STUFF, HUH... THAT'S ALL YOU WANT TO ASK?
I'LL INTRO-DUCE YOU SOME-TIME.
SHE'LL GET A KICK OUT OF YOU, I'M SURE.

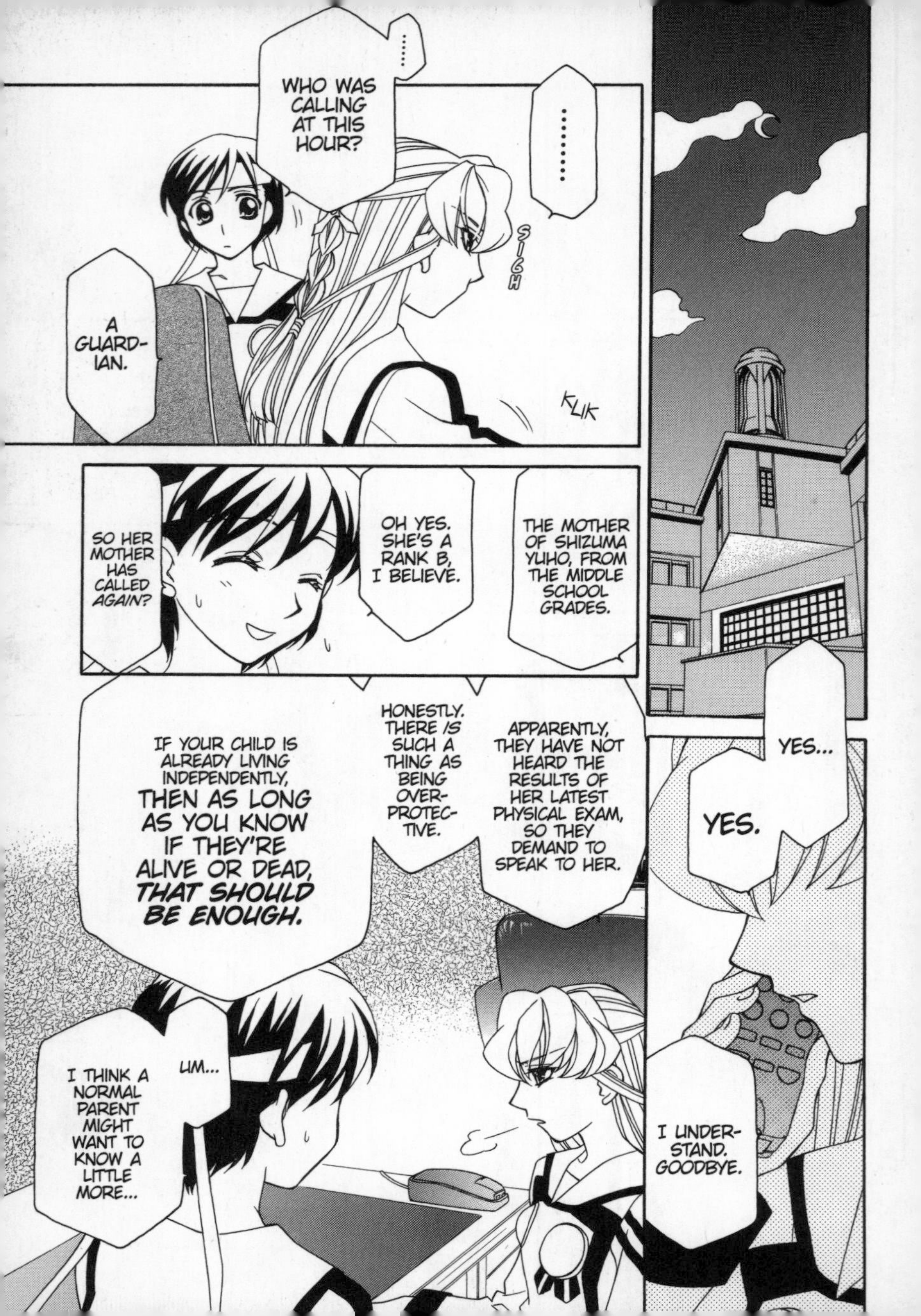
YES...
YES.
I UNDER-STAND. GOODBYE.
......
WHO WAS CALLING AT THIS HOUR?
......
SIGH
A GUARD-IAN.
KLIK
THE MOTHER OF SHIZUMA YUHO, FROM THE MIDDLE SCHOOL GRADES.
OH YES. SHE'S A RANK B, I BELIEVE.
SO HER MOTHER HAS CALLED *AGAIN*?
APPARENTLY, THEY HAVE NOT HEARD THE RESULTS OF HER LATEST PHYSICAL EXAM, SO THEY DEMAND TO SPEAK TO HER.
HONESTLY. THERE *IS* SUCH A THING AS BEING OVER-PROTEC-TIVE.
IF YOUR CHILD IS ALREADY LIVING INDEPENDENTLY, **THEN AS LONG AS YOU KNOW IF THEY'RE ALIVE OR DEAD, *THAT SHOULD BE ENOUGH.***
UM...
I THINK A NORMAL PARENT MIGHT WANT TO KNOW A LITTLE MORE...

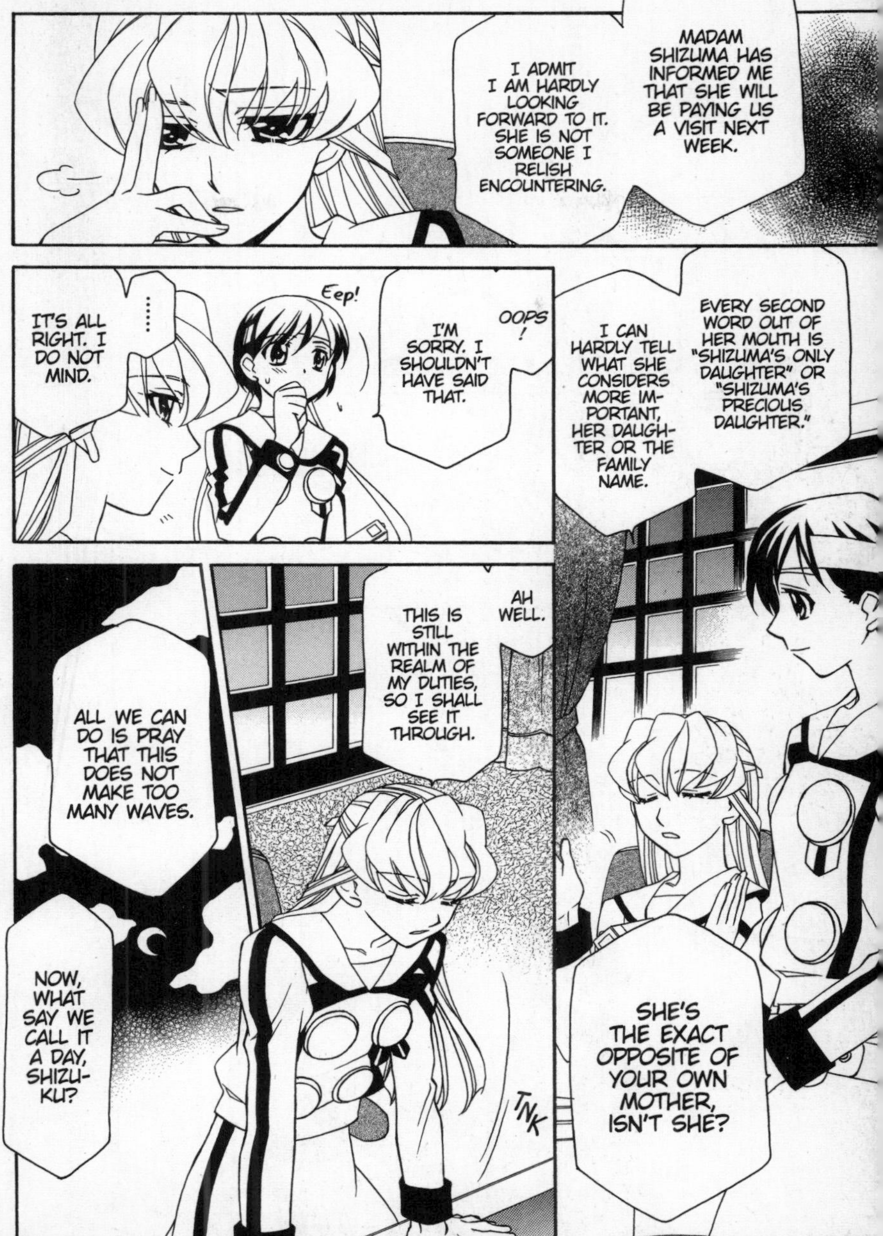
MADAM SHIZUMA HAS INFORMED ME THAT SHE WILL BE PAYING US A VISIT NEXT WEEK.
I ADMIT I AM HARDLY LOOKING FORWARD TO IT. SHE IS NOT SOMEONE I RELISH ENCOUNTERING.
EVERY SECOND WORD OUT OF HER MOUTH IS "SHIZUMA'S ONLY DAUGHTER" OR "SHIZUMA'S PRECIOUS DAUGHTER."
I CAN HARDLY TELL WHAT SHE CONSIDERS MORE IM-PORTANT, HER DAUGH-TER OR THE FAMILY NAME.
SHE'S THE EXACT OPPOSITE OF YOUR OWN MOTHER, ISN'T SHE?
OOPS!
I'M SORRY. I SHOULDN'T HAVE SAID THAT.
Eep!
......
IT'S ALL RIGHT. I DO NOT MIND.
AH WELL.
THIS IS STILL WITHIN THE REALM OF MY DUTIES, SO I SHALL SEE IT THROUGH.
ALL WE CAN DO IS PRAY THAT THIS DOES NOT MAKE TOO MANY WAVES.
NOW, WHAT SAY WE CALL IT A DAY, SHIZU-KU?
TNK

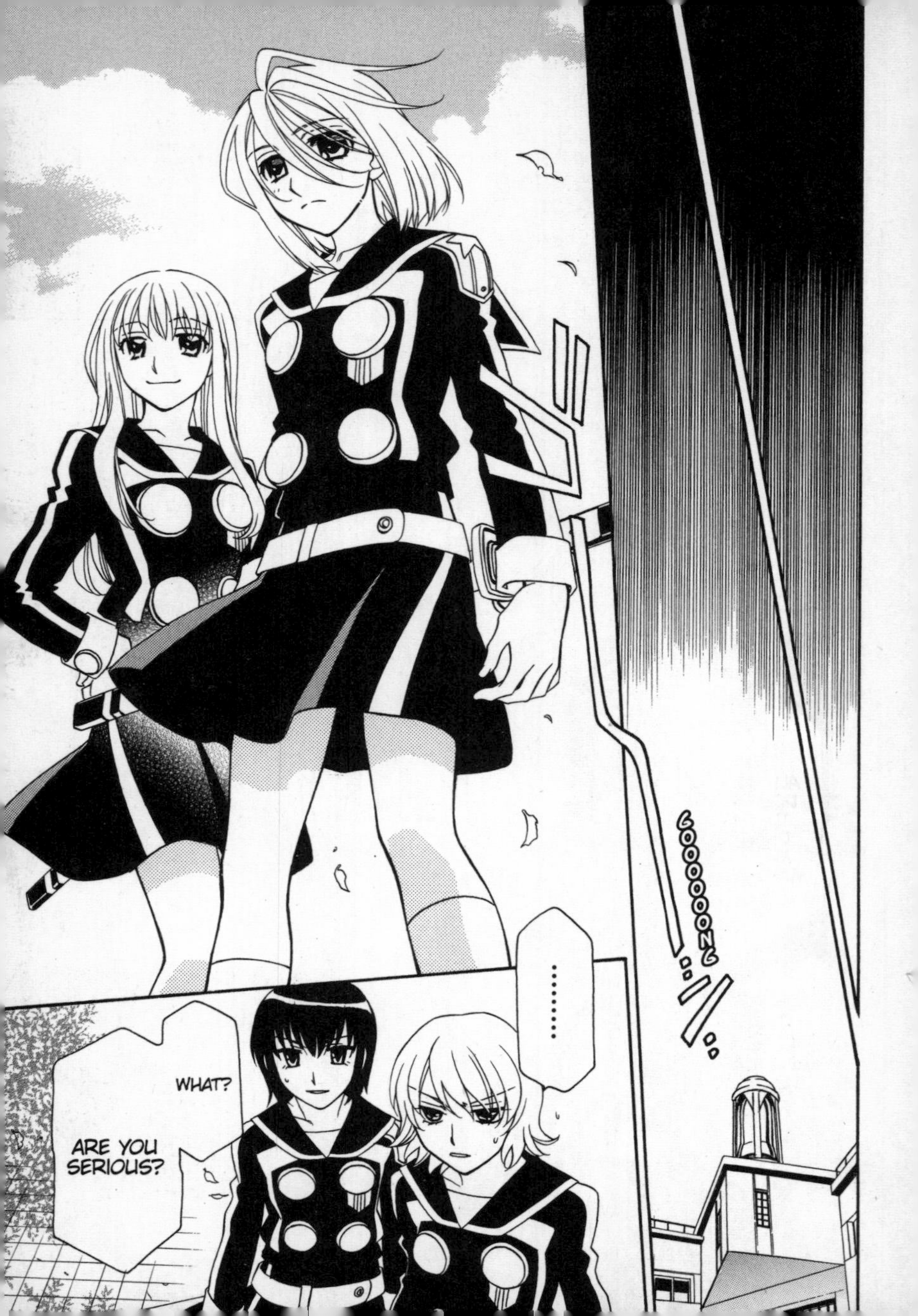
GOOOOOOONG
......
WHAT? ARE YOU SERIOUS?

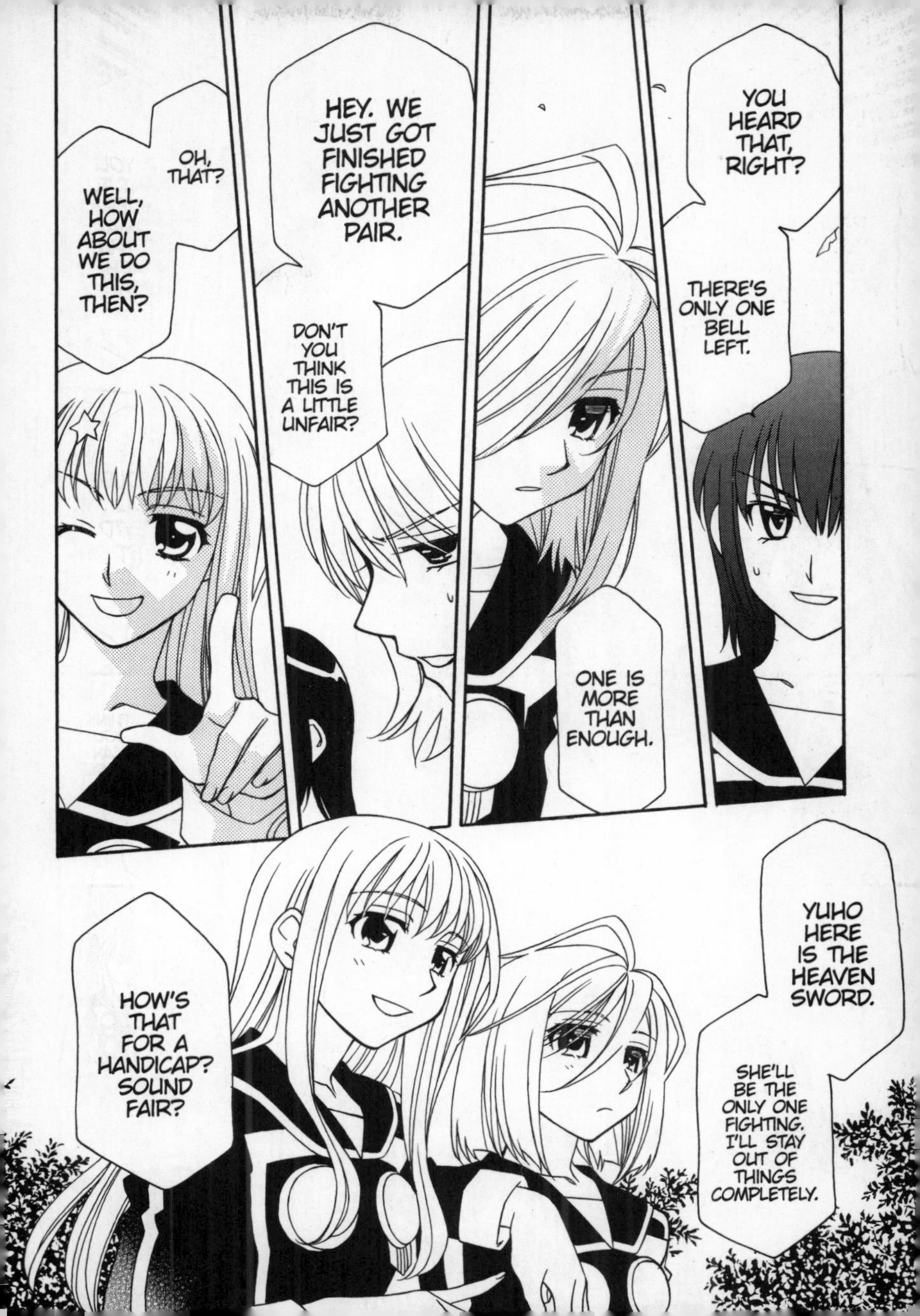
YOU HEARD THAT, RIGHT?
THERE'S ONLY ONE BELL LEFT.
ONE IS MORE THAN ENOUGH.
HEY. WE JUST GOT FINISHED FIGHTING ANOTHER PAIR.
DON'T YOU THINK THIS IS A LITTLE UNFAIR?
OH, THAT?
WELL, HOW ABOUT WE DO THIS, THEN?
YUHO HERE IS THE HEAVEN SWORD.
SHE'LL BE THE ONLY ONE FIGHTING. I'LL STAY OUT OF THINGS COMPLETELY.
HOW'S THAT FOR A HANDICAP? SOUND FAIR?

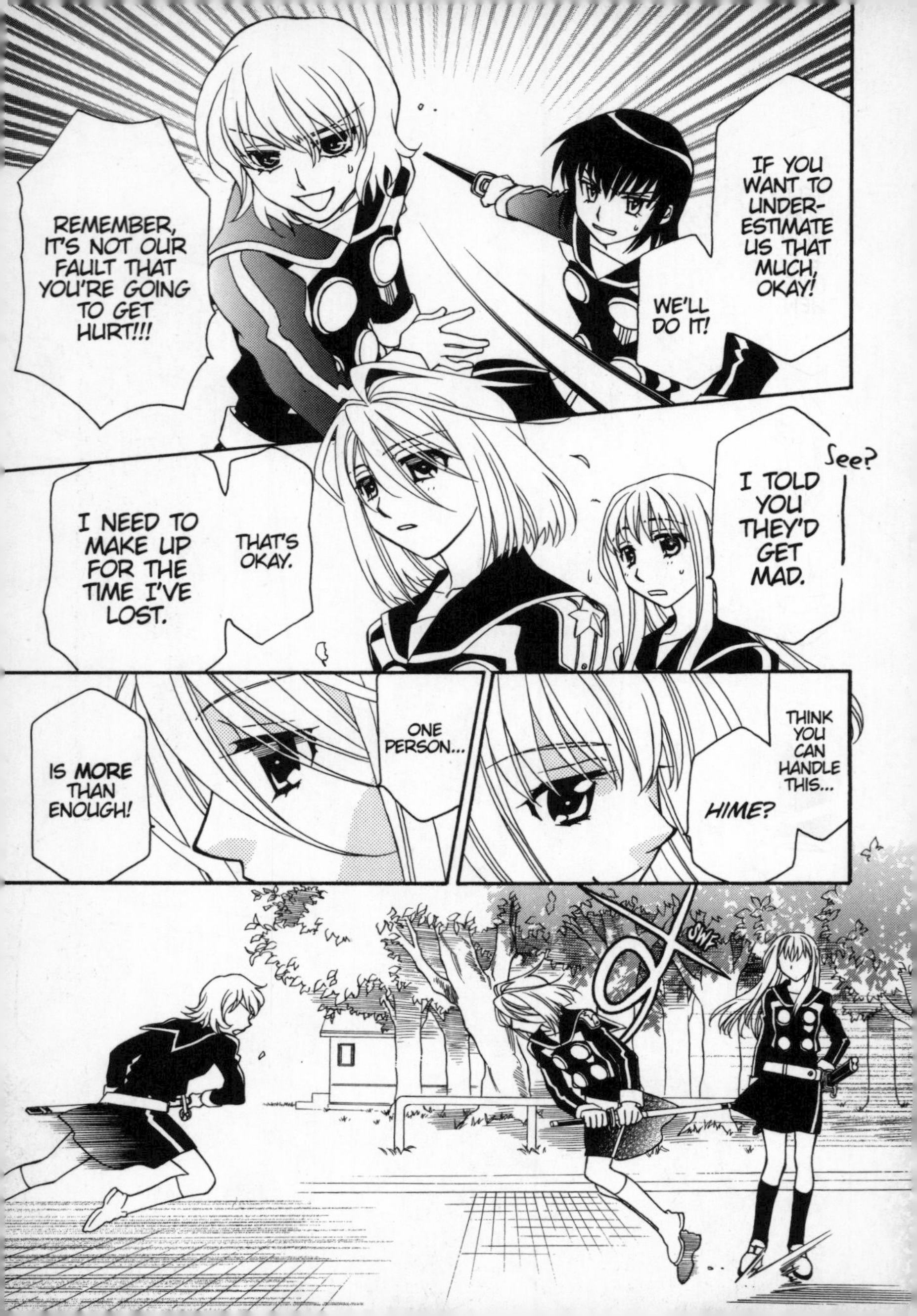
IF YOU WANT TO UNDER-ESTIMATE US THAT MUCH, OKAY!
WE'LL DO IT!
REMEMBER, IT'S NOT OUR FAULT THAT YOU'RE GOING TO GET HURT!!!
See?
I TOLD YOU THEY'D GET MAD.
THAT'S OKAY.
I NEED TO MAKE UP FOR THE TIME I'VE LOST.
THINK YOU CAN HANDLE THIS...
HIME?
ONE PERSON...
IS MORE THAN ENOUGH!
SWF

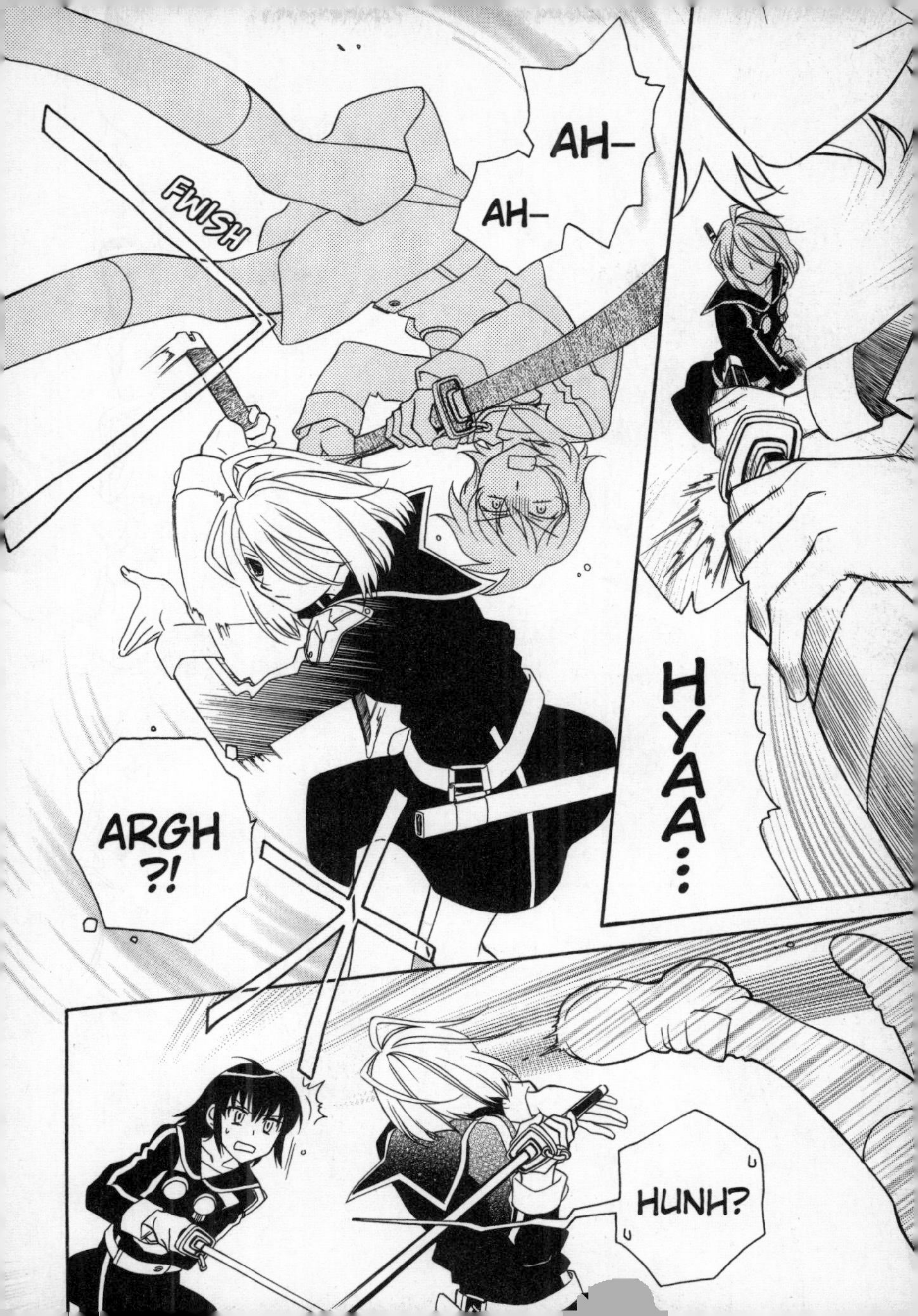
HYAA...
AH–
AH–
FWISH
ARGH ?!
HUNH?

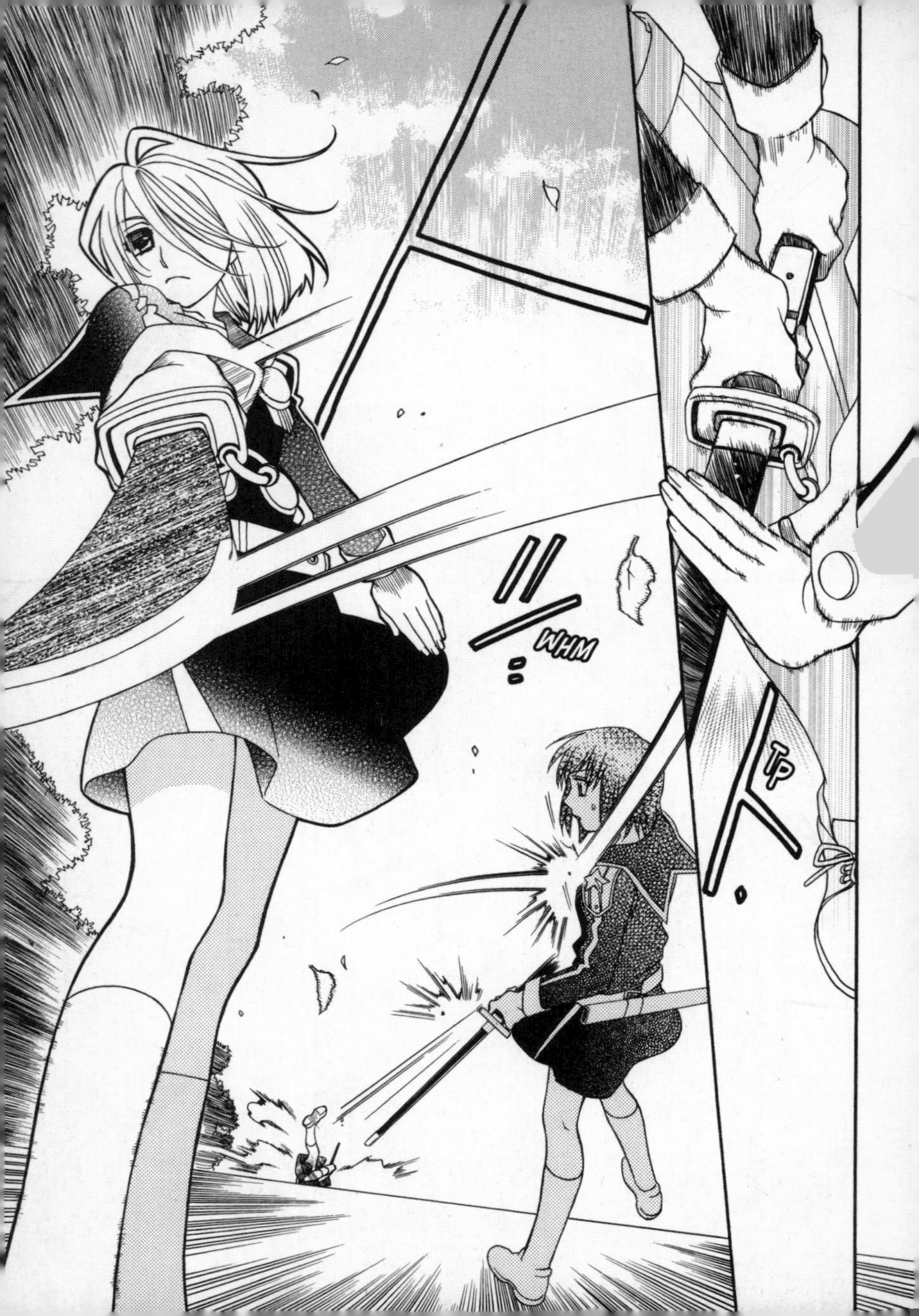
WHM
TP

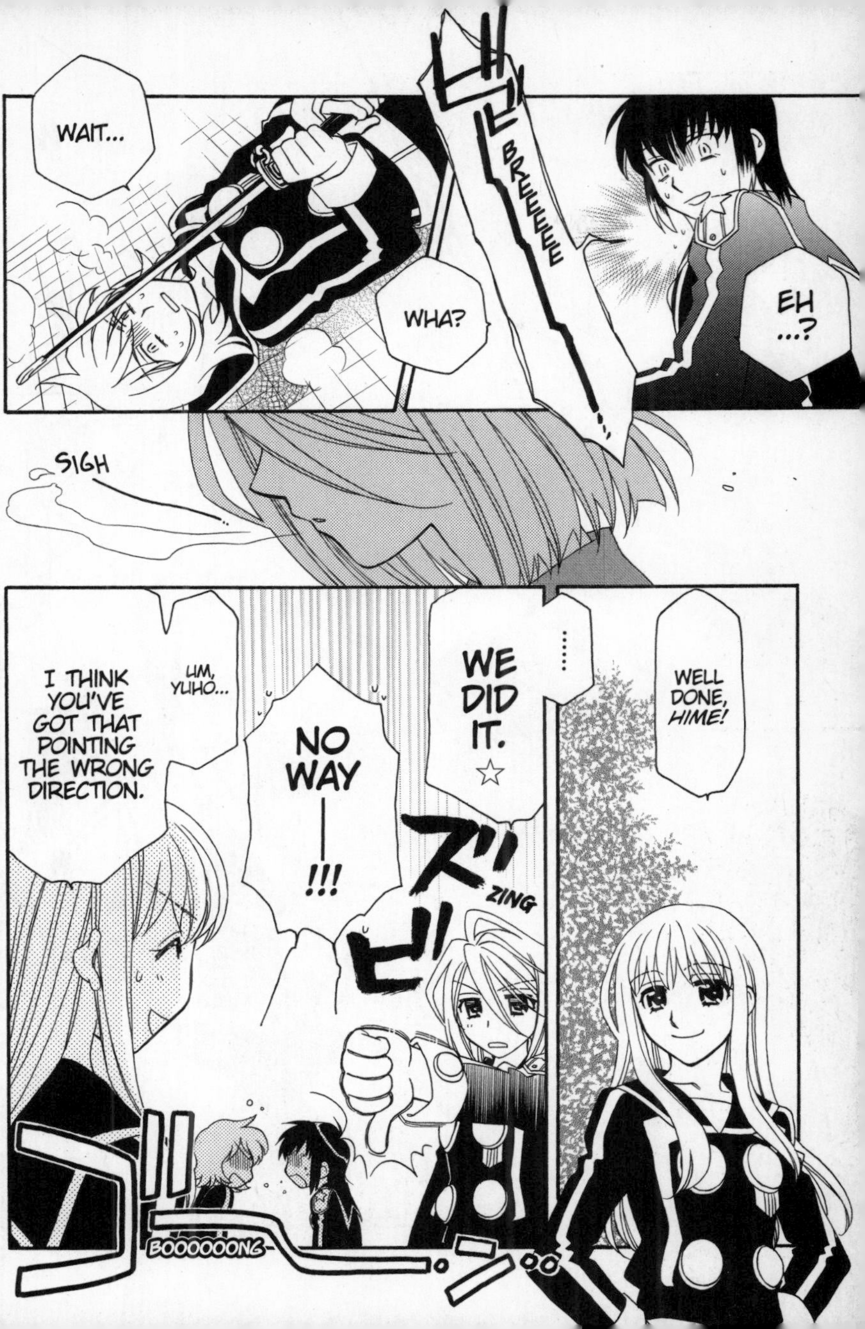
EH ...?
BREEEEEE
WHA?
WAIT...
SIGH
WELL DONE, HIME!
......
WE DID IT. ☆
NO WAY—!!!
ZING
UM, YUHO...
I THINK YOU'VE GOT THAT POINTING THE WRONG DIRECTION.
BOOOOOONG

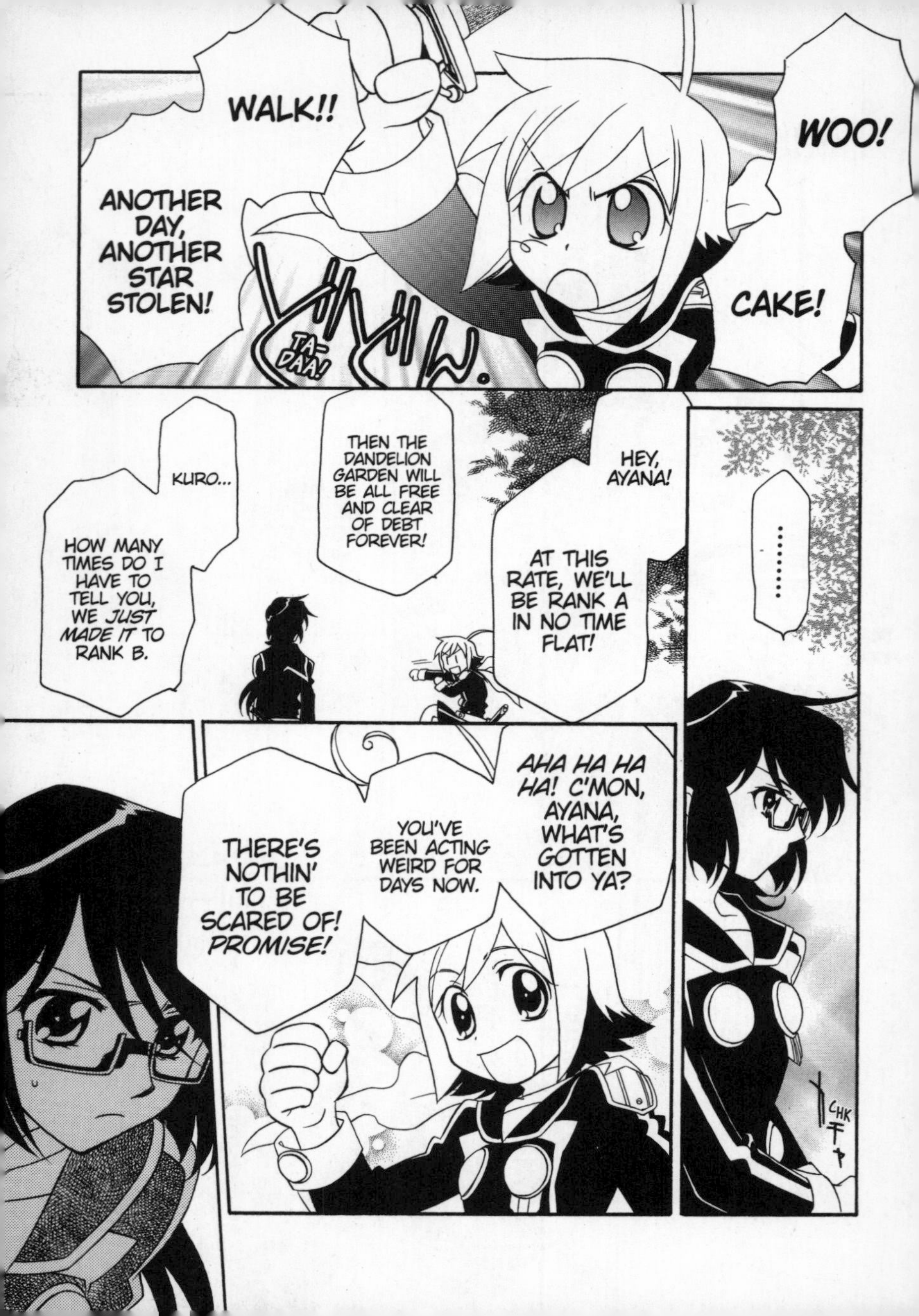
WOO!
CAKE!
WALK!!
ANOTHER DAY, ANOTHER STAR STOLEN!
TA-DAA!
......
HEY, AYANA!
AT THIS RATE, WE'LL BE RANK A IN NO TIME FLAT!
THEN THE DANDELION GARDEN WILL BE ALL FREE AND CLEAR OF DEBT FOREVER!
KURO...
HOW MANY TIMES DO I HAVE TO TELL YOU, WE *JUST* MADE IT TO RANK B.
CHK
AHA HA HA HA HA! C'MON, AYANA, WHAT'S GOTTEN INTO YA?
YOU'VE BEEN ACTING WEIRD FOR DAYS NOW.
THERE'S NOTHIN' TO BE SCARED OF! *PROMISE!*

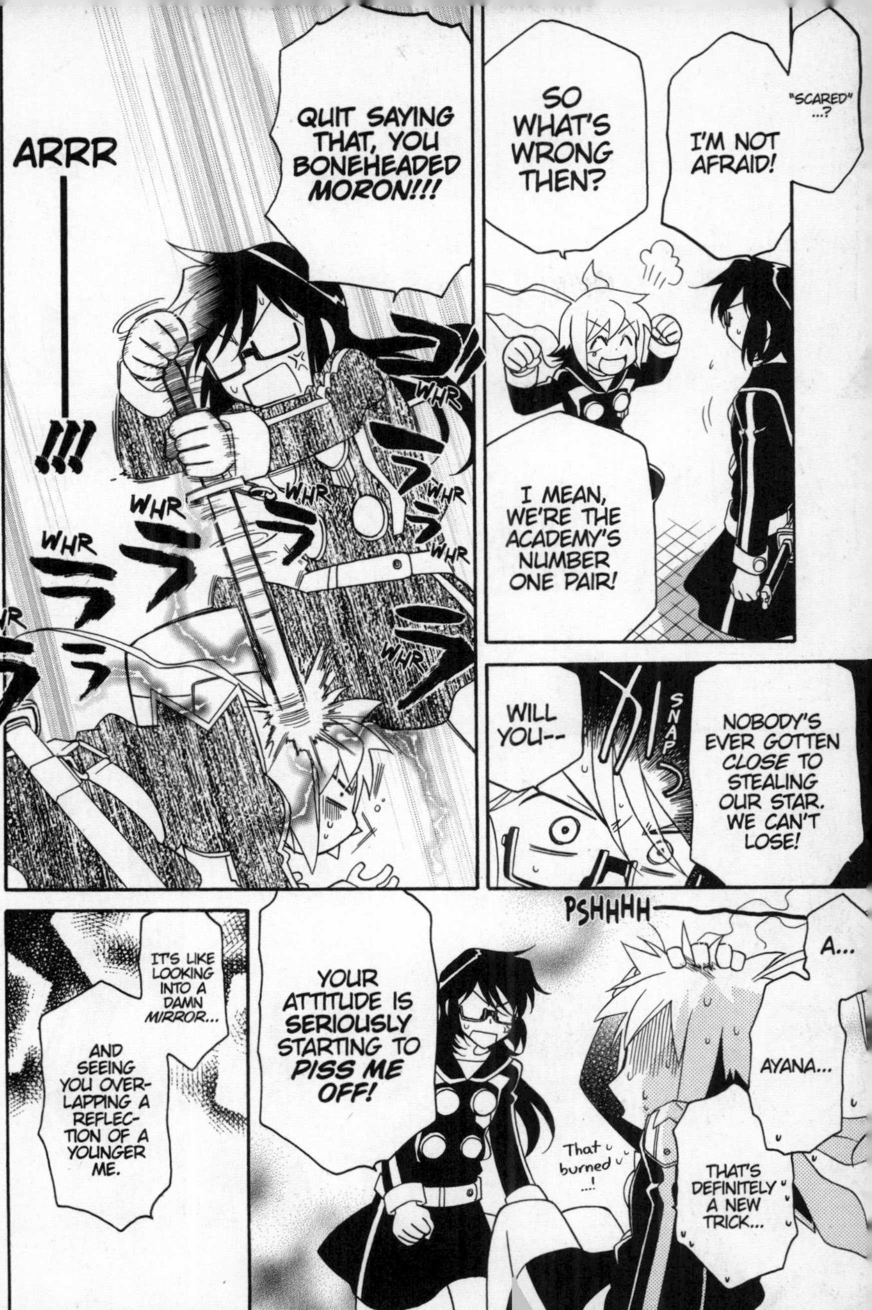
"SCARED" ...?
I'M NOT AFRAID!
SO WHAT'S WRONG THEN?
I MEAN, WE'RE THE ACADEMY'S NUMBER ONE PAIR!
NOBODY'S EVER GOTTEN CLOSE TO STEALING OUR STAR. WE CAN'T LOSE!
SNAP
WILL YOU--
QUIT SAYING THAT, YOU BONEHEADED MORON!!!
ARRR—!!!
WHR WHR WHR WHR WHR WHR WHR WHR
PSHHHH—
A...
AYANA...
THAT'S DEFINITELY A NEW TRICK...
That burned...!
YOUR ATTITUDE IS SERIOUSLY STARTING TO PISS ME OFF!
IT'S LIKE LOOKING INTO A DAMN MIRROR...
AND SEEING YOU OVERLAPPING A REFLECTION OF A YOUNGER ME.

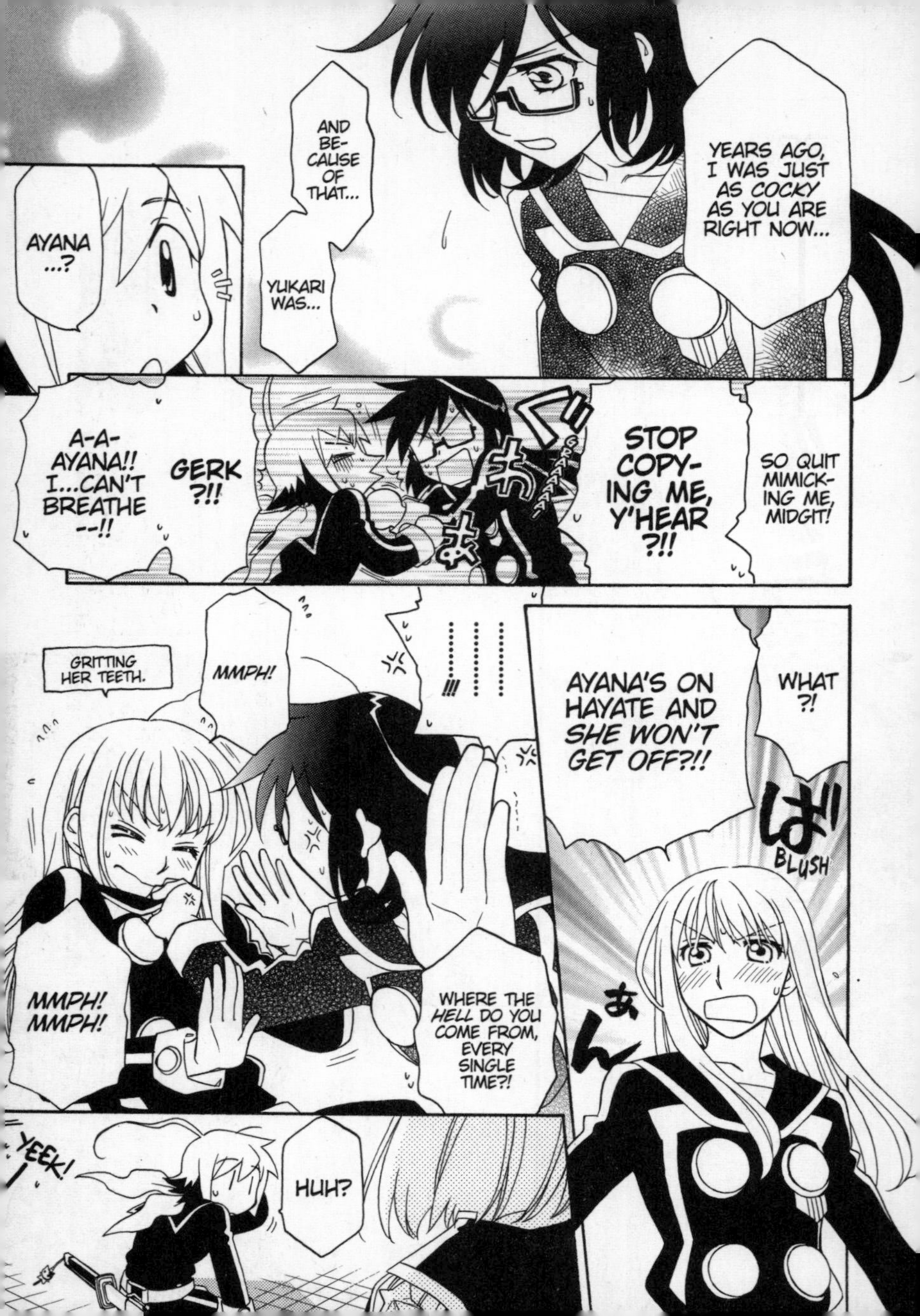
YEARS AGO, I WAS JUST AS COCKY AS YOU ARE RIGHT NOW...
AND BE-CAUSE OF THAT...
YUKARI WAS...
AYANA ...?
SO QUIT MIMICK-ING ME, MIDGIT!
STOP COPY-ING ME, Y'HEAR ?!!
GRAAAAA
GERK ?!!
A-A-AYANA!! I...CAN'T BREATHE --!!
WHAT ?!
AYANA'S ON HAYATE AND SHE WON'T GET OFF?!!
BLUSH
......!!!
MMPH!
GRITTING HER TEETH.
WHERE THE HELL DO YOU COME FROM, EVERY SINGLE TIME?!
MMPH! MMPH!
HUH?
YEEK!

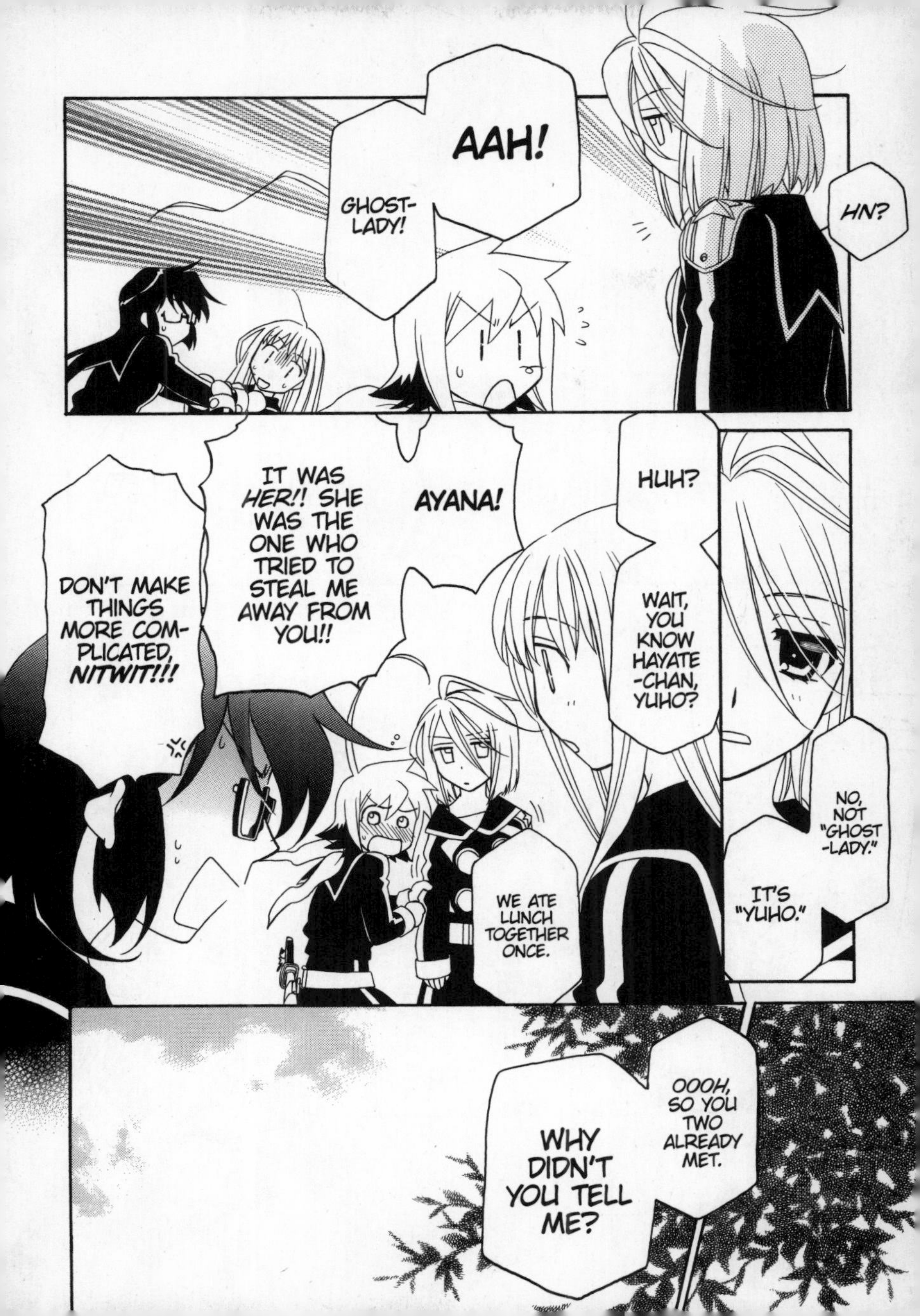
AAH!
GHOST-LADY!
HN?
NO, NOT "GHOST-LADY."
IT'S "YUHO."
HUH?
WAIT, YOU KNOW HAYATE-CHAN, YUHO?
WE ATE LUNCH TOGETHER ONCE.
AYANA!
IT WAS *HER*!! SHE WAS THE ONE WHO TRIED TO STEAL ME AWAY FROM YOU!!
DON'T MAKE THINGS MORE COM-PLICATED, *NITWIT*!!!
OOOH, SO YOU TWO ALREADY MET.
WHY DIDN'T YOU TELL ME?

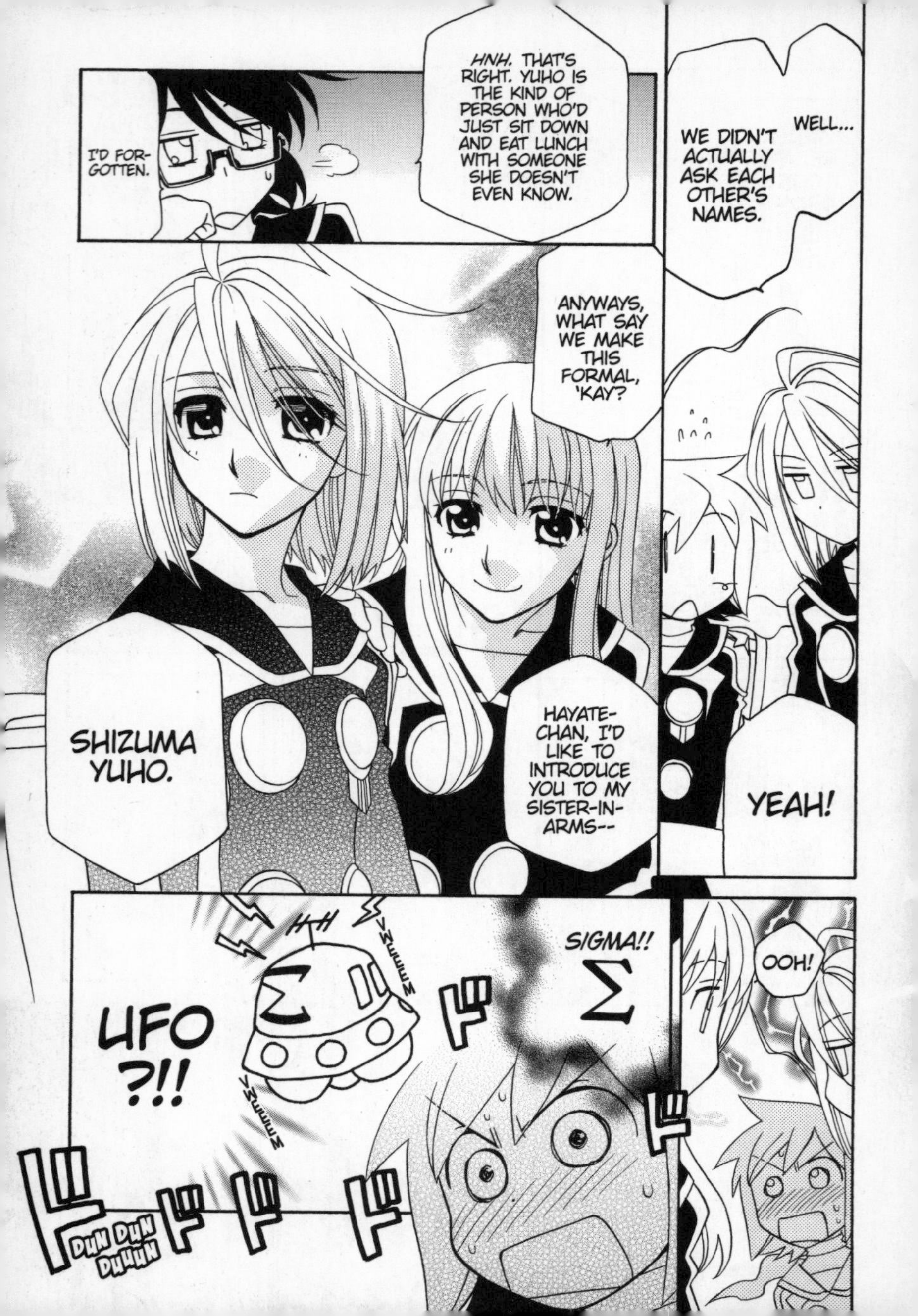

WELL...
WE DIDN'T ACTUALLY ASK EACH OTHER'S NAMES.
YEAH!
HNH. THAT'S RIGHT. YUHO IS THE KIND OF PERSON WHO'D JUST SIT DOWN AND EAT LUNCH WITH SOMEONE SHE DOESN'T EVEN KNOW.
I'D FOR-GOTTEN.
ANYWAYS, WHAT SAY WE MAKE THIS FORMAL, 'KAY?
HAYATE-CHAN, I'D LIKE TO INTRODUCE YOU TO MY SISTER-IN-ARMS--
SHIZUMA YUHO.
OOH!
SIGMA!!
Σ
VWEEEM
Σ
UFO ?!!
VWEEEM
DUN DUN DUHUN

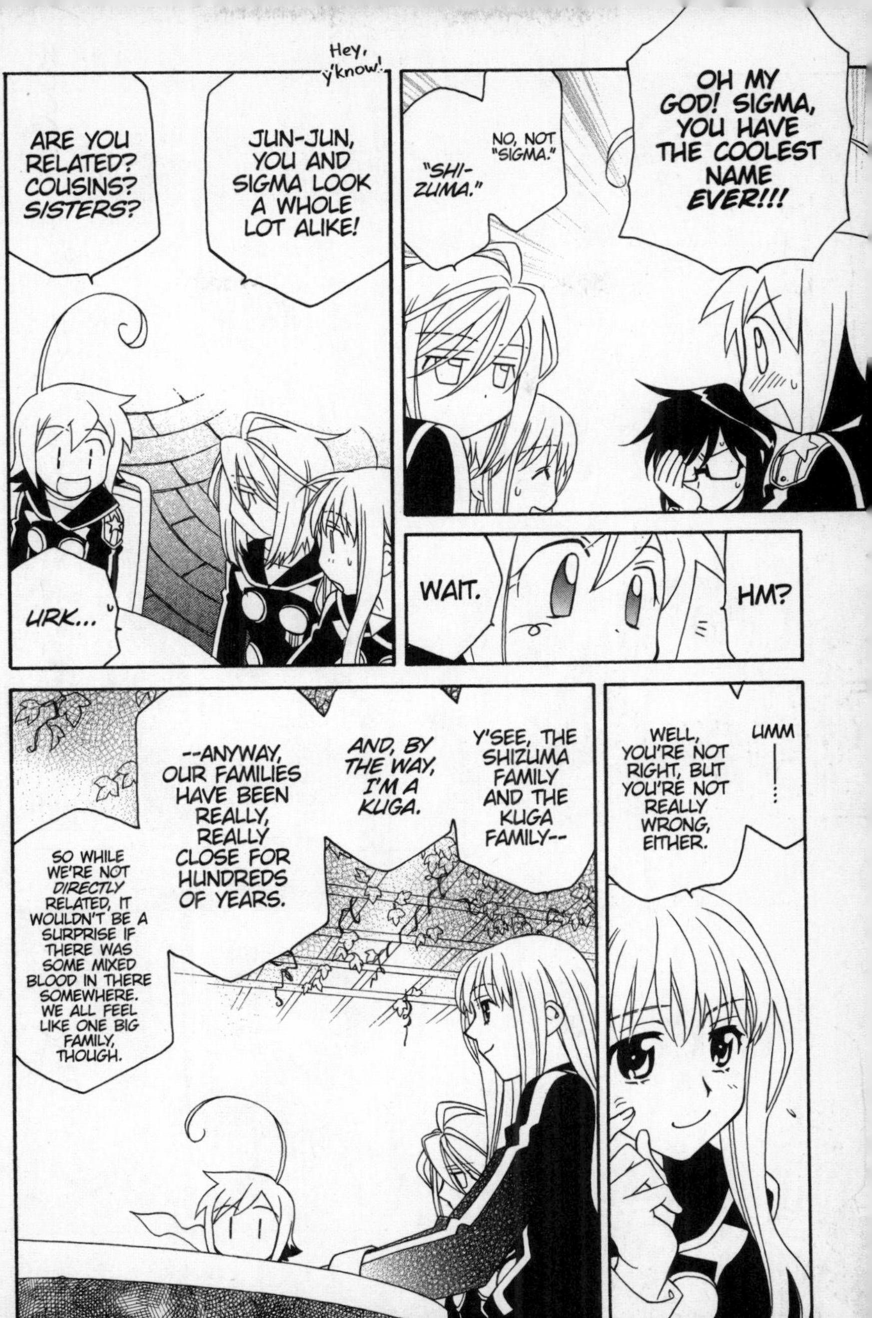
OH MY GOD! SIGMA, YOU HAVE THE COOLEST NAME *EVER!!!*
NO, NOT "SIGMA."
"SHI-ZUMA."
HM?
WAIT.
Hey, y'know!
JUN-JUN, YOU AND SIGMA LOOK A WHOLE LOT ALIKE!
ARE YOU RELATED? COUSINS? SISTERS?
URK...
UMM ...
WELL, YOU'RE NOT RIGHT, BUT YOU'RE NOT REALLY WRONG, EITHER.
Y'SEE, THE SHIZUMA FAMILY AND THE KUGA FAMILY--
AND, BY THE WAY, I'M A KUGA.
--ANYWAY, OUR FAMILIES HAVE BEEN REALLY, REALLY CLOSE FOR HUNDREDS OF YEARS.
SO WHILE WE'RE NOT *DIRECTLY* RELATED, IT WOULDN'T BE A SURPRISE IF THERE WAS SOME MIXED BLOOD IN THERE SOMEWHERE. WE ALL FEEL LIKE ONE BIG FAMILY, THOUGH.

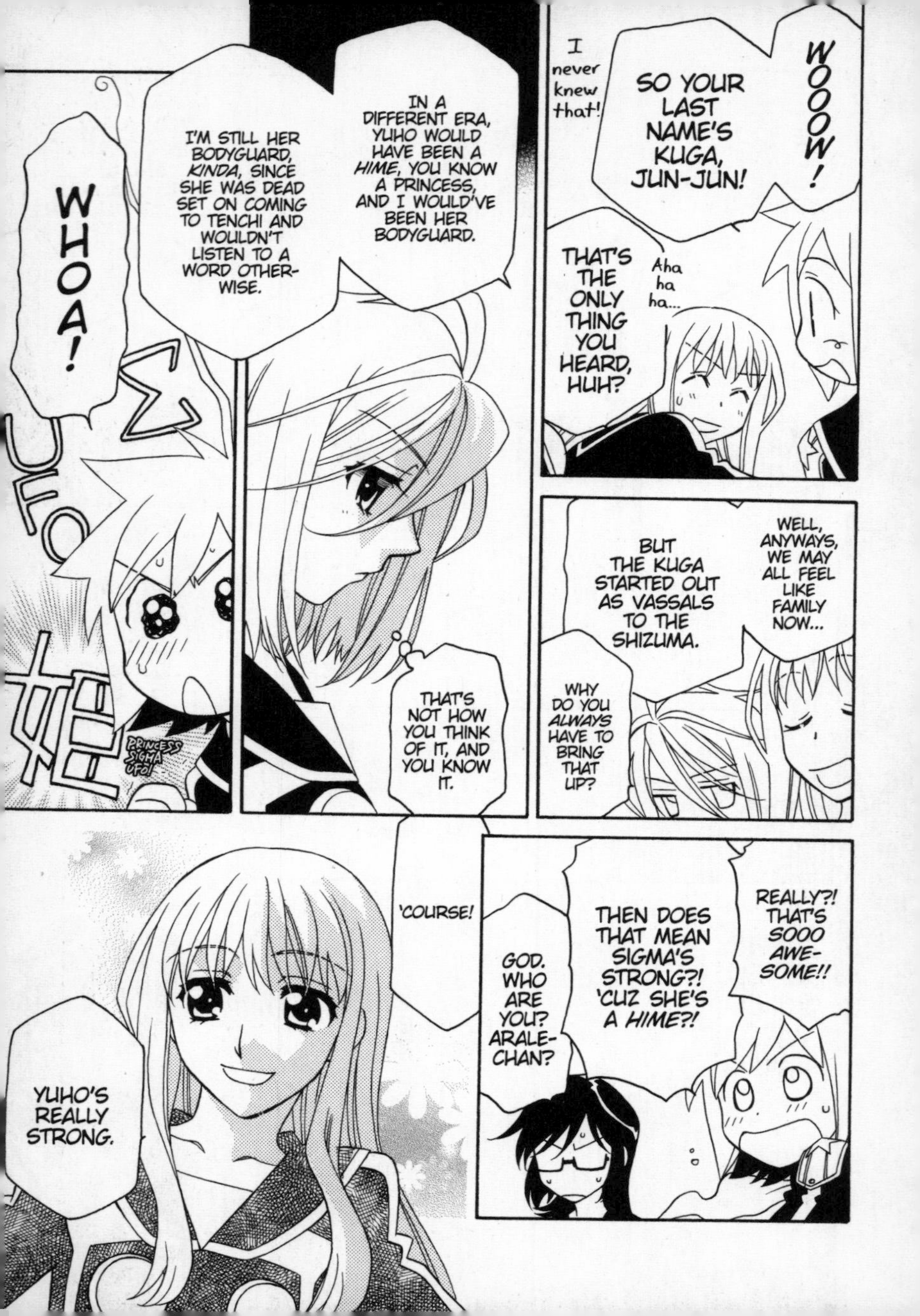
WOOOOW!
SO YOUR LAST NAME'S KUGA, JUN-JUN!
I never knew that!
THAT'S THE ONLY THING YOU HEARD, HUH?
Aha ha ha...
WELL, ANYWAYS, WE MAY ALL FEEL LIKE FAMILY NOW...
BUT THE KUGA STARTED OUT AS VASSALS TO THE SHIZUMA.
WHY DO YOU *ALWAYS* HAVE TO BRING THAT UP?
IN A DIFFERENT ERA, YUHO WOULD HAVE BEEN A *HIME*, YOU KNOW A PRINCESS, AND I WOULD'VE BEEN HER BODYGUARD.
I'M STILL HER BODYGUARD, *KINDA*, SINCE SHE WAS DEAD SET ON COMING TO TENCHI AND WOULDN'T LISTEN TO A WORD OTHER-WISE.
THAT'S NOT HOW YOU THINK OF IT, AND YOU KNOW IT.
WHOA!
PRINCESS SIGMA UFO!
REALLY?! THAT'S SOOO AWE-SOME!!
THEN DOES THAT MEAN SIGMA'S STRONG?! 'CUZ SHE'S A *HIME*?!
GOD. WHO ARE YOU? ARALE-CHAN?
'COURSE!
YUHO'S REALLY STRONG.

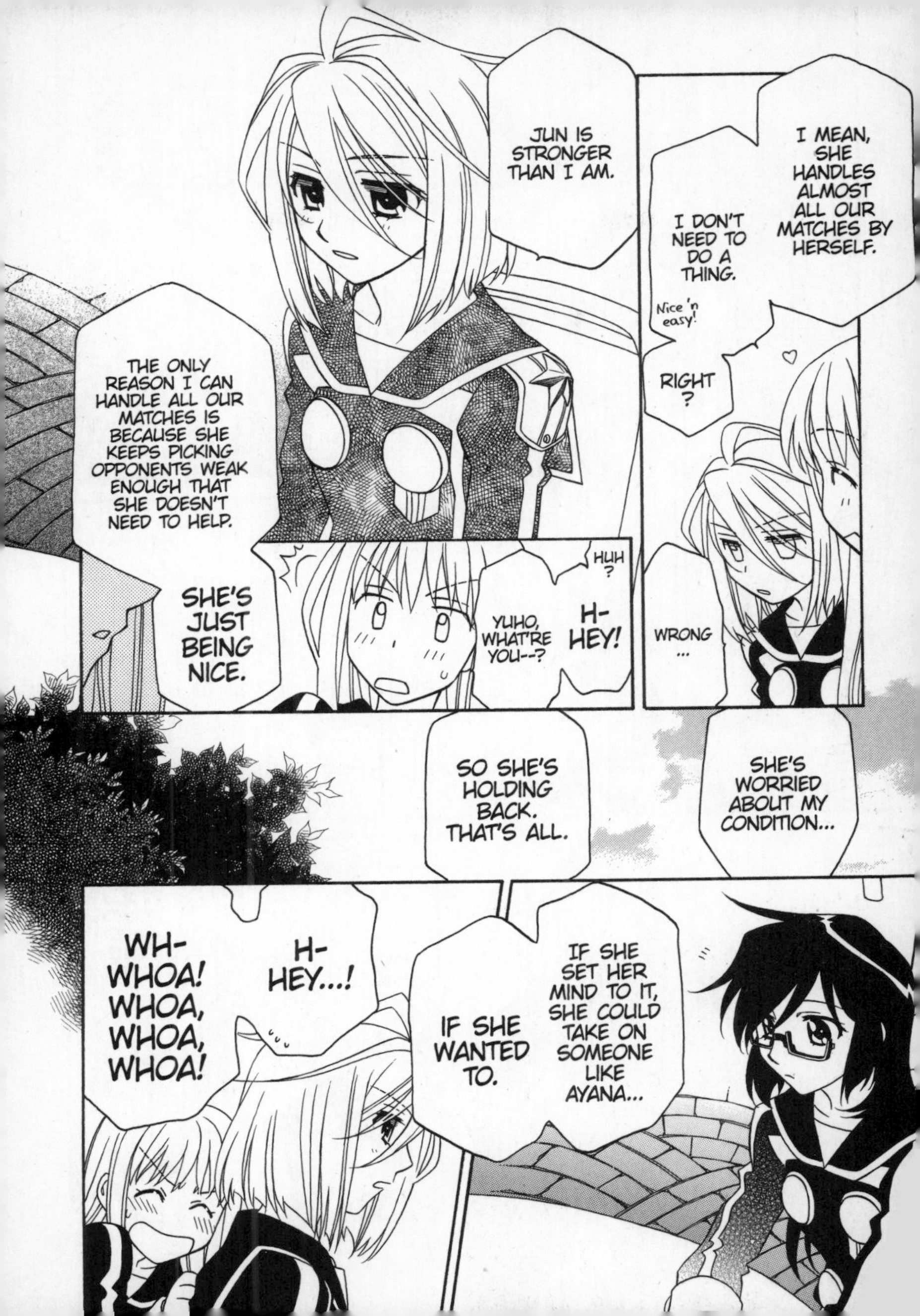
I MEAN, SHE HANDLES ALMOST ALL OUR MATCHES BY HERSELF.
I DON'T NEED TO DO A THING.
Nice 'n easy!
RIGHT?
WRONG...
JUN IS STRONGER THAN I AM.
THE ONLY REASON I CAN HANDLE ALL OUR MATCHES IS BECAUSE SHE KEEPS PICKING OPPONENTS WEAK ENOUGH THAT SHE DOESN'T NEED TO HELP.
HUH?
H-HEY!
YUHO, WHAT'RE YOU--?
SHE'S JUST BEING NICE.
SHE'S WORRIED ABOUT MY CONDITION...
SO SHE'S HOLDING BACK. THAT'S ALL.
IF SHE SET HER MIND TO IT, SHE COULD TAKE ON SOMEONE LIKE AYANA...
IF SHE WANTED TO.
H-HEY...!
WH-WHOA! WHOA, WHOA, WHOA!

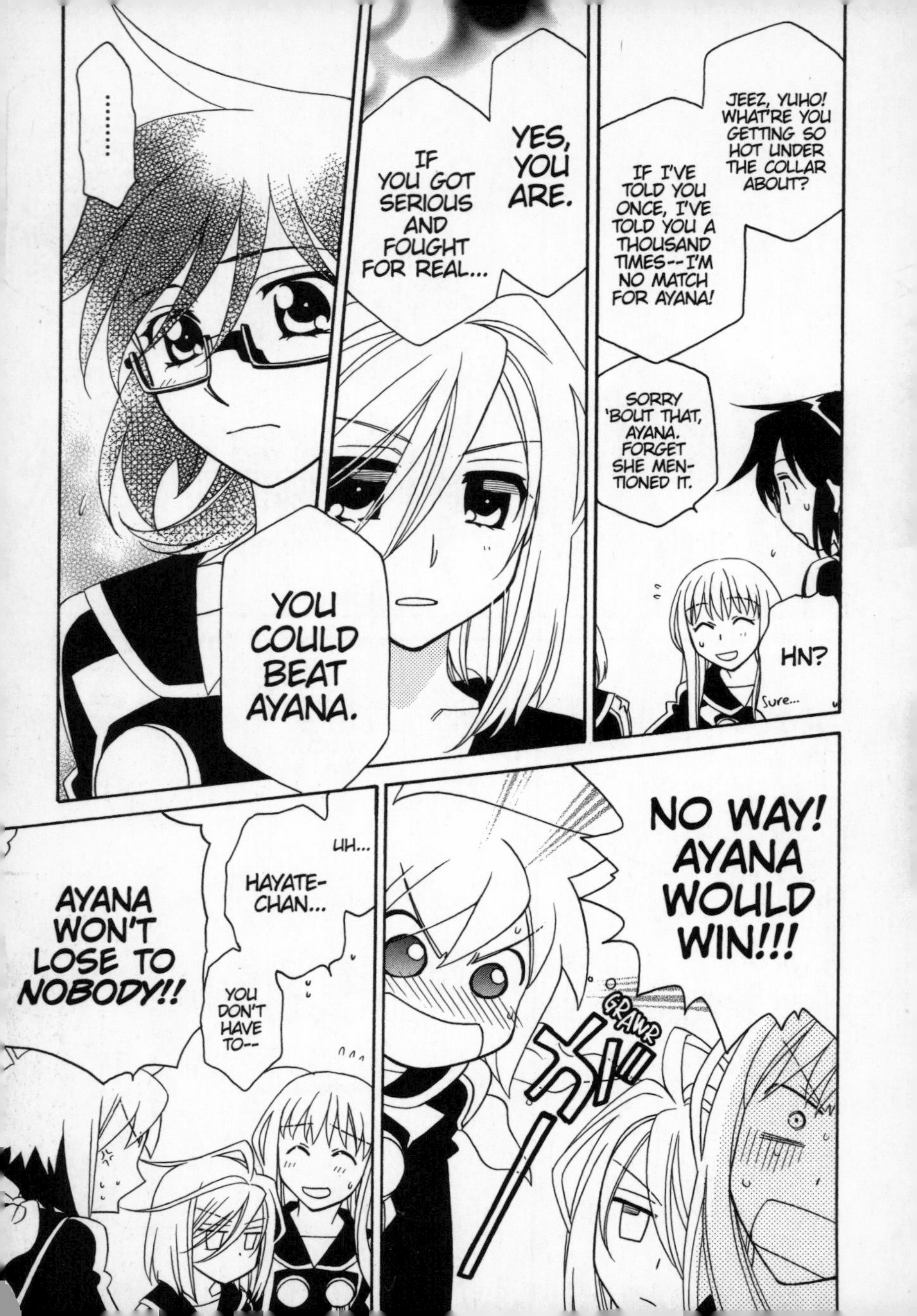
JEEZ, YUHO! WHAT'RE YOU GETTING SO HOT UNDER THE COLLAR ABOUT?
IF I'VE TOLD YOU ONCE, I'VE TOLD YOU A THOUSAND TIMES--I'M NO MATCH FOR AYANA!
SORRY 'BOUT THAT, AYANA. FORGET SHE MENTIONED IT.
HN?
Sure...
YES, YOU ARE.
IF YOU GOT SERIOUS AND FOUGHT FOR REAL...
YOU COULD BEAT AYANA.
......
NO WAY! AYANA WOULD WIN!!!
GRAWR
UH...
HAYATE-CHAN...
AYANA WON'T LOSE TO NOBODY!!
YOU DON'T HAVE TO--

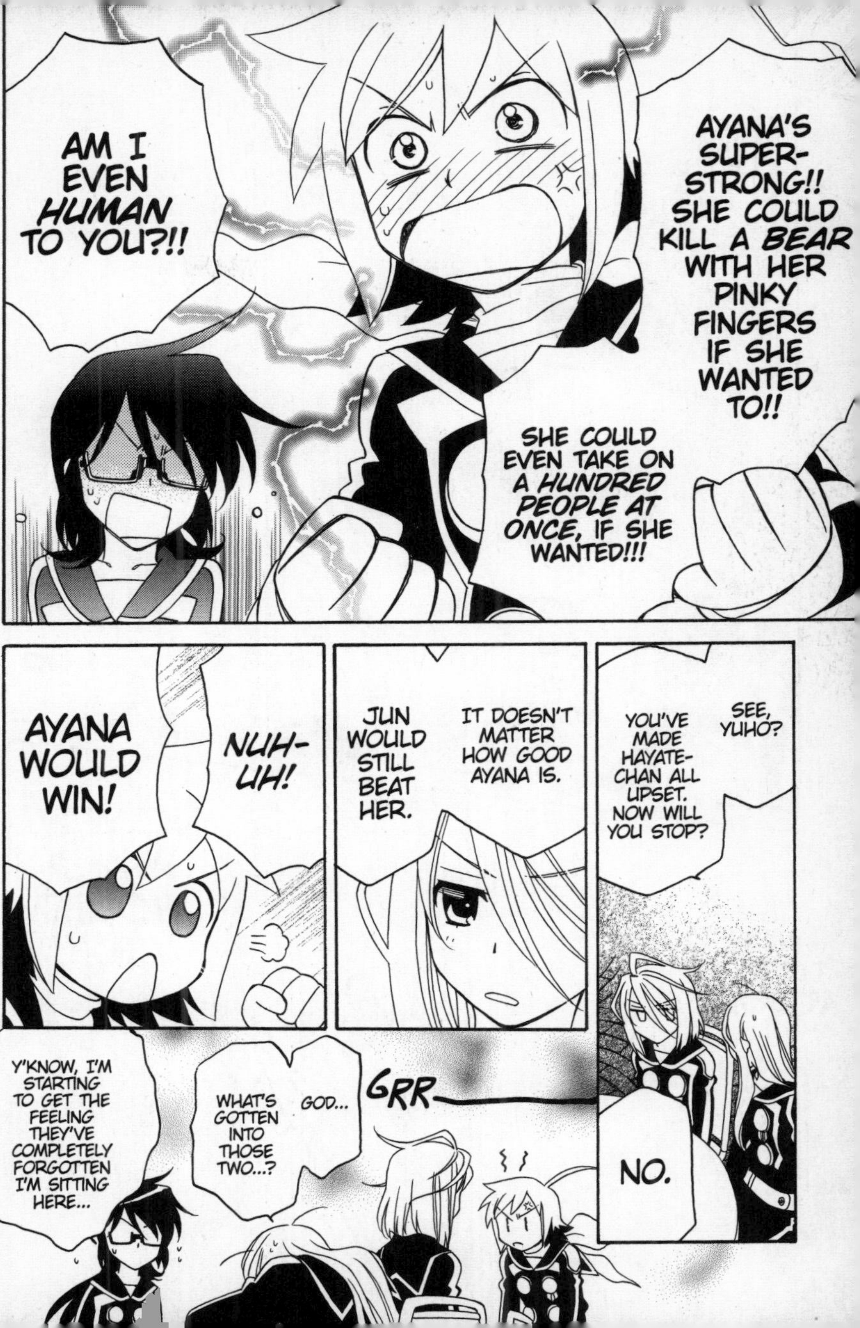
AYANA'S SUPER-STRONG!! SHE COULD KILL A *BEAR* WITH HER PINKY FINGERS IF SHE WANTED TO!!
SHE COULD EVEN TAKE ON A *HUNDRED PEOPLE AT ONCE*, IF SHE WANTED!!!
AM I EVEN *HUMAN* TO YOU?!!
SEE, YUHO?
YOU'VE MADE HAYATE-CHAN ALL UPSET. NOW WILL YOU STOP?
IT DOESN'T MATTER HOW GOOD AYANA IS.
JUN WOULD STILL BEAT HER.
NUH-UH!
AYANA WOULD WIN!
NO.
GRR—
GOD...
WHAT'S GOTTEN INTO THOSE TWO...?
Y'KNOW, I'M STARTING TO GET THE FEELING THEY'VE COMPLETELY FORGOTTEN I'M SITTING HERE...

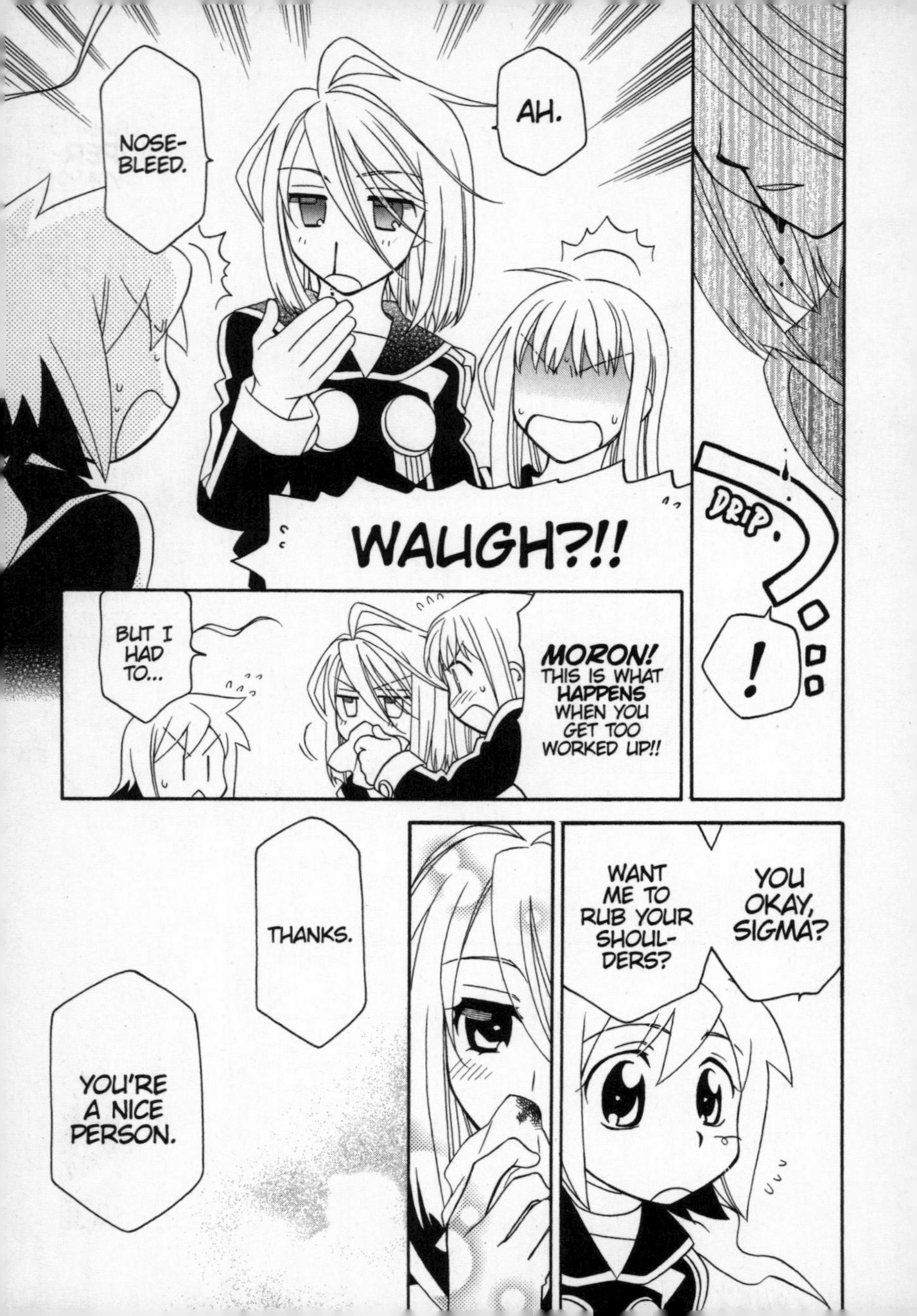
DRIP.
!
AH.
NOSE-BLEED.
WAUGH?!!
MORON! THIS IS WHAT HAPPENS WHEN YOU GET TOO WORKED UP!!
BUT I HAD TO...
YOU OKAY, SIGMA?
WANT ME TO RUB YOUR SHOULDERS?
THANKS.
YOU'RE A NICE PERSON.

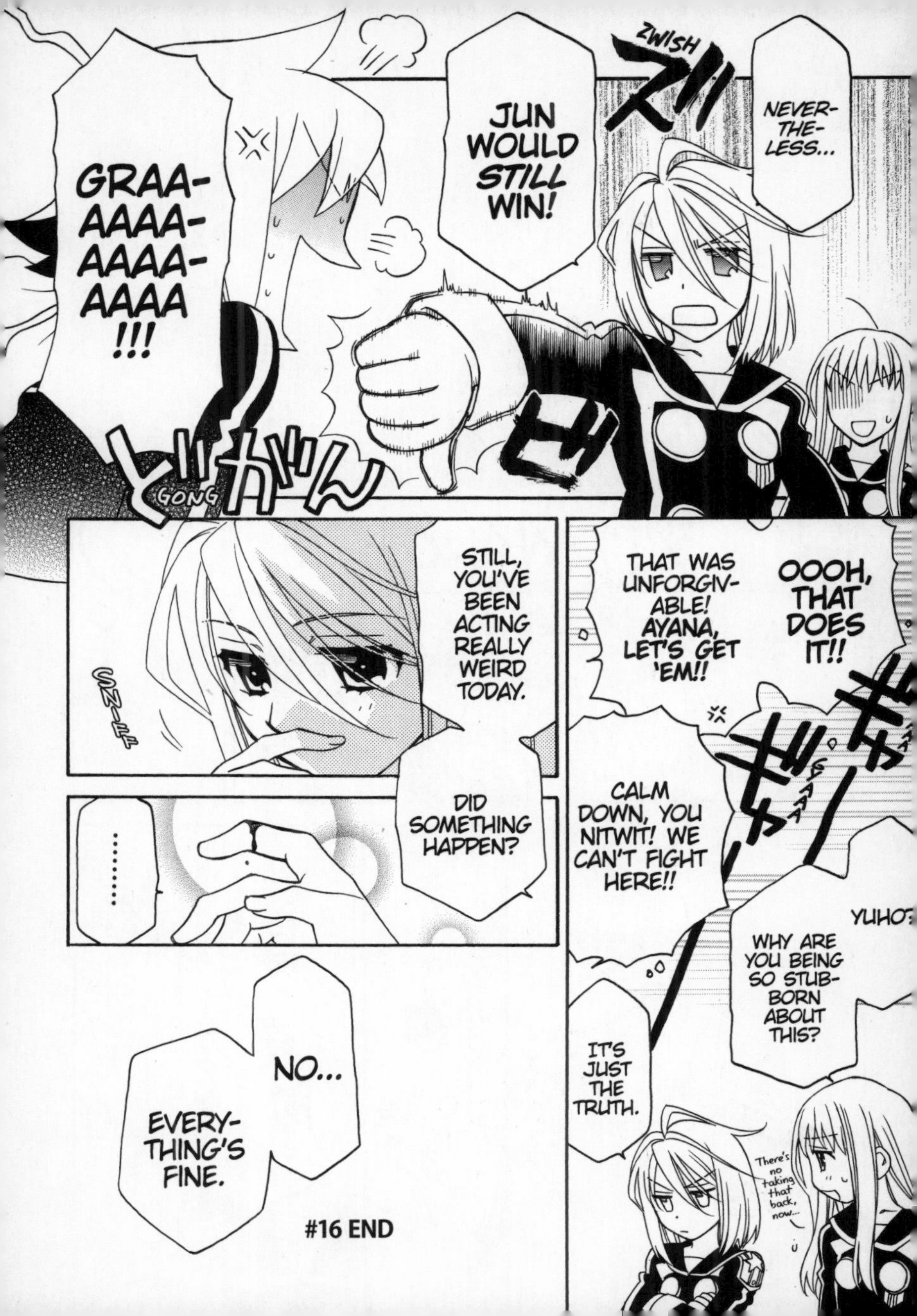
NEVER-THE-LESS...
ZWISH
JUN WOULD STILL WIN!
GRAA-AAAA-AAAA-AAAA!!!
GONG
OOOH, THAT DOES IT!!
THAT WAS UNFORGIV-ABLE! AYANA, LET'S GET 'EM!!
CALM DOWN, YOU NITWIT! WE CAN'T FIGHT HERE!!
YUHO?
WHY ARE YOU BEING SO STUB-BORN ABOUT THIS?
IT'S JUST THE TRUTH.
There's no taking that back, now...
STILL, YOU'VE BEEN ACTING REALLY WEIRD TODAY.
SNIFF
DID SOMETHING HAPPEN?
......
NO...
EVERY-THING'S FINE.
#16 END

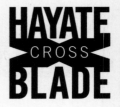

From here on, should
there come a time
when you just can't
take the serious
atmosphere anymore,
please remember this
cross-eyed, reversed-
highlights Shigeru.

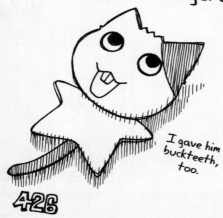

I gave him
buckteeth,
too.

426

TENCHI ACADEMY SWORD-BEARER LIST

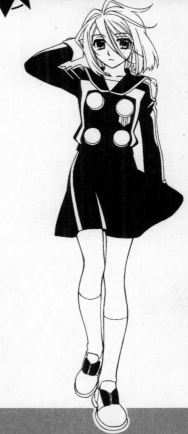

■ DATA ■

Middle School, Class 3-B
Height: 152cm (5'0")
Weight: 38kg (84lbs.)
Birth Date: June 22
Zodiac: Cancer
Blood Type: A
Favorite Word: *Junpuu Manpan* (Morning Star)

■ 静馬夕歩(Shizuma Yuho)■

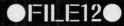

●FILE12●

#17 Life Has Its Ups, Downs, and Idiots

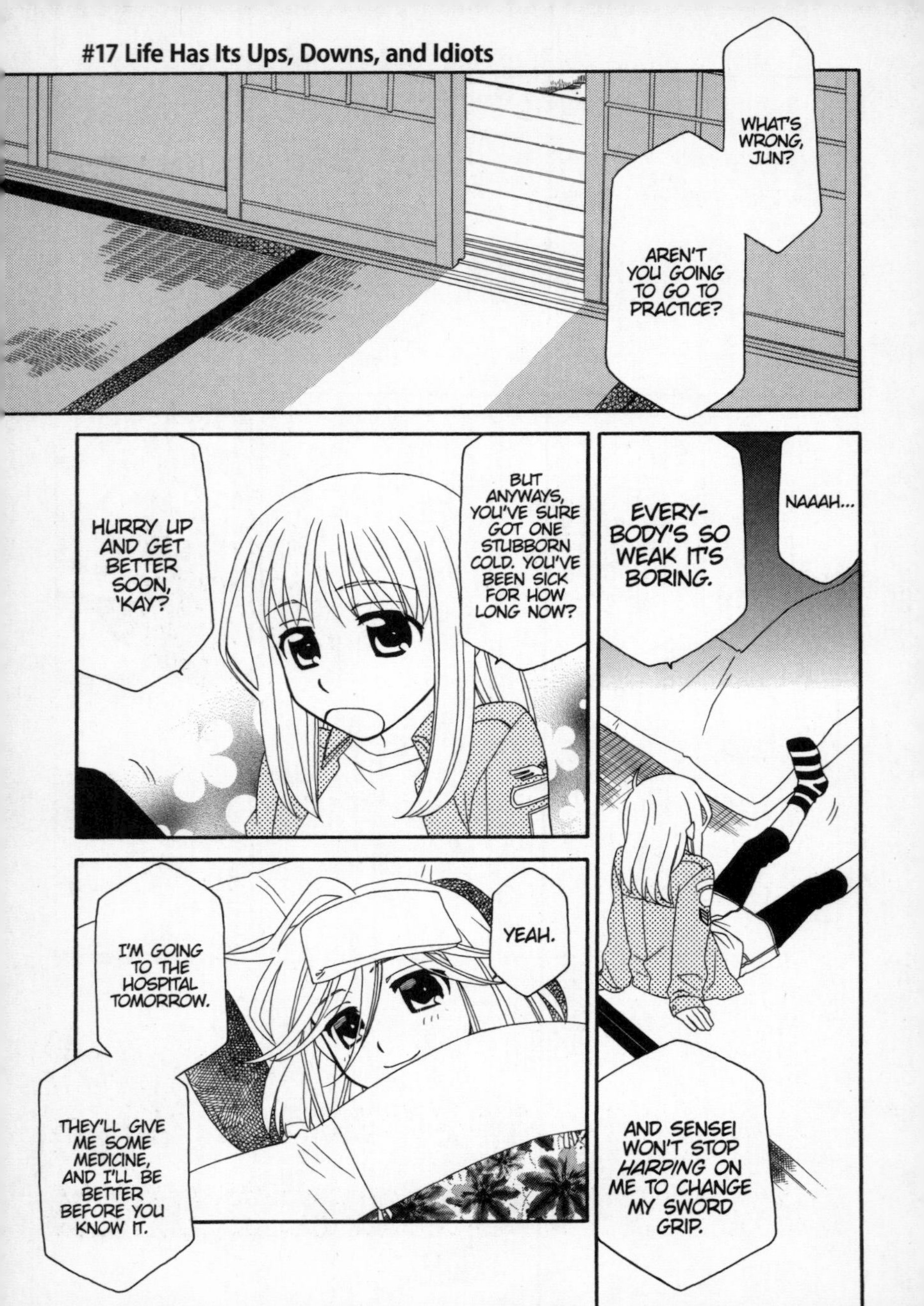
WHAT'S WRONG, JUN?
AREN'T YOU GOING TO GO TO PRACTICE?
NAAAH...
EVERY-BODY'S SO WEAK IT'S BORING.
AND SENSEI WON'T STOP *HARPING* ON ME TO CHANGE MY SWORD GRIP.
BUT ANYWAYS, YOU'VE SURE GOT ONE STUBBORN COLD. YOU'VE BEEN SICK FOR HOW LONG NOW?
HURRY UP AND GET BETTER SOON, 'KAY?
YEAH.
I'M GOING TO THE HOSPITAL TOMORROW.
THEY'LL GIVE ME SOME MEDICINE, AND I'LL BE BETTER BEFORE YOU KNOW IT.

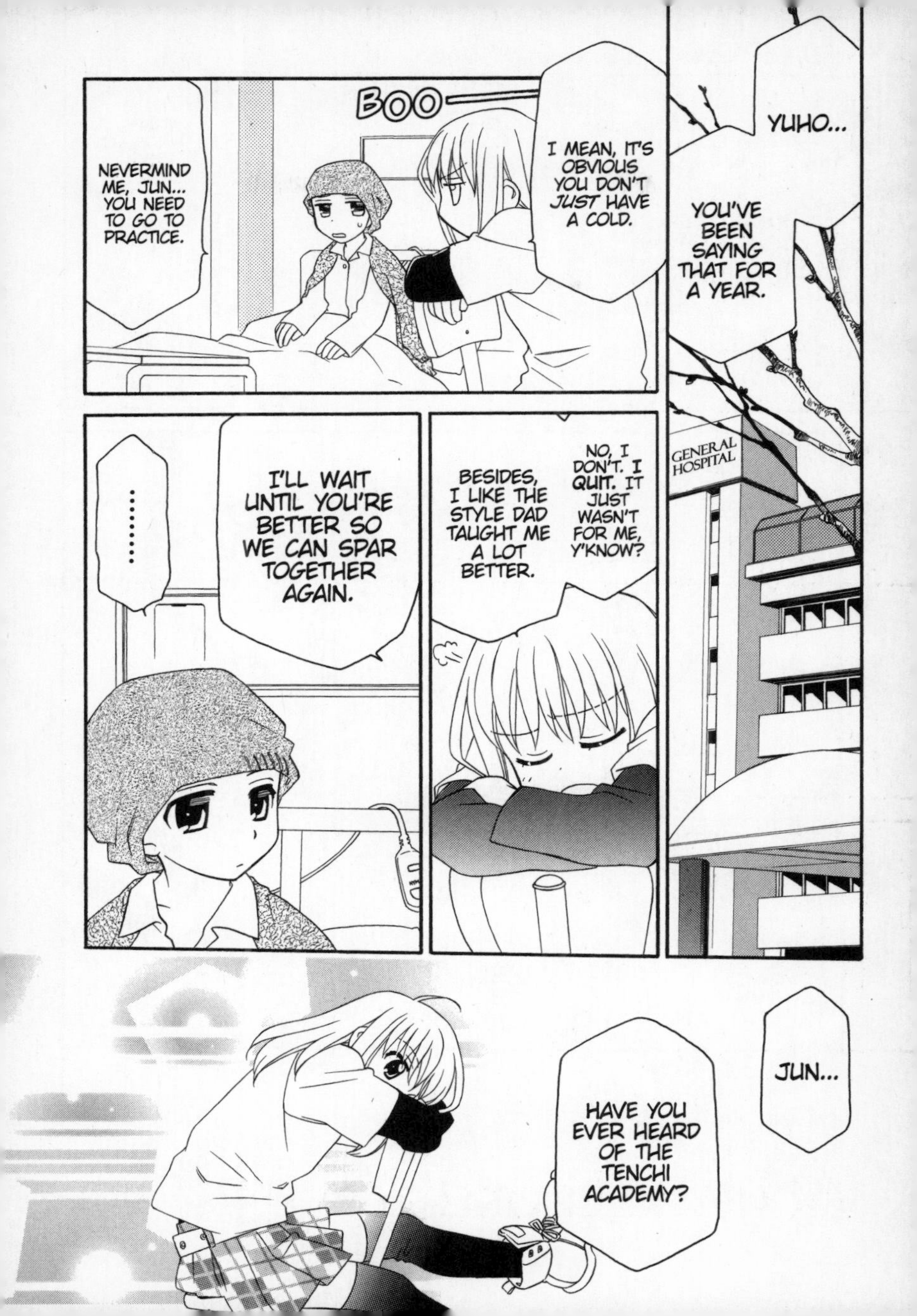
YUHO...
YOU'VE BEEN SAYING THAT FOR A YEAR.
GENERAL HOSPITAL
I MEAN, IT'S OBVIOUS YOU DON'T *JUST* HAVE A COLD.
BOO—
NEVERMIND ME, JUN... YOU NEED TO GO TO PRACTICE.
NO, I DON'T. I **QUIT**. IT JUST WASN'T FOR ME, Y'KNOW?
BESIDES, I LIKE THE STYLE DAD TAUGHT ME A LOT BETTER.
I'LL WAIT UNTIL YOU'RE BETTER SO WE CAN SPAR TOGETHER AGAIN.
....
JUN...
HAVE YOU EVER HEARD OF THE TENCHI ACADEMY?

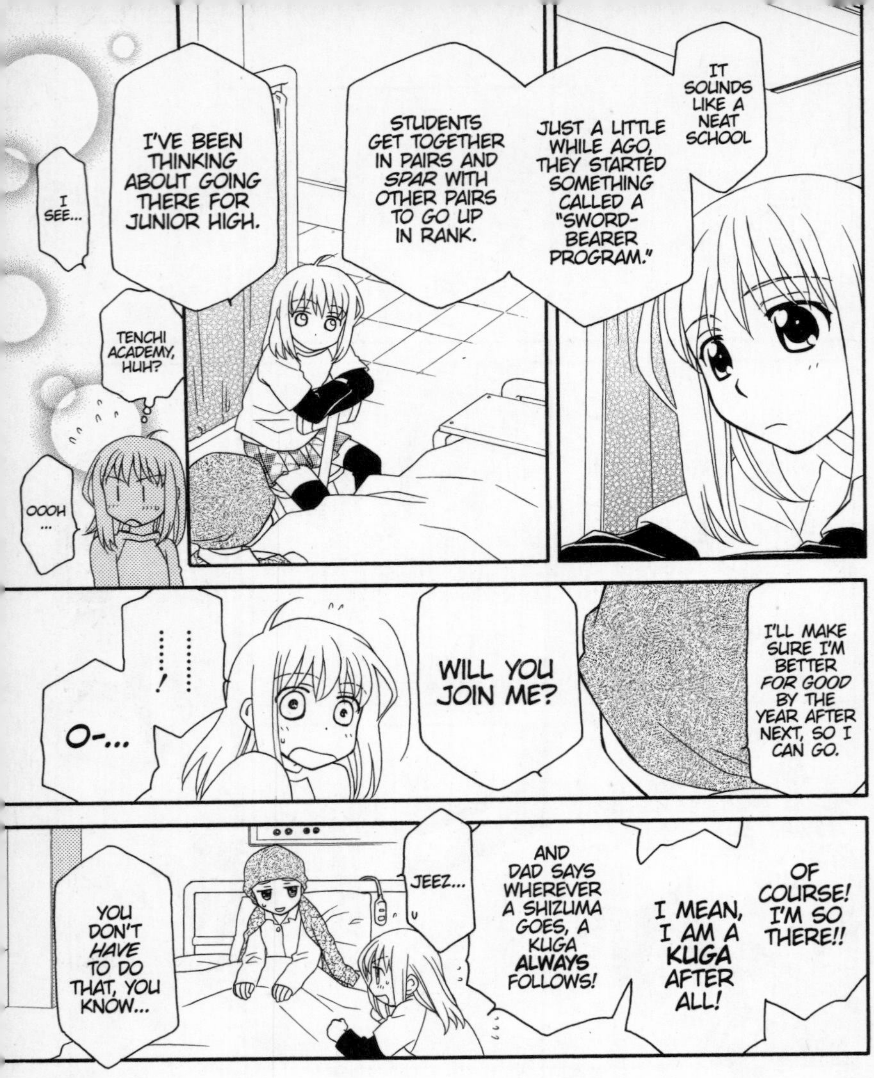
IT SOUNDS LIKE A NEAT SCHOOL
JUST A LITTLE WHILE AGO, THEY STARTED SOMETHING CALLED A "SWORD-BEARER PROGRAM."
STUDENTS GET TOGETHER IN PAIRS AND *SPAR* WITH OTHER PAIRS TO GO UP IN RANK.
I'VE BEEN THINKING ABOUT GOING THERE FOR JUNIOR HIGH.
I SEE...
TENCHI ACADEMY, HUH?
OOOH ...
I'LL MAKE SURE I'M BETTER *FOR GOOD* BY THE YEAR AFTER NEXT, SO I CAN GO.
WILL YOU JOIN ME?
......!
O-...
OF COURSE! I'M SO THERE!!
I MEAN, I AM A **KUGA** AFTER ALL!
AND DAD SAYS WHEREVER A SHIZUMA GOES, A KUGA **ALWAYS** FOLLOWS!
JEEZ...
YOU DON'T *HAVE* TO DO THAT, YOU KNOW...

#17 Life Has Its Ups, Downs, and Idiots

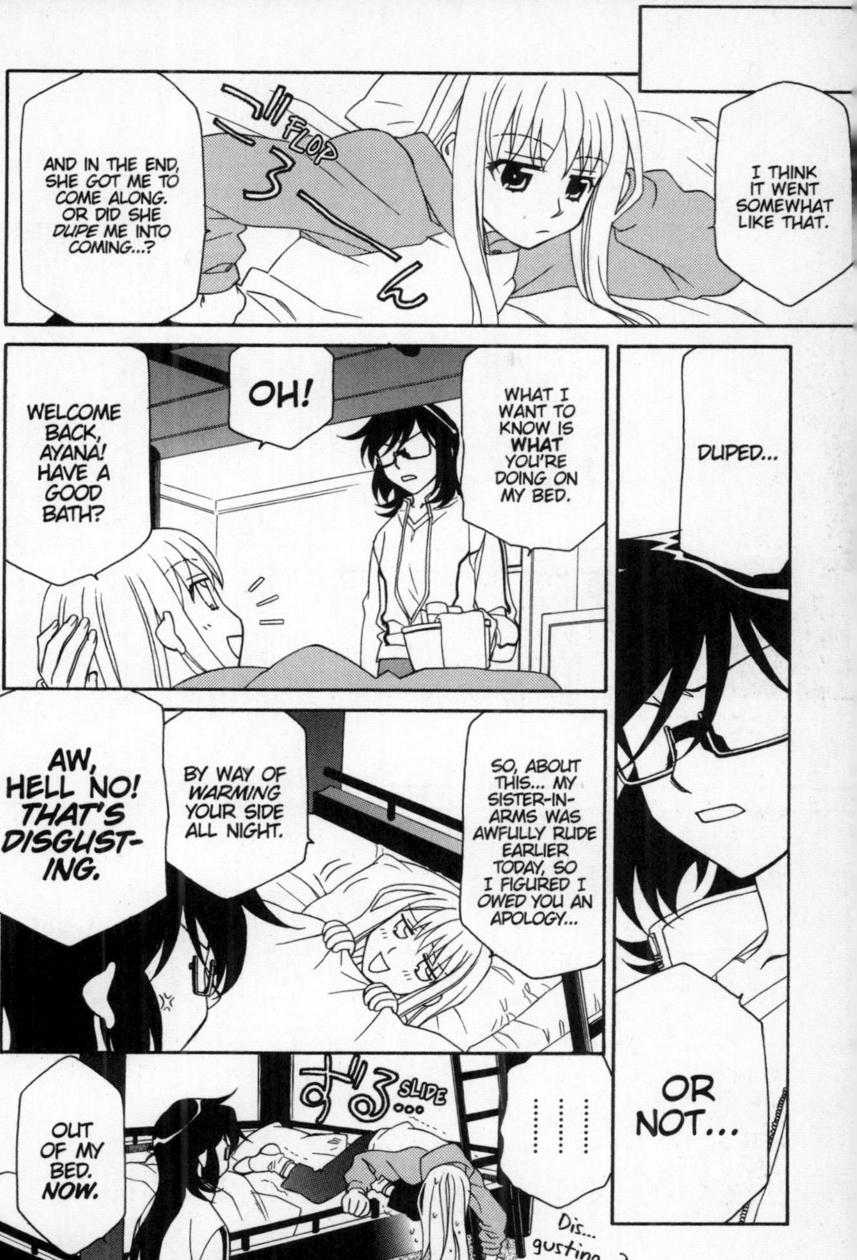

I THINK IT WENT SOMEWHAT LIKE THAT.
FLOP
AND IN THE END, SHE GOT ME TO COME ALONG. OR DID SHE *DUPE* ME INTO COMING...?
DUPED...
OR NOT...
WHAT I WANT TO KNOW IS **WHAT** YOU'RE DOING ON MY BED.
OH!
WELCOME BACK, AYANA! HAVE A GOOD BATH?
SO, ABOUT THIS... MY SISTER-IN-ARMS WAS AWFULLY RUDE EARLIER TODAY, SO I FIGURED I OWED YOU AN APOLOGY...
BY WAY OF *WARMING* YOUR SIDE ALL NIGHT.
AW, HELL NO! *THAT'S DISGUSTING.*
......
SLIDE...
OUT OF MY BED. **NOW.**
Dis... gusting...?

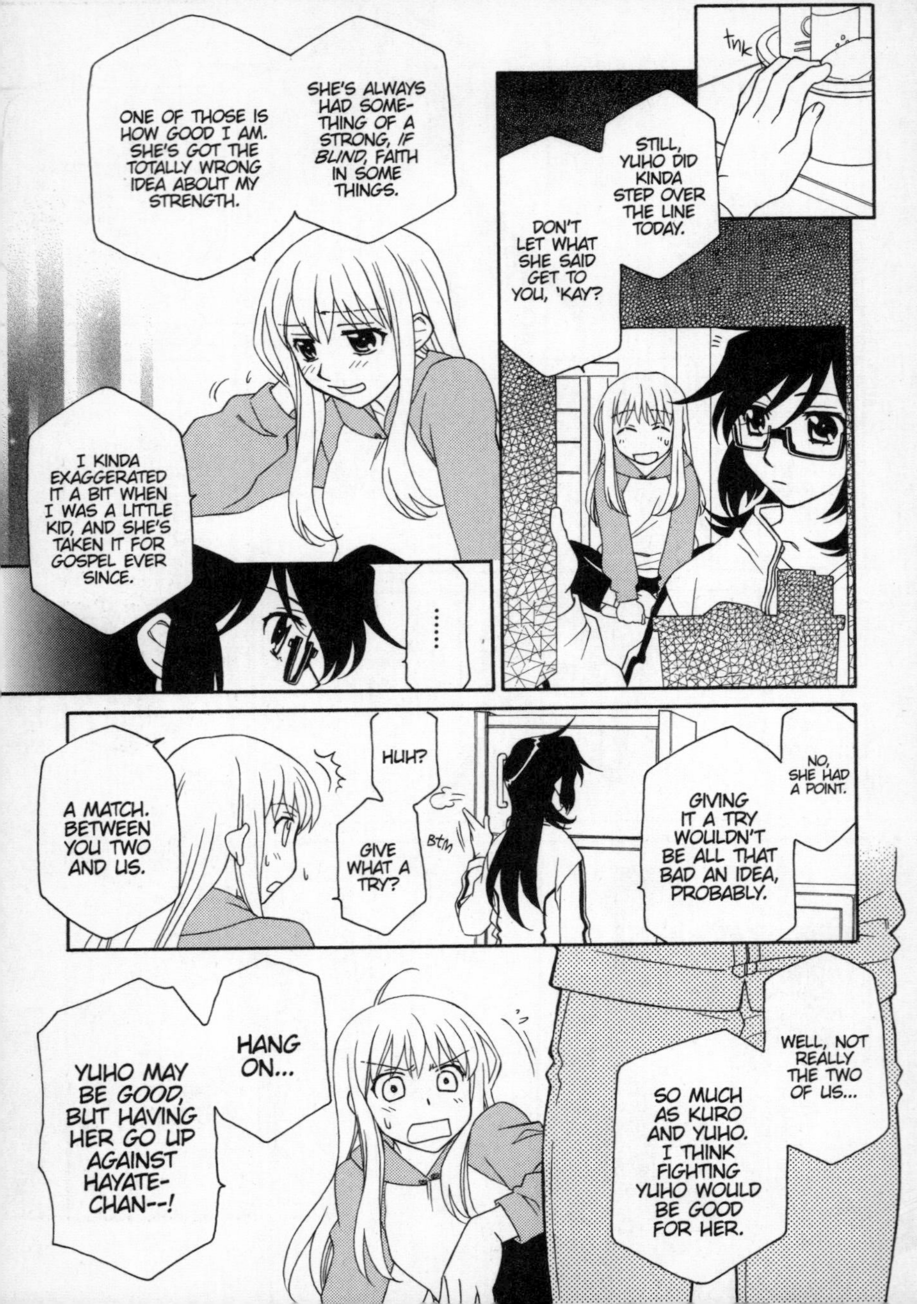
tnk
STILL, YUHO DID KINDA STEP OVER THE LINE TODAY.
DON'T LET WHAT SHE SAID GET TO YOU, 'KAY?
SHE'S ALWAYS HAD SOME-THING OF A STRONG, *IF BLIND*, FAITH IN SOME THINGS.
ONE OF THOSE IS HOW GOOD I AM. SHE'S GOT THE TOTALLY WRONG IDEA ABOUT MY STRENGTH.
I KINDA EXAGGERATED IT A BIT WHEN I WAS A LITTLE KID, AND SHE'S TAKEN IT FOR GOSPEL EVER SINCE.
......
NO, SHE HAD A POINT.
GIVING IT A TRY WOULDN'T BE ALL THAT BAD AN IDEA, PROBABLY.
HUH?
Btm
GIVE WHAT A TRY?
A MATCH. BETWEEN YOU TWO AND US.
WELL, NOT REALLY THE TWO OF US...
SO MUCH AS KURO AND YUHO. I THINK FIGHTING YUHO WOULD BE GOOD FOR HER.
HANG ON...
YUHO MAY BE *GOOD*, BUT HAVING HER GO UP AGAINST HAYATE-CHAN--!

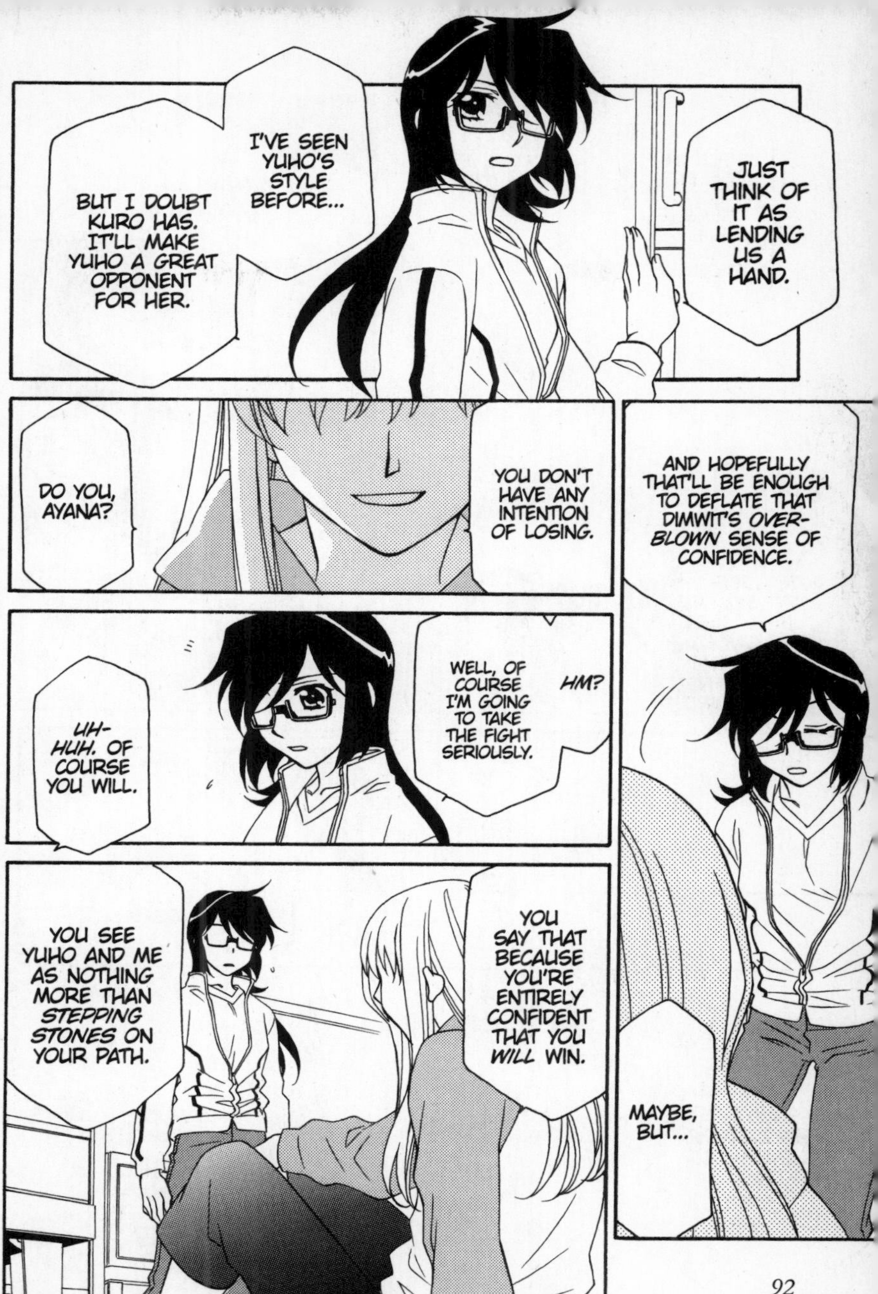
JUST THINK OF IT AS LENDING US A HAND.
I'VE SEEN YUHO'S STYLE BEFORE...
BUT I DOUBT KURO HAS. IT'LL MAKE YUHO A GREAT OPPONENT FOR HER.
AND HOPEFULLY THAT'LL BE ENOUGH TO DEFLATE THAT DIMWIT'S *OVER-BLOWN* SENSE OF CONFIDENCE.
MAYBE, BUT...
YOU DON'T HAVE ANY INTENTION OF LOSING.
DO YOU, AYANA?
HM?
WELL, OF COURSE I'M GOING TO TAKE THE FIGHT SERIOUSLY.
UH-HUH. OF COURSE YOU WILL.
YOU SAY THAT BECAUSE YOU'RE ENTIRELY CONFIDENT THAT YOU *WILL* WIN.
YOU SEE YUHO AND ME AS NOTHING MORE THAN *STEPPING STONES* ON YOUR PATH.

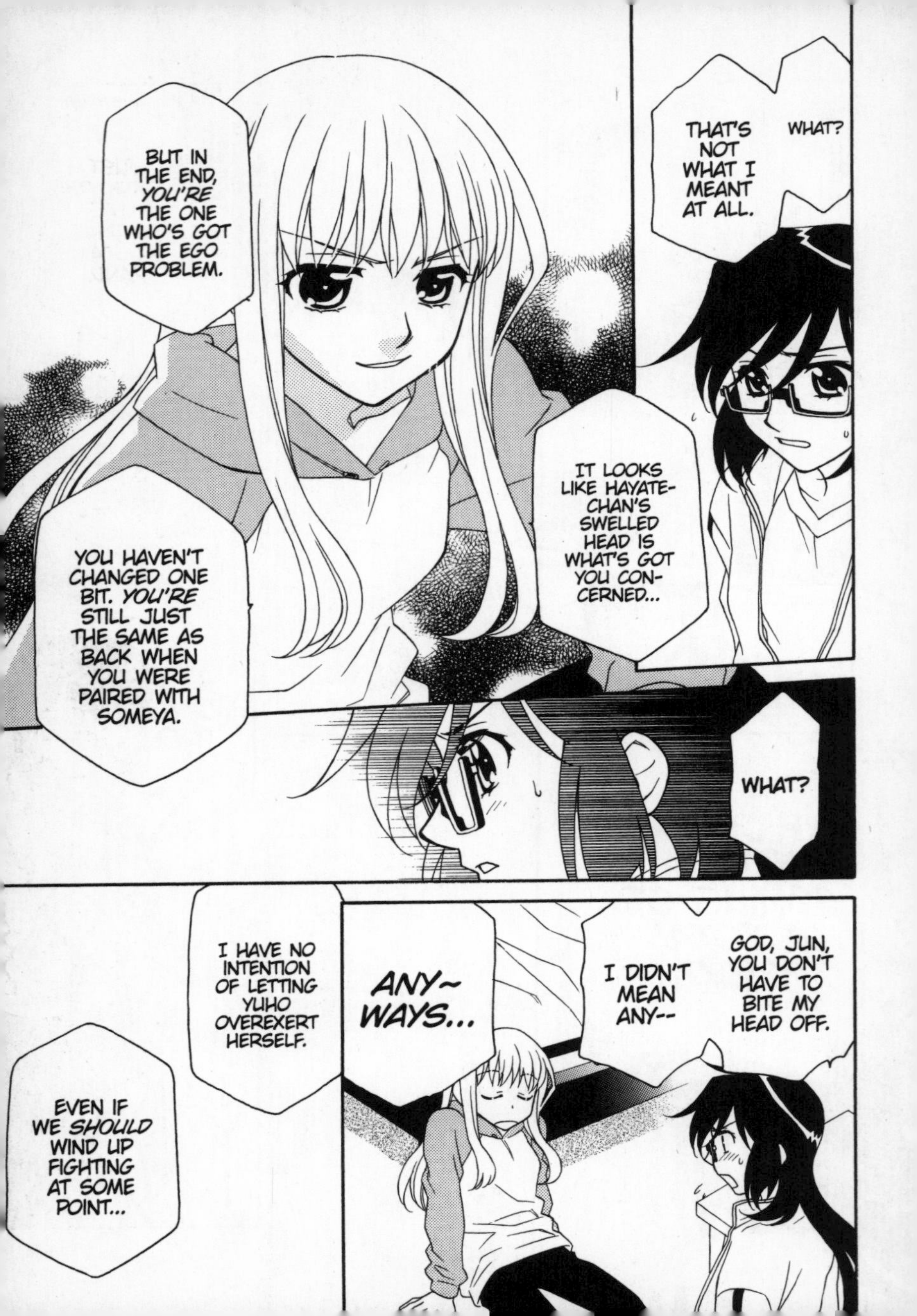
WHAT?
THAT'S NOT WHAT I MEANT AT ALL.
WHAT?
IT LOOKS LIKE HAYATE-CHAN'S SWELLED HEAD IS WHAT'S GOT YOU CONCERNED...
BUT IN THE END, *YOU'RE* THE ONE WHO'S GOT THE EGO PROBLEM.
YOU HAVEN'T CHANGED ONE BIT. *YOU'RE* STILL JUST THE SAME AS BACK WHEN YOU WERE PAIRED WITH SOMEYA.
GOD, JUN, YOU DON'T HAVE TO BITE MY HEAD OFF.
I DIDN'T MEAN ANY--
ANY~ WAYS...
I HAVE NO INTENTION OF LETTING YUHO OVEREXERT HERSELF.
EVEN IF WE *SHOULD* WIND UP FIGHTING AT SOME POINT...

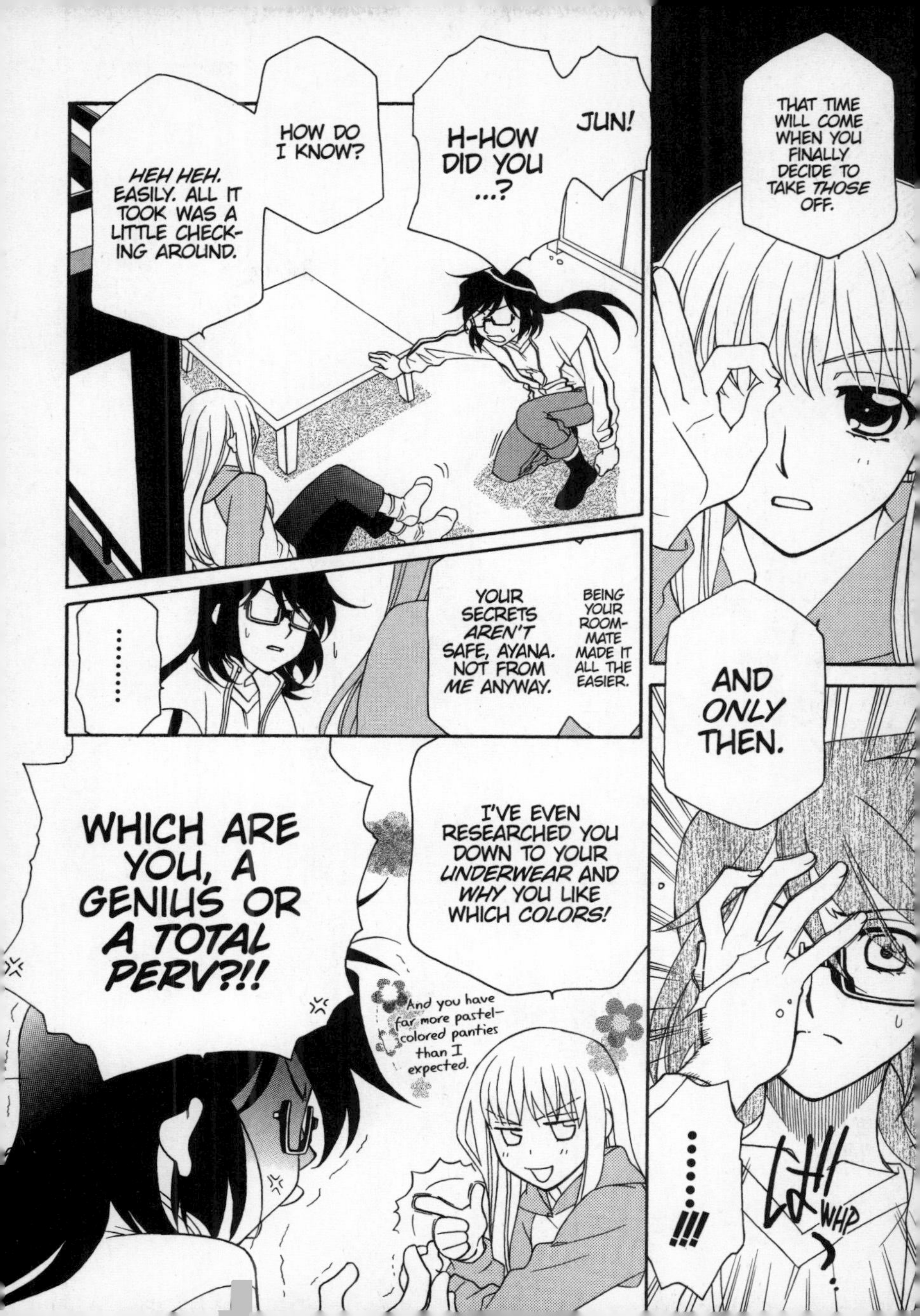
THAT TIME WILL COME WHEN YOU FINALLY DECIDE TO TAKE *THOSE* OFF.
AND *ONLY* THEN.
……!!!
WHP
JUN!
H-HOW DID YOU …?
HOW DO I KNOW?
HEH HEH. EASILY. ALL IT TOOK WAS A LITTLE CHECKING AROUND.
BEING YOUR ROOMMATE MADE IT ALL THE EASIER.
YOUR SECRETS *AREN'T* SAFE, AYANA. NOT FROM *ME* ANYWAY.
……
I'VE EVEN RESEARCHED YOU DOWN TO YOUR *UNDERWEAR* AND *WHY* YOU LIKE WHICH *COLORS!*
And you have far more pastel-colored panties than I expected.
WHICH ARE YOU, A GENIUS OR *A TOTAL PERV?!!*

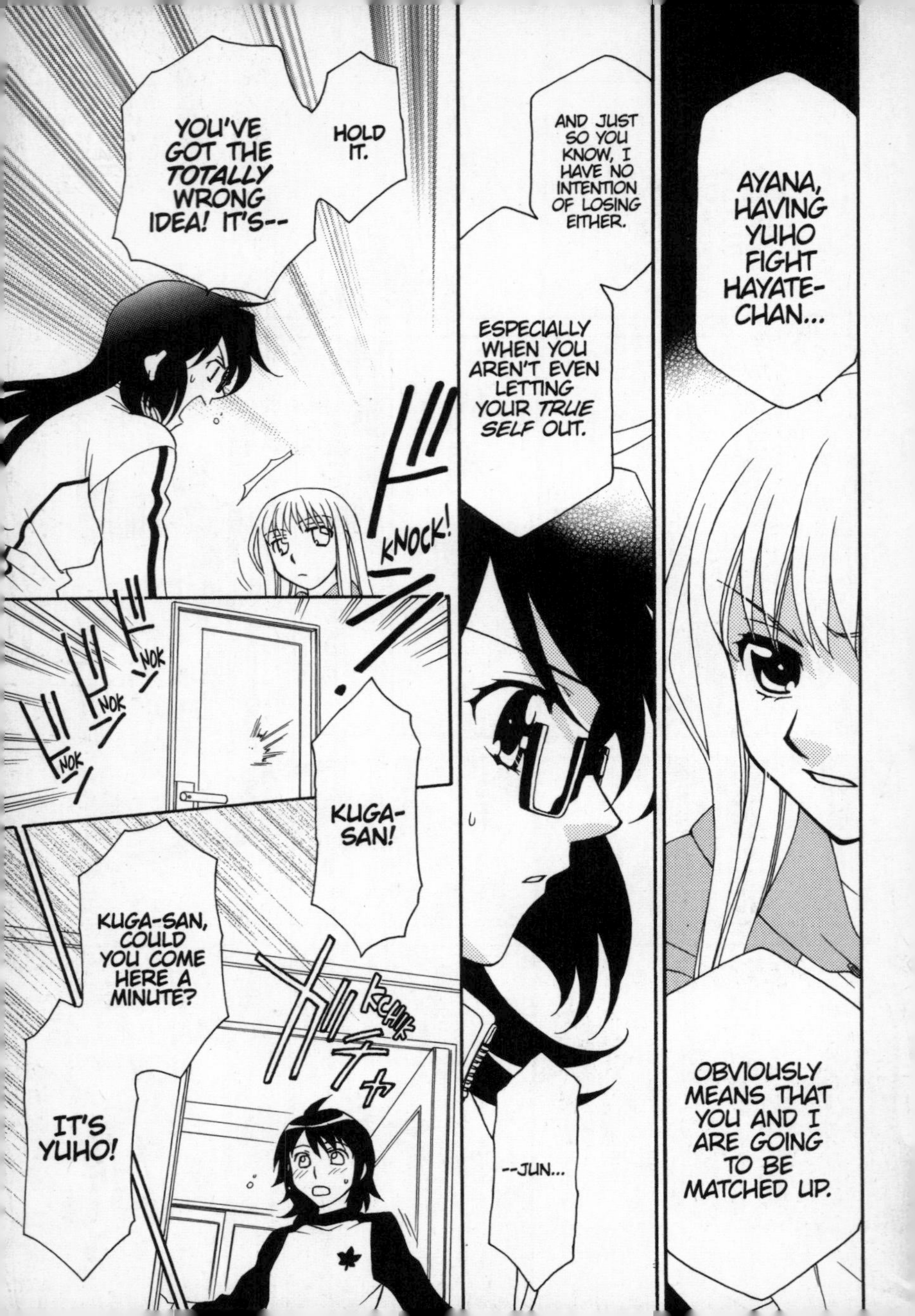
AYANA, HAVING YUHO FIGHT HAYATE-CHAN...
OBVIOUSLY MEANS THAT YOU AND I ARE GOING TO BE MATCHED UP.
AND JUST SO YOU KNOW, I HAVE NO INTENTION OF LOSING EITHER.
ESPECIALLY WHEN YOU AREN'T EVEN LETTING YOUR TRUE SELF OUT.
--JUN...
HOLD IT.
YOU'VE GOT THE TOTALLY WRONG IDEA! IT'S--
KNOCK!
NOK
NOK
NOK
KUGA-SAN!
KUGA-SAN, COULD YOU COME HERE A MINUTE?
KCHAK
IT'S YUHO!

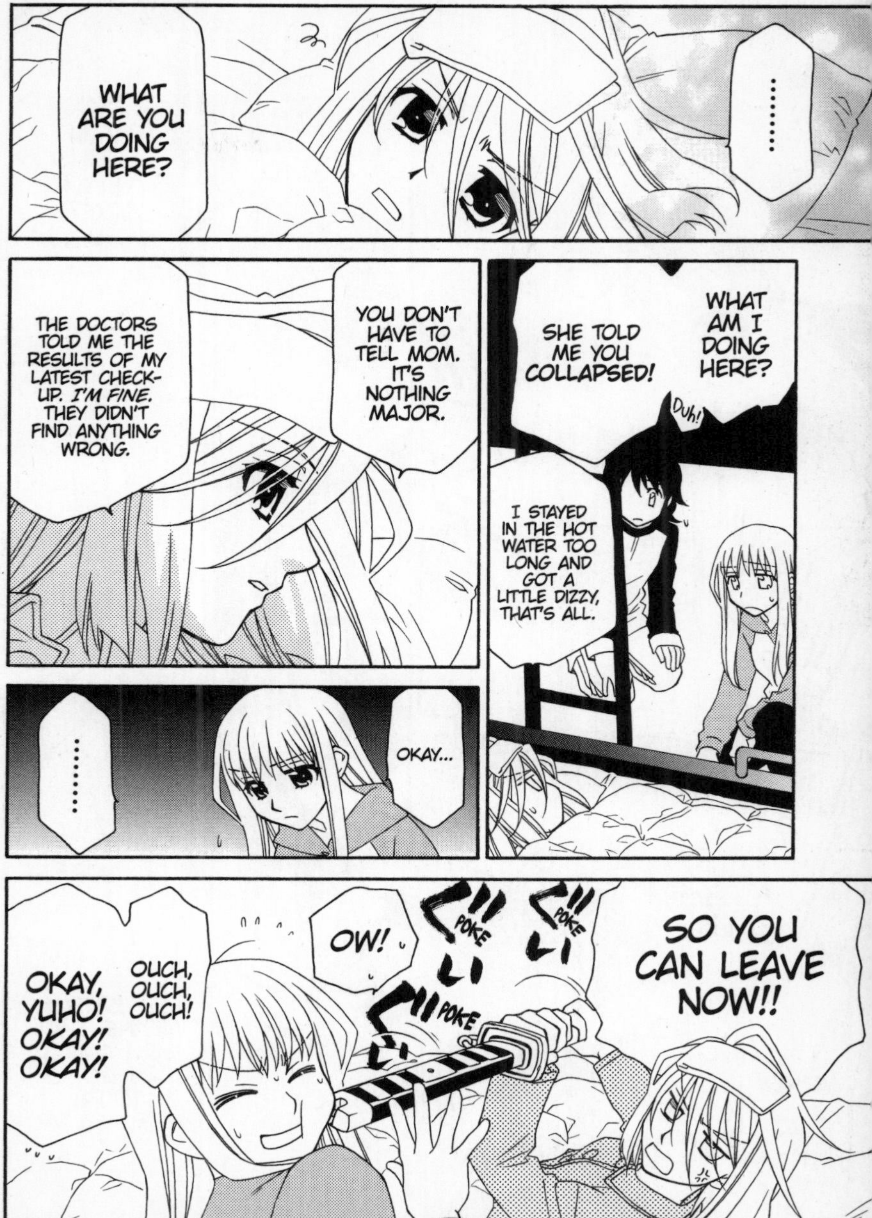
……
WHAT ARE YOU DOING HERE?
WHAT AM I DOING HERE?
SHE TOLD ME YOU COLLAPSED!
Duh!
I STAYED IN THE HOT WATER TOO LONG AND GOT A LITTLE DIZZY, THAT'S ALL.
YOU DON'T HAVE TO TELL MOM. IT'S NOTHING MAJOR.
THE DOCTORS TOLD ME THE RESULTS OF MY LATEST CHECK-UP. *I'M FINE.* THEY DIDN'T FIND ANYTHING WRONG.
OKAY...
……
SO YOU CAN LEAVE NOW!!
POKE
POKE
POKE
OW!
OUCH, OUCH, OUCH!
OKAY, YUHO! OKAY! OKAY!

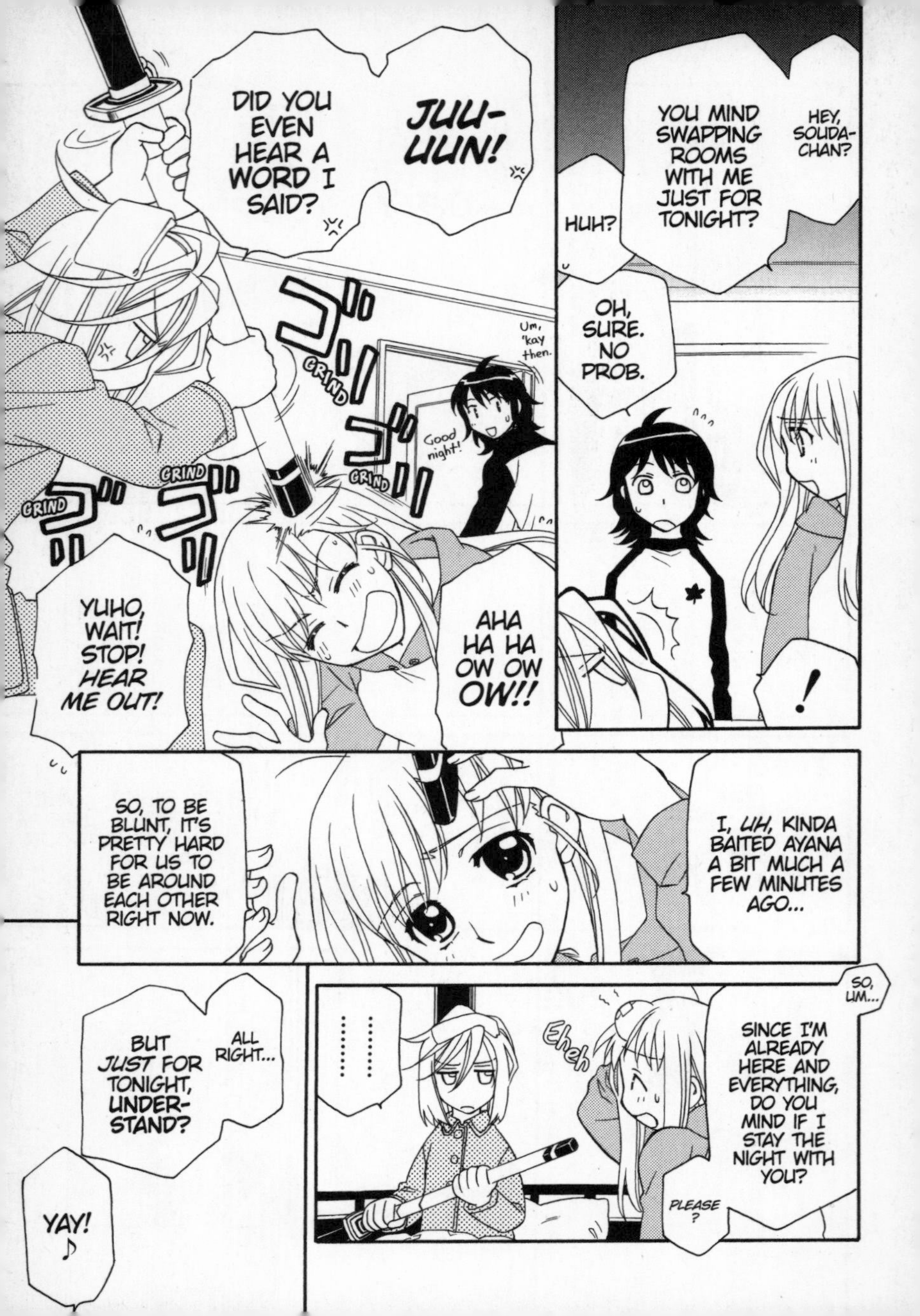
HEY, SOUDA-CHAN?
YOU MIND SWAPPING ROOMS WITH ME JUST FOR TONIGHT?
HUH?
OH, SURE. NO PROB.
!
JUU-UUN!
DID YOU EVEN HEAR A WORD I SAID?
GRIND
GRIND
GRIND
GRIND
Um, 'kay then.
Good night!
AHA HA HA OW OW OW!!
YUHO, WAIT! STOP! *HEAR ME OUT!*
I, *UH*, KINDA BAITED AYANA A BIT MUCH A FEW MINUTES AGO...
SO, TO BE BLUNT, IT'S PRETTY HARD FOR US TO BE AROUND EACH OTHER RIGHT NOW.
SO, UM...
SINCE I'M ALREADY HERE AND EVERYTHING, DO YOU MIND IF I STAY THE NIGHT WITH YOU?
PLEASE?
Eheh
......
ALL RIGHT...
BUT *JUST* FOR TONIGHT, UNDERSTAND?
YAY! ♪

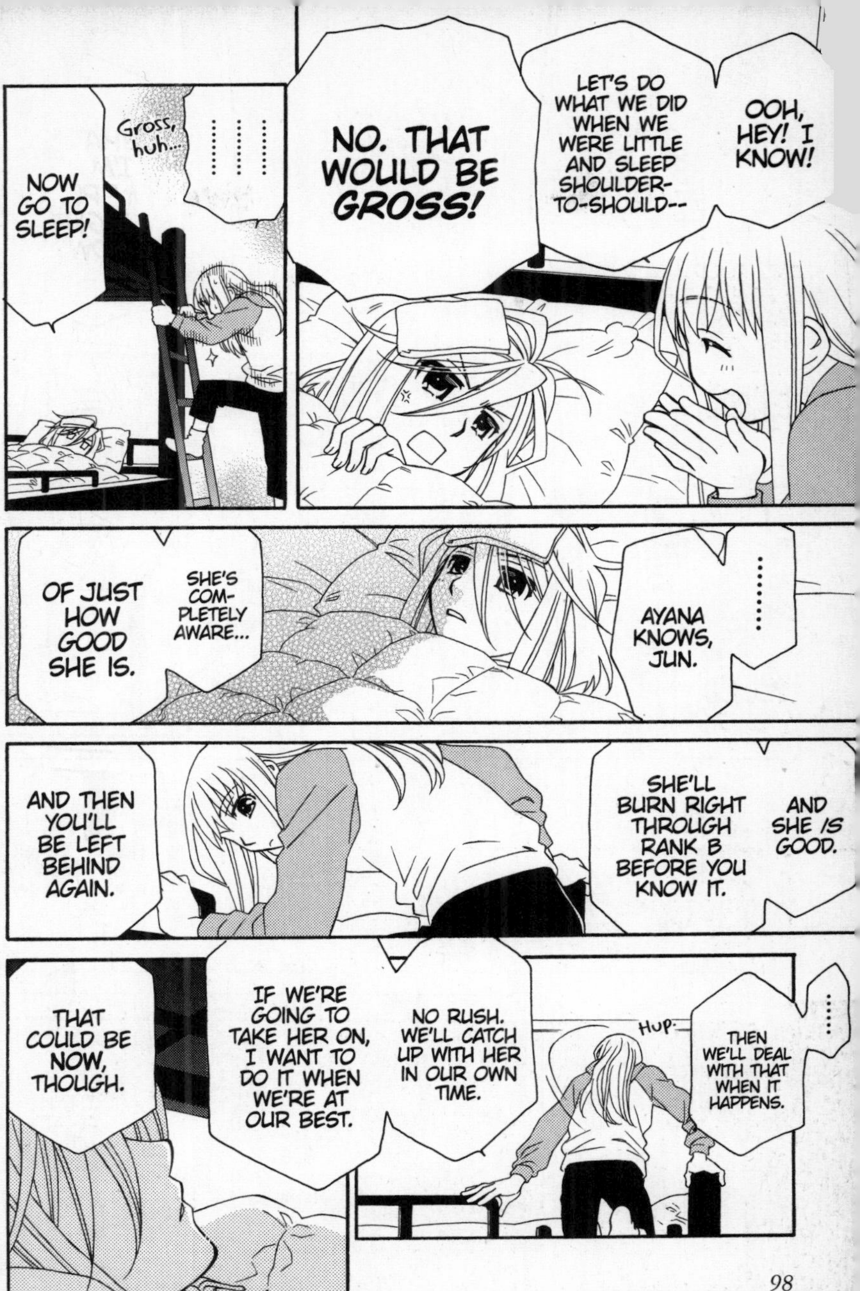
OOH, HEY! I KNOW!
LET'S DO WHAT WE DID WHEN WE WERE LITTLE AND SLEEP SHOULDER-TO-SHOULD--
NO. THAT WOULD BE *GROSS!*
......
Gross, huh...
NOW GO TO SLEEP!
......
AYANA KNOWS, JUN.
SHE'S COMPLETELY AWARE...
OF JUST HOW GOOD SHE IS.
AND SHE *IS* GOOD.
SHE'LL BURN RIGHT THROUGH RANK B BEFORE YOU KNOW IT.
AND THEN YOU'LL BE LEFT BEHIND AGAIN.
......
THEN WE'LL DEAL WITH THAT WHEN IT HAPPENS.
Hup.
NO RUSH. WE'LL CATCH UP WITH HER IN OUR OWN TIME.
IF WE'RE GOING TO TAKE HER ON, I WANT TO DO IT WHEN WE'RE AT OUR BEST.
THAT COULD BE NOW, THOUGH.

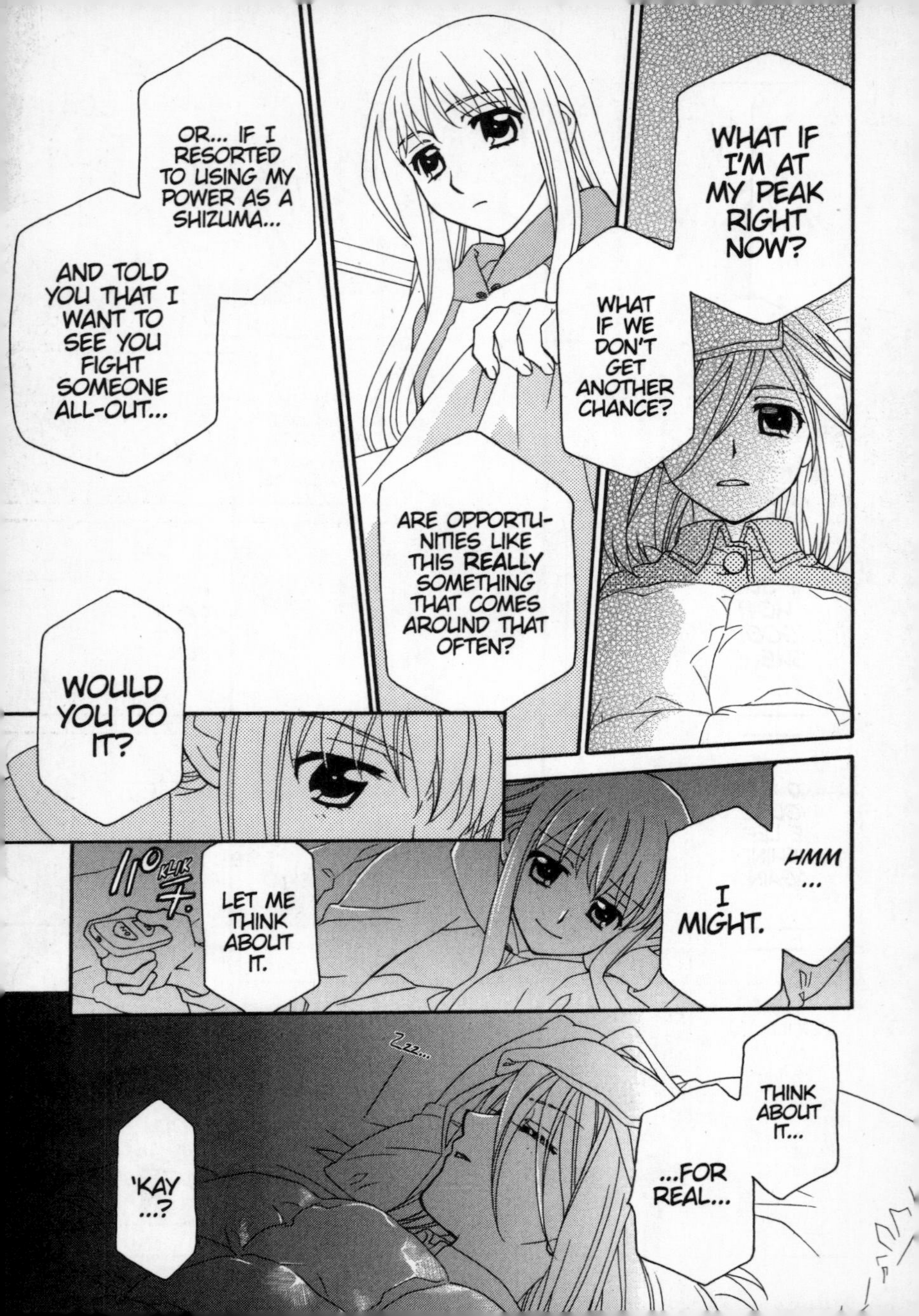
WHAT IF I'M AT MY PEAK RIGHT NOW?
WHAT IF WE DON'T GET ANOTHER CHANCE?
ARE OPPORTUNITIES LIKE THIS REALLY SOMETHING THAT COMES AROUND THAT OFTEN?
OR... IF I RESORTED TO USING MY POWER AS A SHIZUMA...
AND TOLD YOU THAT I WANT TO SEE YOU FIGHT SOMEONE ALL-OUT...
WOULD YOU DO IT?
HMM...
I MIGHT.
LET ME THINK ABOUT IT.
KLIK
THINK ABOUT IT...
...FOR REAL...
Zzz...
'KAY...?

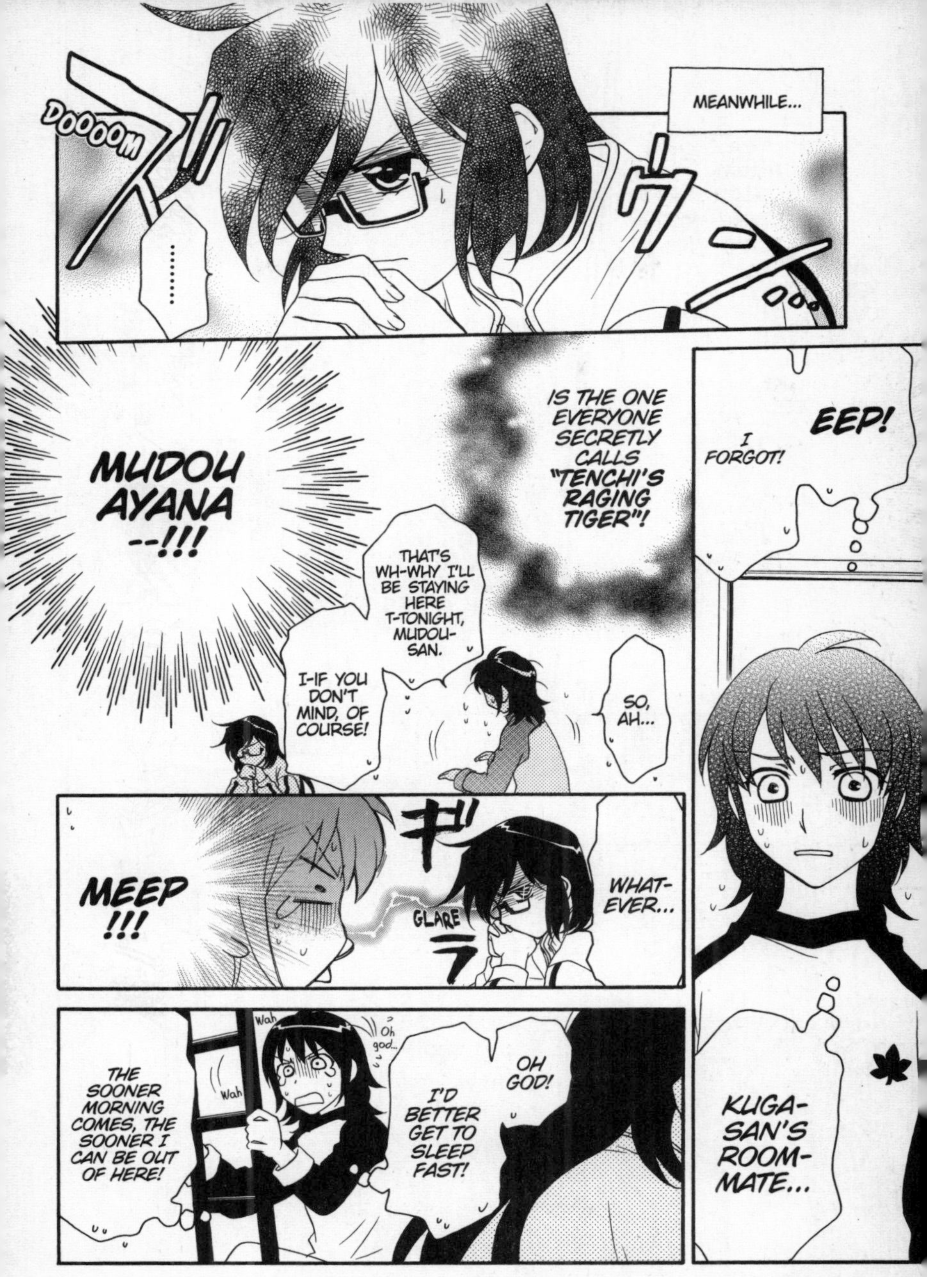
MEANWHILE...
DOOOOM
......
EEP!
I FORGOT!
KUGA-SAN'S ROOMMATE...
IS THE ONE EVERYONE SECRETLY CALLS "TENCHI'S RAGING TIGER"!
MUDOU AYANA --!!!
SO, AH...
THAT'S WH-WHY I'LL BE STAYING HERE T-TONIGHT, MUDOU-SAN.
I-IF YOU DON'T MIND, OF COURSE!
WHAT-EVER...
GLARE
MEEP !!!
OH GOD!
I'D BETTER GET TO SLEEP FAST!
Oh god...
Wah
Wah
THE SOONER MORNING COMES, THE SOONER I CAN BE OUT OF HERE!

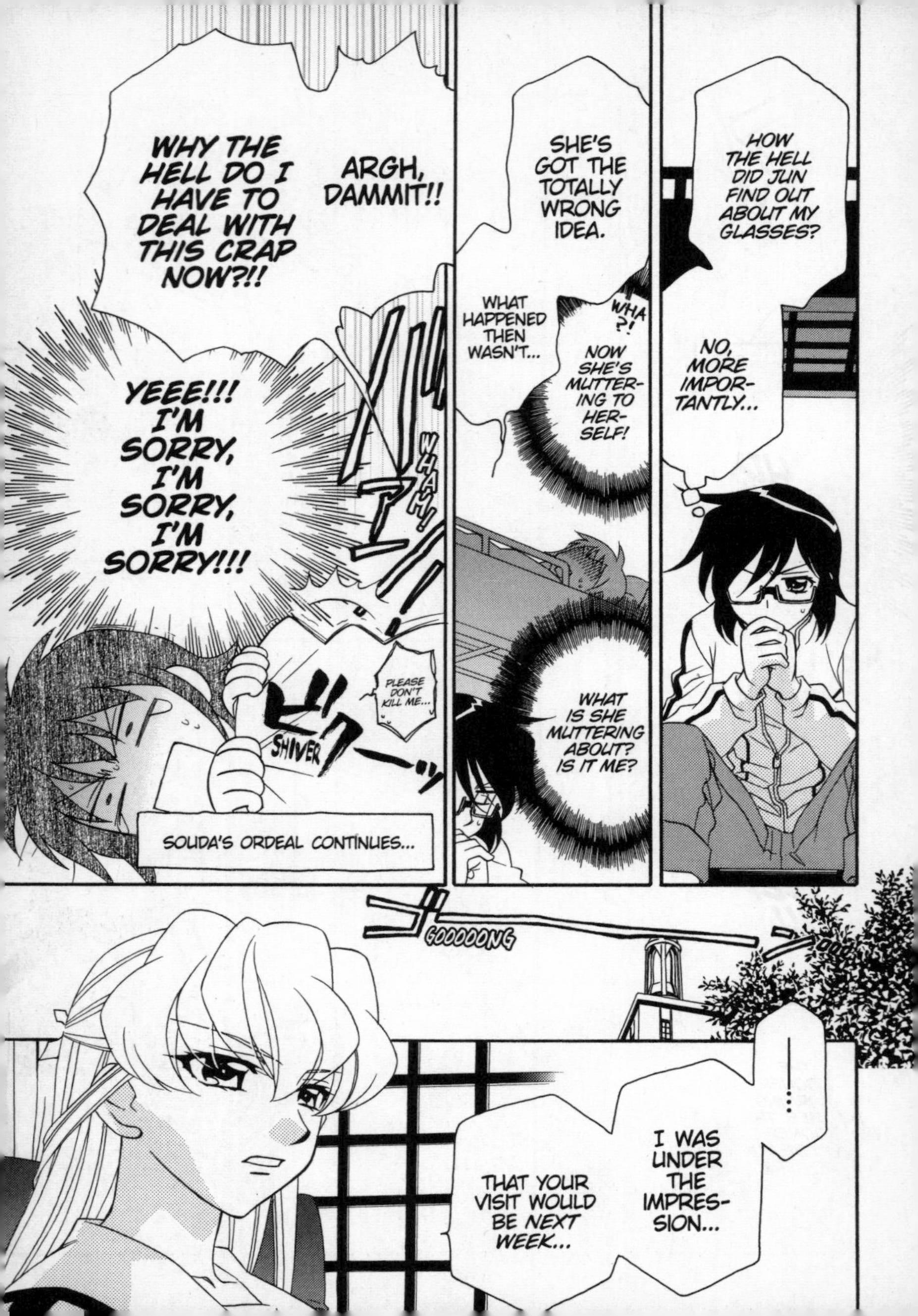
HOW THE HELL DID JUN FIND OUT ABOUT MY GLASSES?
NO, MORE IMPORTANTLY...
SHE'S GOT THE TOTALLY WRONG IDEA.
WHA?!
NOW SHE'S MUTTERING TO HERSELF!
WHAT HAPPENED THEN WASN'T...
WHAT IS SHE MUTTERING ABOUT? IS IT ME?
ARGH, DAMMIT!!
WHY THE HELL DO I HAVE TO DEAL WITH THIS CRAP NOW?!!
WHAM!
YEEE!!! I'M SORRY, I'M SORRY, I'M SORRY!!!
PLEASE DON'T KILL ME...
SHIVER
SOUDA'S ORDEAL CONTINUES...
GOOOOONG
...!
I WAS UNDER THE IMPRESSION...
THAT YOUR VISIT WOULD BE NEXT WEEK...

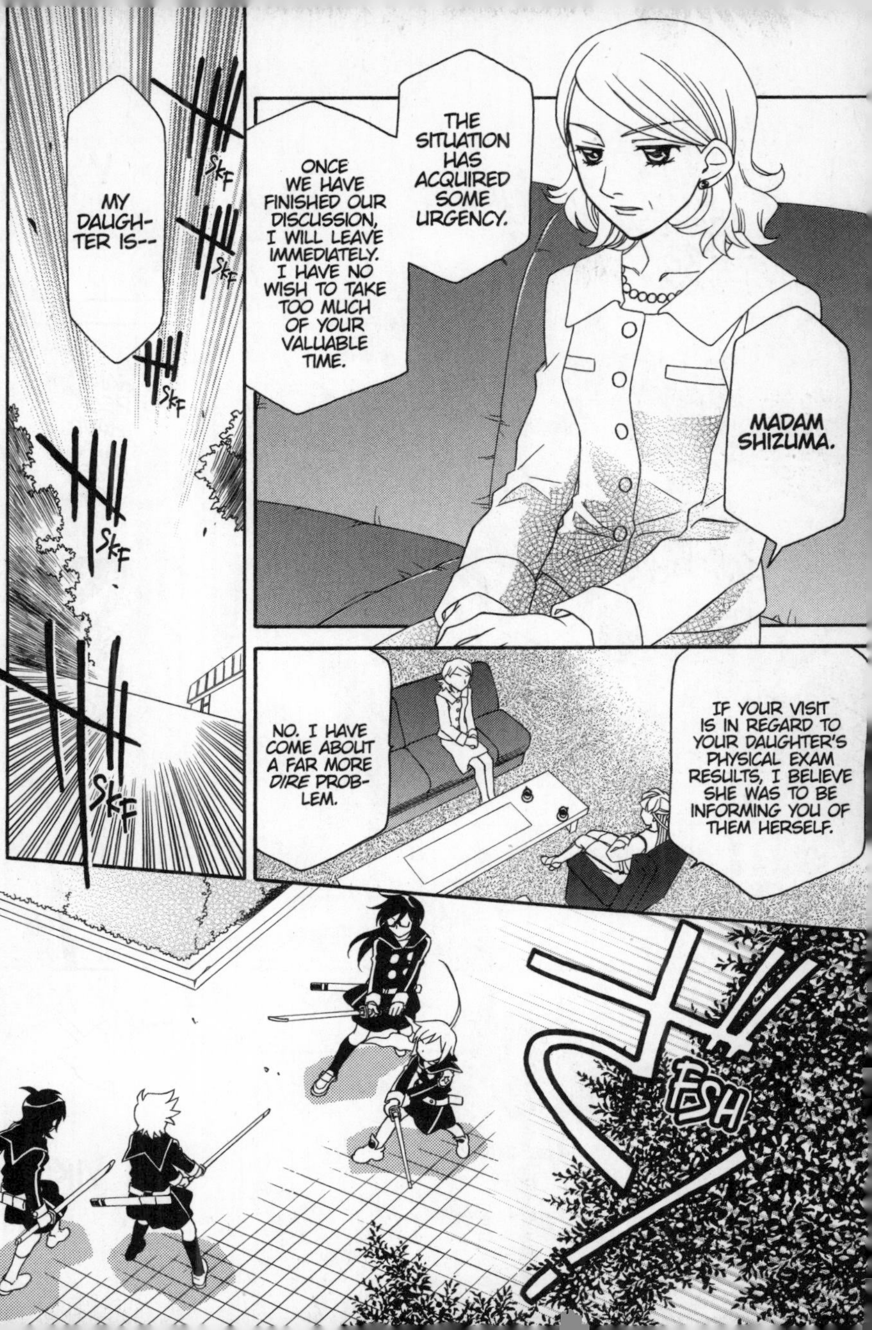
THE SITUATION HAS ACQUIRED SOME URGENCY.
ONCE WE HAVE FINISHED OUR DISCUSSION, I WILL LEAVE IMMEDIATELY. I HAVE NO WISH TO TAKE TOO MUCH OF YOUR VALUABLE TIME.
MADAM SHIZUMA.
IF YOUR VISIT IS IN REGARD TO YOUR DAUGHTER'S PHYSICAL EXAM RESULTS, I BELIEVE SHE WAS TO BE INFORMING YOU OF THEM HERSELF.
NO. I HAVE COME ABOUT A FAR MORE *DIRE* PROBLEM.
SKF
SKF
MY DAUGHTER IS--
SKF
SKF
SKF
FSH

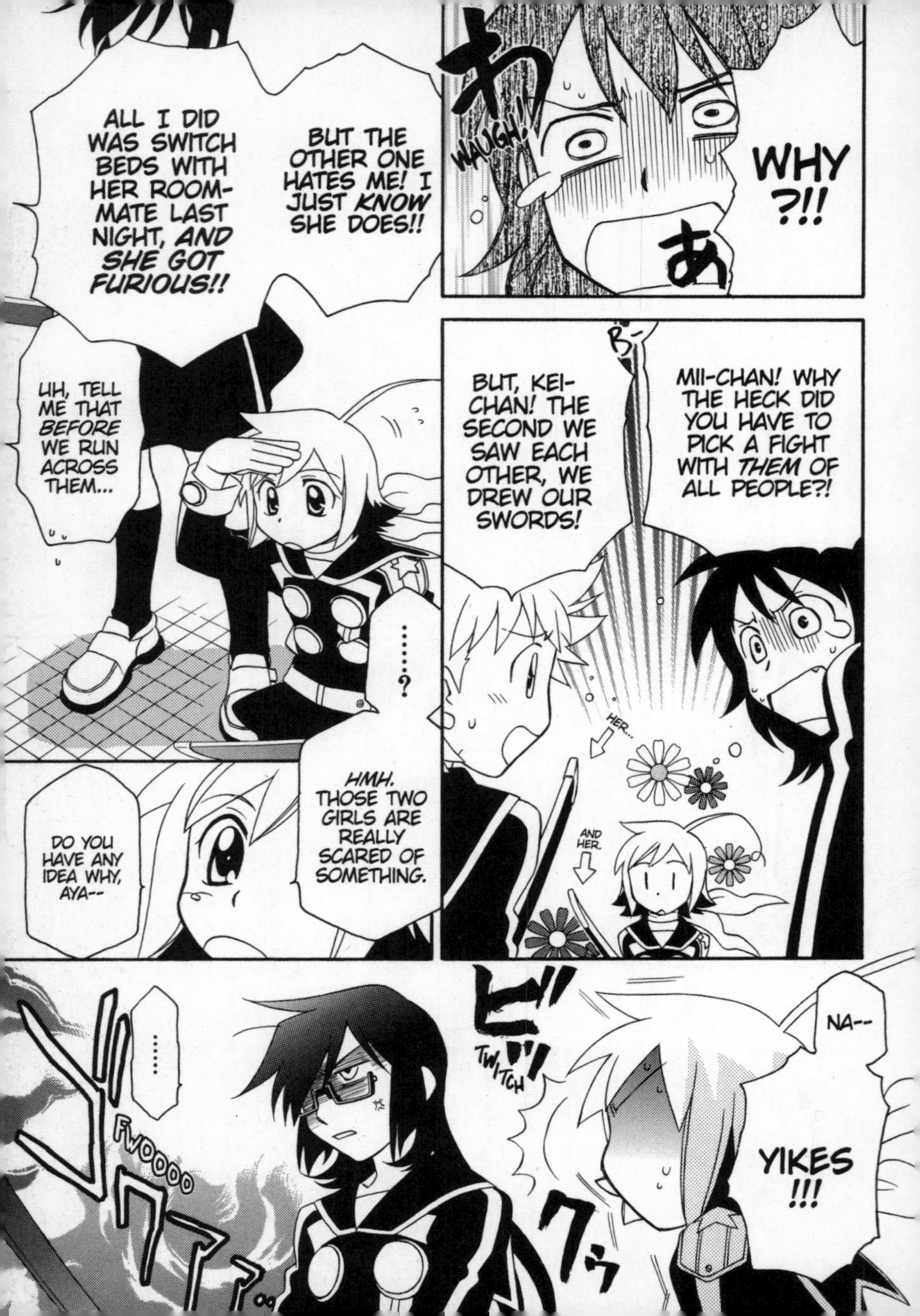

わ
WAUGH!!
WHY?!!
あ
BUT THE OTHER ONE HATES ME! I JUST *KNOW* SHE DOES!!
ALL I DID WAS SWITCH BEDS WITH HER ROOM-MATE LAST NIGHT, *AND SHE GOT FURIOUS!!*
B--
MII-CHAN! WHY THE HECK DID YOU HAVE TO PICK A FIGHT WITH *THEM* OF ALL PEOPLE?!
BUT, KEI-CHAN! THE SECOND WE SAW EACH OTHER, WE DREW OUR SWORDS!
HER...
AND HER.
UH, TELL ME THAT *BEFORE* WE RUN ACROSS THEM...
......?
HMH. THOSE TWO GIRLS ARE REALLY SCARED OF SOMETHING.
DO YOU HAVE ANY IDEA WHY, AYA--
NA--
YIKES!!!
ビ
TWITCH
......
FWOOOO

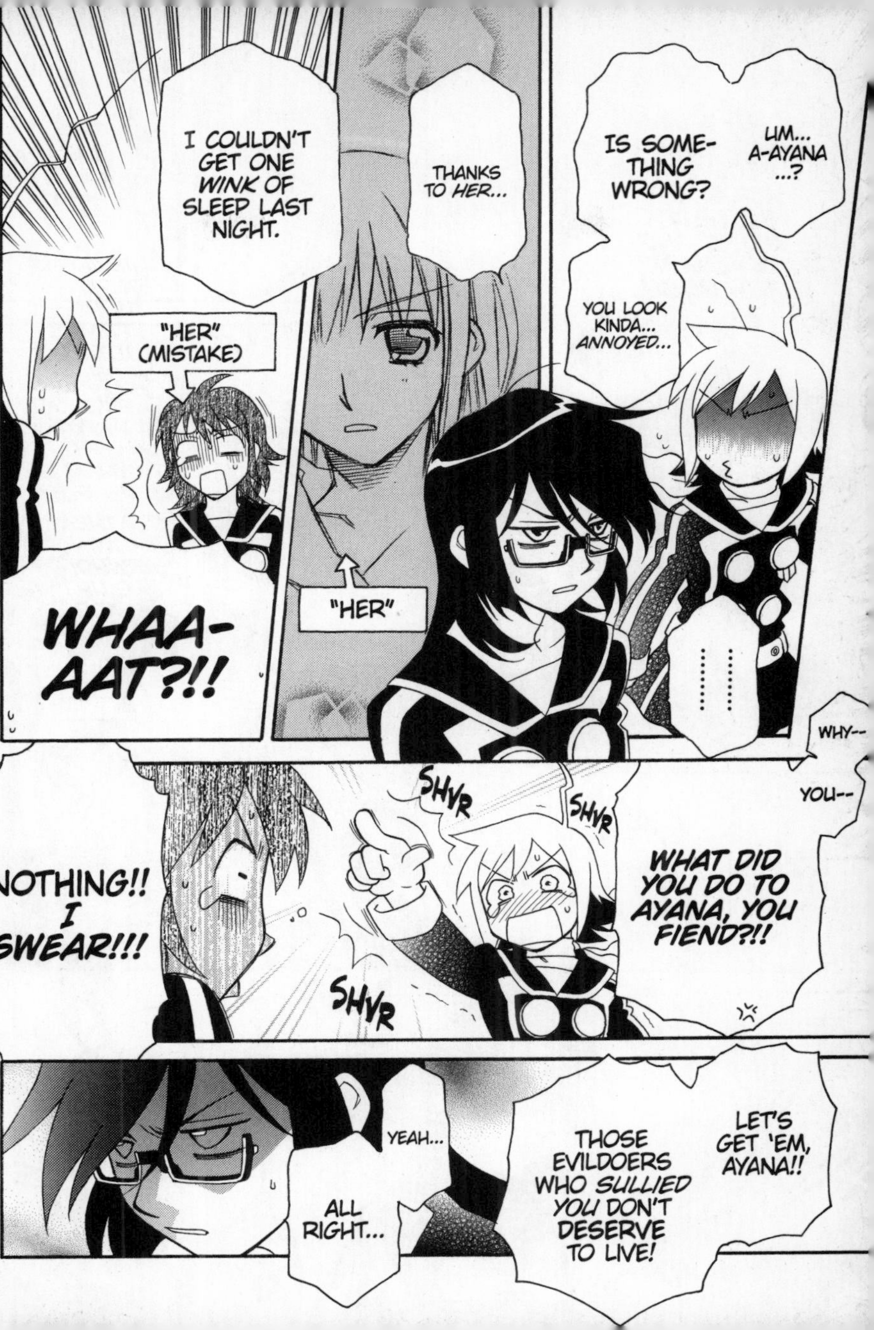
UM... A-AYANA ...?
IS SOME-THING WRONG?
YOU LOOK KINDA... ANNOYED...
......
THANKS TO HER...
"HER"
I COULDN'T GET ONE WINK OF SLEEP LAST NIGHT.
"HER" (MISTAKE)
WHAAA-AAT?!!
WHY--
YOU--
WHAT DID YOU DO TO AYANA, YOU FIEND?!!
SHVR
SHVR
SHVR
NOTHING!! I SWEAR!!!
LET'S GET 'EM, AYANA!!
THOSE EVILDOERS WHO SULLIED YOU DON'T DESERVE TO LIVE!
YEAH...
ALL RIGHT...

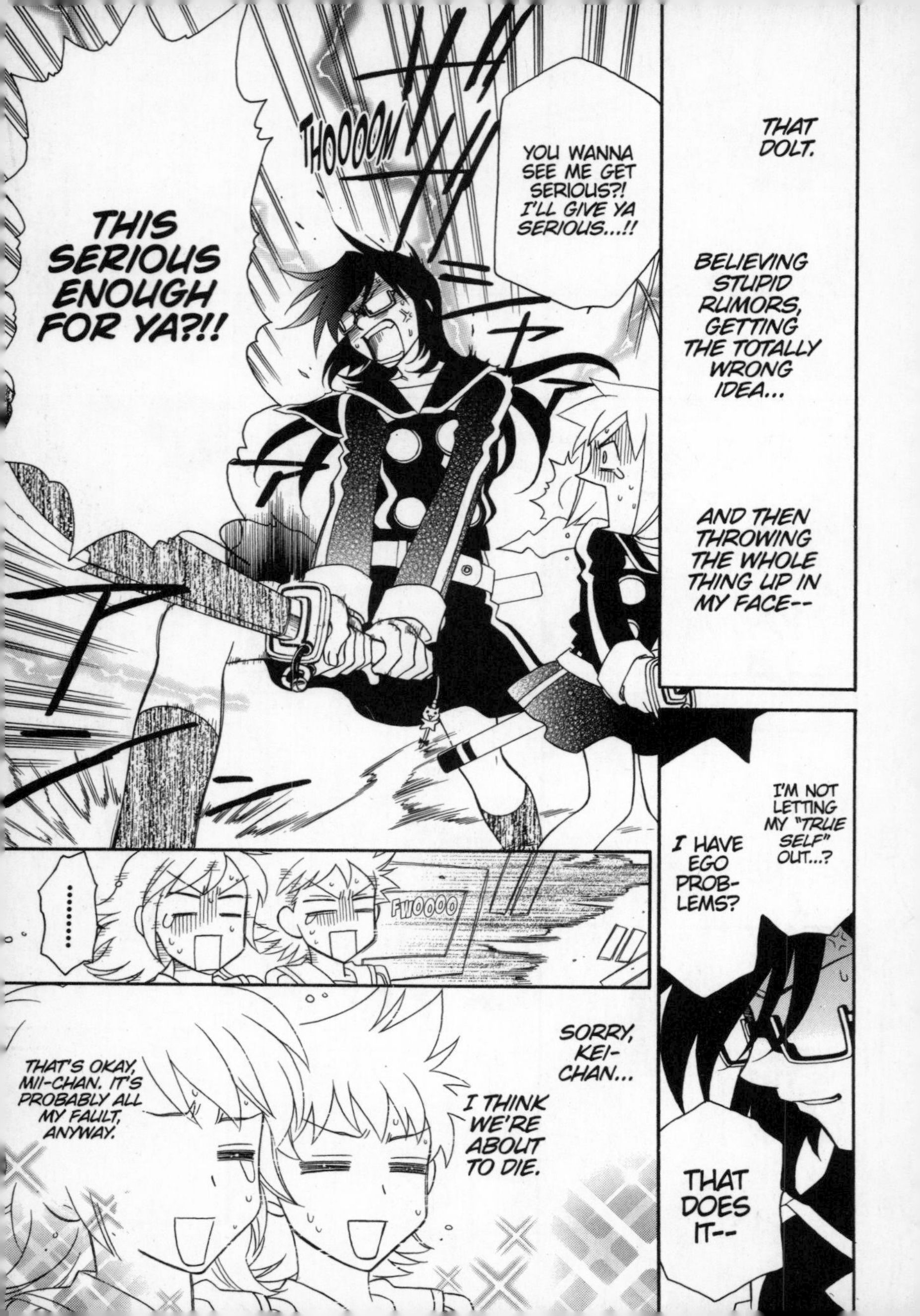
THAT DOLT.
BELIEVING STUPID RUMORS, GETTING THE TOTALLY WRONG IDEA...
AND THEN THROWING THE WHOLE THING UP IN MY FACE--
YOU WANNA SEE ME GET SERIOUS?! I'LL GIVE YA SERIOUS...!!
THOOOOM
THIS SERIOUS ENOUGH FOR YA?!!
I'M NOT LETTING MY "TRUE SELF" OUT...?
I HAVE EGO PROB-LEMS?
THAT DOES IT--
FWOOOO
......
SORRY, KEI-CHAN...
I THINK WE'RE ABOUT TO DIE.
THAT'S OKAY, MII-CHAN. IT'S PROBABLY ALL MY FAULT, ANYWAY.

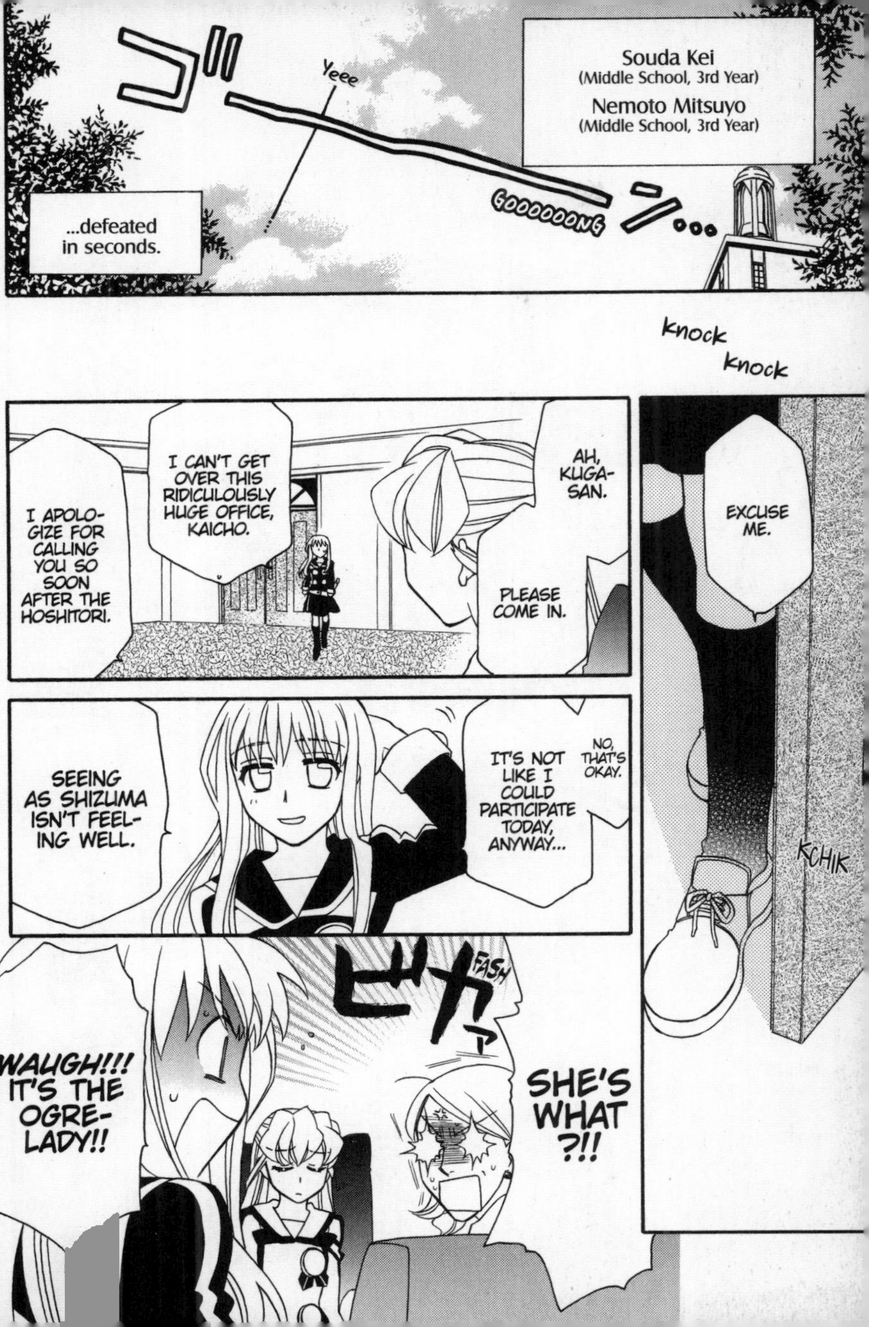
Souda Kei
(Middle School, 3rd Year)
Nemoto Mitsuyo
(Middle School, 3rd Year)
GOOOOOONG
Yeee
...defeated in seconds.
knock knock
EXCUSE ME.
KCHIK
AH, KUGA-SAN.
PLEASE COME IN.
I CAN'T GET OVER THIS RIDICULOUSLY HUGE OFFICE, KAICHO.
I APOLOGIZE FOR CALLING YOU SO SOON AFTER THE HOSHITORI.
NO, THAT'S OKAY.
IT'S NOT LIKE I COULD PARTICIPATE TODAY, ANYWAY...
SEEING AS SHIZUMA ISN'T FEELING WELL.
FASH
SHE'S WHAT?!!
WAUGH!!! IT'S THE OGRE-LADY!!

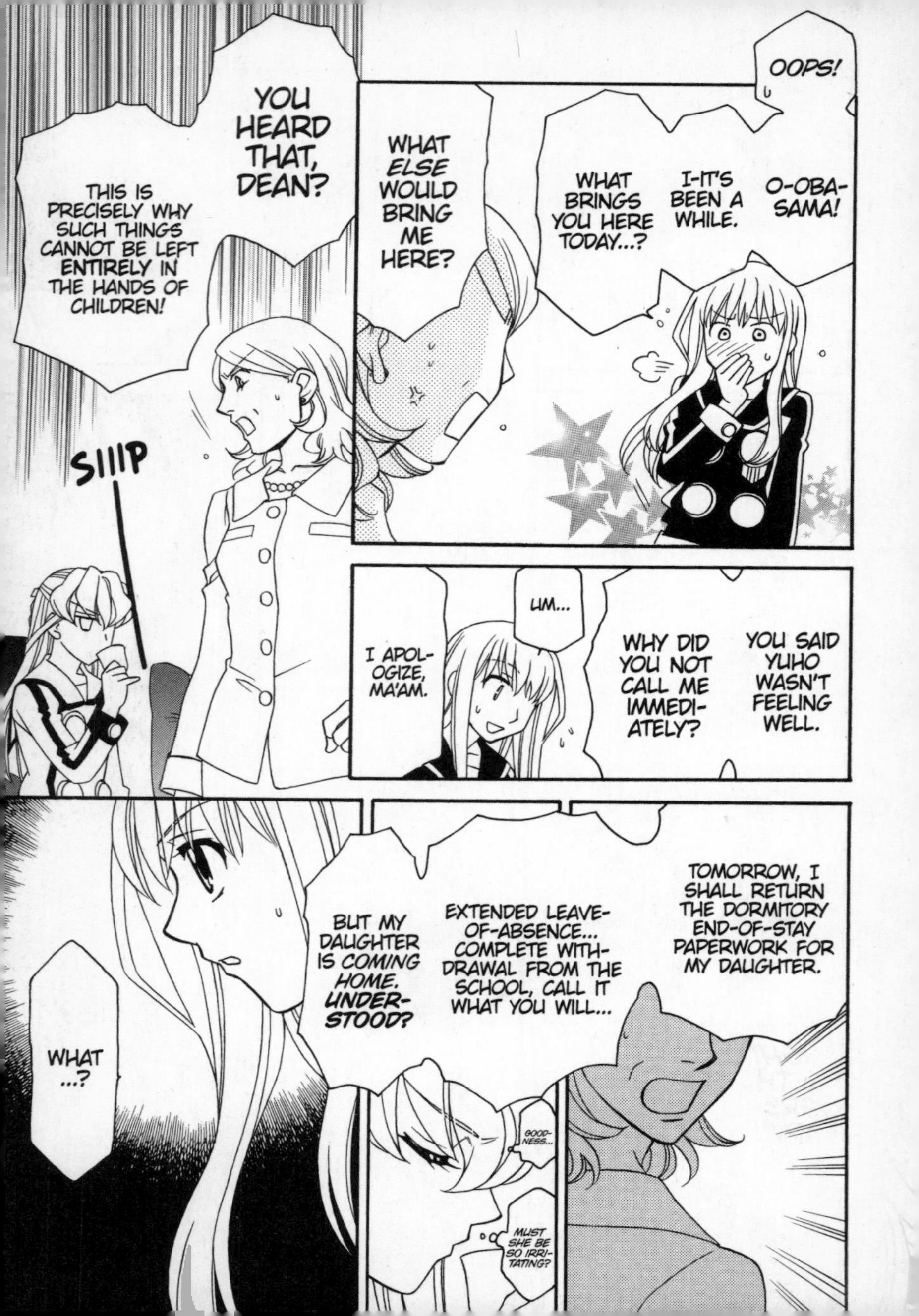
OOPS!
O-OBA-SAMA!
I-IT'S BEEN A WHILE.
WHAT BRINGS YOU HERE TODAY...?
WHAT ELSE WOULD BRING ME HERE?
YOU SAID YUHO WASN'T FEELING WELL.
WHY DID YOU NOT CALL ME IMMEDI-ATELY?
UM...
I APOLOG-OGIZE, MA'AM.
YOU HEARD THAT, DEAN?
THIS IS PRECISELY WHY SUCH THINGS CANNOT BE LEFT ENTIRELY IN THE HANDS OF CHILDREN!
SIIIP
TOMORROW, I SHALL RETURN THE DORMITORY END-OF-STAY PAPERWORK FOR MY DAUGHTER.
EXTENDED LEAVE-OF-ABSENCE... COMPLETE WITH-DRAWAL FROM THE SCHOOL, CALL IT WHAT YOU WILL...
BUT MY DAUGHTER IS COMING HOME. UNDER-STOOD?
GOOD-NESS...
MUST SHE BE SO IRRI-TATING?
WHAT ...?

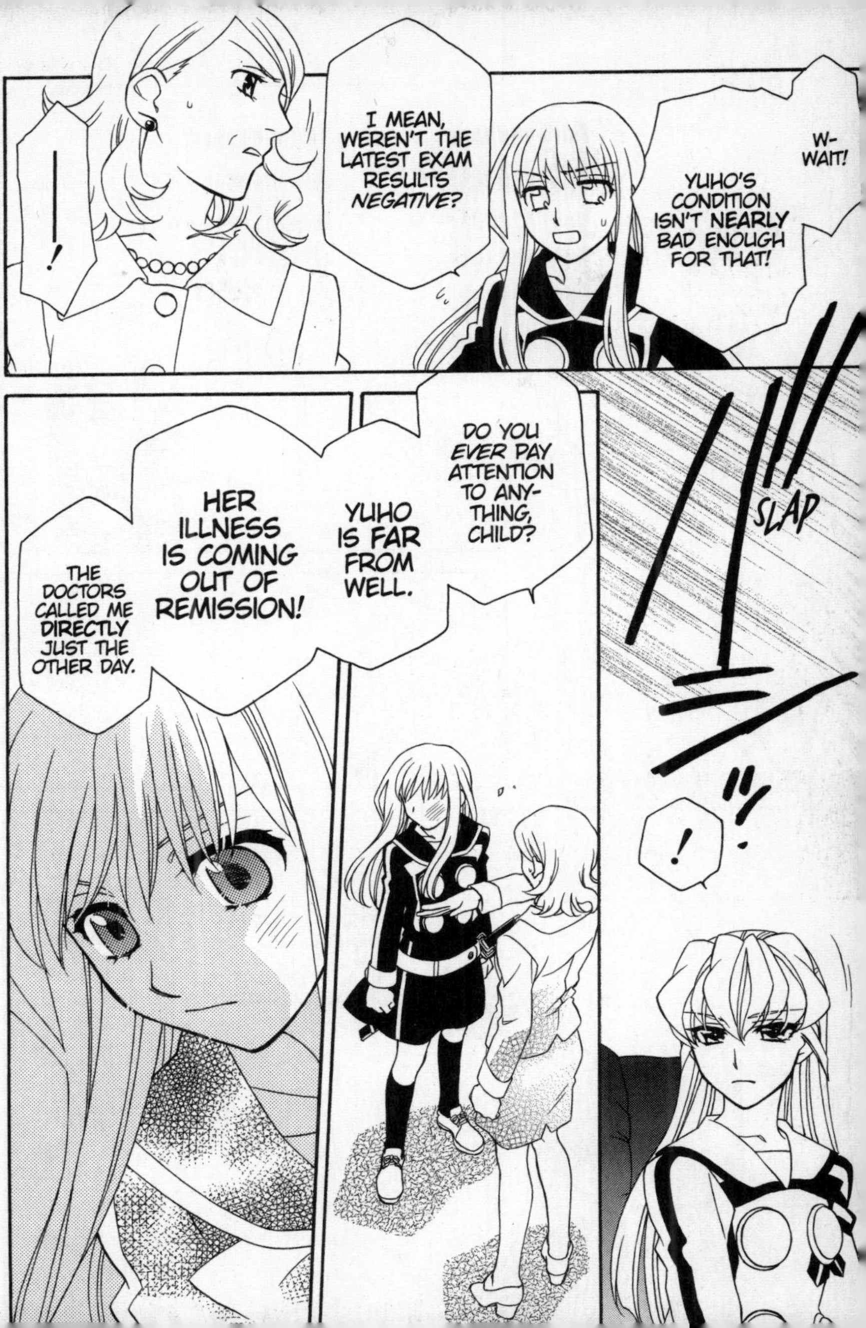

W-WAIT!
YUHO'S CONDITION ISN'T NEARLY BAD ENOUGH FOR THAT!
I MEAN, WEREN'T THE LATEST EXAM RESULTS *NEGATIVE*?
—!
SLAP
!
DO YOU *EVER* PAY ATTENTION TO ANY-THING, CHILD?
YUHO IS FAR FROM WELL.
HER ILLNESS IS COMING OUT OF REMISSION!
THE DOCTORS CALLED ME **DIRECTLY** JUST THE OTHER DAY.

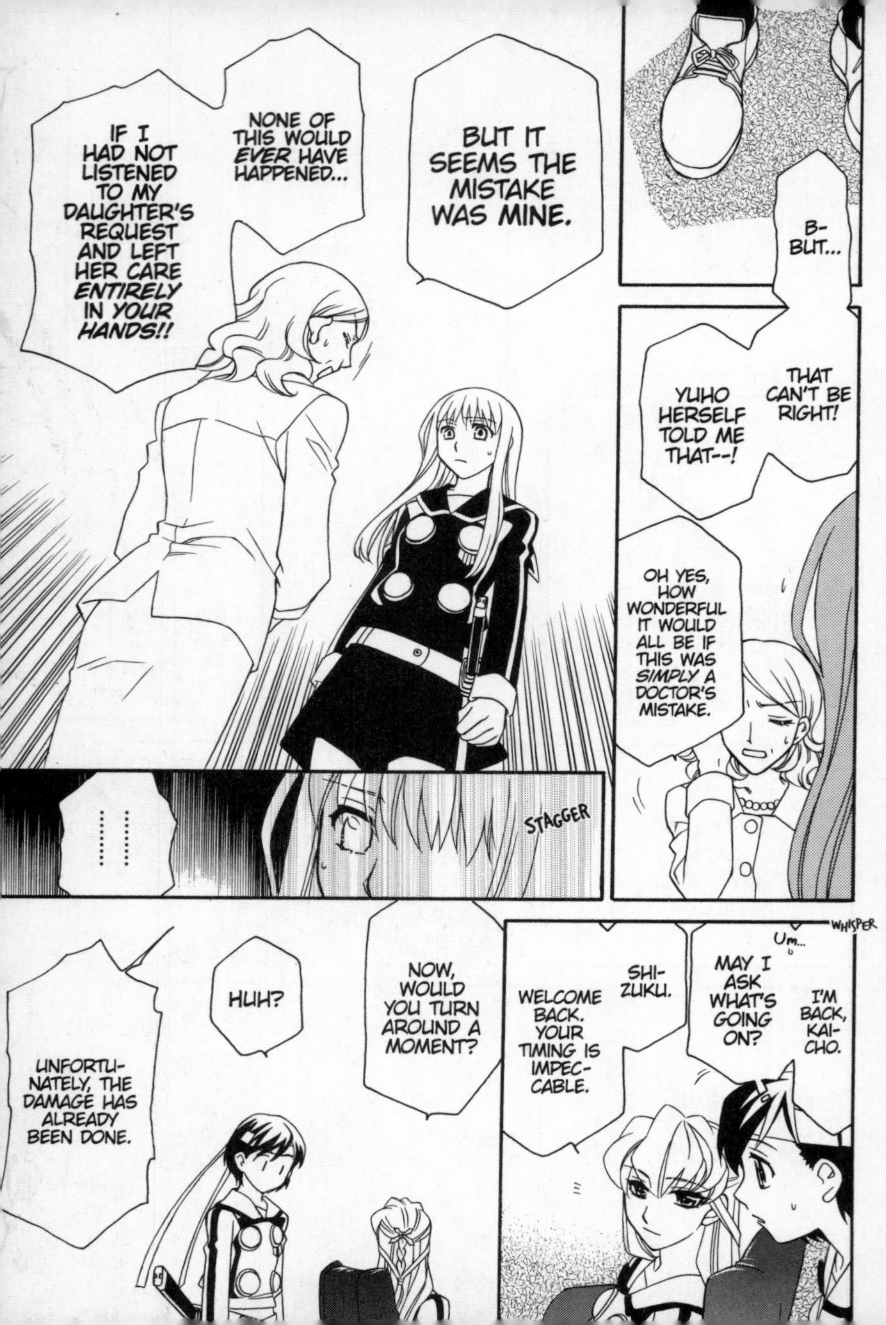
B-BUT...
THAT CAN'T BE RIGHT!
YUHO HERSELF TOLD ME THAT--!
OH YES, HOW WONDERFUL IT WOULD ALL BE IF THIS WAS *SIMPLY* A DOCTOR'S MISTAKE.
BUT IT SEEMS THE MISTAKE WAS MINE.
NONE OF THIS WOULD *EVER* HAVE HAPPENED...
IF I HAD NOT LISTENED TO MY DAUGHTER'S REQUEST AND LEFT HER CARE *ENTIRELY* IN *YOUR HANDS!!*
STAGGER
......
......
WHISPER
Um...
I'M BACK, KAI-CHO.
MAY I ASK WHAT'S GOING ON?
SHI-ZUKU.
WELCOME BACK. YOUR TIMING IS IMPECCABLE.
NOW, WOULD YOU TURN AROUND A MOMENT?
HUH?
UNFORTUNATELY, THE DAMAGE HAS ALREADY BEEN DONE.

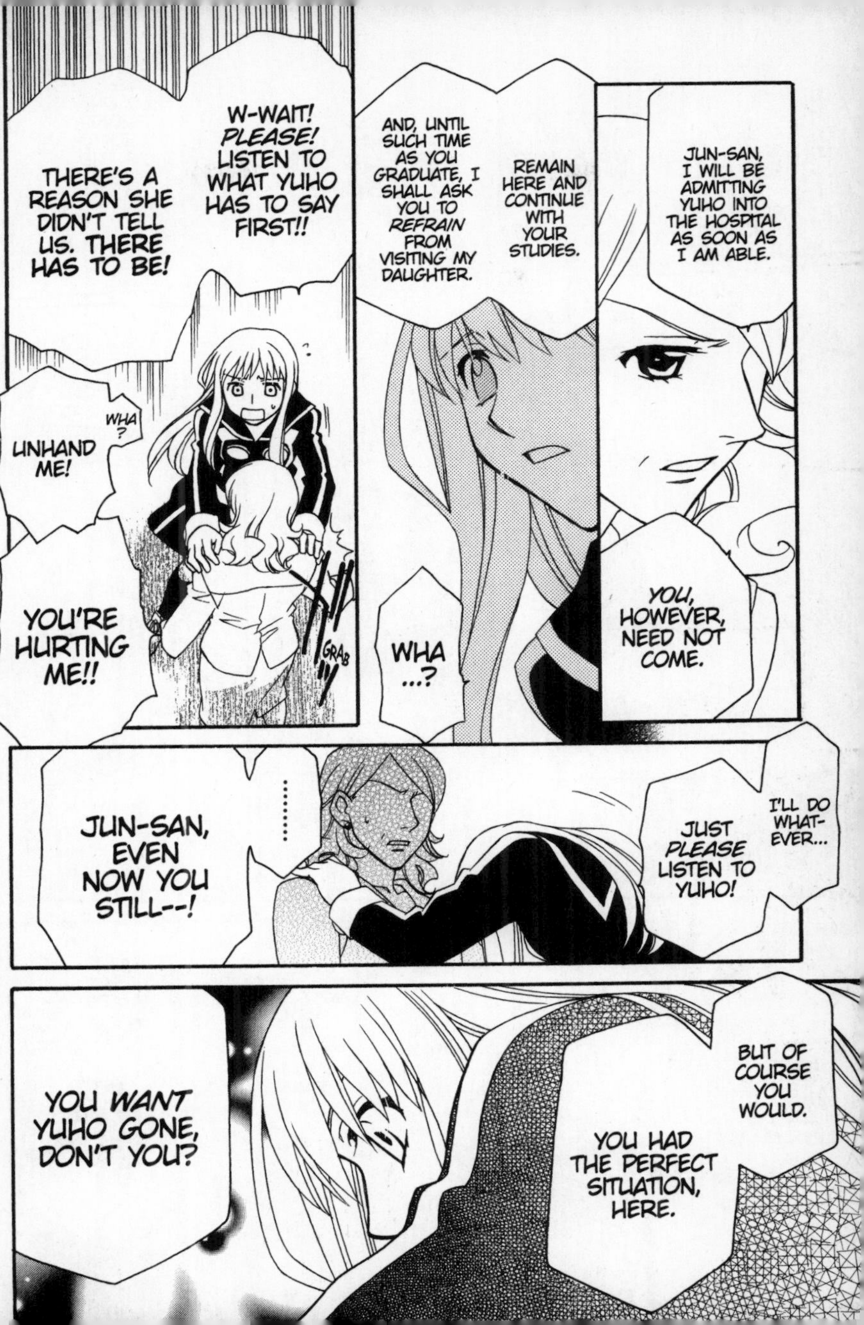
JUN-SAN, I WILL BE ADMITTING YUHO INTO THE HOSPITAL AS SOON AS I AM ABLE.
YOU, HOWEVER, NEED NOT COME.
REMAIN HERE AND CONTINUE WITH YOUR STUDIES.
AND, UNTIL SUCH TIME AS YOU GRADUATE, I SHALL ASK YOU TO *REFRAIN* FROM VISITING MY DAUGHTER.
WHA ...?
W-WAIT! *PLEASE!* LISTEN TO WHAT YUHO HAS TO SAY FIRST!!
THERE'S A REASON SHE DIDN'T TELL US. THERE HAS TO BE!
WHA ?
UNHAND ME!
YOU'RE HURTING ME!!
GRAB
I'LL DO WHAT-EVER...
JUST *PLEASE* LISTEN TO YUHO!
......
JUN-SAN, EVEN NOW YOU STILL--!
BUT OF COURSE YOU WOULD.
YOU HAD THE PERFECT SITUATION, HERE.
YOU *WANT* YUHO GONE, DON'T YOU?

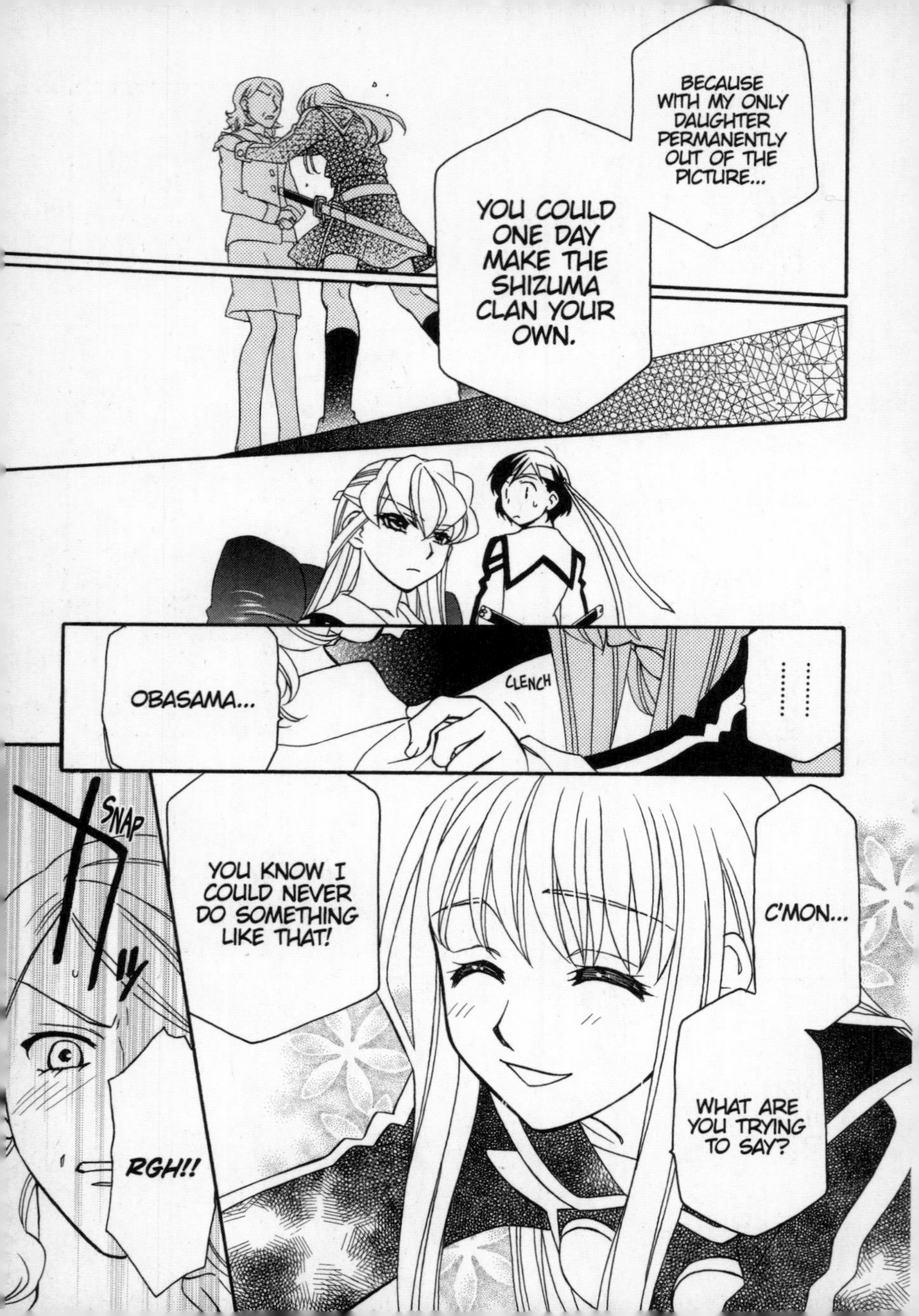
BECAUSE WITH MY ONLY DAUGHTER PERMANENTLY OUT OF THE PICTURE...
YOU COULD ONE DAY MAKE THE SHIZUMA CLAN YOUR OWN.
......
CLENCH
OBASAMA...
C'MON...
WHAT ARE YOU TRYING TO SAY?
YOU KNOW I COULD NEVER DO SOMETHING LIKE THAT!
SNAP
RGH!!

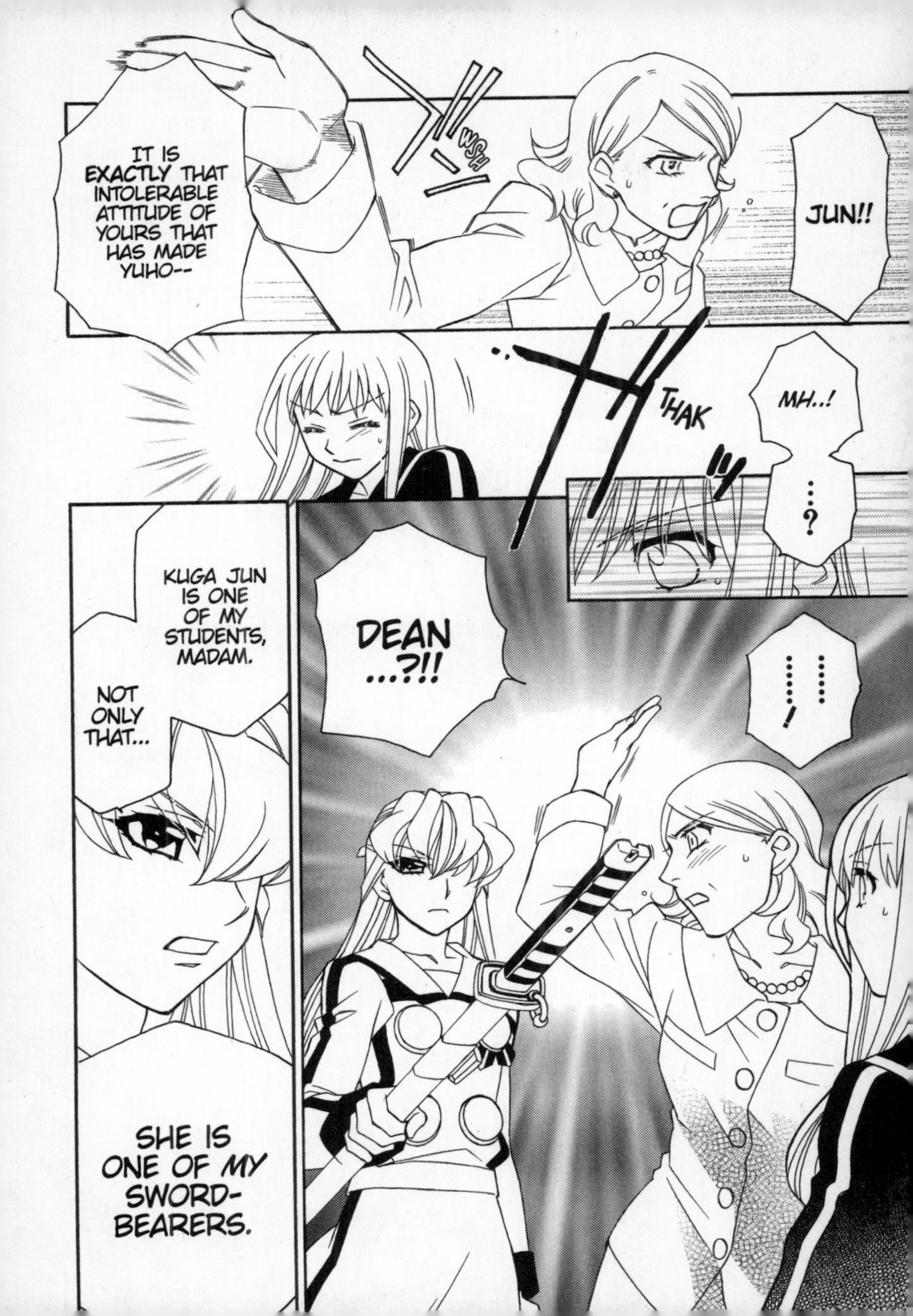
IT IS EXACTLY THAT INTOLERABLE ATTITUDE OF YOURS THAT HAS MADE YUHO--
WSH
JUN!!
MH..!
THAK
...?
DEAN ...?!!
......!
KUGA JUN IS ONE OF MY STUDENTS, MADAM.
NOT ONLY THAT...
SHE IS ONE OF MY SWORD-BEARERS.

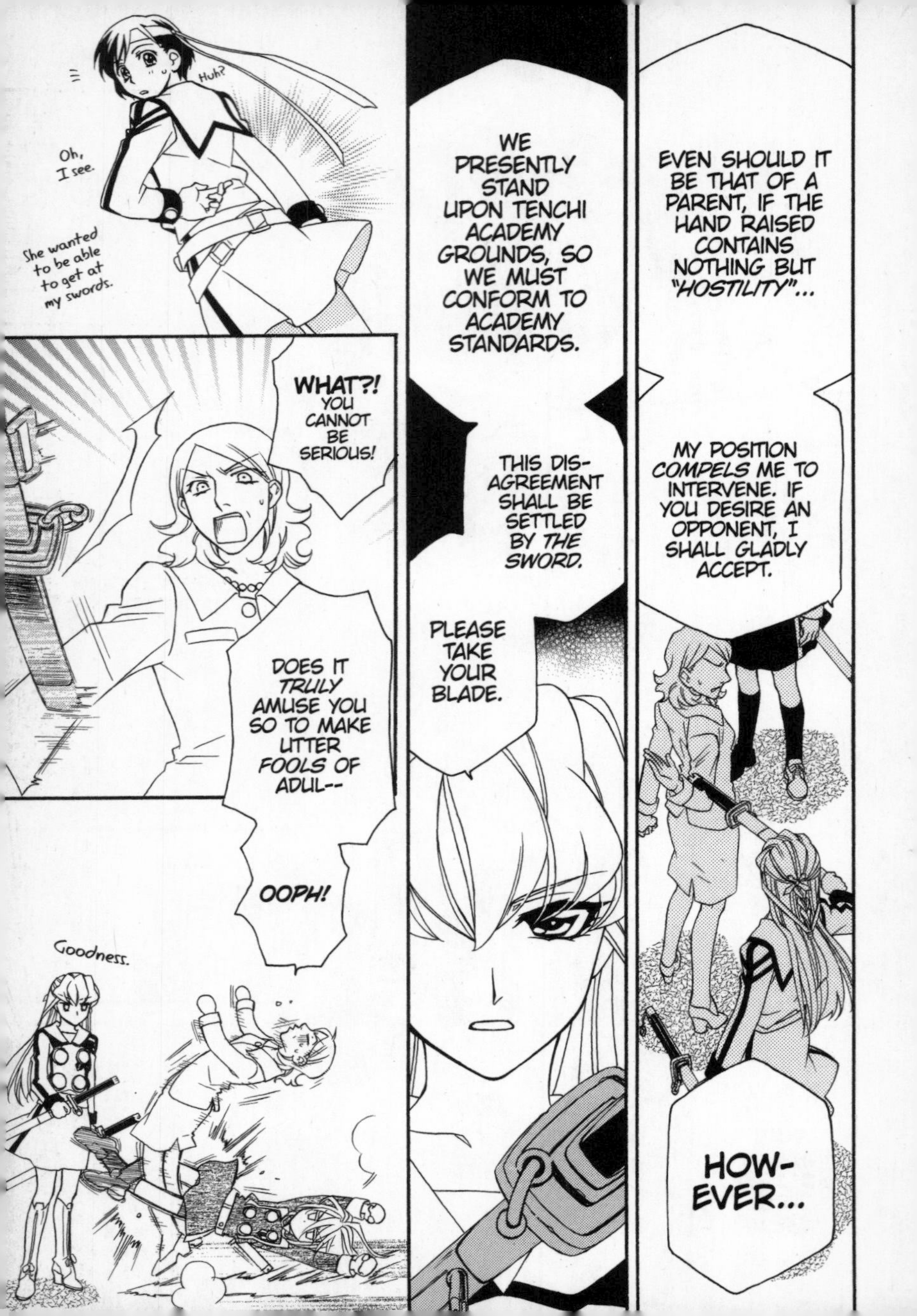
EVEN SHOULD IT BE THAT OF A PARENT, IF THE HAND RAISED CONTAINS NOTHING BUT "HOSTILITY"...
MY POSITION COMPELS ME TO INTERVENE. IF YOU DESIRE AN OPPONENT, I SHALL GLADLY ACCEPT.
HOW-EVER...
WE PRESENTLY STAND UPON TENCHI ACADEMY GROUNDS, SO WE MUST CONFORM TO ACADEMY STANDARDS.
THIS DIS-AGREEMENT SHALL BE SETTLED BY THE SWORD.
PLEASE TAKE YOUR BLADE.
Huh?
Oh, I see.
She wanted to be able to get at my swords.
WHAT?! YOU CANNOT BE SERIOUS!
DOES IT TRULY AMUSE YOU SO TO MAKE UTTER FOOLS OF ADUL--
OOPH!
Goodness.

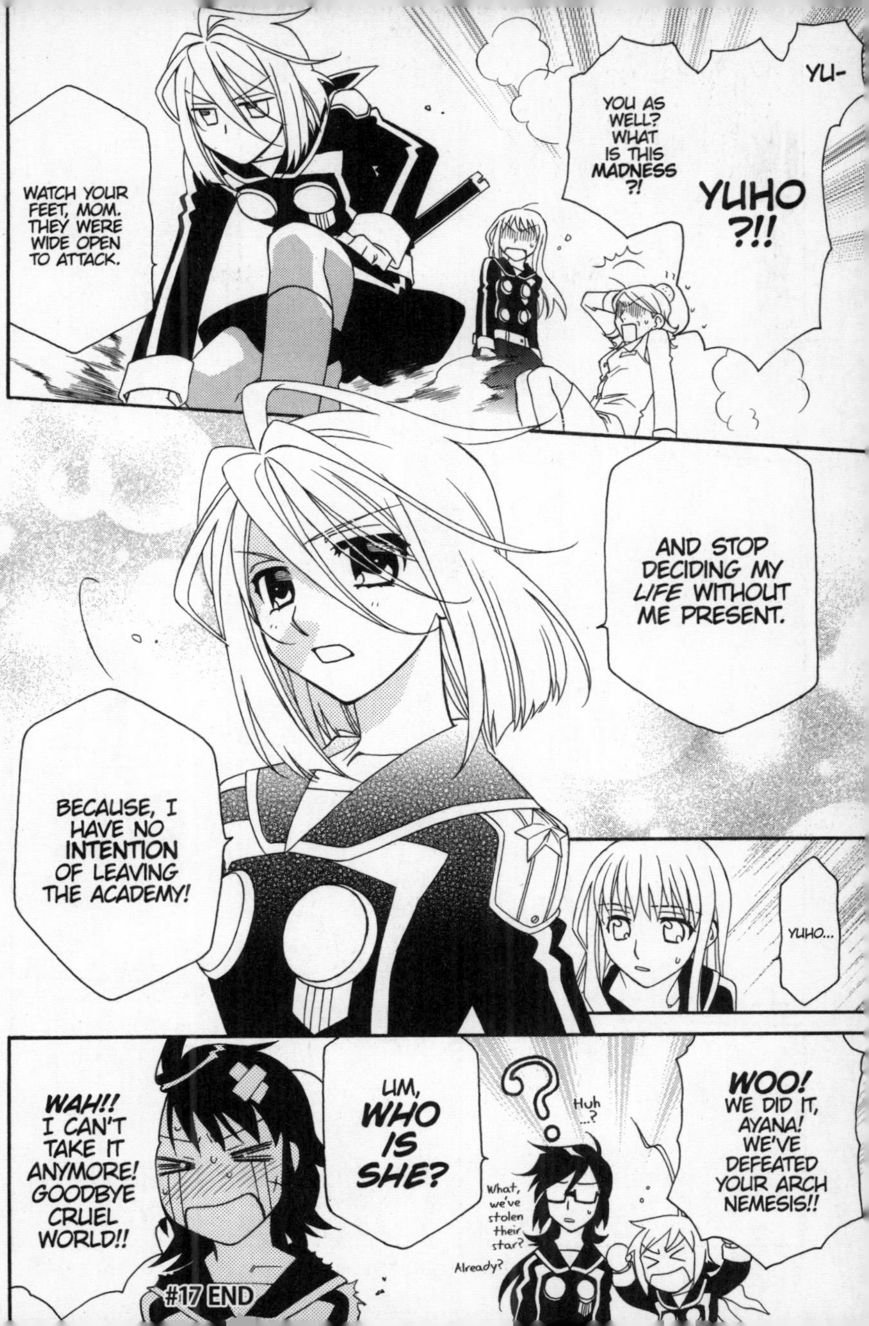
YU-
YUHO ?!!
YOU AS WELL? WHAT IS THIS MADNESS ?!
WATCH YOUR FEET, MOM. THEY WERE WIDE OPEN TO ATTACK.
AND STOP DECIDING MY *LIFE* WITHOUT ME PRESENT.
BECAUSE, I HAVE NO INTENTION OF LEAVING THE ACADEMY!
YUHO...
WOO! WE DID IT, AYANA! WE'VE DEFEATED YOUR ARCH NEMESIS!!
Huh ...?
What, we've stolen their star?
Already?
UM, WHO IS SHE?
WAH!! I CAN'T TAKE IT ANYMORE! GOODBYE CRUEL WORLD!!
#17 END

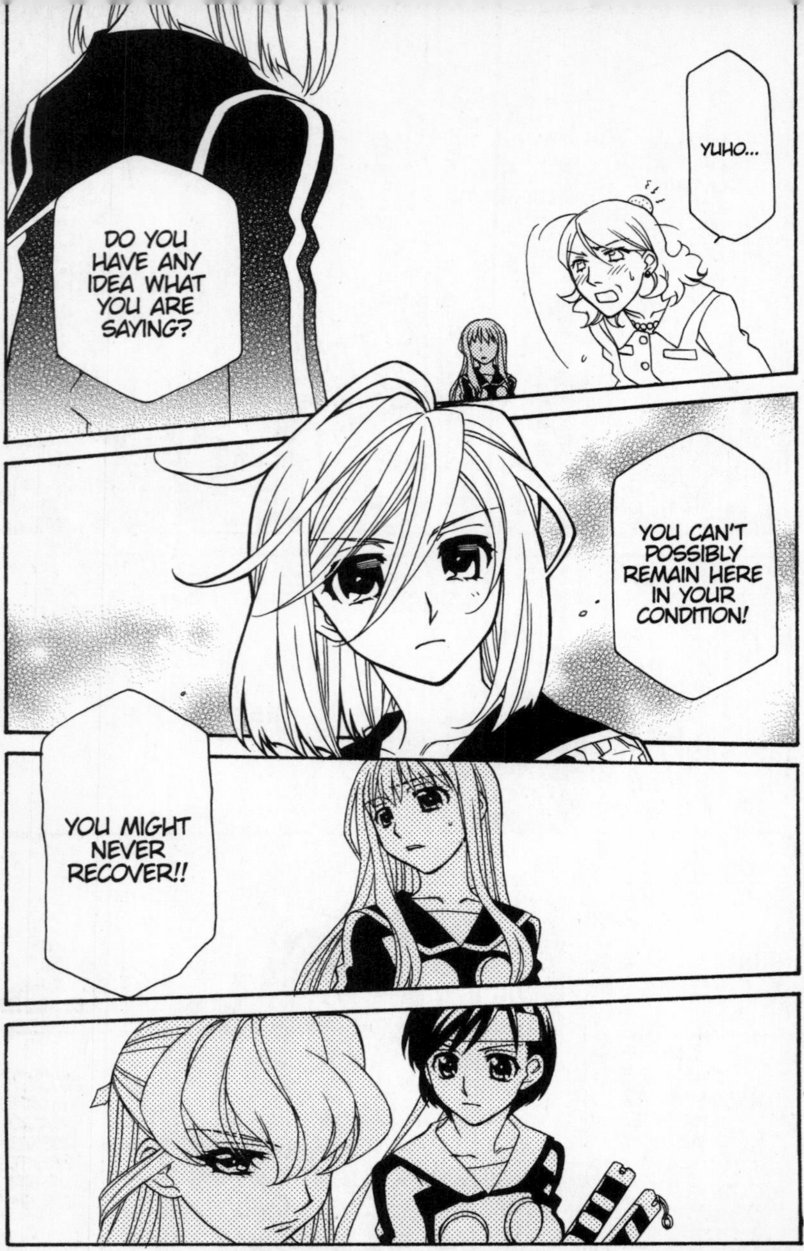
YUHO...
DO YOU HAVE ANY IDEA WHAT YOU ARE SAYING?
YOU CAN'T POSSIBLY REMAIN HERE IN YOUR CONDITION!
YOU MIGHT NEVER RECOVER!!

#18 Stubbornness and Idiocy: Two Sides of the Same Coin

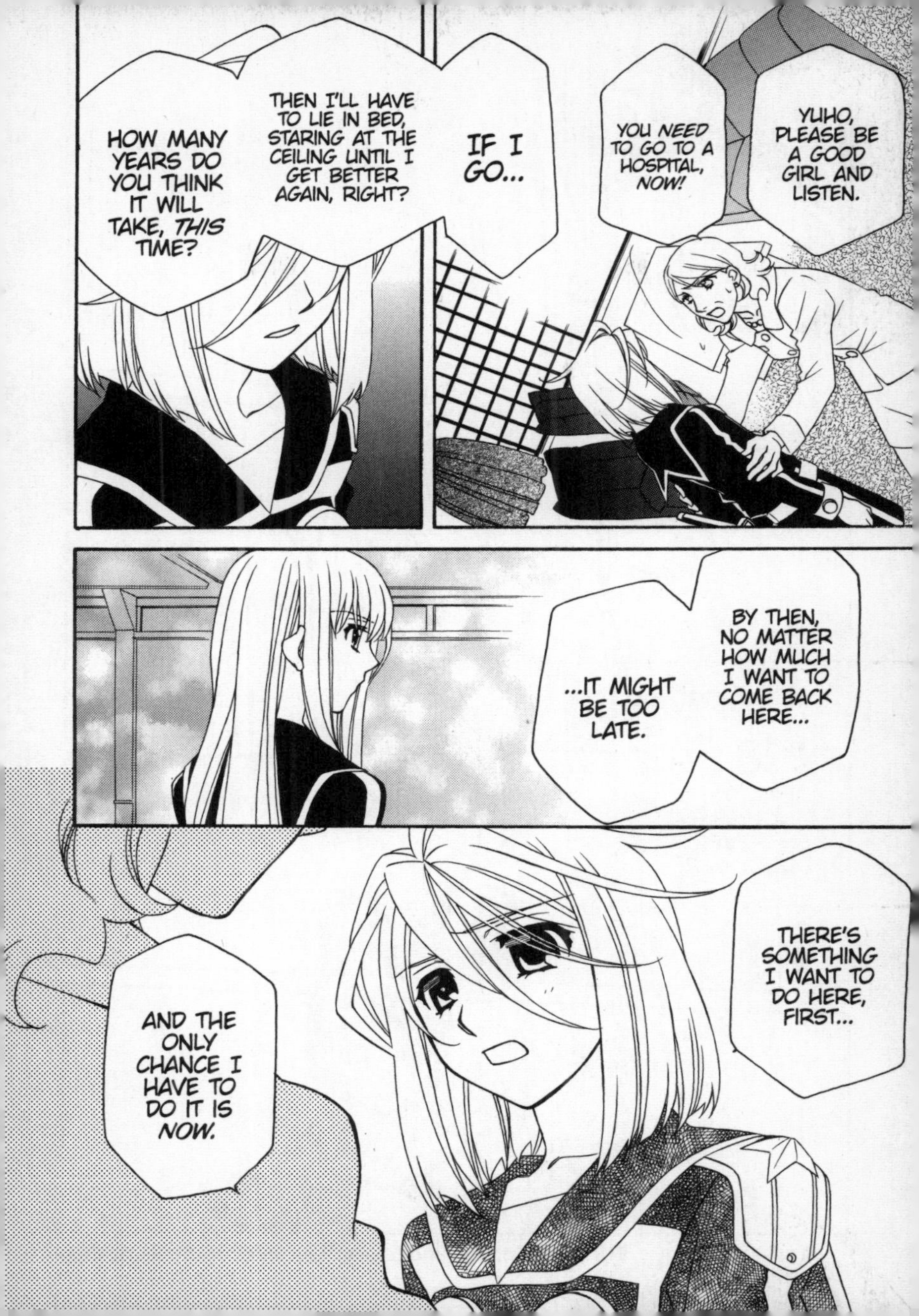
YUHO, PLEASE BE A GOOD GIRL AND LISTEN.
YOU *NEED* TO GO TO A HOSPITAL, *NOW!*
IF I GO...
THEN I'LL HAVE TO LIE IN BED, STARING AT THE CEILING UNTIL I GET BETTER AGAIN, RIGHT?
HOW MANY YEARS DO YOU THINK IT WILL TAKE, *THIS* TIME?
BY THEN, NO MATTER HOW MUCH I WANT TO COME BACK HERE...
...IT MIGHT BE TOO LATE.
THERE'S SOMETHING I WANT TO DO HERE, FIRST...
AND THE ONLY CHANCE I HAVE TO DO IT IS *NOW.*

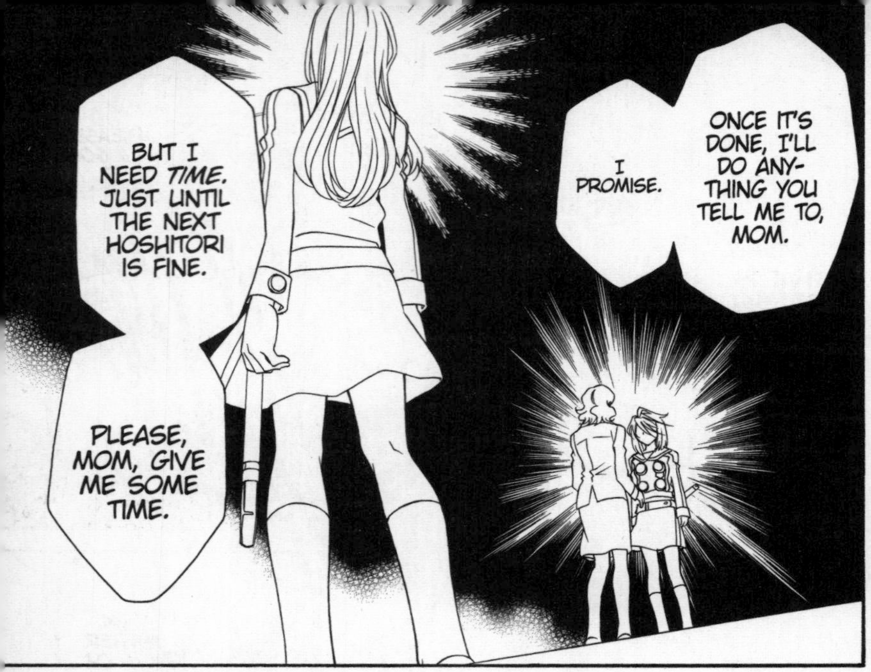
ONCE IT'S DONE, I'LL DO ANY-THING YOU TELL ME TO, MOM.
I PROMISE.
BUT I NEED *TIME.* JUST UNTIL THE NEXT HOSHITORI IS FINE.
PLEASE, MOM, GIVE ME SOME TIME.

#18 Stubbornness and Idiocy: Two Sides of the Same Coin

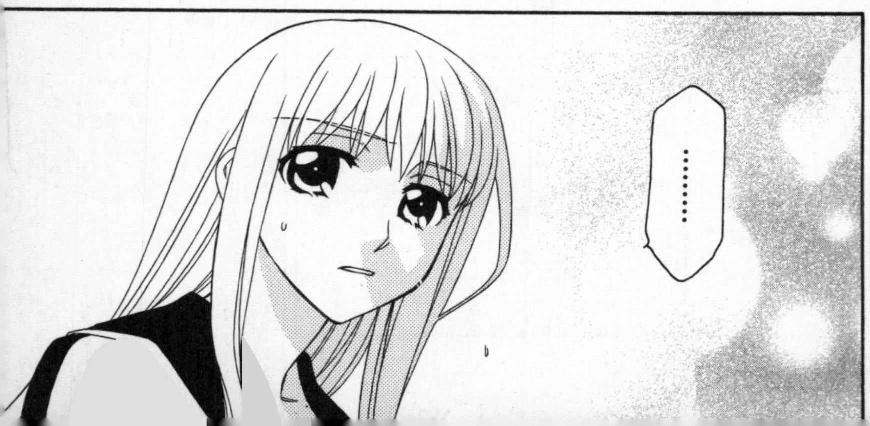
....

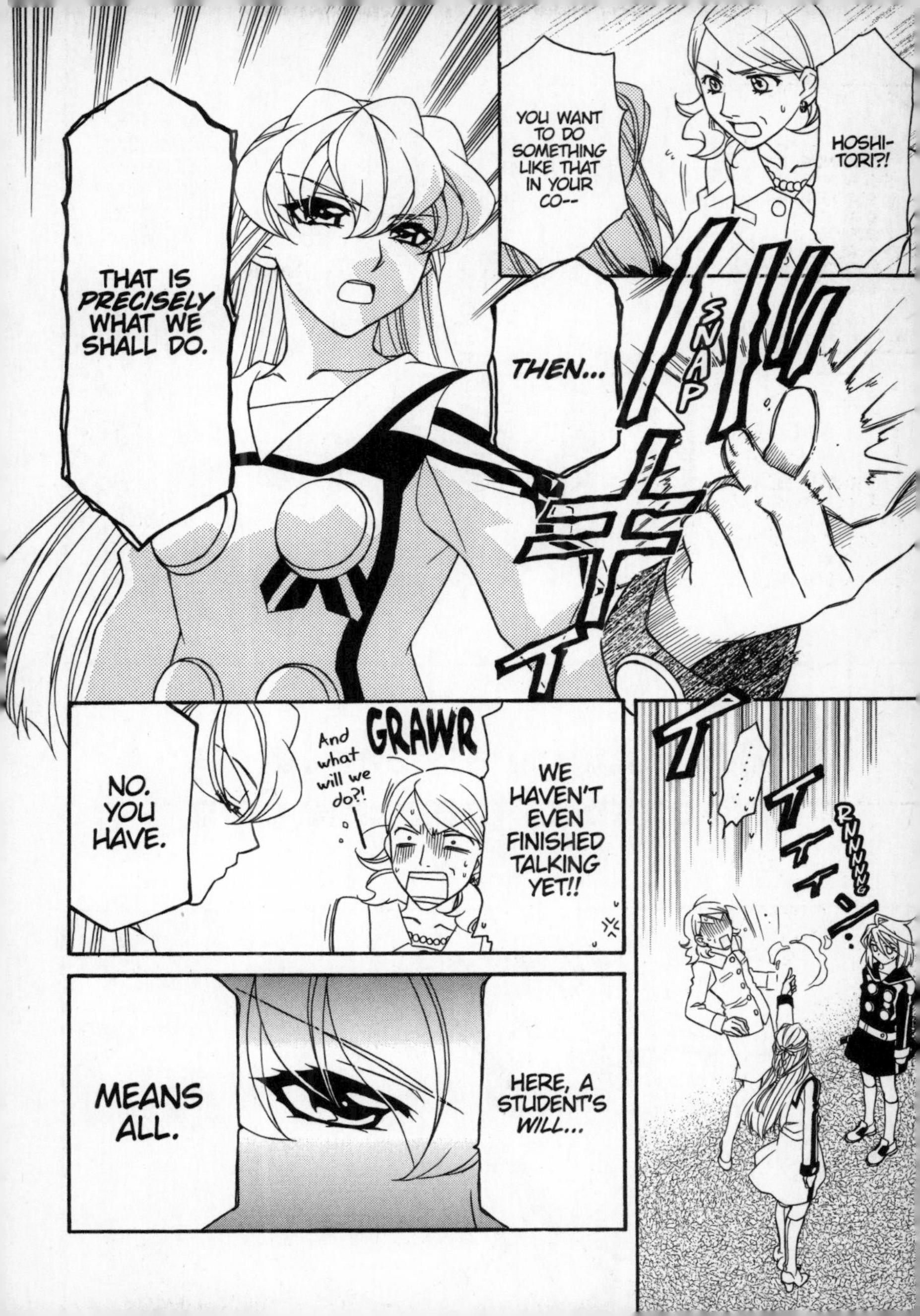
HOSHI-TORI?!
YOU WANT TO DO SOMETHING LIKE THAT IN YOUR CO--
THAT IS *PRECISELY* WHAT WE SHALL DO.
THEN...
SNAP
......
RNNNNG
WE HAVEN'T EVEN FINISHED TALKING YET!!
GRAWR
And what will we do?!
NO. YOU HAVE.
HERE, A STUDENT'S *WILL*...
MEANS ALL.

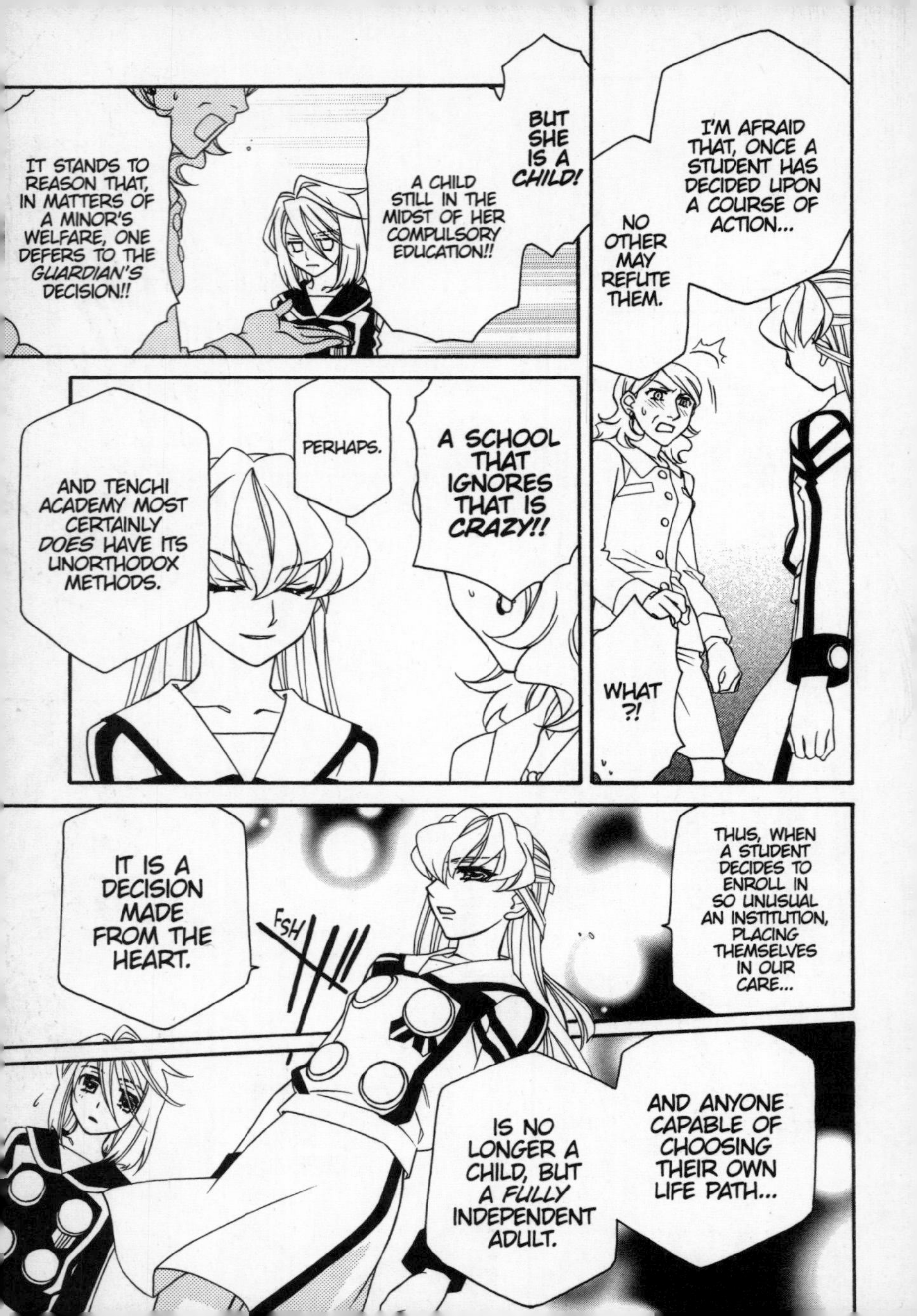

I'M AFRAID THAT, ONCE A STUDENT HAS DECIDED UPON A COURSE OF ACTION...
NO OTHER MAY REFUTE THEM.
WHAT?!
BUT SHE IS A CHILD!
A CHILD STILL IN THE MIDST OF HER COMPULSORY EDUCATION!!
IT STANDS TO REASON THAT, IN MATTERS OF A MINOR'S WELFARE, ONE DEFERS TO THE GUARDIAN'S DECISION!!
A SCHOOL THAT IGNORES THAT IS CRAZY!!
PERHAPS.
AND TENCHI ACADEMY MOST CERTAINLY DOES HAVE ITS UNORTHODOX METHODS.
THUS, WHEN A STUDENT DECIDES TO ENROLL IN SO UNUSUAL AN INSTITUTION, PLACING THEMSELVES IN OUR CARE...
IT IS A DECISION MADE FROM THE HEART.
FSH
AND ANYONE CAPABLE OF CHOOSING THEIR OWN LIFE PATH...
IS NO LONGER A CHILD, BUT A FULLY INDEPENDENT ADULT.

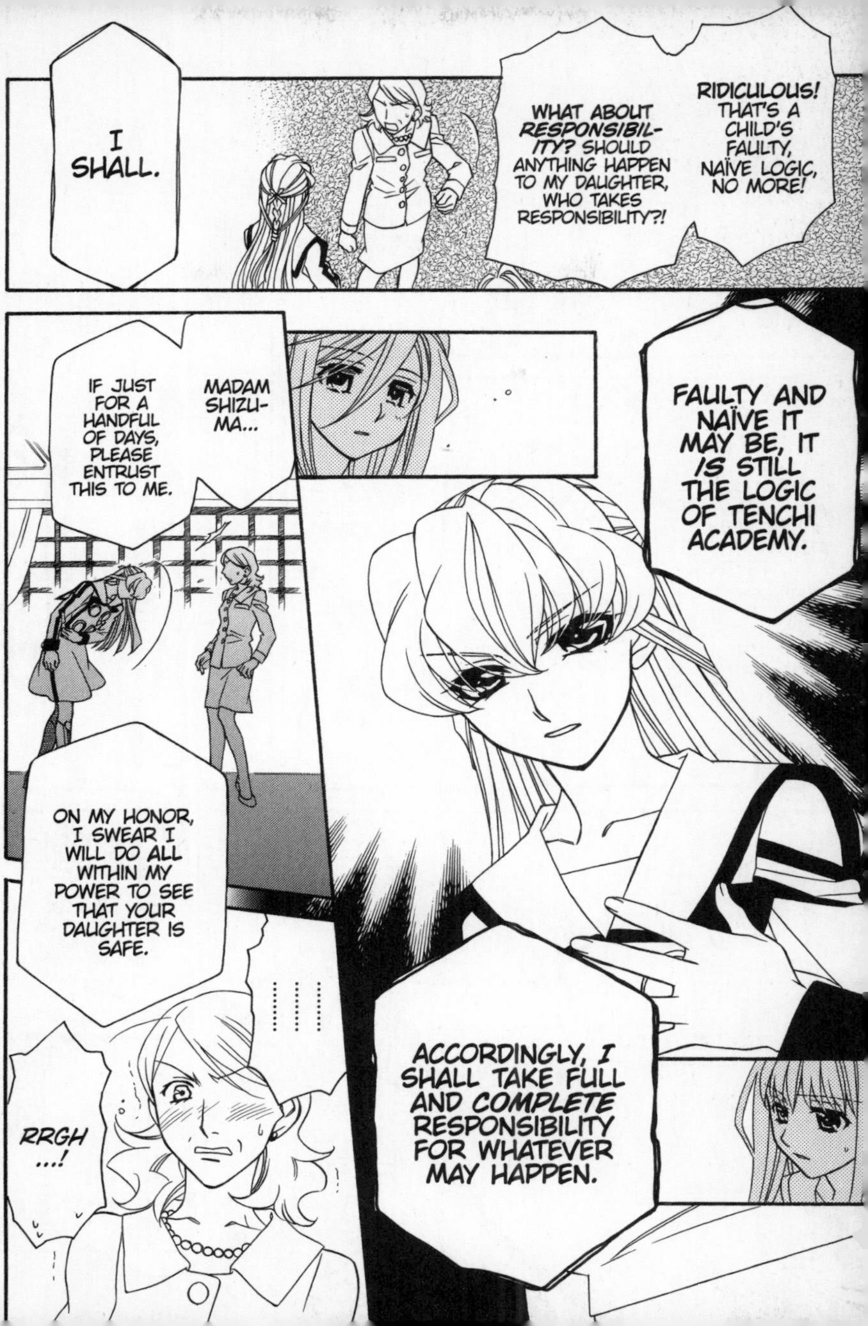
RIDICULOUS! THAT'S A CHILD'S FAULTY, NAÏVE LOGIC, NO MORE!
WHAT ABOUT *RESPONSIBILITY?* SHOULD ANYTHING HAPPEN TO MY DAUGHTER, WHO TAKES RESPONSIBILITY?!
I SHALL.
FAULTY AND NAÏVE IT MAY BE, IT *IS* STILL THE LOGIC OF TENCHI ACADEMY.
MADAM SHIZUMA...
IF JUST FOR A HANDFUL OF DAYS, PLEASE ENTRUST THIS TO ME.
ON MY HONOR, I SWEAR I WILL DO ALL WITHIN MY POWER TO SEE THAT YOUR DAUGHTER IS SAFE.
ACCORDINGLY, *I* SHALL TAKE FULL AND *COMPLETE* RESPONSIBILITY FOR WHATEVER MAY HAPPEN.
......
RRGH ...!

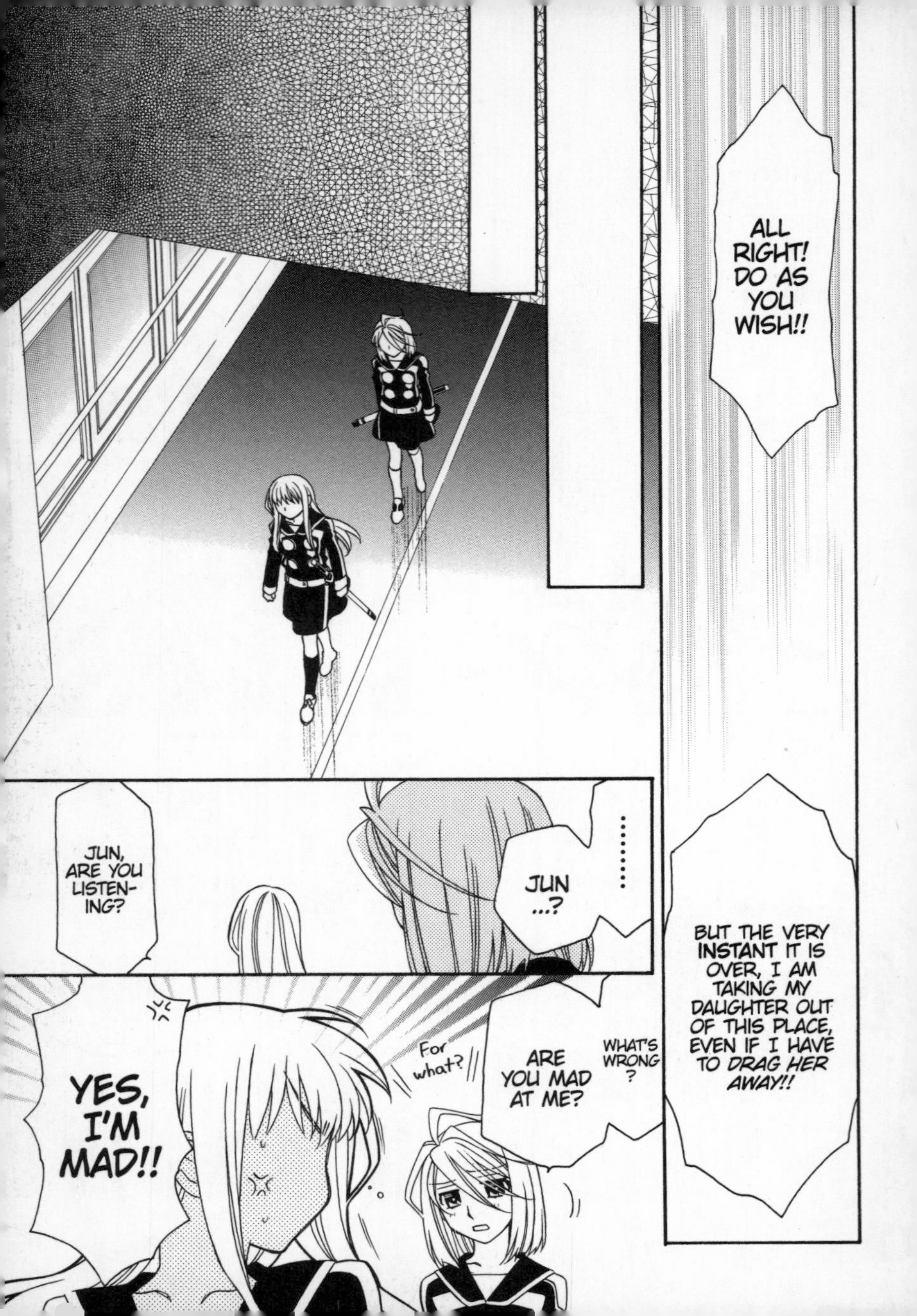
ALL RIGHT! DO AS YOU WISH!!
BUT THE VERY INSTANT IT IS OVER, I AM TAKING MY DAUGHTER OUT OF THIS PLACE, EVEN IF I HAVE TO *DRAG HER AWAY*!!
......
JUN ...?
JUN, ARE YOU LISTEN-ING?
WHAT'S WRONG?
ARE YOU MAD AT ME?
For what?
YES, I'M MAD!!

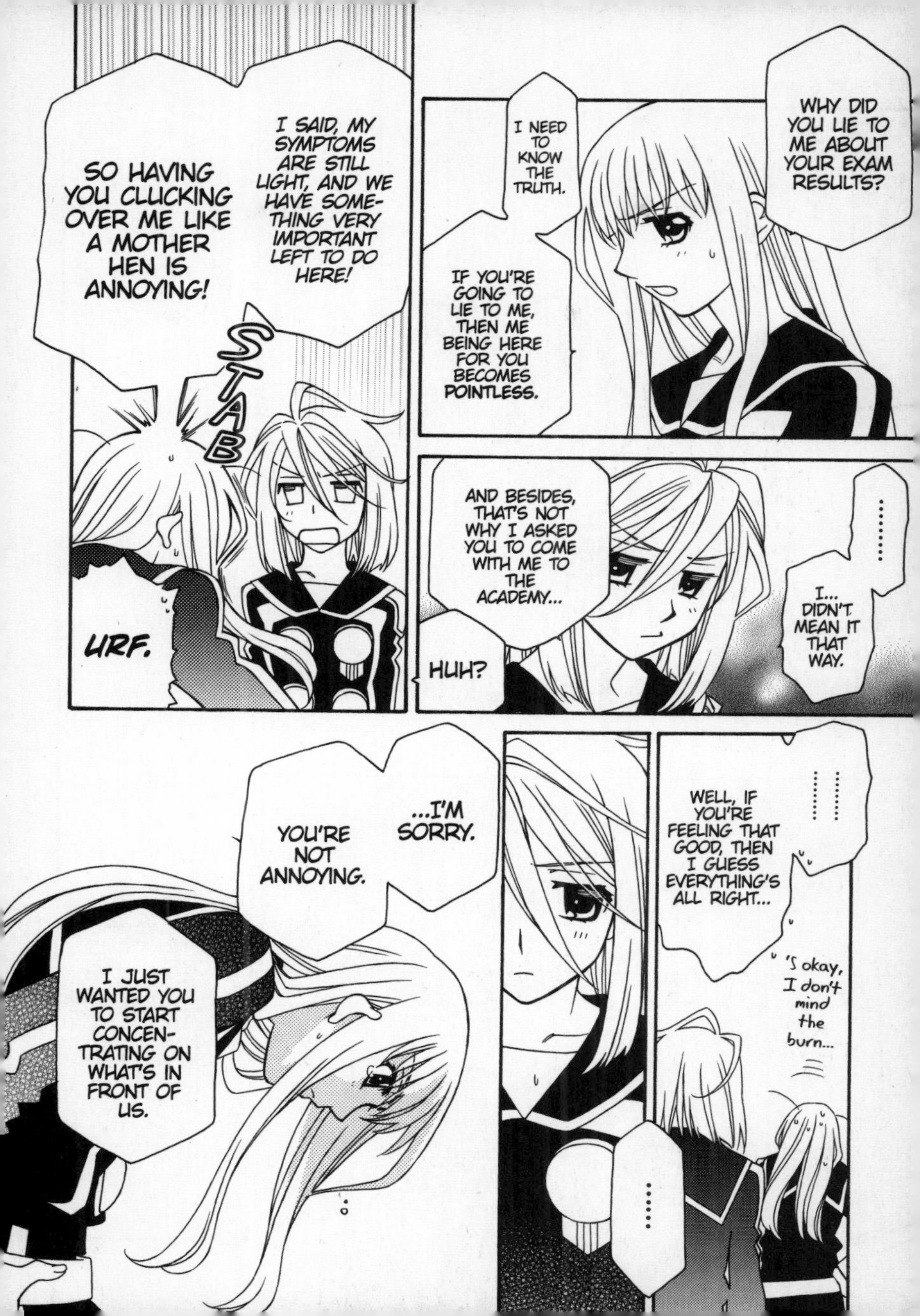
WHY DID YOU LIE TO ME ABOUT YOUR EXAM RESULTS?
I NEED TO KNOW THE TRUTH.
IF YOU'RE GOING TO LIE TO ME, THEN ME BEING HERE FOR YOU BECOMES POINTLESS.
......
I... DIDN'T MEAN IT THAT WAY.
AND BESIDES, THAT'S NOT WHY I ASKED YOU TO COME WITH ME TO THE ACADEMY...
HUH?
I SAID, MY SYMPTOMS ARE STILL LIGHT, AND WE HAVE SOME-THING VERY IMPORTANT LEFT TO DO HERE!
SO HAVING YOU CLUCKING OVER ME LIKE A MOTHER HEN IS ANNOYING!
STAB
URF.
......
WELL, IF YOU'RE FEELING THAT GOOD, THEN I GUESS EVERYTHING'S ALL RIGHT...
'S okay, I don't mind the burn...
......
...I'M SORRY.
YOU'RE NOT ANNOYING.
I JUST WANTED YOU TO START CONCEN-TRATING ON WHAT'S IN FRONT OF US.

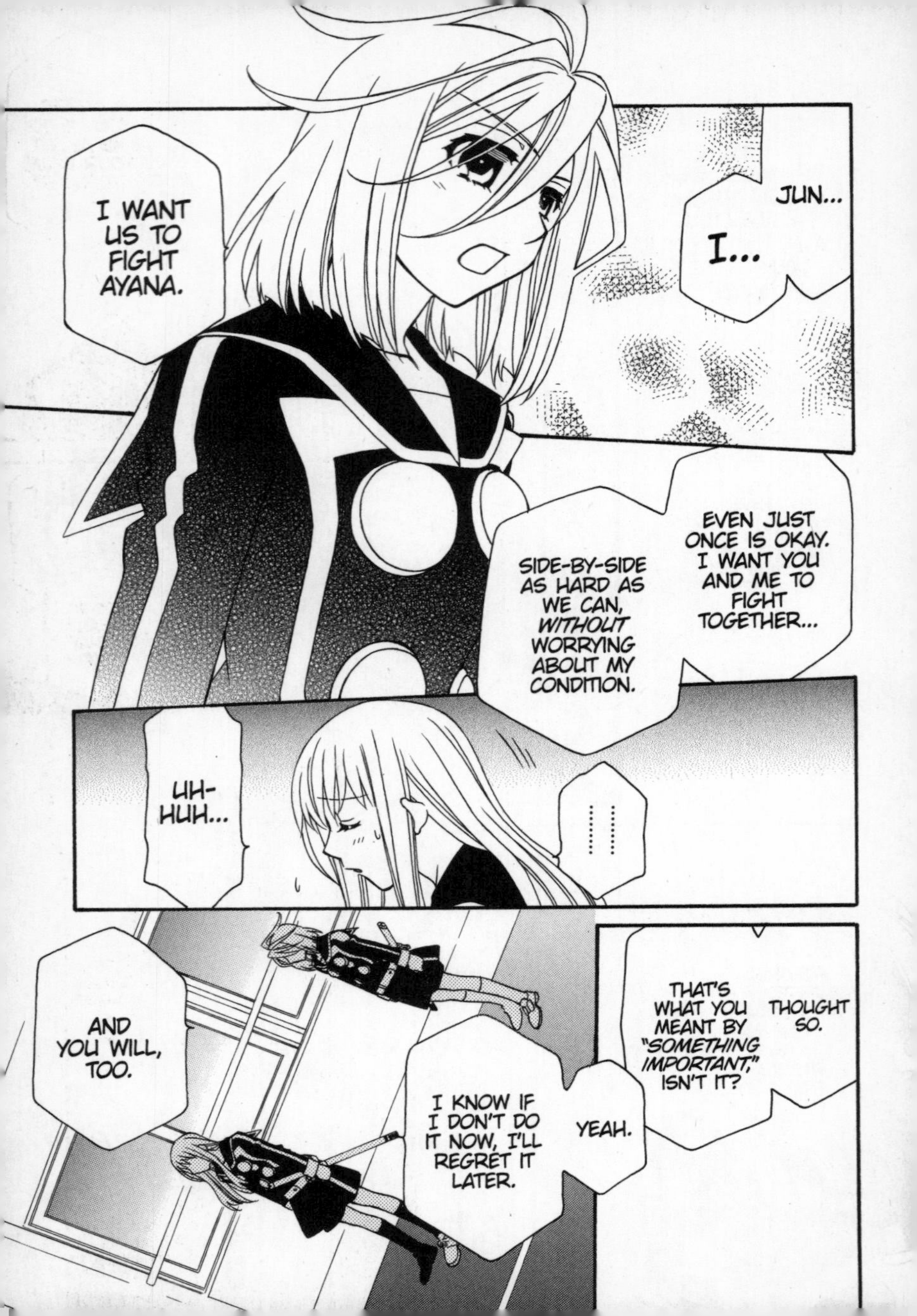
JUN... I...
I WANT US TO FIGHT AYANA.
EVEN JUST ONCE IS OKAY. I WANT YOU AND ME TO FIGHT TOGETHER...
SIDE-BY-SIDE AS HARD AS WE CAN, *WITHOUT* WORRYING ABOUT MY CONDITION.
......
UH-HUH...
THOUGHT SO.
THAT'S WHAT YOU MEANT BY "*SOMETHING IMPORTANT,*" ISN'T IT?
YEAH.
I KNOW IF I DON'T DO IT NOW, I'LL REGRET IT LATER.
AND YOU WILL, TOO.

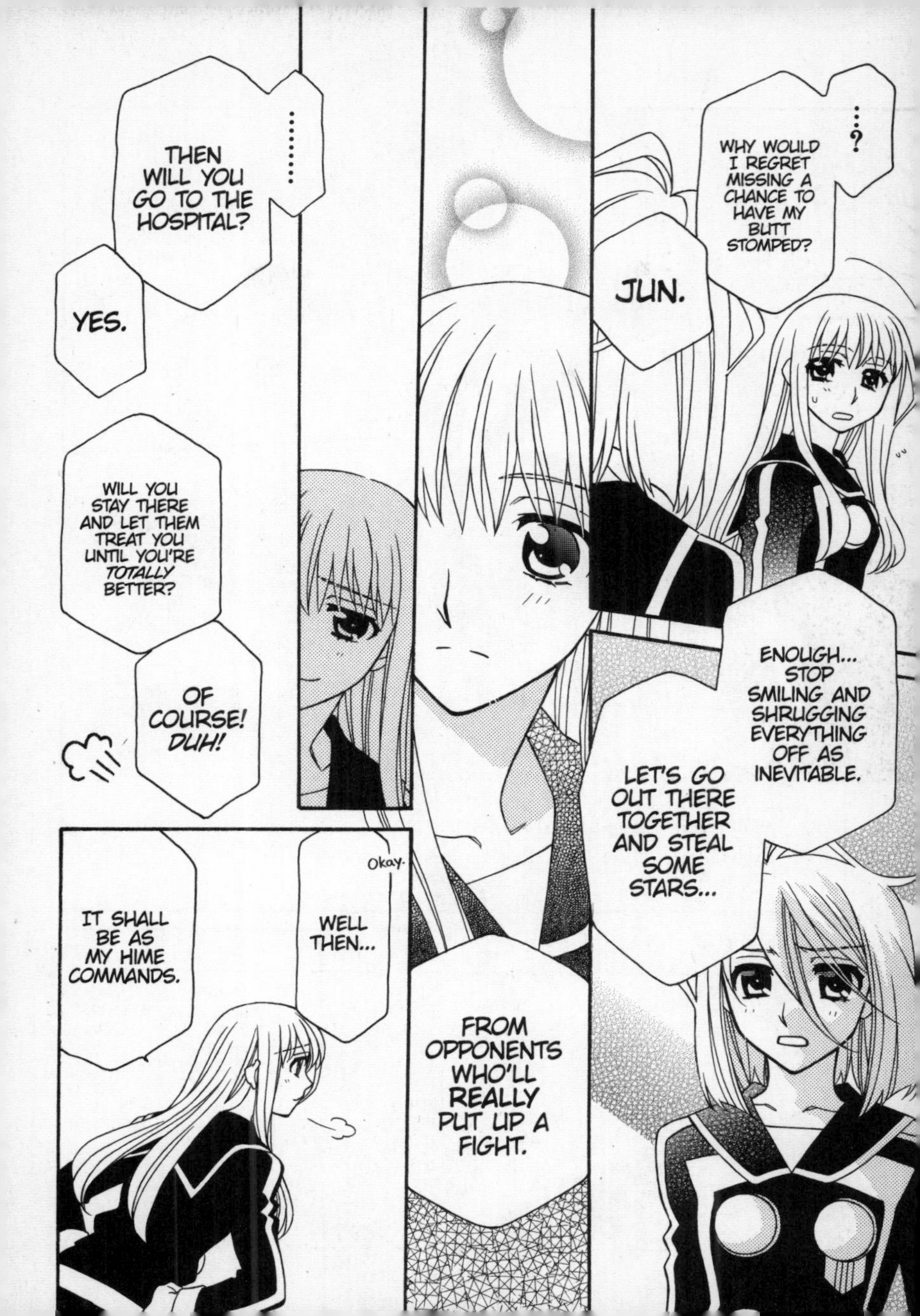
…?
WHY WOULD I REGRET MISSING A CHANCE TO HAVE MY BUTT STOMPED?
JUN.
ENOUGH... STOP SMILING AND SHRUGGING EVERYTHING OFF AS INEVITABLE.
LET'S GO OUT THERE TOGETHER AND STEAL SOME STARS...
FROM OPPONENTS WHO'LL REALLY PUT UP A FIGHT.
………
THEN WILL YOU GO TO THE HOSPITAL?
YES.
WILL YOU STAY THERE AND LET THEM TREAT YOU UNTIL YOU'RE *TOTALLY* BETTER?
OF COURSE! DUH!
Okay.
WELL THEN...
IT SHALL BE AS MY HIME COMMANDS.

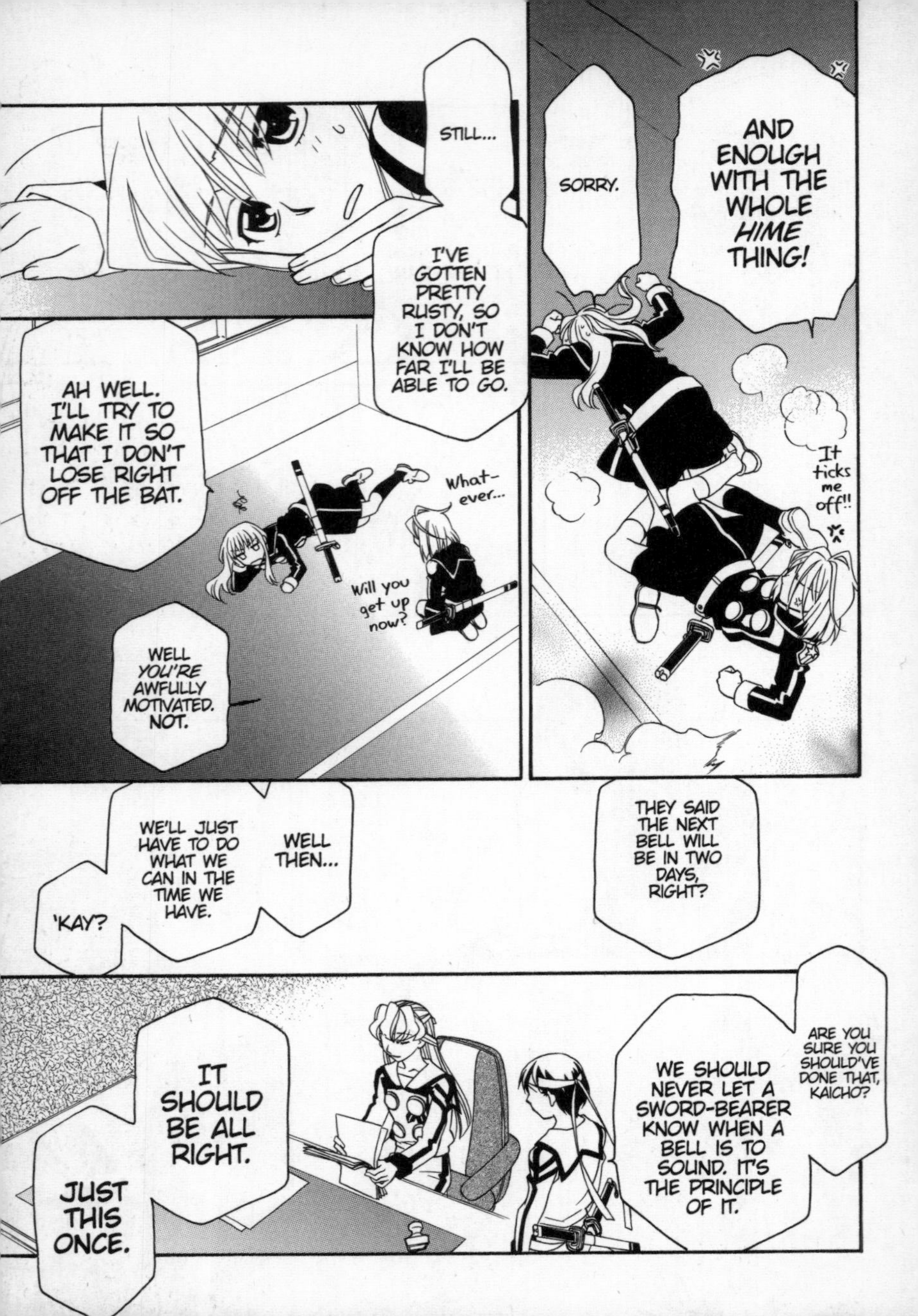
AND ENOUGH WITH THE WHOLE *HIME* THING!
SORRY.
It ticks me off!!
STILL...
I'VE GOTTEN PRETTY RUSTY, SO I DON'T KNOW HOW FAR I'LL BE ABLE TO GO.
AH WELL. I'LL TRY TO MAKE IT SO THAT I DON'T LOSE RIGHT OFF THE BAT.
What-ever...
Will you get up now?
WELL *YOU'RE* AWFULLY MOTIVATED. NOT.
THEY SAID THE NEXT BELL WILL BE IN TWO DAYS, RIGHT?
WELL THEN...
WE'LL JUST HAVE TO DO WHAT WE CAN IN THE TIME WE HAVE.
'KAY?
ARE YOU SURE YOU SHOULD'VE DONE THAT, KAICHO?
WE SHOULD NEVER LET A SWORD-BEARER KNOW WHEN A BELL IS TO SOUND. IT'S THE PRINCIPLE OF IT.
IT SHOULD BE ALL RIGHT.
JUST THIS ONCE.

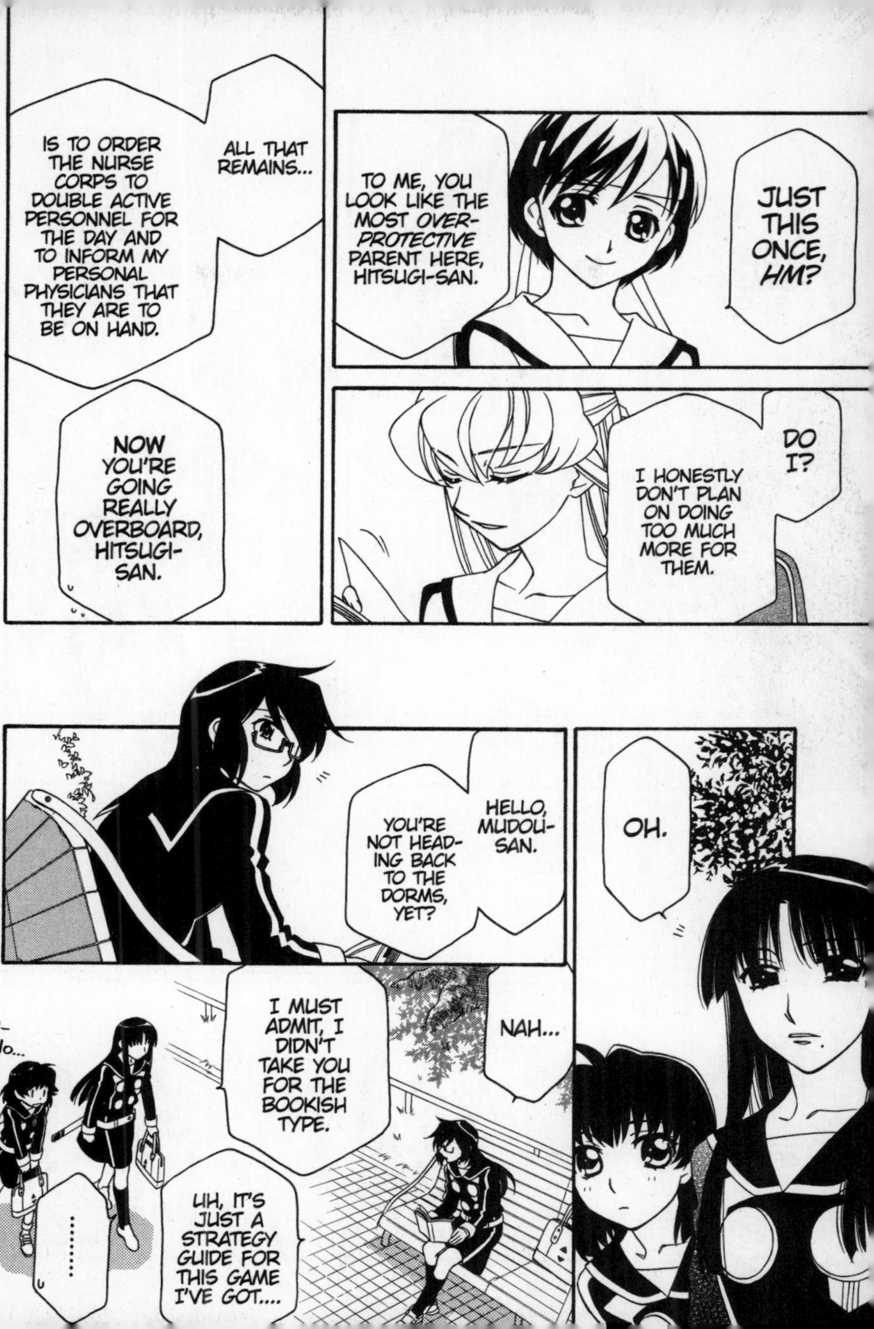
JUST THIS ONCE, *HM?*
TO ME, YOU LOOK LIKE THE MOST *OVER-PROTECTIVE* PARENT HERE, HITSUGI-SAN.
DO I?
I HONESTLY DON'T PLAN ON DOING TOO MUCH MORE FOR THEM.
ALL THAT REMAINS...
IS TO ORDER THE NURSE CORPS TO DOUBLE ACTIVE PERSONNEL FOR THE DAY AND TO INFORM MY PERSONAL PHYSICIANS THAT THEY ARE TO BE ON HAND.
NOW YOU'RE GOING REALLY OVERBOARD, HITSUGI-SAN.
OH.
HELLO, MUDOU-SAN.
YOU'RE NOT HEADING BACK TO THE DORMS, YET?
NAH...
I MUST ADMIT, I DIDN'T TAKE YOU FOR THE BOOKISH TYPE.
UH, IT'S JUST A STRATEGY GUIDE FOR THIS GAME I'VE GOT....
H-hello...
......

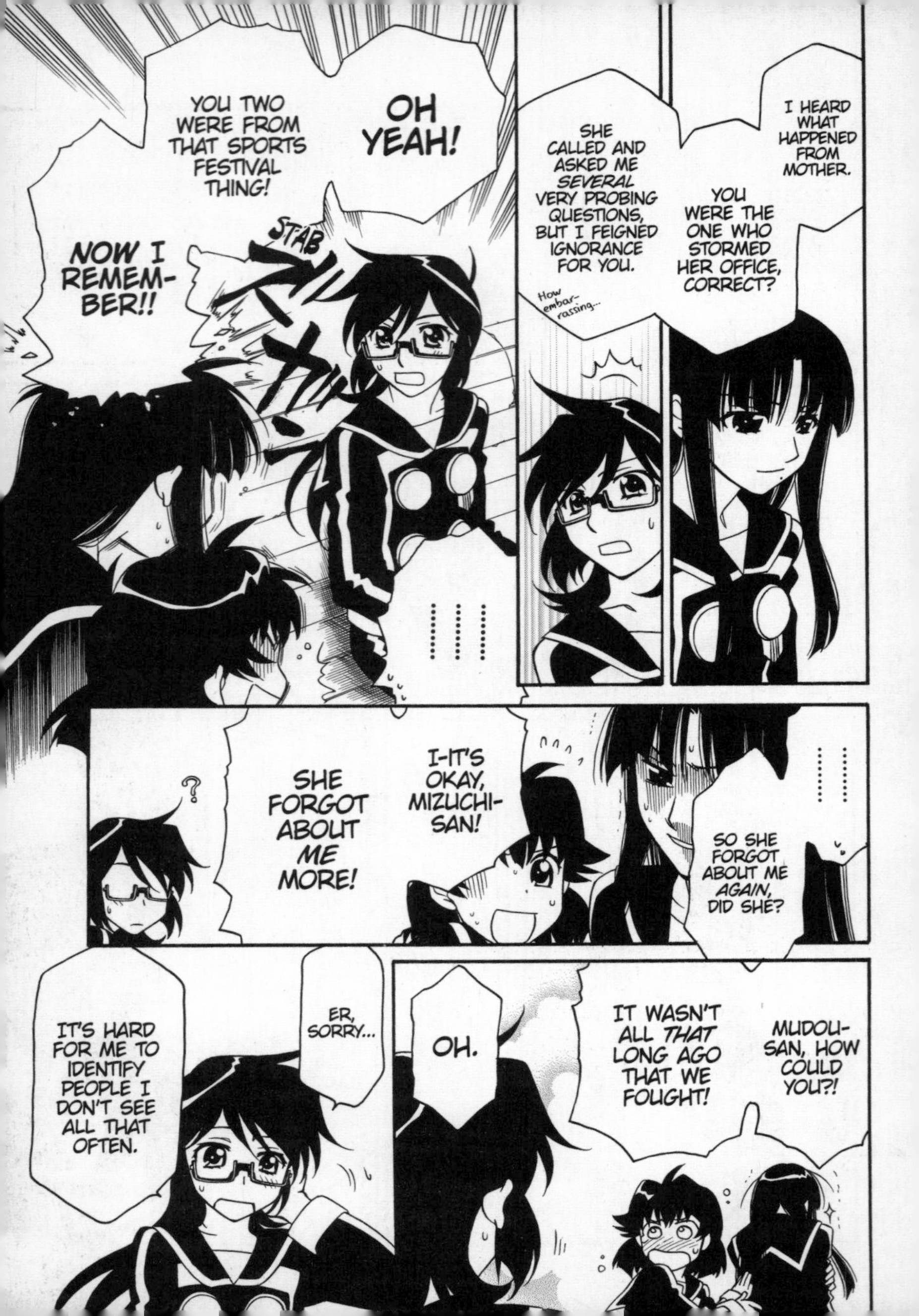
I HEARD WHAT HAPPENED FROM MOTHER.
YOU WERE THE ONE WHO STORMED HER OFFICE, CORRECT?
SHE CALLED AND ASKED ME *SEVERAL* VERY PROBING QUESTIONS, BUT I FEIGNED IGNORANCE FOR YOU.
How embarrassing...
OH YEAH!
YOU TWO WERE FROM THAT SPORTS FESTIVAL THING!
STAB
NOW I REMEMBER!!
......
......
SO SHE FORGOT ABOUT ME *AGAIN*, DID SHE?
I-IT'S OKAY, MIZUCHI-SAN!
SHE FORGOT ABOUT *ME* MORE!
?
MUDOU-SAN, HOW COULD YOU?!
IT WASN'T ALL *THAT* LONG AGO THAT WE FOUGHT!
OH.
ER, SORRY...
IT'S HARD FOR ME TO IDENTIFY PEOPLE I DON'T SEE ALL THAT OFTEN.

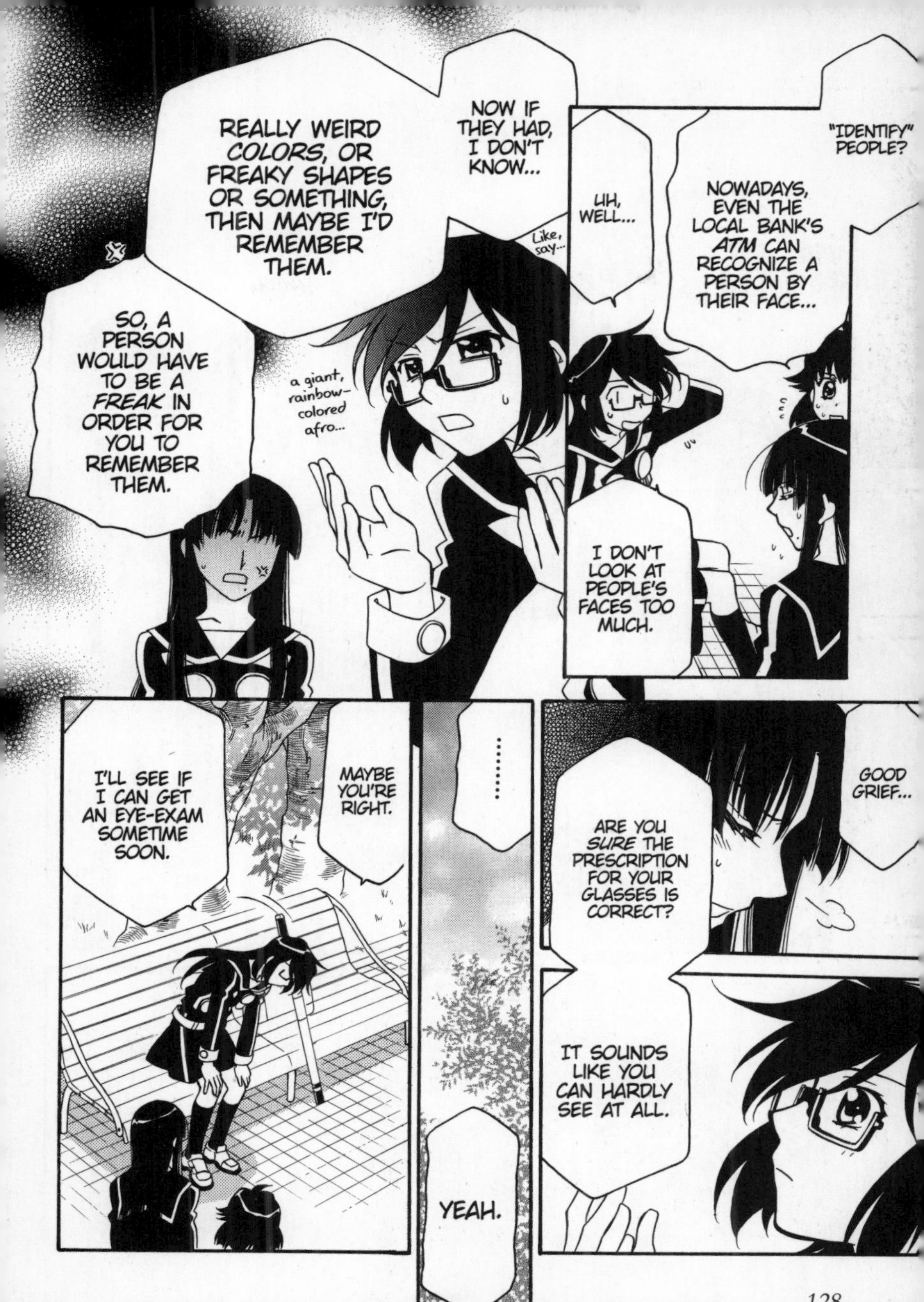

"IDENTIFY" PEOPLE?
NOWADAYS, EVEN THE LOCAL BANK'S *ATM* CAN RECOGNIZE A PERSON BY THEIR FACE...
UH, WELL...
I DON'T LOOK AT PEOPLE'S FACES TOO MUCH.
NOW IF THEY HAD, I DON'T KNOW...
REALLY WEIRD *COLORS*, OR FREAKY SHAPES OR SOMETHING, THEN MAYBE I'D REMEMBER THEM.
Like, say...
a giant, rainbow-colored afro...
SO, A PERSON WOULD HAVE TO BE A *FREAK* IN ORDER FOR YOU TO REMEMBER THEM.
GOOD GRIEF...
ARE YOU *SURE* THE PRESCRIPTION FOR YOUR GLASSES IS CORRECT?
IT SOUNDS LIKE YOU CAN HARDLY SEE AT ALL.
......
YEAH.
MAYBE YOU'RE RIGHT.
I'LL SEE IF I CAN GET AN EYE-EXAM SOMETIME SOON.

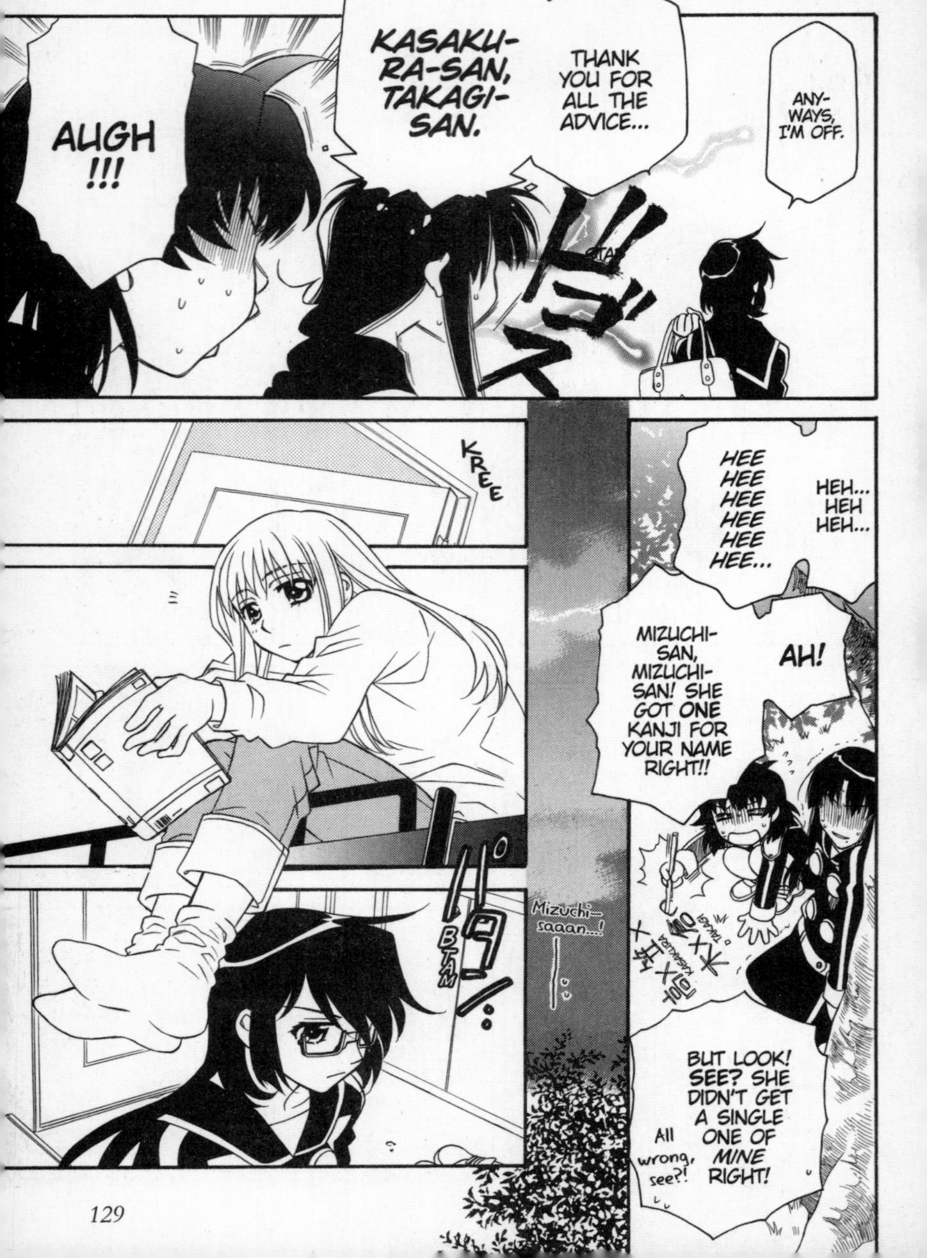
ANY-WAYS, I'M OFF.
KASAKU-RA-SAN, TAKAGI-SAN.
THANK YOU FOR ALL THE ADVICE...
AUGH !!!
HEE HEE HEE HEE HEE HEE...
HEH... HEH HEH...
AH!
MIZUCHI-SAN, MIZUCHI-SAN! SHE GOT ONE KANJI FOR YOUR NAME RIGHT!!
BUT LOOK! SEE? SHE DIDN'T GET A SINGLE ONE OF MINE RIGHT!
All wrong, see?!
Mizuchi-saaan...!
KREEE
BTAM

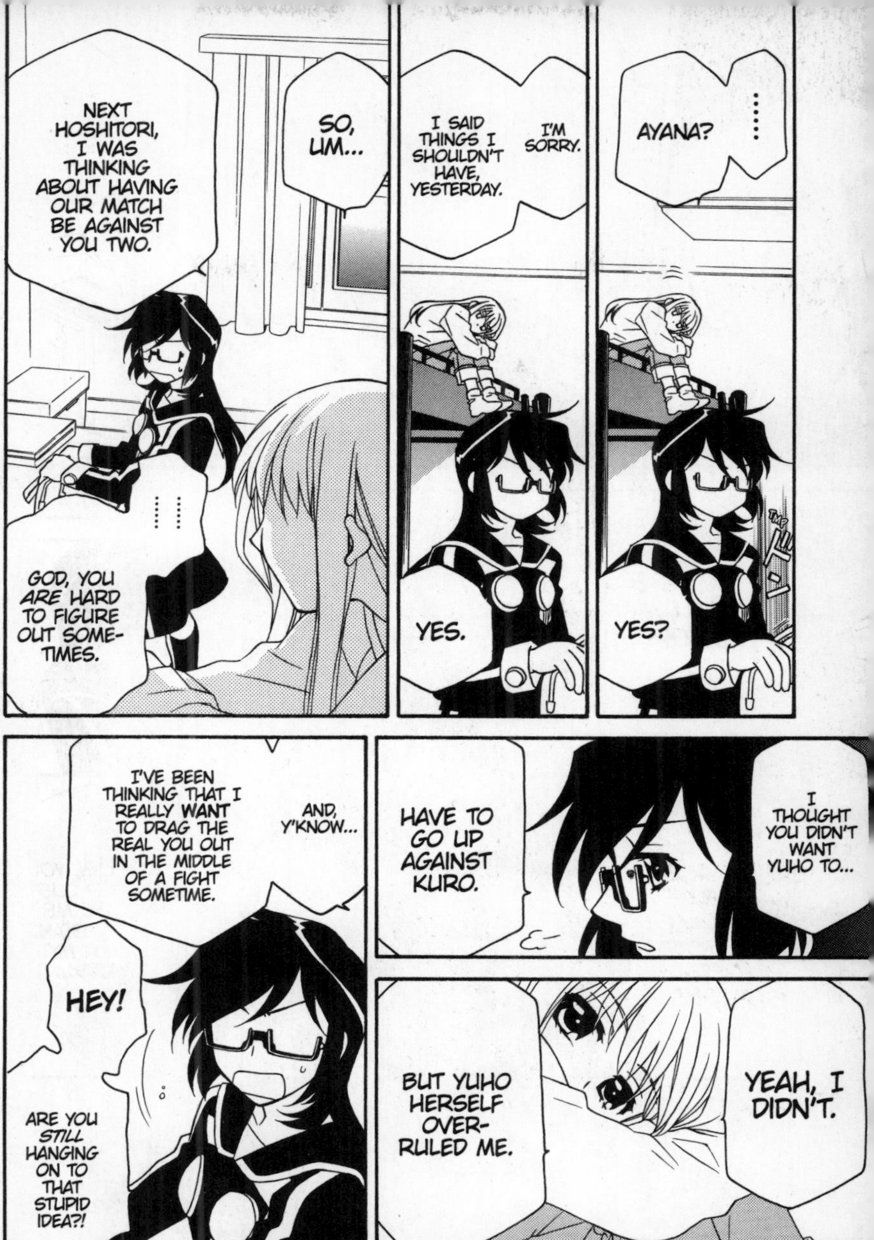
......
AYANA?
TMP
YES?
I'M SORRY.
I SAID THINGS I SHOULDN'T HAVE, YESTERDAY.
YES.
SO, UM...
NEXT HOSHITORI, I WAS THINKING ABOUT HAVING OUR MATCH BE AGAINST YOU TWO.
......
GOD, YOU *ARE* HARD TO FIGURE OUT SOME-TIMES.
I THOUGHT YOU DIDN'T WANT YUHO TO...
HAVE TO GO UP AGAINST KURO.
YEAH, I DIDN'T.
BUT YUHO HERSELF OVER-RULED ME.
AND, Y'KNOW...
I'VE BEEN THINKING THAT I REALLY WANT TO DRAG THE REAL YOU OUT IN THE MIDDLE OF A FIGHT SOMETIME.
HEY!
ARE YOU *STILL* HANGING ON TO THAT STUPID IDEA?!

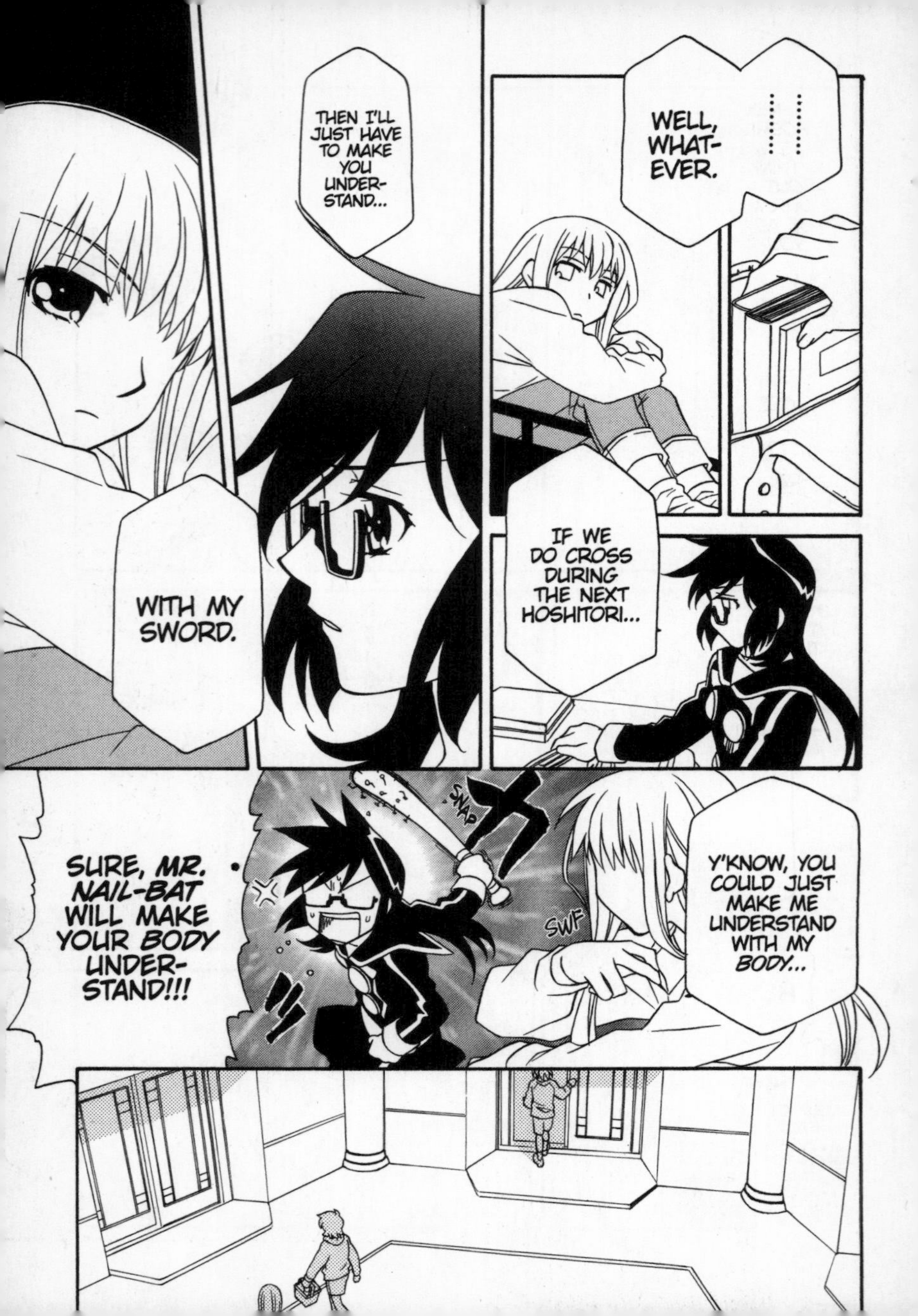

......
WELL, WHAT-EVER.
IF WE DO CROSS DURING THE NEXT HOSHITORI...
THEN I'LL JUST HAVE TO MAKE YOU UNDER-STAND...
WITH MY SWORD.
Y'KNOW, YOU COULD JUST MAKE ME UNDERSTAND WITH MY *BODY*...
SNAP
SWF
SURE, MR. *NAIL-BAT* WILL MAKE YOUR *BODY* UNDER-STAND!!!

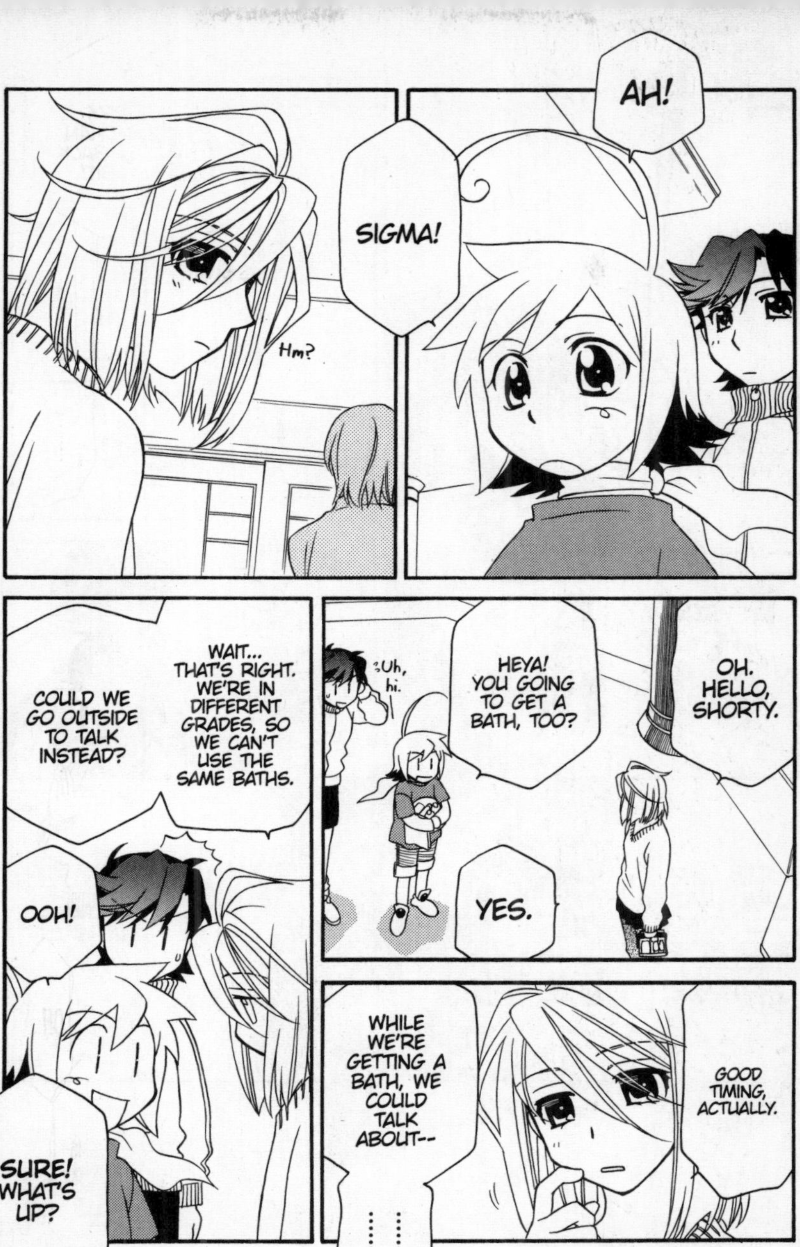
AH!
SIGMA!
Hm?
OH. HELLO, SHORTY.
HEYA! YOU GOING TO GET A BATH, TOO?
Uh, hi.
YES.
GOOD TIMING, ACTUALLY.
WHILE WE'RE GETTING A BATH, WE COULD TALK ABOUT--
......
WAIT... THAT'S RIGHT. WE'RE IN DIFFERENT GRADES, SO WE CAN'T USE THE SAME BATHS.
COULD WE GO OUTSIDE TO TALK INSTEAD?
OOH!
SURE! WHAT'S UP?

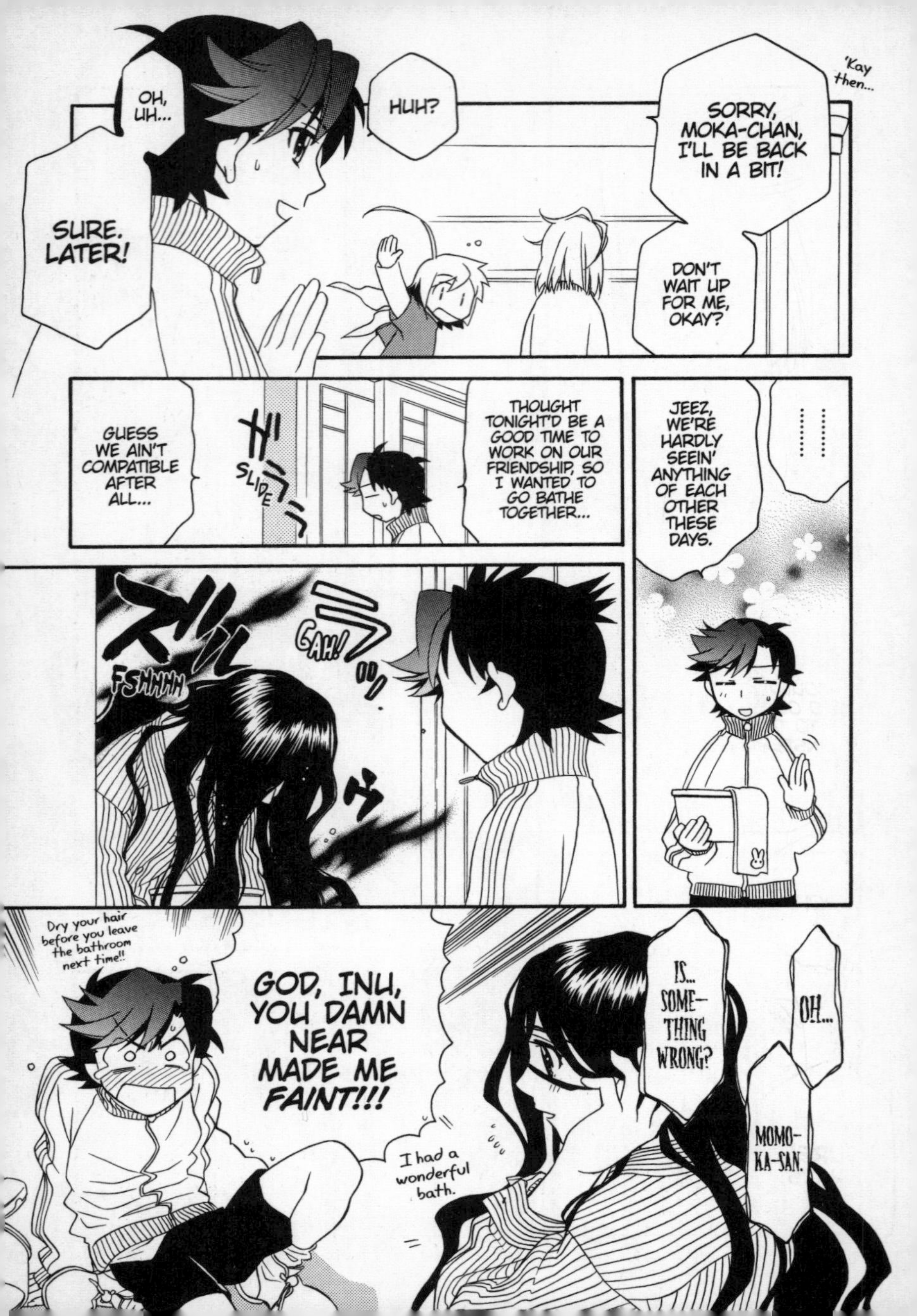
'Kay then...
SORRY, MOKA-CHAN, I'LL BE BACK IN A BIT!
DON'T WAIT UP FOR ME, OKAY?
HUH?
OH, UH...
SURE. LATER!
......
JEEZ, WE'RE HARDLY SEEIN' ANYTHING OF EACH OTHER THESE DAYS.
THOUGHT TONIGHT'D BE A GOOD TIME TO WORK ON OUR FRIENDSHIP, SO I WANTED TO GO BATHE TOGETHER...
SLIDE
GUESS WE AIN'T COMPATIBLE AFTER ALL...
GAH!
FSHHHH
OH...
MOMO-KA-SAN.
IS... SOME-THING WRONG?
I had a wonderful bath.
GOD, INU, YOU DAMN NEAR MADE ME FAINT!!!
Dry your hair before you leave the bathroom next time!!

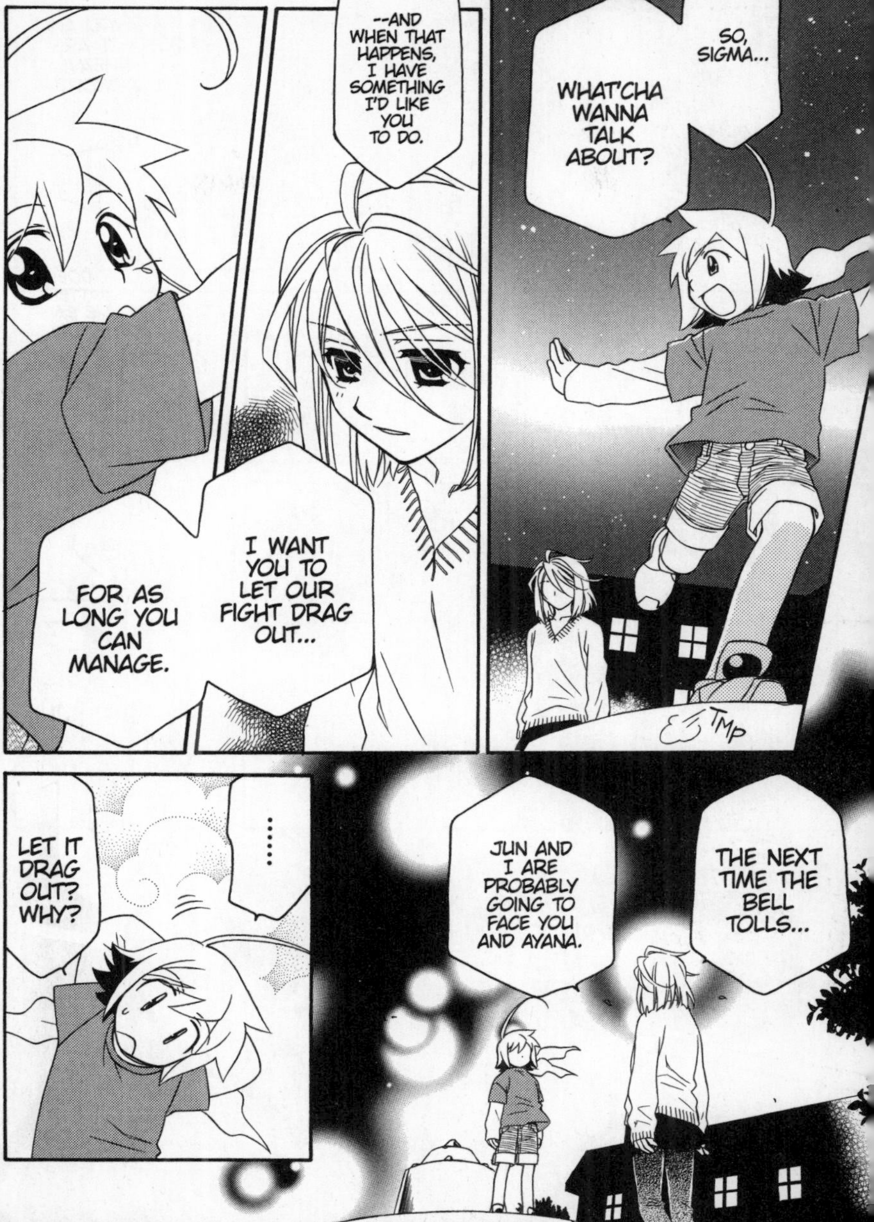
SO, SIGMA...
WHAT'CHA WANNA TALK ABOUT?
TMP
--AND WHEN THAT HAPPENS, I HAVE SOMETHING I'D LIKE YOU TO DO.
I WANT YOU TO LET OUR FIGHT DRAG OUT...
FOR AS LONG YOU CAN MANAGE.
THE NEXT TIME THE BELL TOLLS...
JUN AND I ARE PROBABLY GOING TO FACE YOU AND AYANA.
......
LET IT DRAG OUT? WHY?

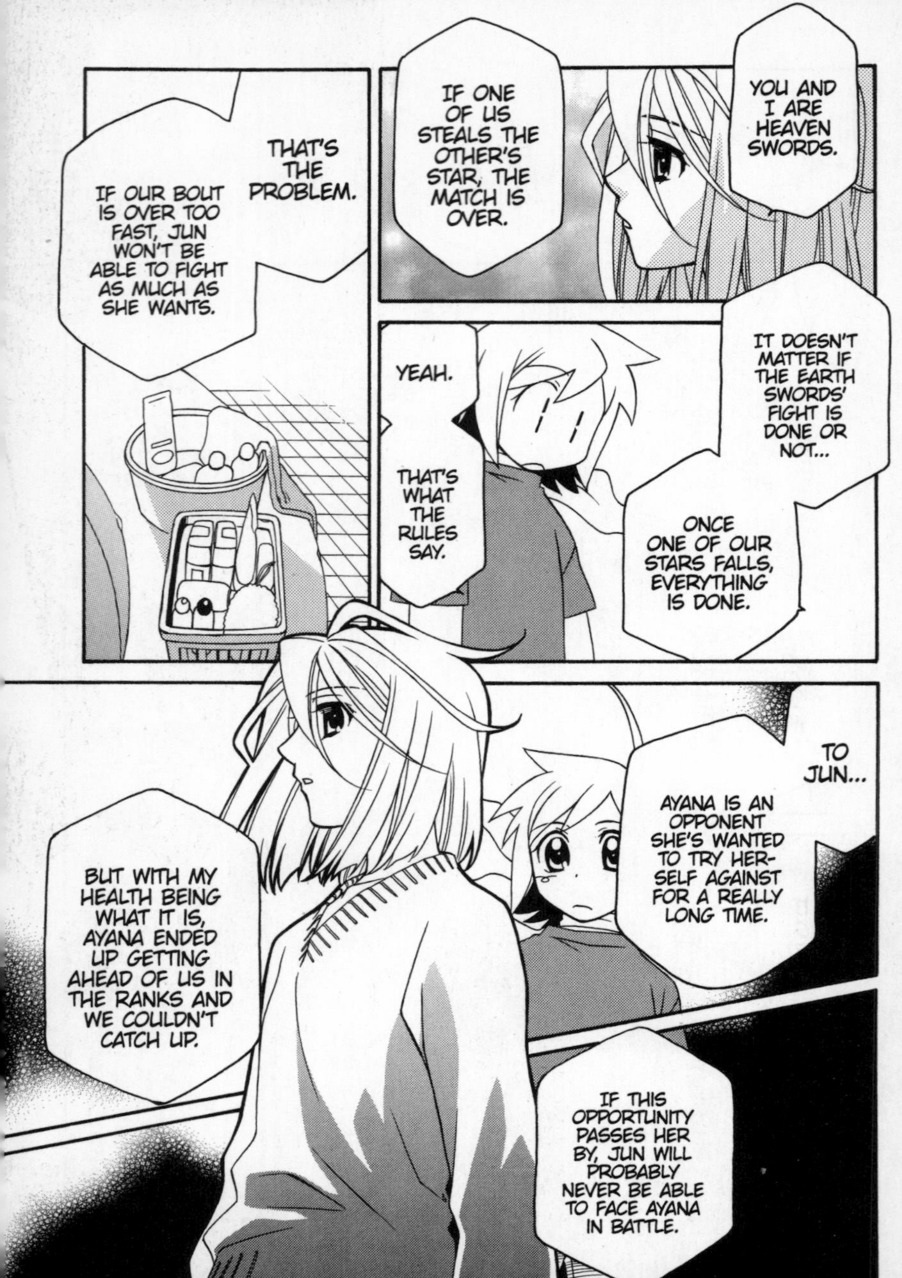
YOU AND I ARE HEAVEN SWORDS.
IF ONE OF US STEALS THE OTHER'S STAR, THE MATCH IS OVER.
IT DOESN'T MATTER IF THE EARTH SWORDS' FIGHT IS DONE OR NOT...
ONCE ONE OF OUR STARS FALLS, EVERYTHING IS DONE.
YEAH.
THAT'S WHAT THE RULES SAY.
THAT'S THE PROBLEM.
IF OUR BOUT IS OVER TOO FAST, JUN WON'T BE ABLE TO FIGHT AS MUCH AS SHE WANTS.
TO JUN...
AYANA IS AN OPPONENT SHE'S WANTED TO TRY HER-SELF AGAINST FOR A REALLY LONG TIME.
BUT WITH MY HEALTH BEING WHAT IT IS, AYANA ENDED UP GETTING AHEAD OF US IN THE RANKS AND WE COULDN'T CATCH UP.
IF THIS OPPORTUNITY PASSES HER BY, JUN WILL PROBABLY NEVER BE ABLE TO FACE AYANA IN BATTLE.

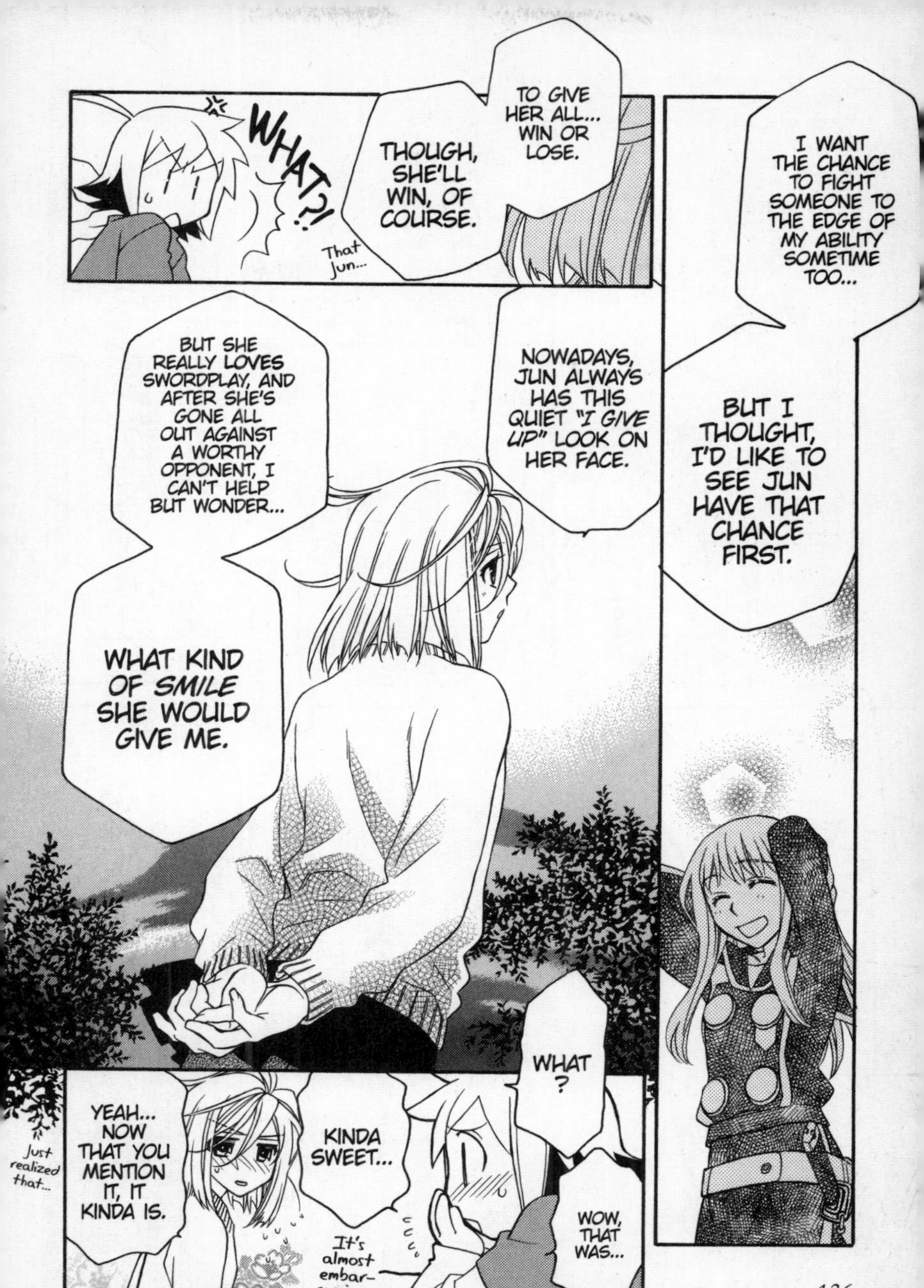
I WANT THE CHANCE TO FIGHT SOMEONE TO THE EDGE OF MY ABILITY SOMETIME TOO...
BUT I THOUGHT, I'D LIKE TO SEE JUN HAVE THAT CHANCE FIRST.
TO GIVE HER ALL... WIN OR LOSE.
THOUGH, SHE'LL WIN, OF COURSE.
WHAT?!
That Jun...
NOWADAYS, JUN ALWAYS HAS THIS QUIET "I GIVE UP" LOOK ON HER FACE.
BUT SHE REALLY LOVES SWORDPLAY, AND AFTER SHE'S GONE ALL OUT AGAINST A WORTHY OPPONENT, I CAN'T HELP BUT WONDER...
WHAT KIND OF SMILE SHE WOULD GIVE ME.
WHAT?
WOW, THAT WAS...
KINDA SWEET...
It's almost embarrassing...
YEAH... NOW THAT YOU MENTION IT, IT KINDA IS.
Just realized that...

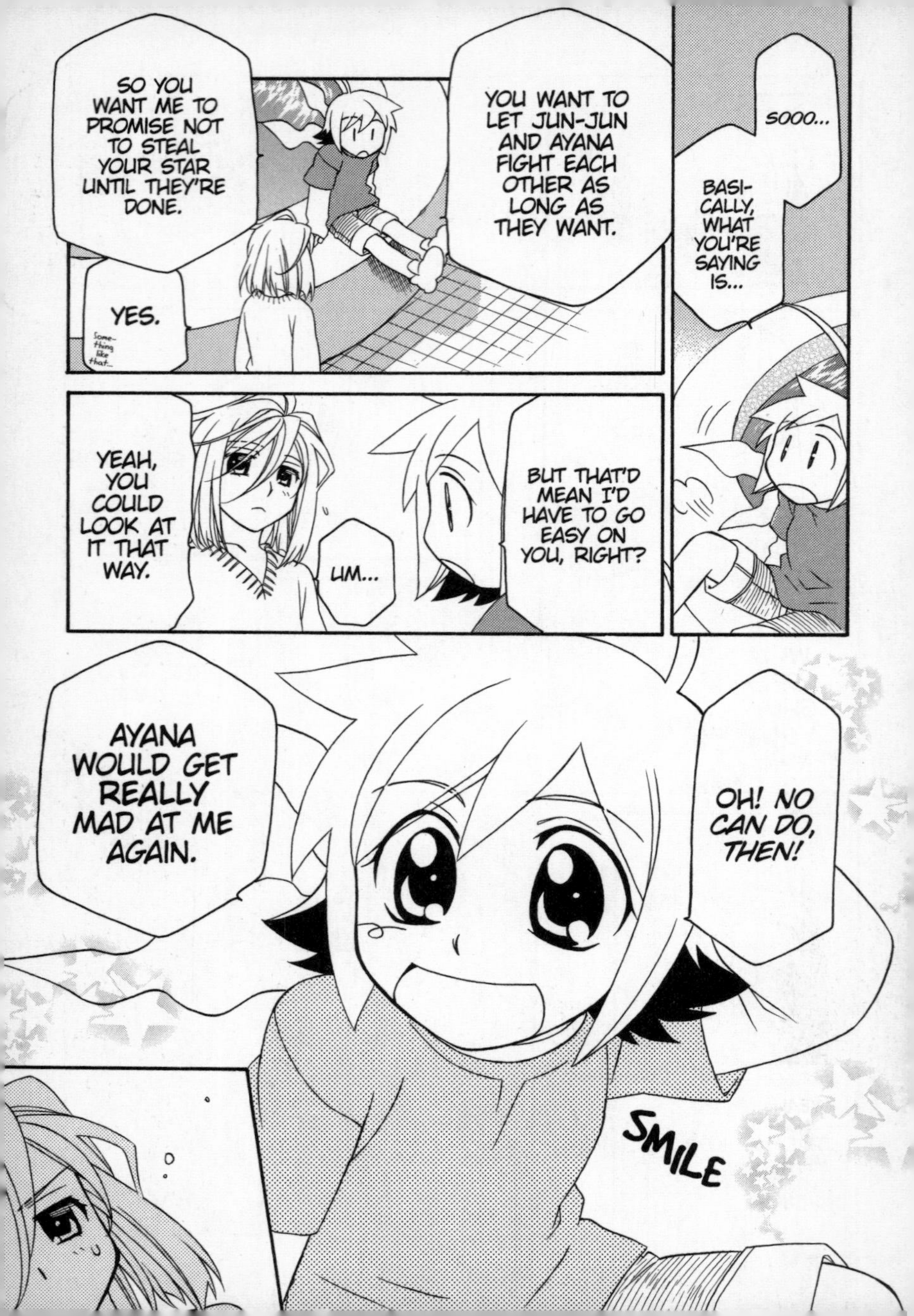

SOOO...
BASICALLY, WHAT YOU'RE SAYING IS...
YOU WANT TO LET JUN-JUN AND AYANA FIGHT EACH OTHER AS LONG AS THEY WANT.
SO YOU WANT ME TO PROMISE NOT TO STEAL YOUR STAR UNTIL THEY'RE DONE.
YES.
Something like that...
BUT THAT'D MEAN I'D HAVE TO GO EASY ON YOU, RIGHT?
UM...
YEAH, YOU COULD LOOK AT IT THAT WAY.
OH! NO CAN DO, THEN!
AYANA WOULD GET REALLY MAD AT ME AGAIN.
SMILE

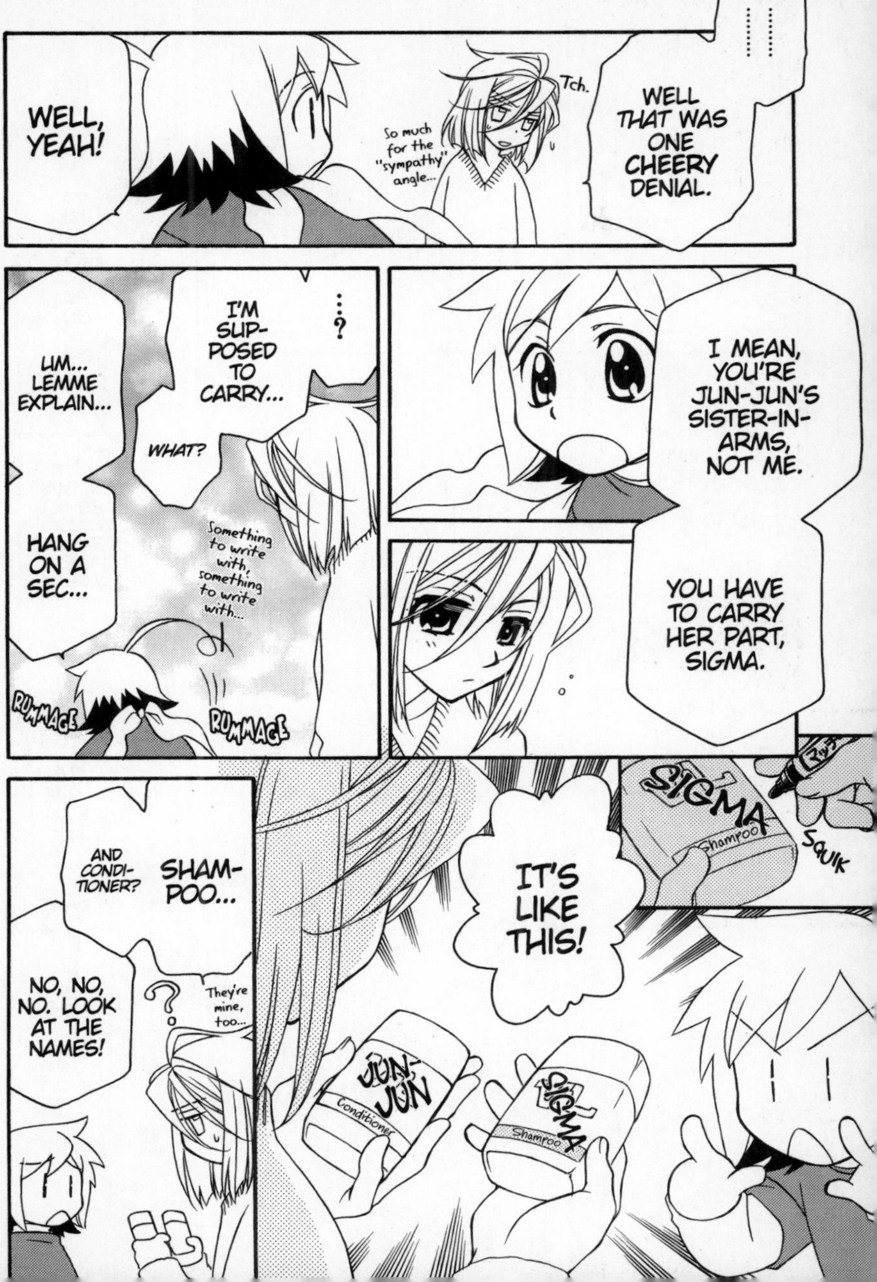
......
WELL THAT WAS ONE CHEERY DENIAL.
Tch.
So much for the "sympathy" angle...
WELL, YEAH!
I MEAN, YOU'RE JUN-JUN'S SISTER-IN-ARMS, NOT ME.
YOU HAVE TO CARRY HER PART, SIGMA.
...?
I'M SUP-POSED TO CARRY...
WHAT?
UM... LEMME EXPLAIN...
Something to write with, something to write with...
HANG ON A SEC...
RUMMAGE
RUMMAGE
SIGMA
Shampoo
SQUIK
IT'S LIKE THIS!
SHAM-POO...
AND CONDI-TIONER?
JUN-JUN
Conditioner
SIGMA
Shampoo
They're mine, too...
NO, NO, NO. LOOK AT THE NAMES!

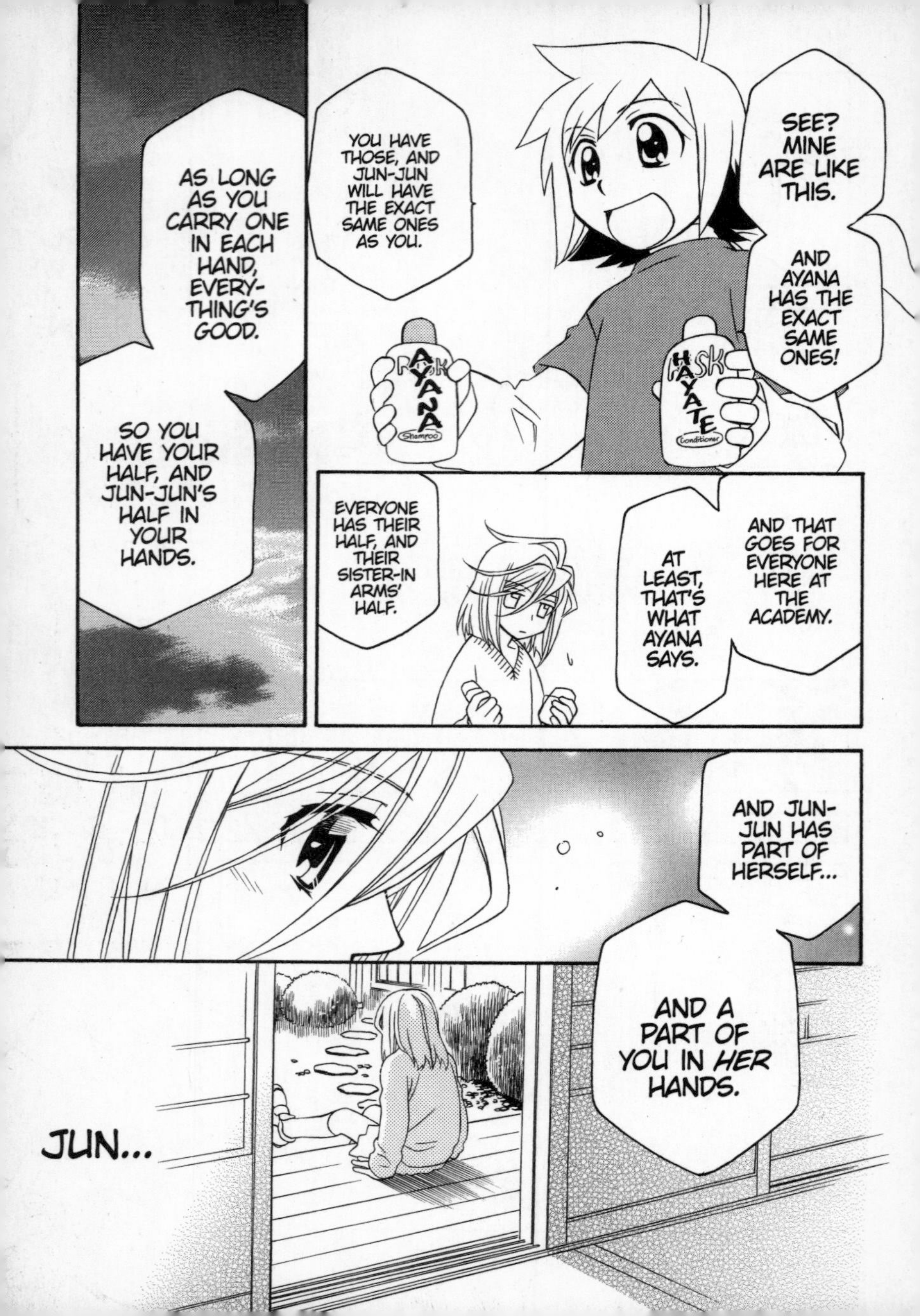
SEE? MINE ARE LIKE THIS.
AND AYANA HAS THE EXACT SAME ONES!
HAYATE
Conditioner
AYANA
Shampoo
YOU HAVE THOSE, AND JUN-JUN WILL HAVE THE EXACT SAME ONES AS YOU.
AND THAT GOES FOR EVERYONE HERE AT THE ACADEMY.
AT LEAST, THAT'S WHAT AYANA SAYS.
EVERYONE HAS THEIR HALF, AND THEIR SISTER-IN ARMS' HALF.
AS LONG AS YOU CARRY ONE IN EACH HAND, EVERY-THING'S GOOD.
SO YOU HAVE YOUR HALF, AND JUN-JUN'S HALF IN YOUR HANDS.
AND JUN-JUN HAS PART OF HERSELF...
AND A PART OF YOU IN *HER* HANDS.
JUN...

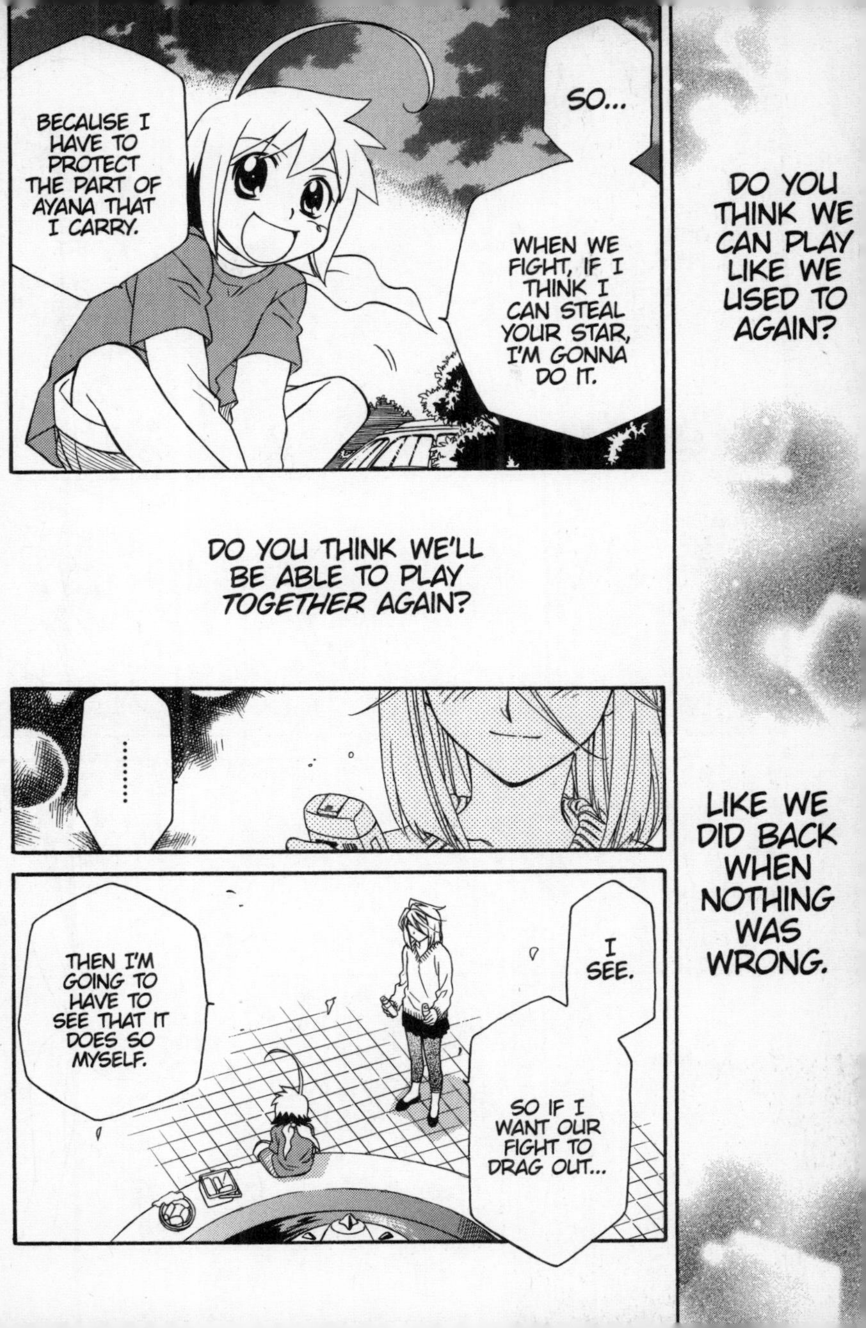
DO YOU THINK WE CAN PLAY LIKE WE USED TO AGAIN?
LIKE WE DID BACK WHEN NOTHING WAS WRONG.
BECAUSE I HAVE TO PROTECT THE PART OF AYANA THAT I CARRY.
SO...
WHEN WE FIGHT, IF I THINK I CAN STEAL YOUR STAR, I'M GONNA DO IT.
DO YOU THINK WE'LL BE ABLE TO PLAY TOGETHER AGAIN?
……
I SEE.
SO IF I WANT OUR FIGHT TO DRAG OUT...
THEN I'M GOING TO HAVE TO SEE THAT IT DOES SO MYSELF.

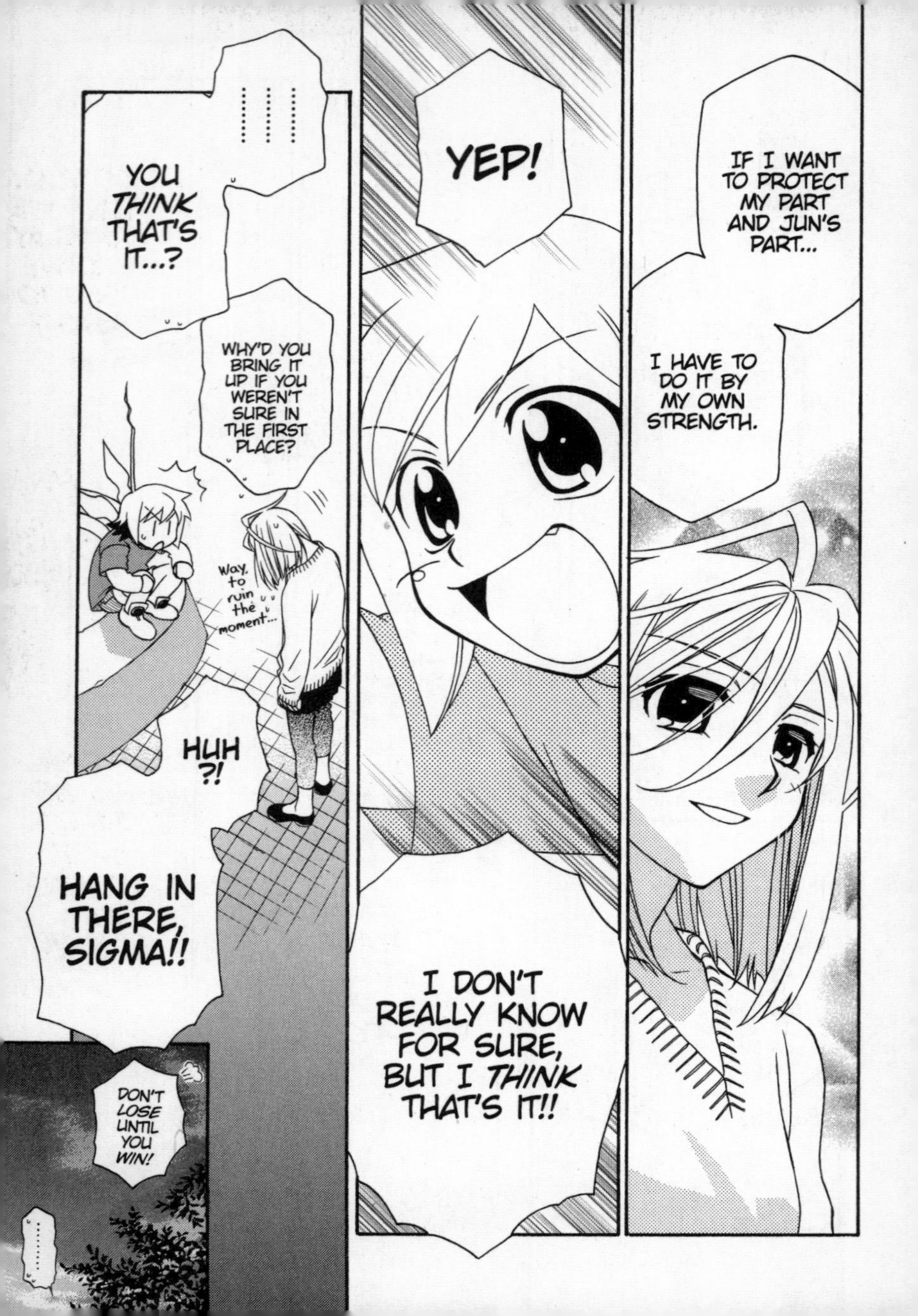
IF I WANT TO PROTECT MY PART AND JUN'S PART...
I HAVE TO DO IT BY MY OWN STRENGTH.
YEP!
I DON'T REALLY KNOW FOR SURE, BUT I *THINK* THAT'S IT!!
......
YOU *THINK* THAT'S IT...?
WHY'D YOU BRING IT UP IF YOU WEREN'T SURE IN THE FIRST PLACE?
Way to ruin the moment...
HUH?!
HANG IN THERE, SIGMA!!
DON'T LOSE UNTIL YOU WIN!
......

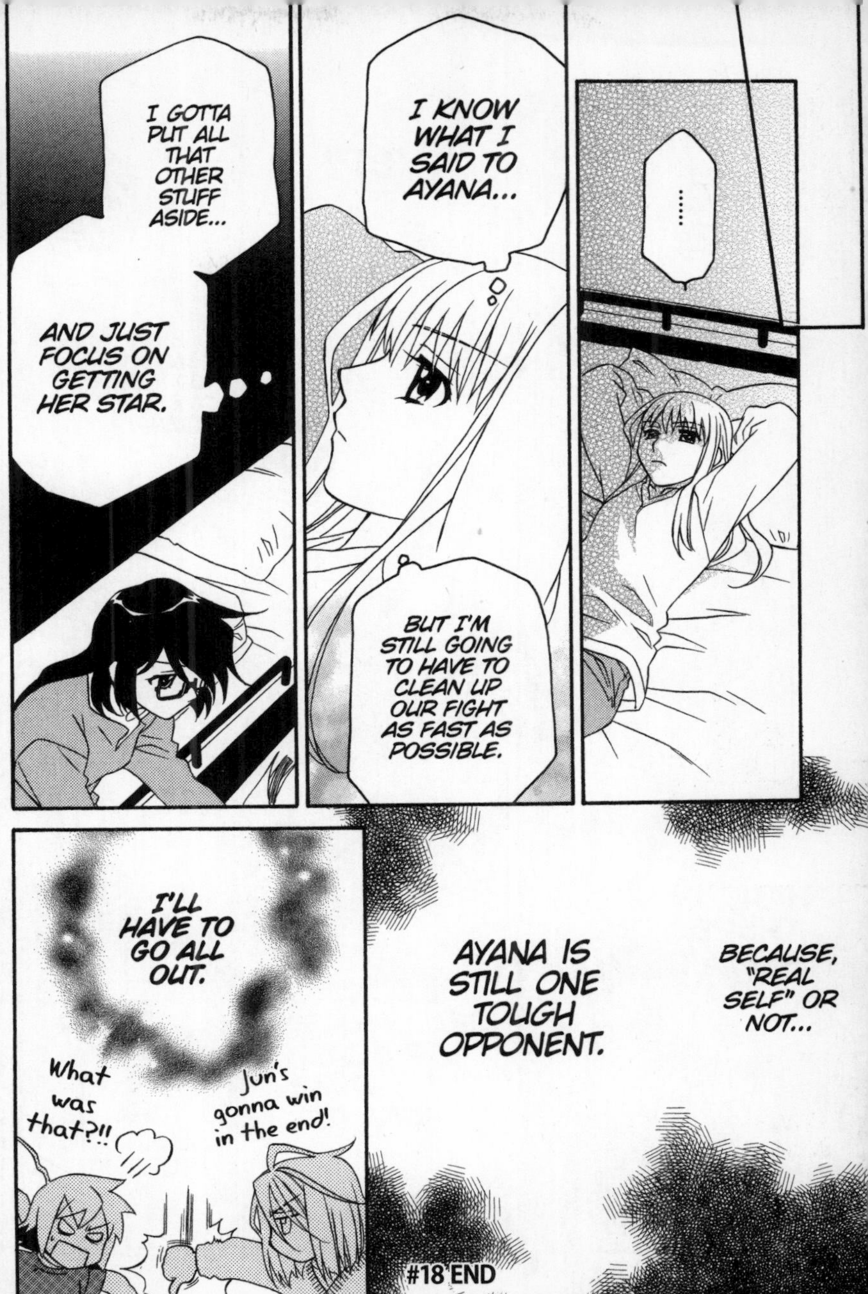
......
I KNOW WHAT I SAID TO AYANA...
BUT I'M STILL GOING TO HAVE TO CLEAN UP OUR FIGHT AS FAST AS POSSIBLE.
I GOTTA PUT ALL THAT OTHER STUFF ASIDE...
AND JUST FOCUS ON GETTING HER STAR.
BECAUSE, "REAL SELF" OR NOT...
AYANA IS STILL ONE TOUGH OPPONENT.
I'LL HAVE TO GO ALL OUT.
Jun's gonna win in the end!
What was that?!!
#18 END

#19 Various Idiots

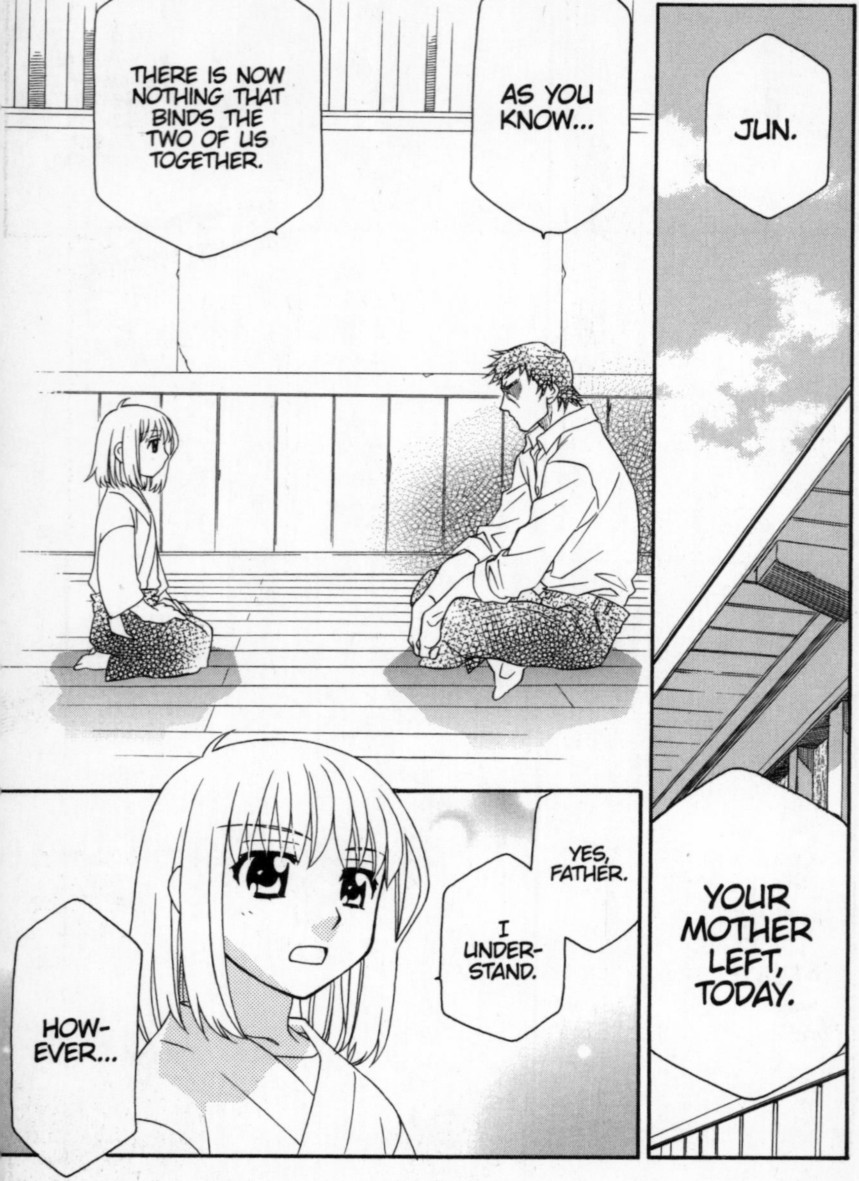
JUN.
YOUR MOTHER LEFT, TODAY.
AS YOU KNOW...
THERE IS NOW NOTHING THAT BINDS THE TWO OF US TOGETHER.
YES, FATHER.
I UNDER-STAND.
HOW-EVER...

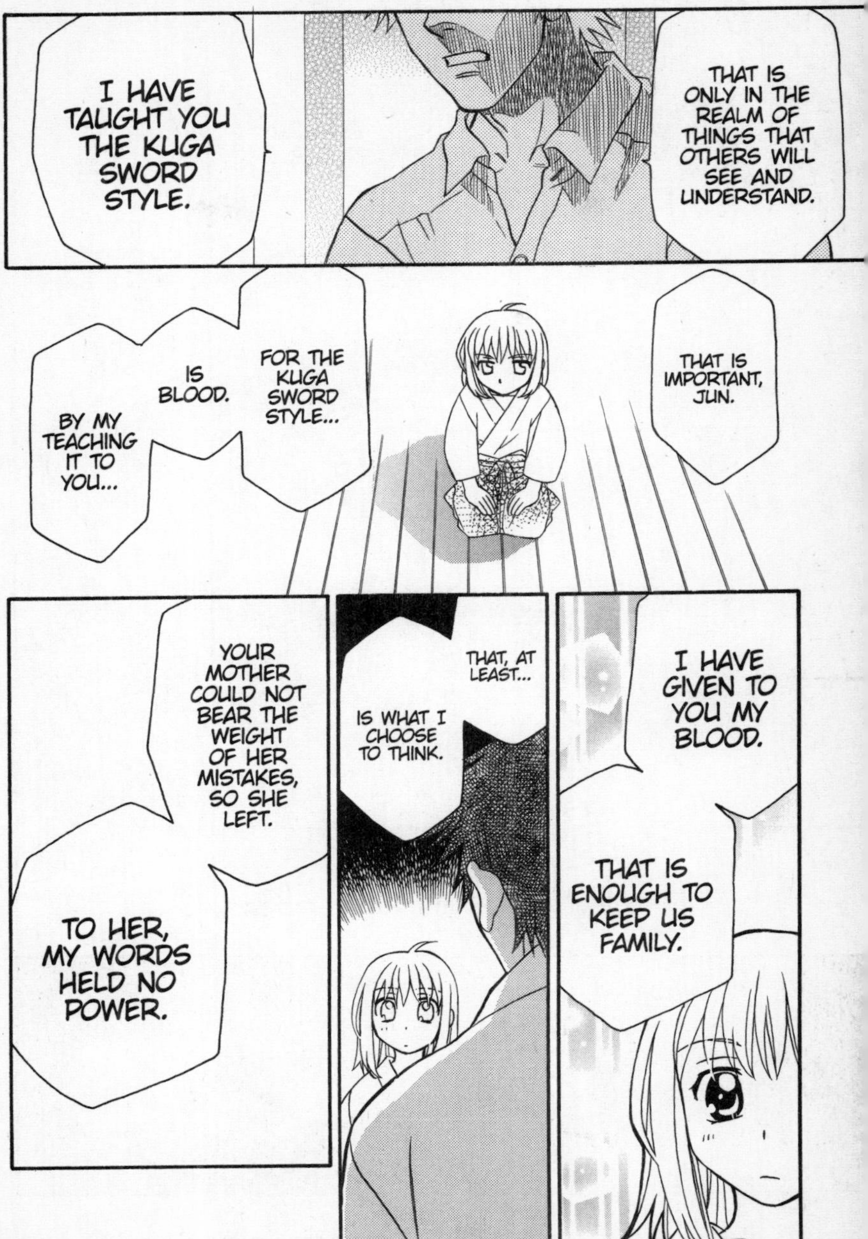
THAT IS ONLY IN THE REALM OF THINGS THAT OTHERS WILL SEE AND UNDERSTAND.
I HAVE TAUGHT YOU THE KUGA SWORD STYLE.
THAT IS IMPORTANT, JUN.
FOR THE KUGA SWORD STYLE...
IS BLOOD.
BY MY TEACHING IT TO YOU...
I HAVE GIVEN TO YOU MY BLOOD.
THAT IS ENOUGH TO KEEP US FAMILY.
THAT, AT LEAST...
IS WHAT I CHOOSE TO THINK.
YOUR MOTHER COULD NOT BEAR THE WEIGHT OF HER MISTAKES, SO SHE LEFT.
TO HER, MY WORDS HELD NO POWER.

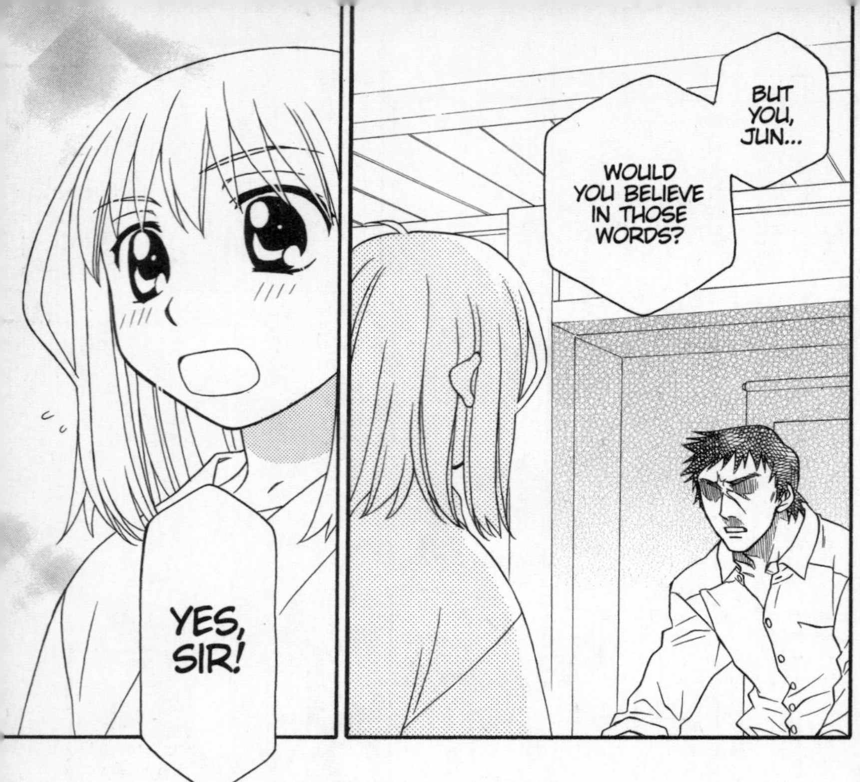
BUT YOU, JUN...
WOULD YOU BELIEVE IN THOSE WORDS?
YES, SIR!

#19 Various Idiots

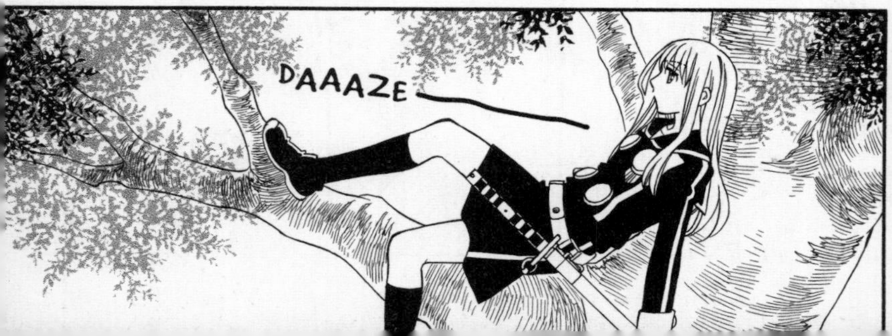
DAAAZE

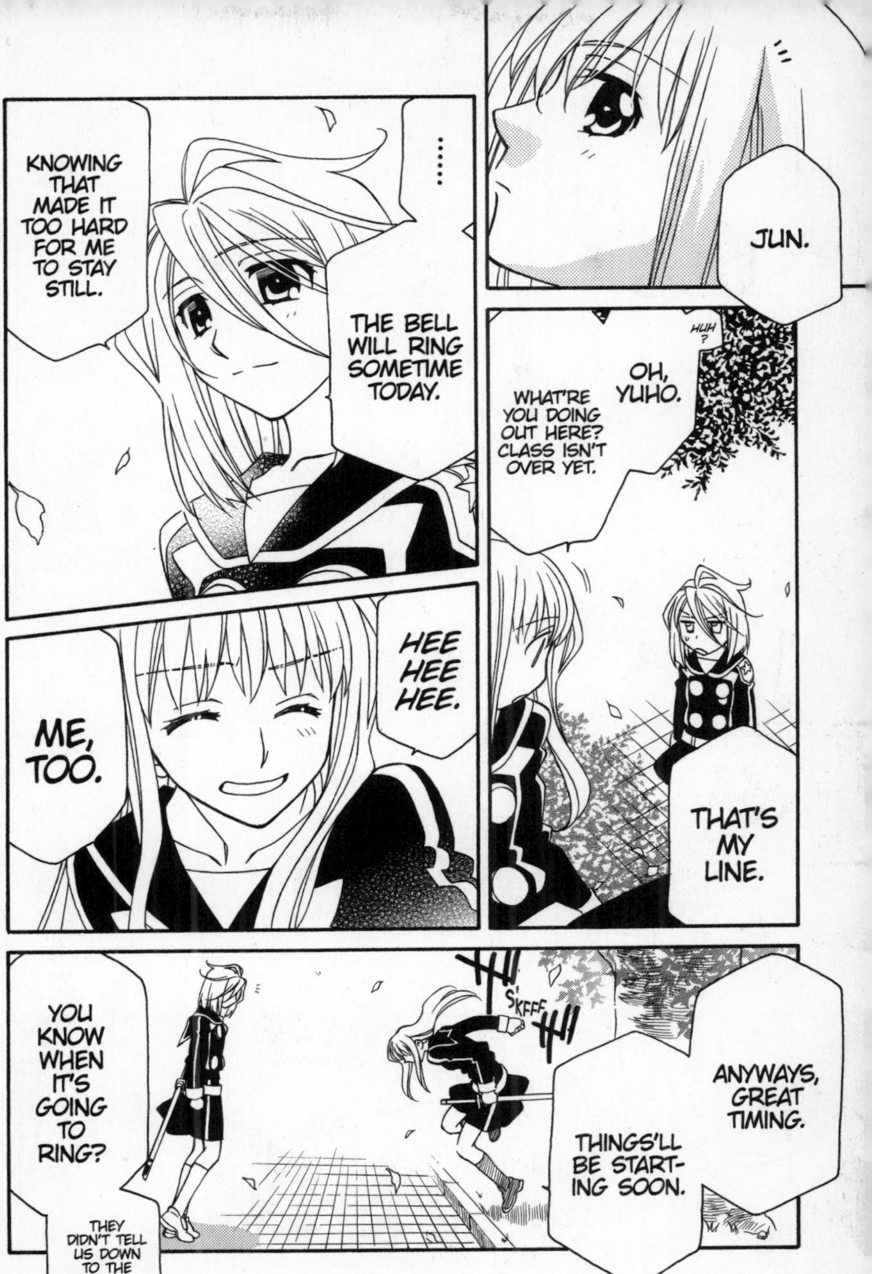
JUN.
HUH?
OH, YUHO.
WHAT'RE YOU DOING OUT HERE? CLASS ISN'T OVER YET.
THAT'S MY LINE.
......
THE BELL WILL RING SOMETIME TODAY.
KNOWING THAT MADE IT TOO HARD FOR ME TO STAY STILL.
HEE HEE HEE.
ME, TOO.
ANYWAYS, GREAT TIMING.
THINGS'LL BE STARTING SOON.
SKFFF
YOU KNOW WHEN IT'S GOING TO RING?
THEY DIDN'T TELL US DOWN TO THE MINUTE...

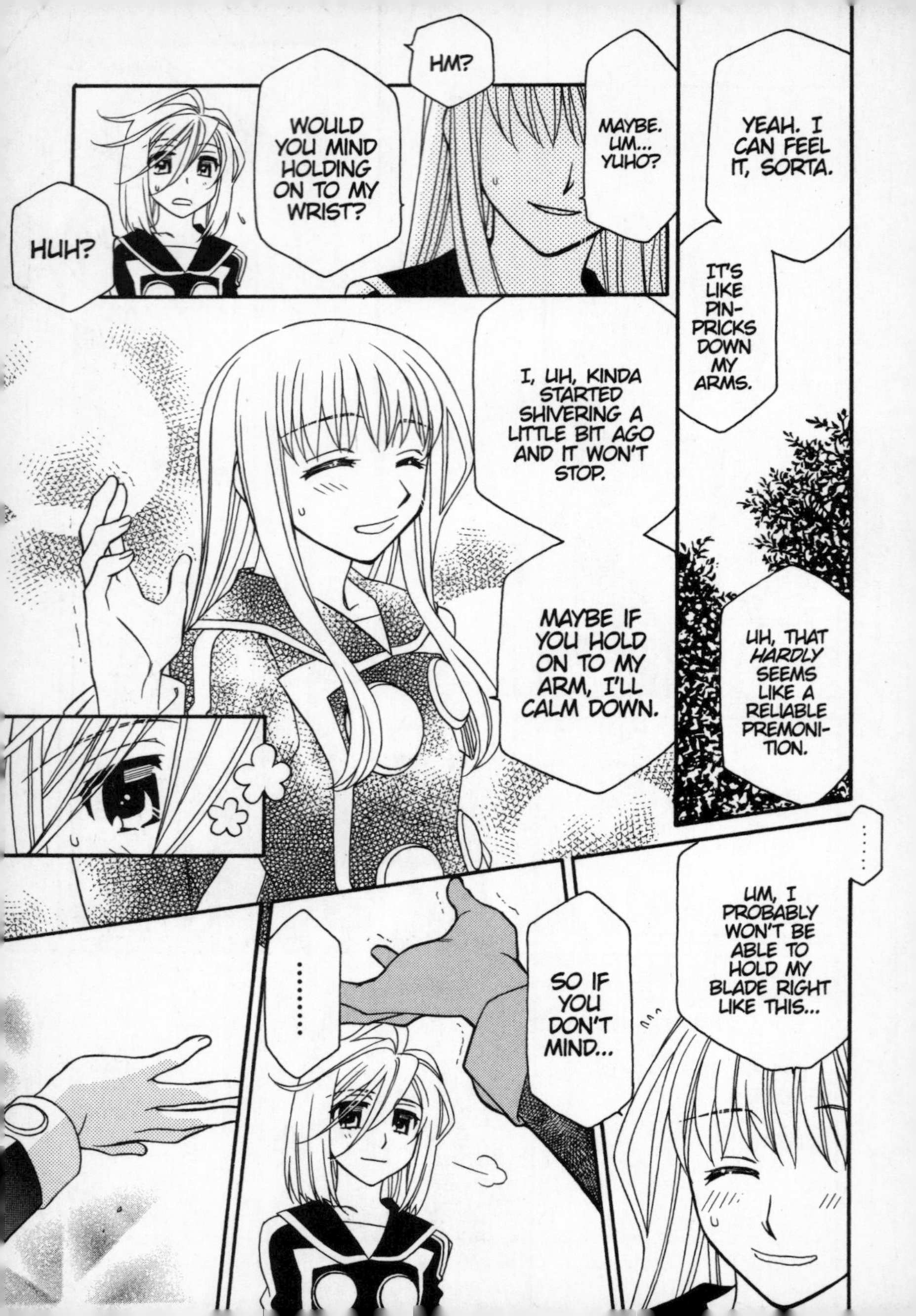
YEAH. I CAN FEEL IT, SORTA.
IT'S LIKE PIN-PRICKS DOWN MY ARMS.
UH, THAT *HARDLY* SEEMS LIKE A RELIABLE PREMONI-TION.
MAYBE. UM... YUHO?
HM?
WOULD YOU MIND HOLDING ON TO MY WRIST?
HUH?
I, UH, KINDA STARTED SHIVERING A LITTLE BIT AGO AND IT WON'T STOP.
MAYBE IF YOU HOLD ON TO MY ARM, I'LL CALM DOWN.
......
UM, I PROBABLY WON'T BE ABLE TO HOLD MY BLADE RIGHT LIKE THIS...
SO IF YOU DON'T MIND...
....

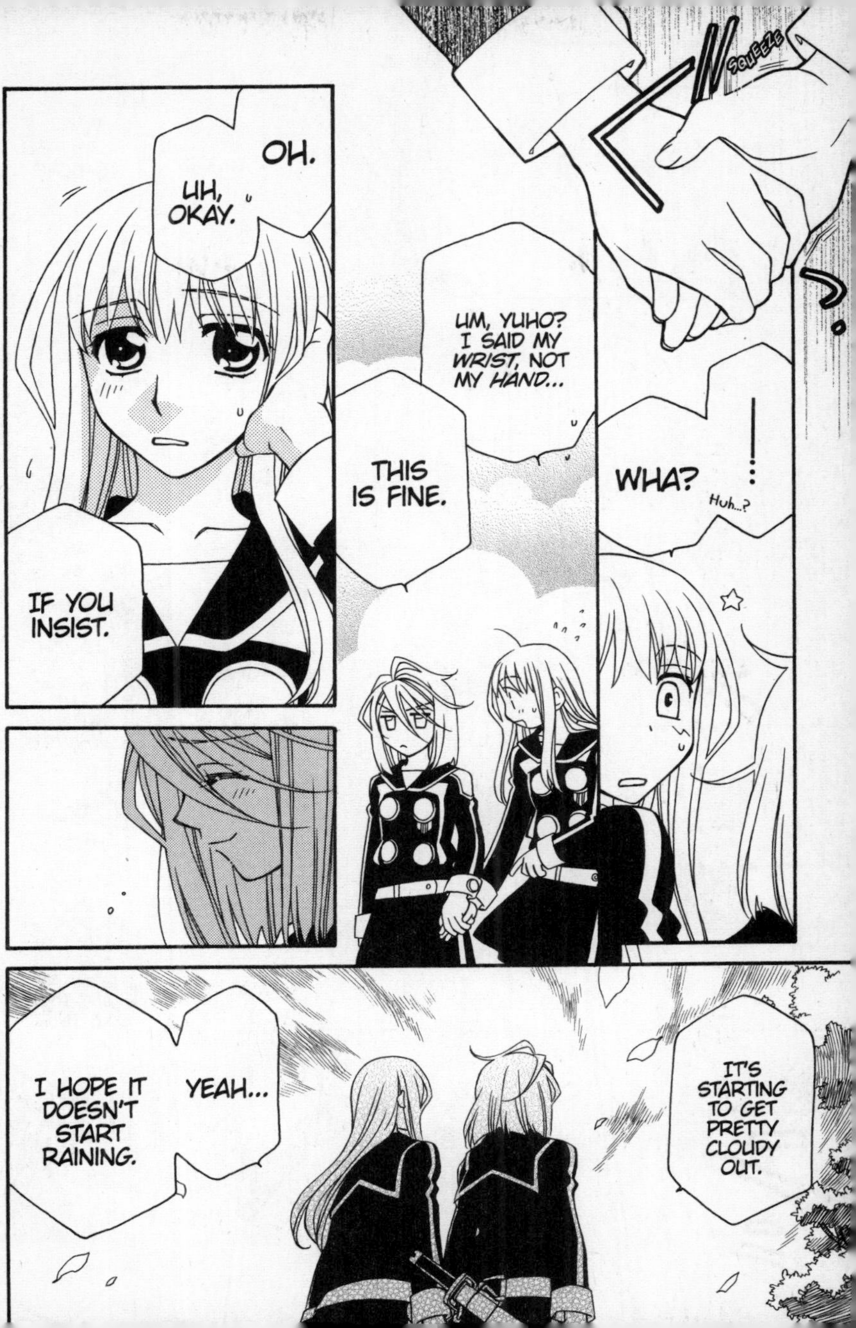
SQUEEZE
!
WHA?
Huh...?
UM, YUHO? I SAID MY *WRIST*, NOT MY *HAND*...
THIS IS FINE.
OH.
UH, OKAY.
IF YOU INSIST.
IT'S STARTING TO GET PRETTY CLOUDY OUT.
YEAH...
I HOPE IT DOESN'T START RAINING.

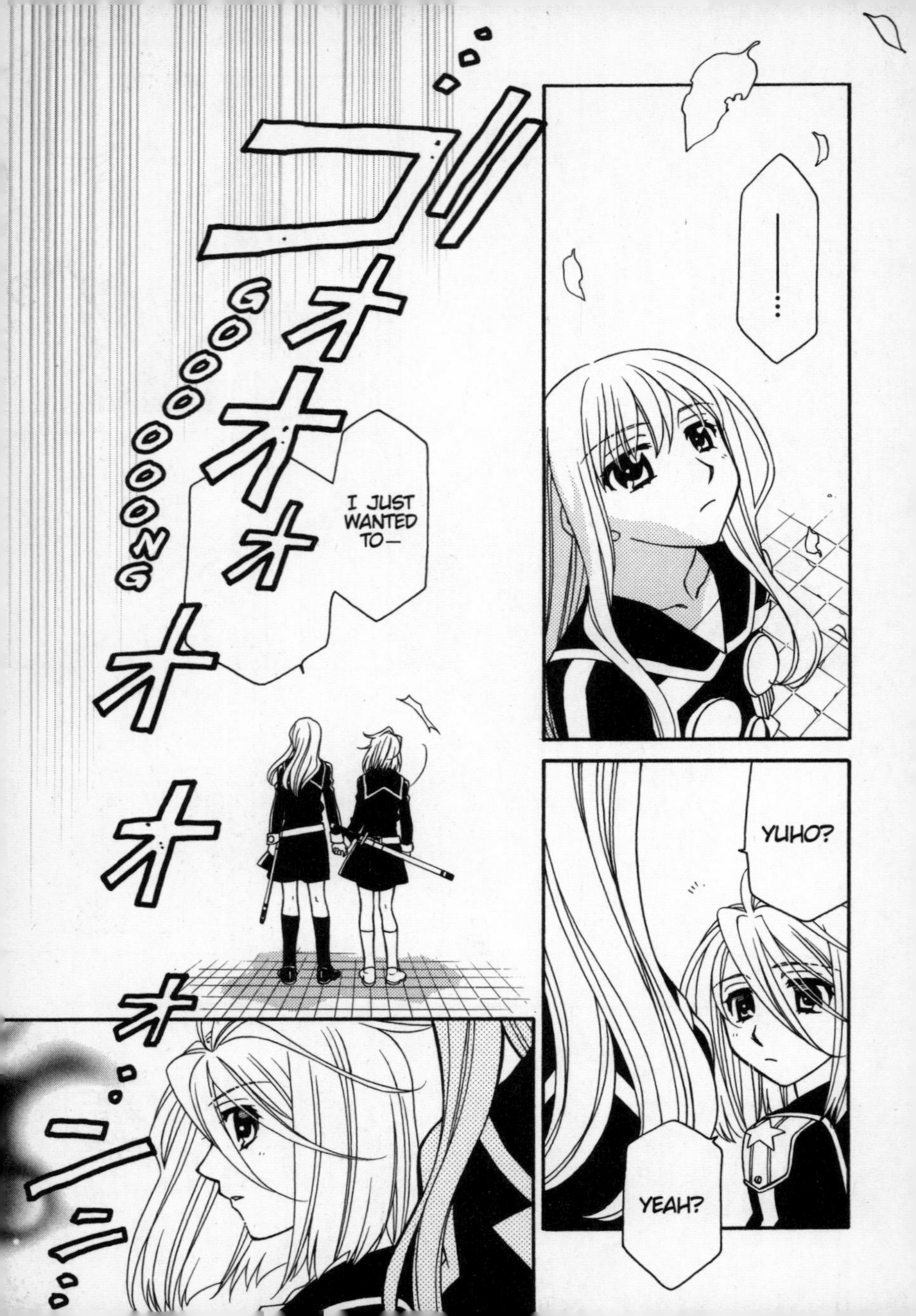
......
GOOOOOOOONG
I JUST WANTED TO—
YUHO?
YEAH?

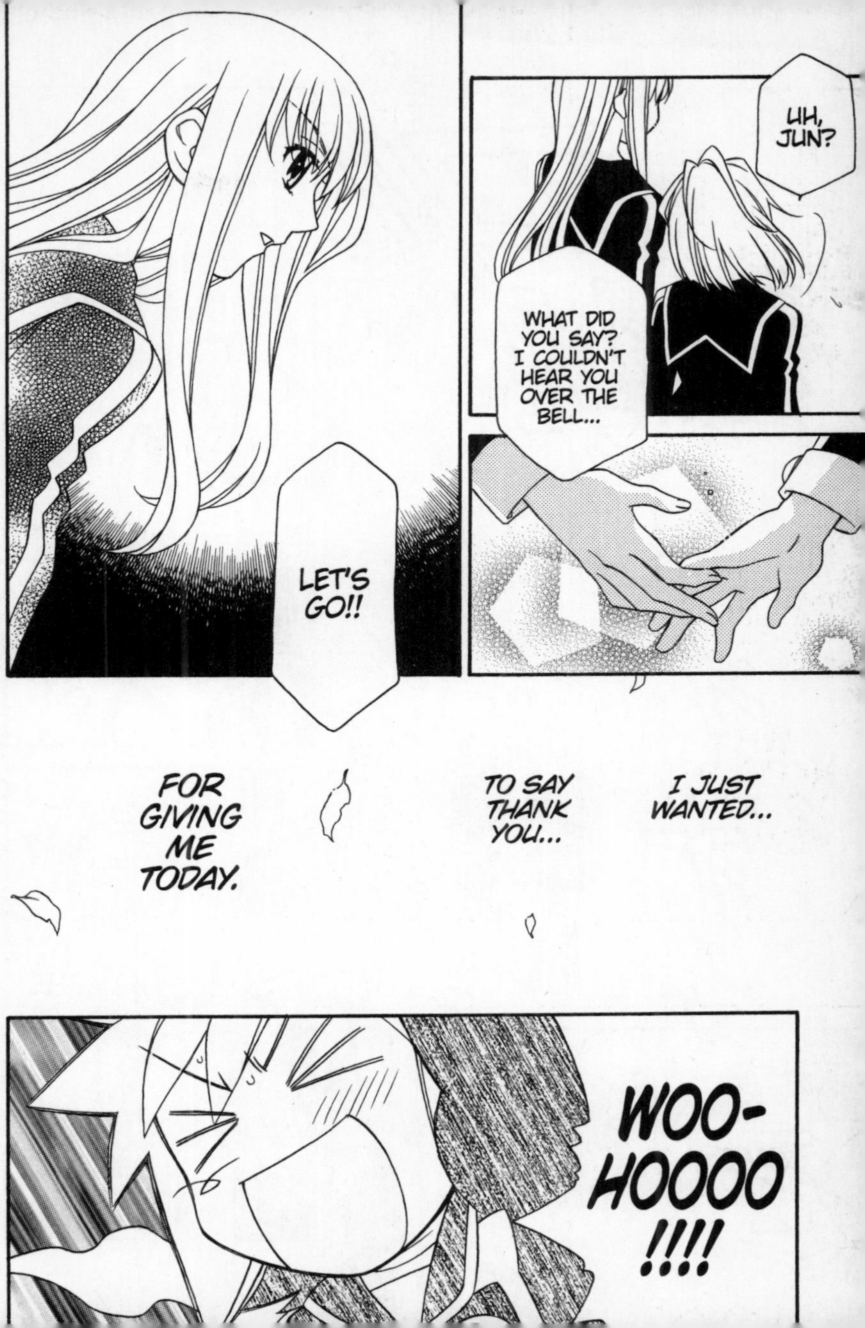
UH, JUN?
WHAT DID YOU SAY? I COULDN'T HEAR YOU OVER THE BELL...
LET'S GO!!
I JUST WANTED...
TO SAY THANK YOU...
FOR GIVING ME TODAY.
WOO-HOOOO!!!!

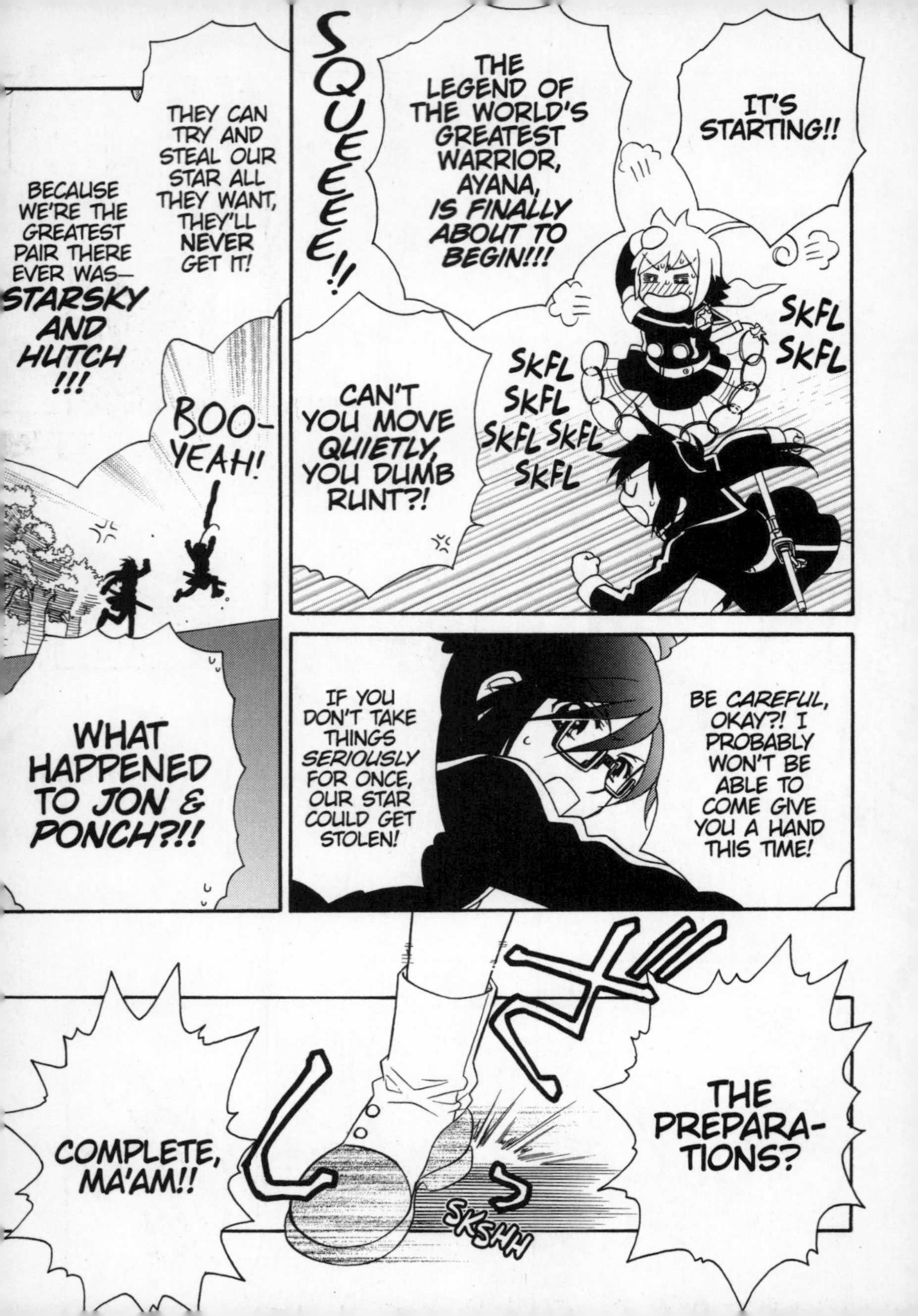
IT'S STARTING!!
THE LEGEND OF THE WORLD'S GREATEST WARRIOR, AYANA, IS FINALLY ABOUT TO BEGIN!!!
SQUEEEEE!!
SKFL SKFL
SKFL SKFL SKFL SKFL SKFL
CAN'T YOU MOVE QUIETLY, YOU DUMB RUNT?!
BE CAREFUL, OKAY?! I PROBABLY WON'T BE ABLE TO COME GIVE YOU A HAND THIS TIME!
IF YOU DON'T TAKE THINGS SERIOUSLY FOR ONCE, OUR STAR COULD GET STOLEN!
THEY CAN TRY AND STEAL OUR STAR ALL THEY WANT, THEY'LL NEVER GET IT!
BECAUSE WE'RE THE GREATEST PAIR THERE EVER WAS— STARSKY AND HUTCH!!!
BOO-YEAH!
WHAT HAPPENED TO JON & PONCH?!!
THE PREPARATIONS?
COMPLETE, MA'AM!!
SKSHH

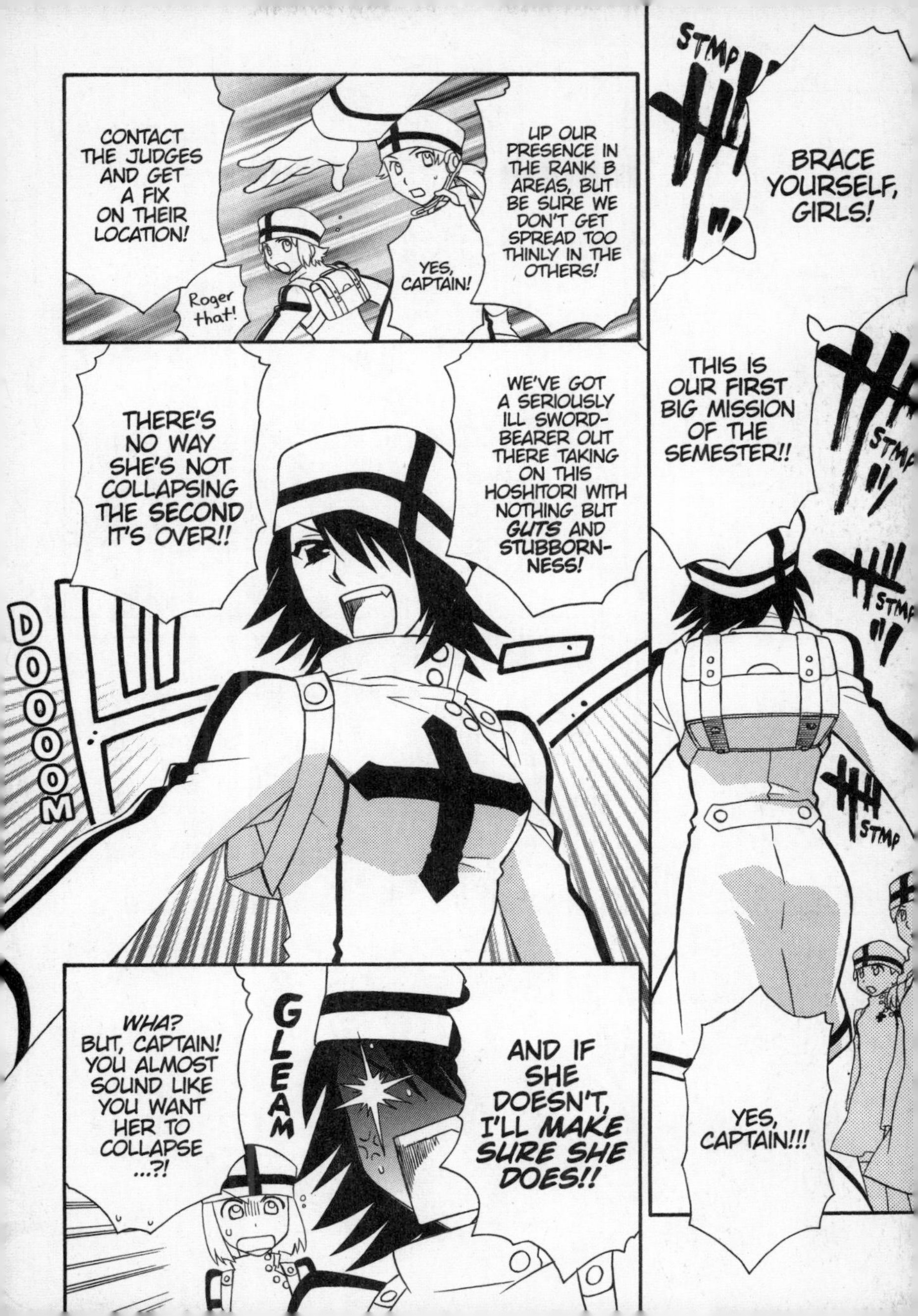
STMP
BRACE YOURSELF, GIRLS!
THIS IS OUR FIRST BIG MISSION OF THE SEMESTER!!
STMP
STMP
STMP
YES, CAPTAIN!!!
UP OUR PRESENCE IN THE RANK B AREAS, BUT BE SURE WE DON'T GET SPREAD TOO THINLY IN THE OTHERS!
YES, CAPTAIN!
CONTACT THE JUDGES AND GET A FIX ON THEIR LOCATION!
Roger that!
WE'VE GOT A SERIOUSLY ILL SWORD-BEARER OUT THERE TAKING ON THIS HOSHITORI WITH NOTHING BUT *GUTS* AND STUBBORN-NESS!
THERE'S NO WAY SHE'S NOT COLLAPSING THE SECOND IT'S OVER!!
DOOOOOM
AND IF SHE DOESN'T, I'LL *MAKE SURE SHE DOES!!*
GLEAM
WHA? BUT, CAPTAIN! YOU ALMOST SOUND LIKE YOU WANT HER TO COLLAPSE ...?!

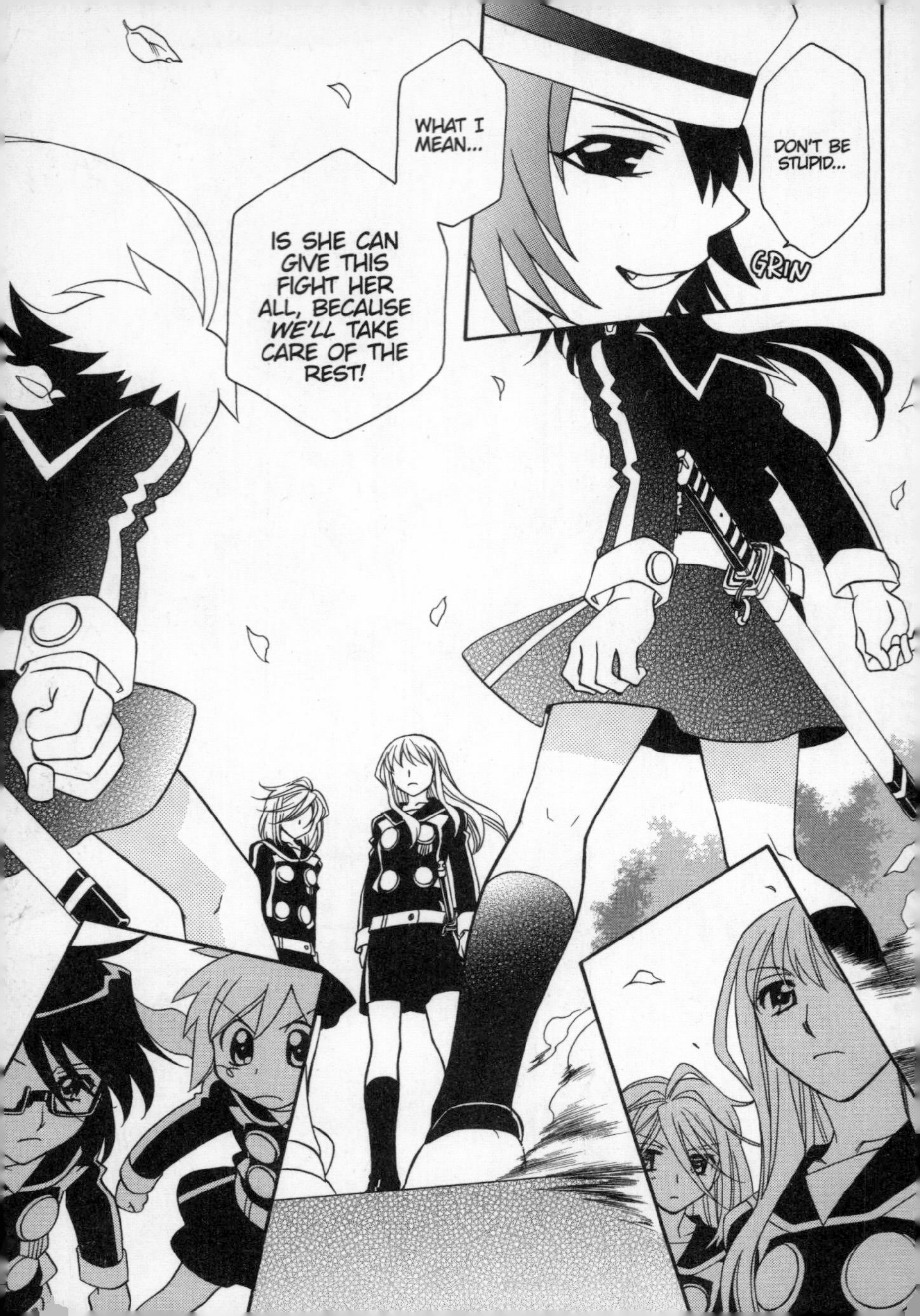
DON'T BE STUPID...
GRIN
WHAT I MEAN...
IS SHE CAN GIVE THIS FIGHT HER ALL, BECAUSE *WE'LL* TAKE CARE OF THE REST!

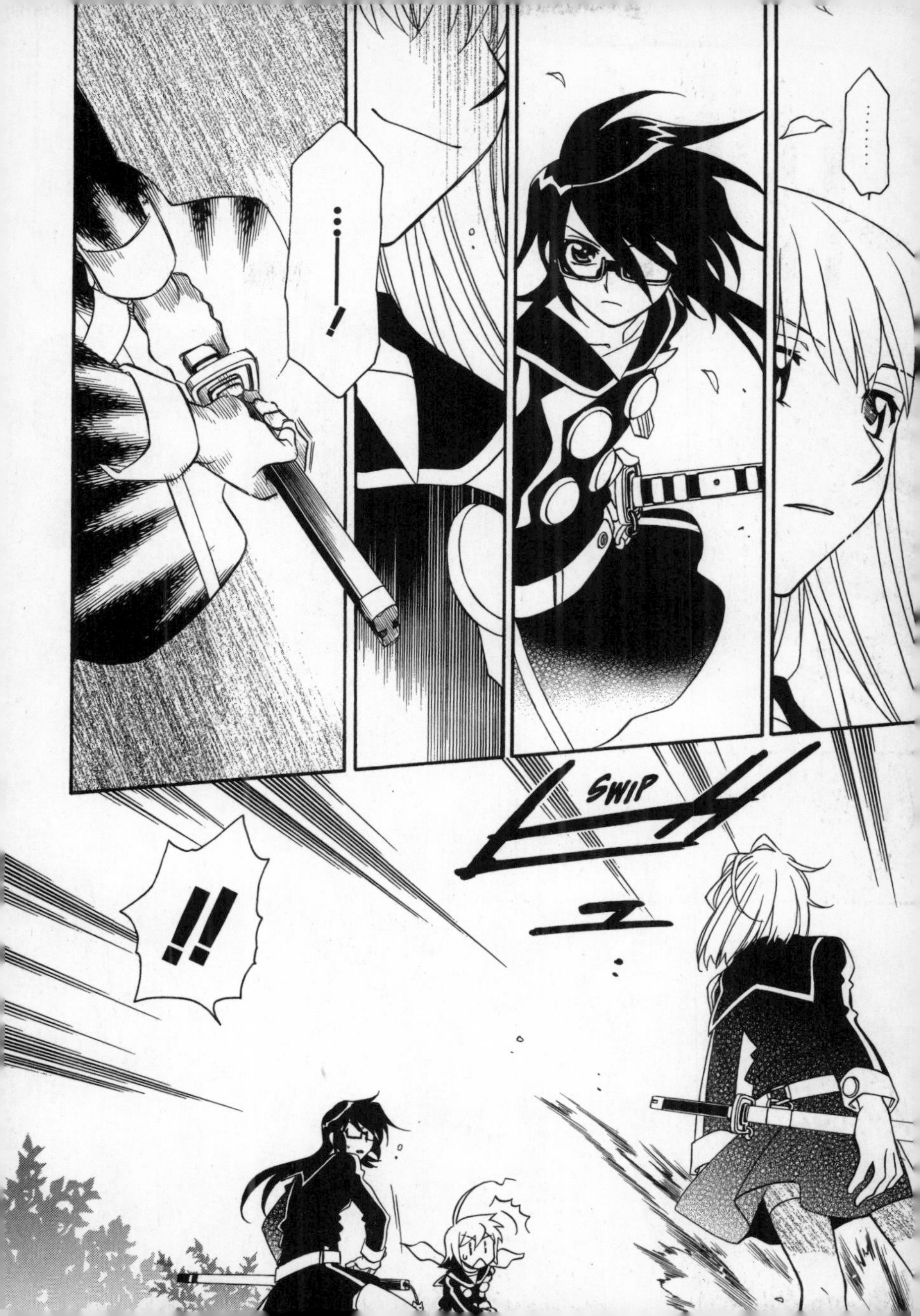
......
...—!
SWIP
!!

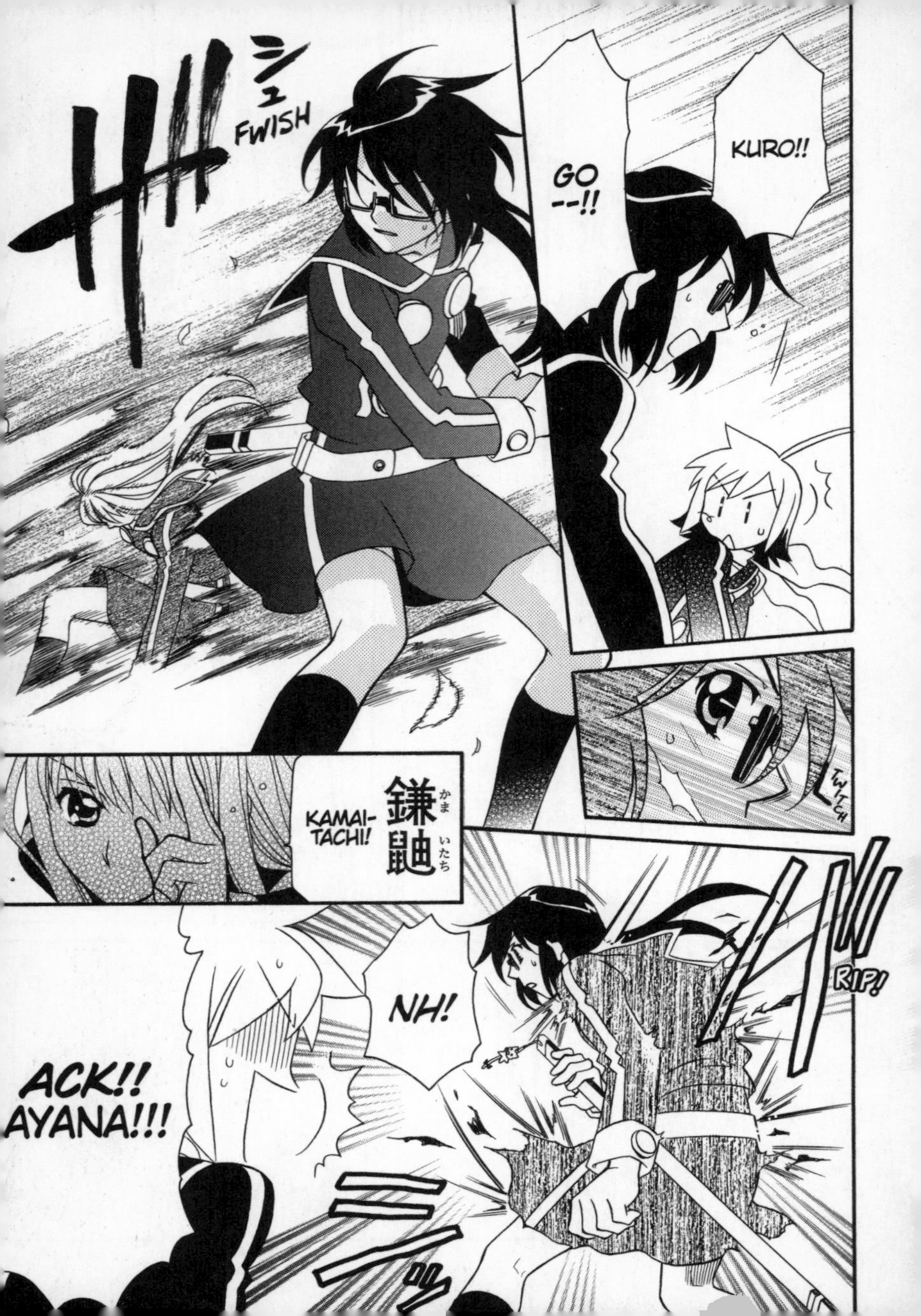
KURO!!
GO --!!
TWITCH
シュ
FWISH
KAMAI-TACHI!
鎌鼬 かまいたち
RIP!
NH!
ACK!! AYANA!!!

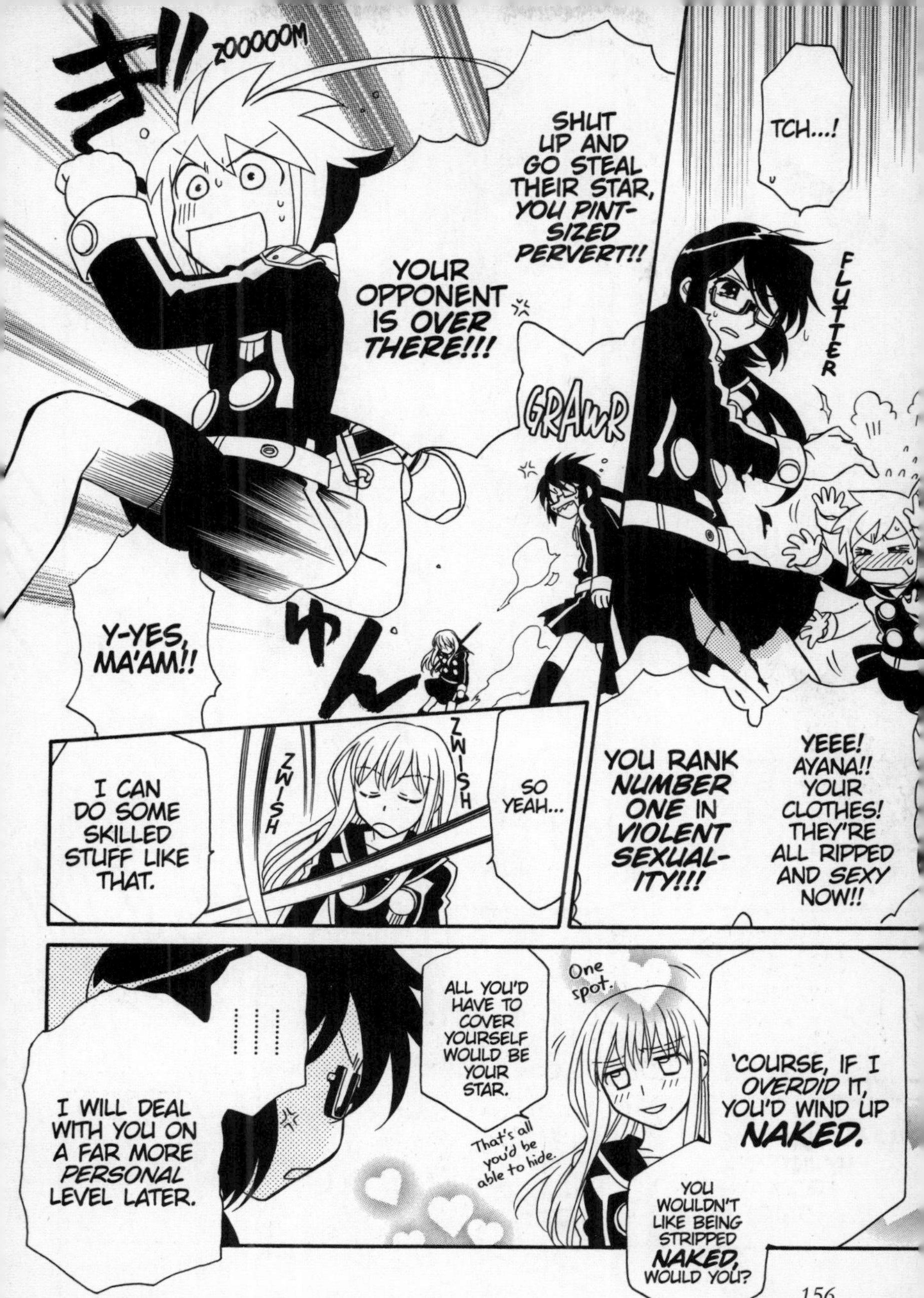
TCH...!
FLUTTER
YEEE! AYANA!! YOUR CLOTHES! THEY'RE ALL RIPPED AND SEXY NOW!!
YOU RANK NUMBER ONE IN VIOLENT SEXUALITY!!!
SHUT UP AND GO STEAL THEIR STAR, YOU PINT-SIZED PERVERT!!
YOUR OPPONENT IS OVER THERE!!!
GRAWR
ZOOOOOM
Y-YES, MA'AM!!
ZWISH
ZWISH
SO YEAH...
I CAN DO SOME SKILLED STUFF LIKE THAT.
'COURSE, IF I OVERDID IT, YOU'D WIND UP NAKED.
YOU WOULDN'T LIKE BEING STRIPPED NAKED, WOULD YOU?
One spot.
ALL YOU'D HAVE TO COVER YOURSELF WOULD BE YOUR STAR.
That's all you'd be able to hide.
......
I WILL DEAL WITH YOU ON A FAR MORE PERSONAL LEVEL LATER.

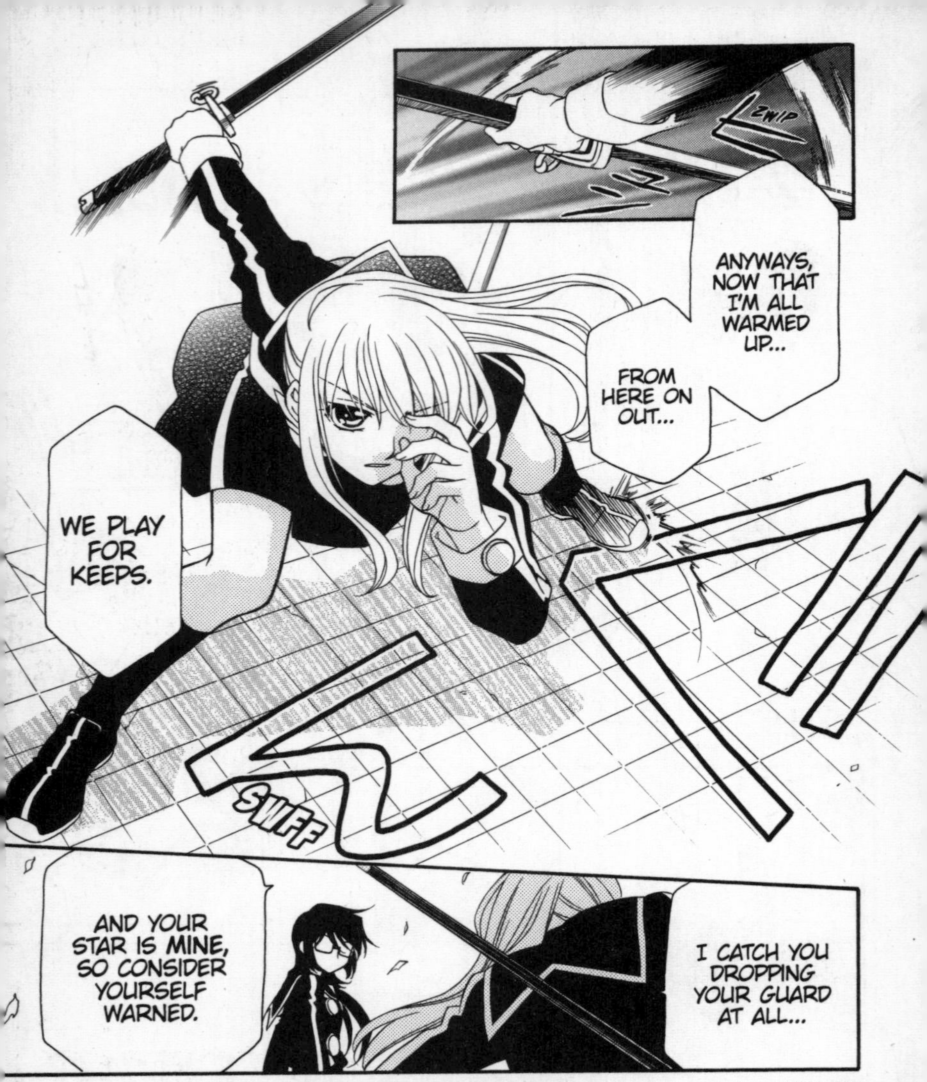
ZWIP
ANYWAYS, NOW THAT I'M ALL WARMED UP...
FROM HERE ON OUT...
WE PLAY FOR KEEPS.
SWFF
I CATCH YOU DROPPING YOUR GUARD AT ALL...
AND YOUR STAR IS MINE, SO CONSIDER YOURSELF WARNED.
HNH.
THAT WAS MY INTENTION FROM THE START.

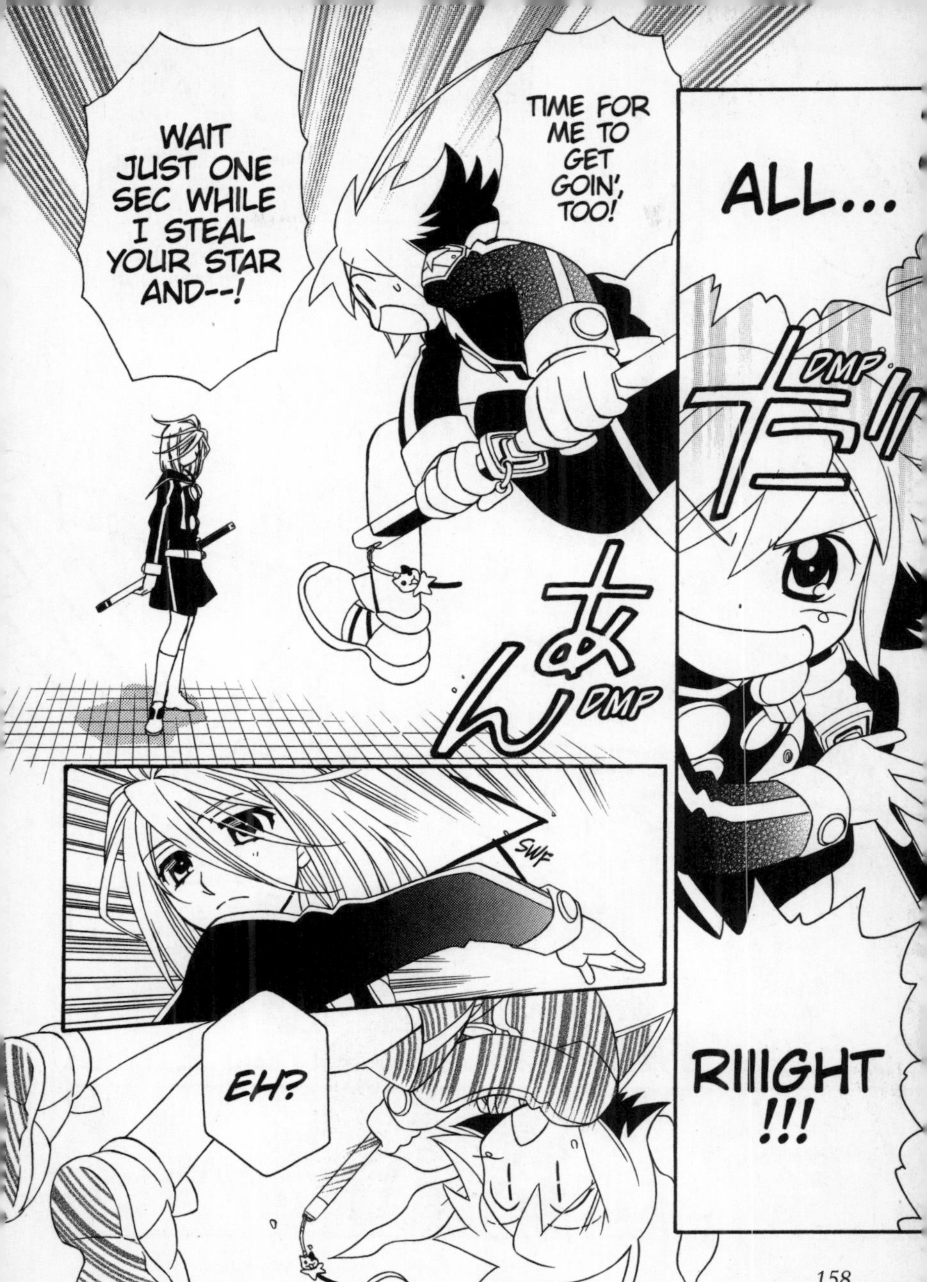
ALL...
DMP
DMP
RIIIGHT !!!
TIME FOR ME TO GET GOIN', TOO!
WAIT JUST ONE SEC WHILE I STEAL YOUR STAR AND--!
SWF
EH?

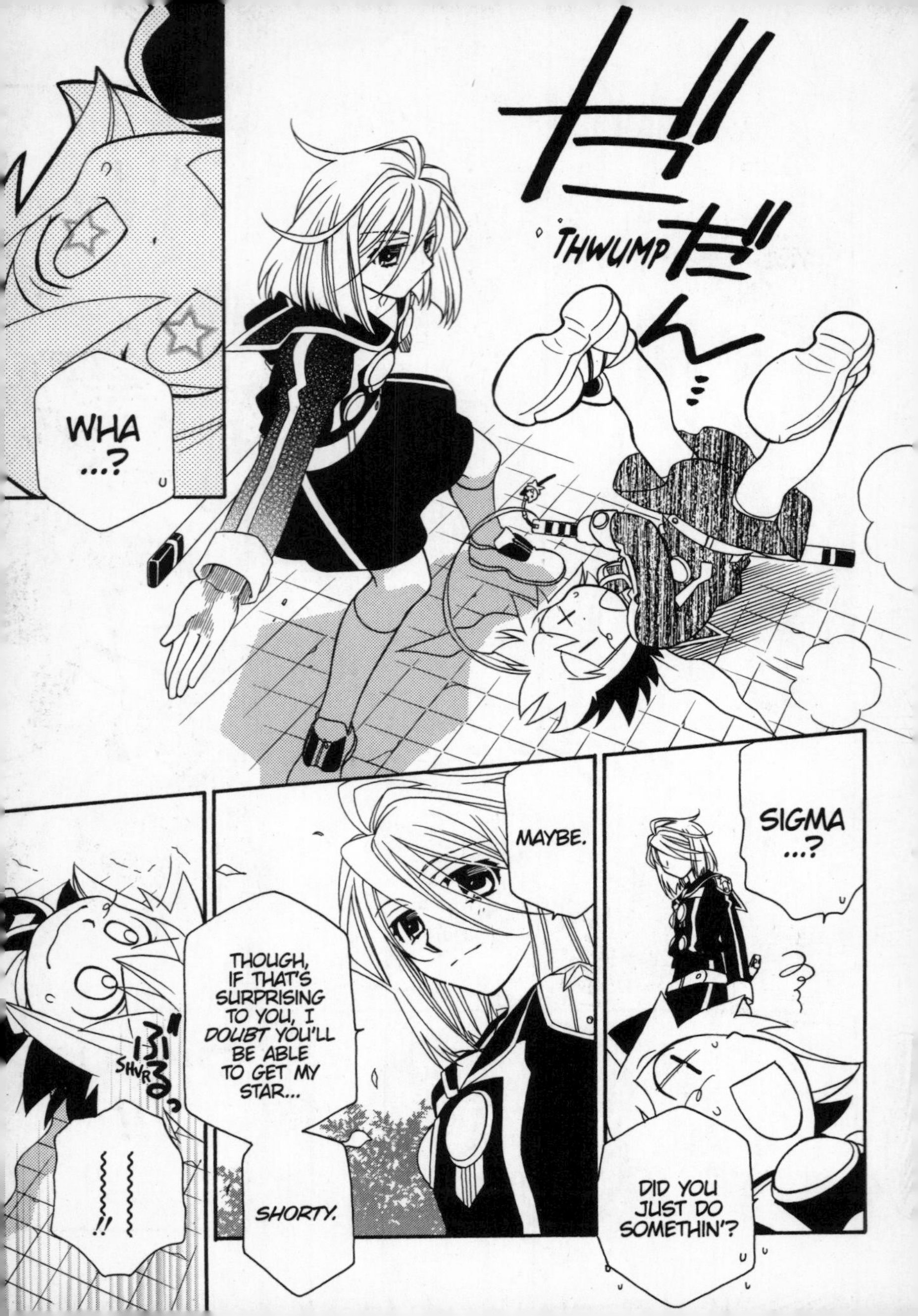
だーだん
THWUMP
WHA ...?
SIGMA ...?
DID YOU JUST DO SOMETHIN'?
MAYBE.
THOUGH, IF THAT'S SURPRISING TO YOU, I DOUBT YOU'LL BE ABLE TO GET MY STAR...
SHORTY.
ぶるっ
SHVR
!!

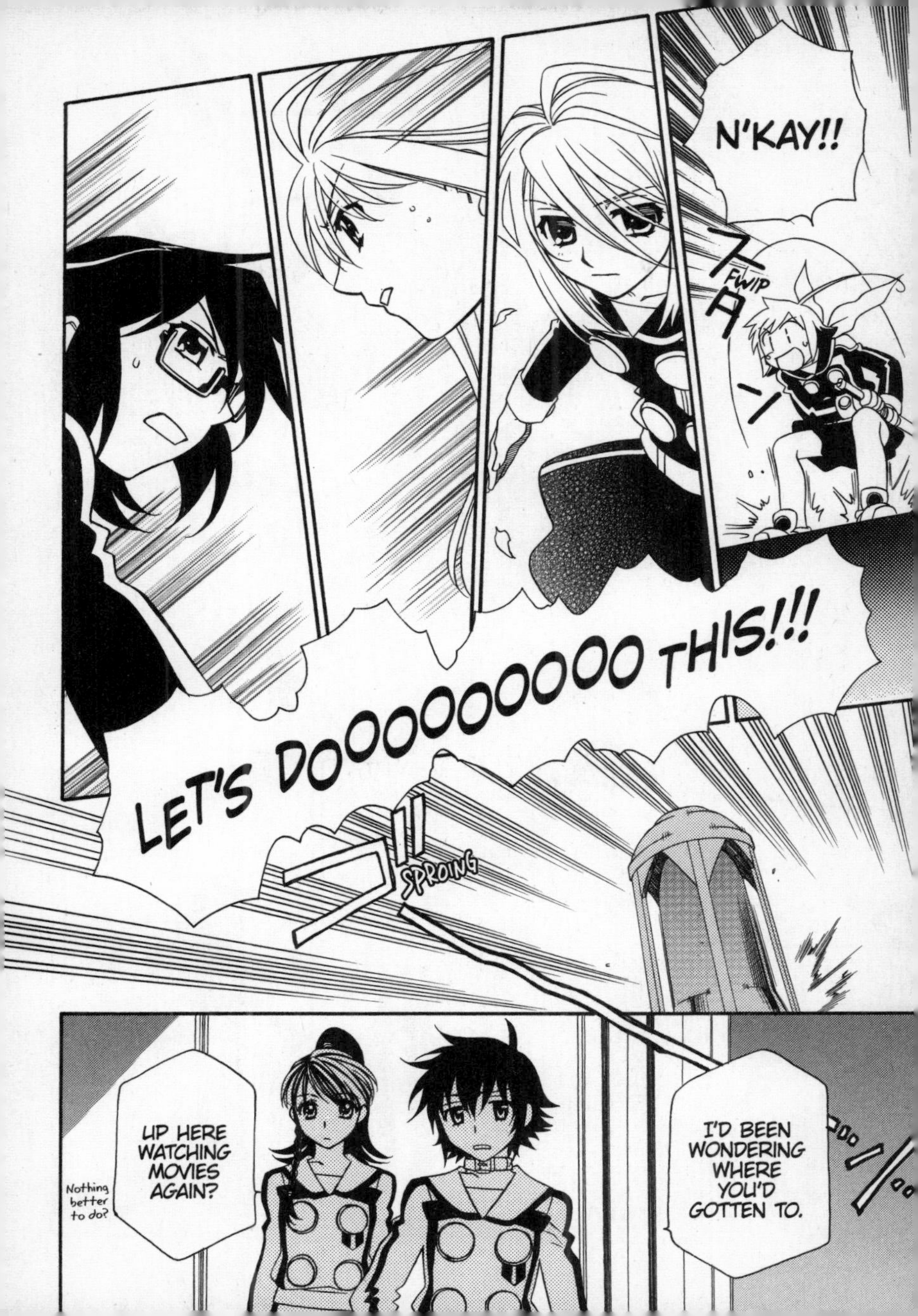
N'KAY!!
FWIP
LET'S DOOOOOOOOO THIS!!!
SPROING
I'D BEEN WONDERING WHERE YOU'D GOTTEN TO.
UP HERE WATCHING MOVIES AGAIN?
Nothing better to do?

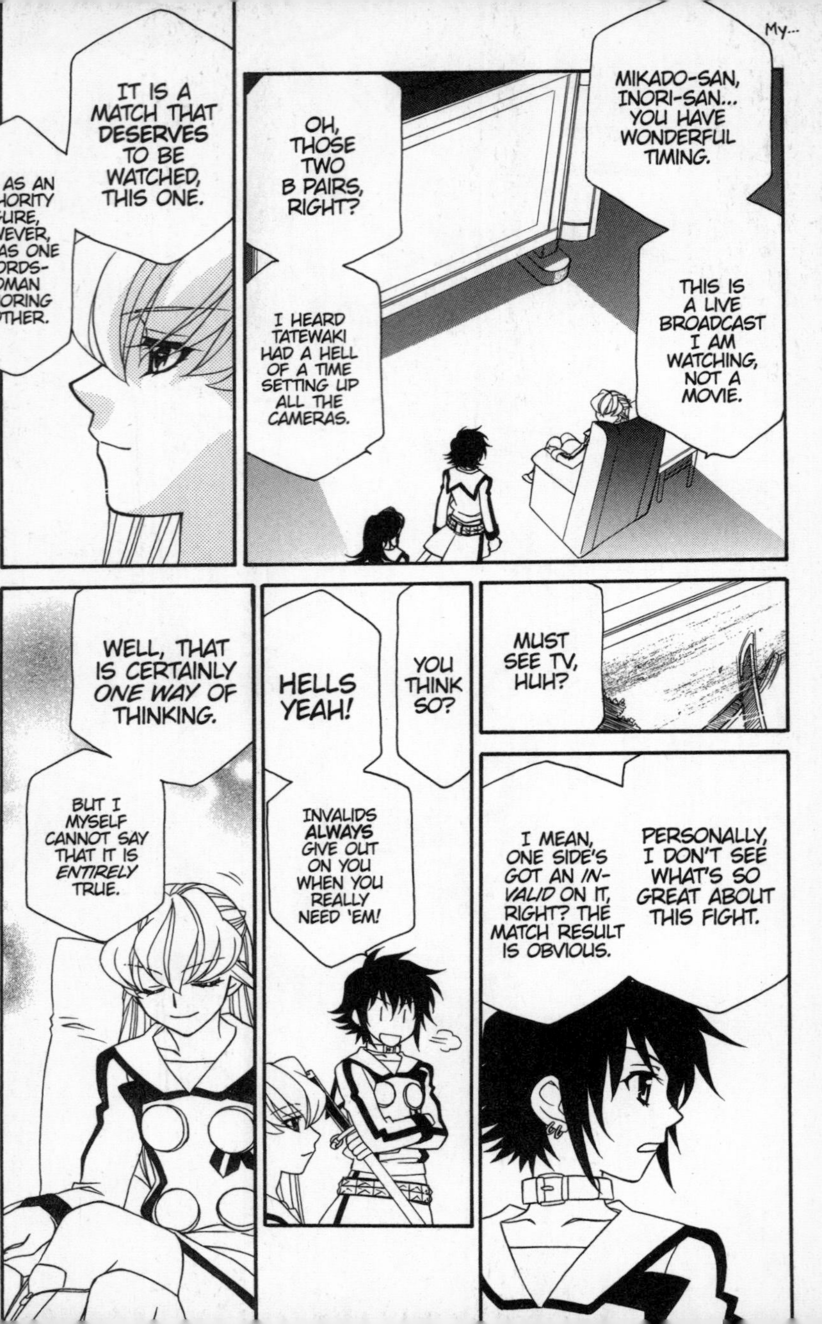
My...
MIKADO-SAN, INORI-SAN... YOU HAVE WONDERFUL TIMING.
OH, THOSE TWO B PAIRS, RIGHT?
THIS IS A LIVE BROADCAST I AM WATCHING, NOT A MOVIE.
I HEARD TATEWAKI HAD A HELL OF A TIME SETTING UP ALL THE CAMERAS.
IT IS A MATCH THAT DESERVES TO BE WATCHED, THIS ONE.
NOT AS AN AUTHORITY FIGURE, HOWEVER, BUT AS ONE SWORDS-WOMAN HONORING ANOTHER.
MUST SEE TV, HUH?
PERSONALLY, I DON'T SEE WHAT'S SO GREAT ABOUT THIS FIGHT.
I MEAN, ONE SIDE'S GOT AN *INVALID* ON IT, RIGHT? THE MATCH RESULT IS OBVIOUS.
YOU THINK SO?
HELLS YEAH!
INVALIDS **ALWAYS** GIVE OUT ON YOU WHEN YOU REALLY NEED 'EM!
WELL, THAT IS CERTAINLY *ONE WAY* OF THINKING.
BUT I MYSELF CANNOT SAY THAT IT IS *ENTIRELY* TRUE.

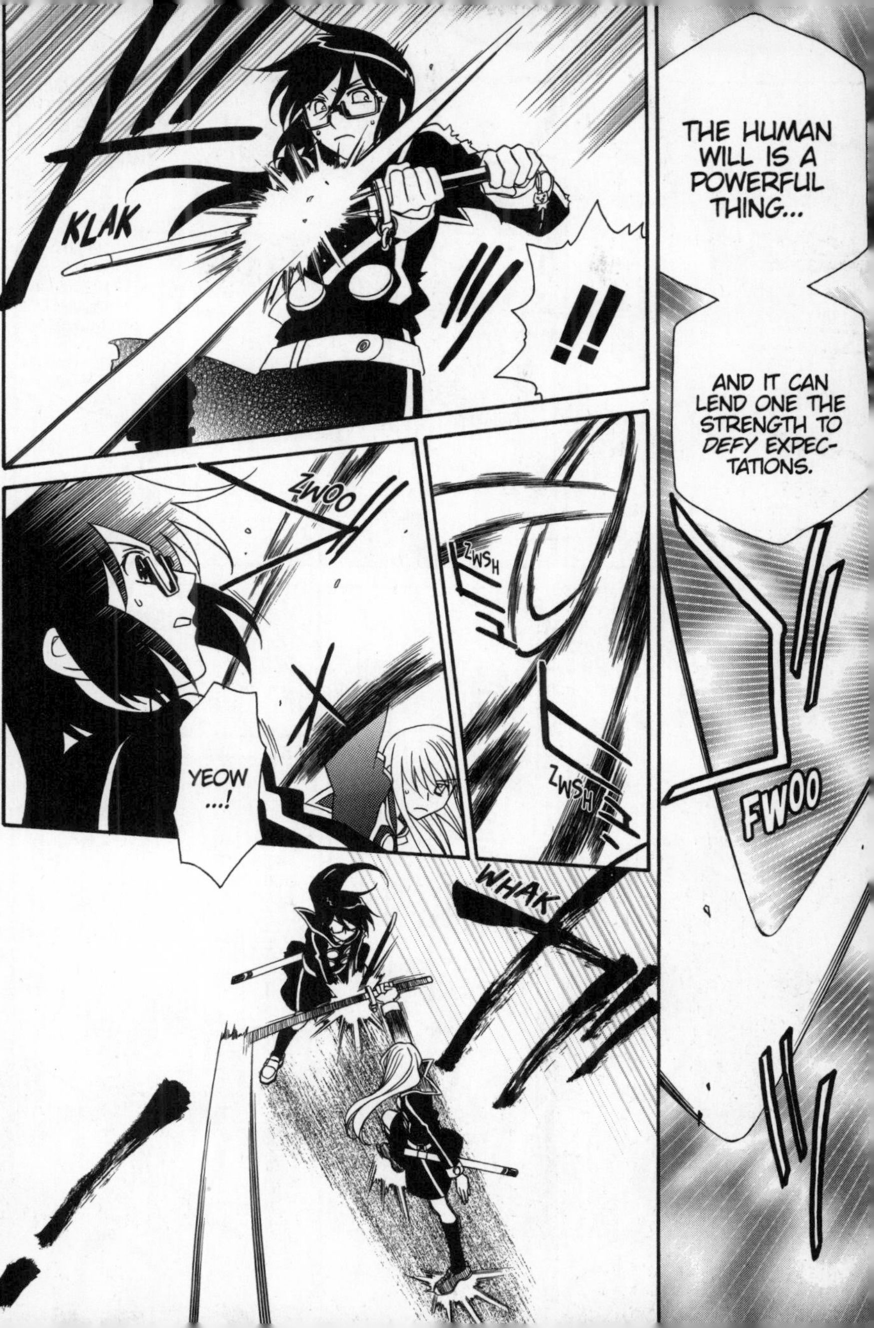
THE HUMAN WILL IS A POWERFUL THING...
AND IT CAN LEND ONE THE STRENGTH TO *DEFY* EXPECTATIONS.
FWOO
KLAK
!!
ZWSH
ZWSH
ZWOO
YEOW ...!
WHAK
!

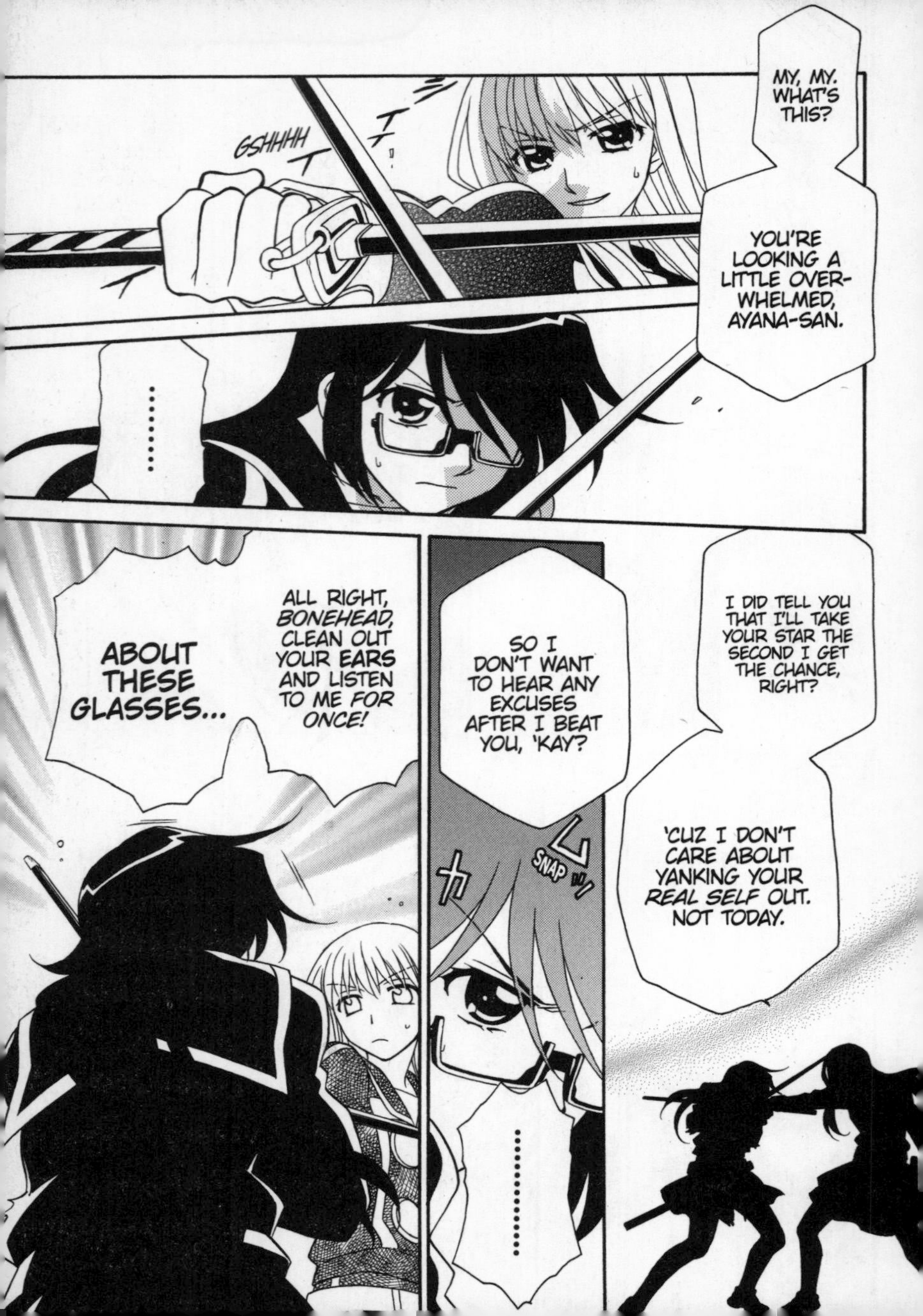
MY, MY. WHAT'S THIS?
GSHHHH
YOU'RE LOOKING A LITTLE OVER-WHELMED, AYANA-SAN.
......
I DID TELL YOU THAT I'LL TAKE YOUR STAR THE SECOND I GET THE CHANCE, RIGHT?
'CUZ I DON'T CARE ABOUT YANKING YOUR *REAL SELF* OUT. NOT TODAY.
SO I DON'T WANT TO HEAR ANY EXCUSES AFTER I BEAT YOU, 'KAY?
SNAP
......
ALL RIGHT, *BONEHEAD*, CLEAN OUT YOUR EARS AND LISTEN TO ME *FOR ONCE!*
ABOUT THESE GLASSES...

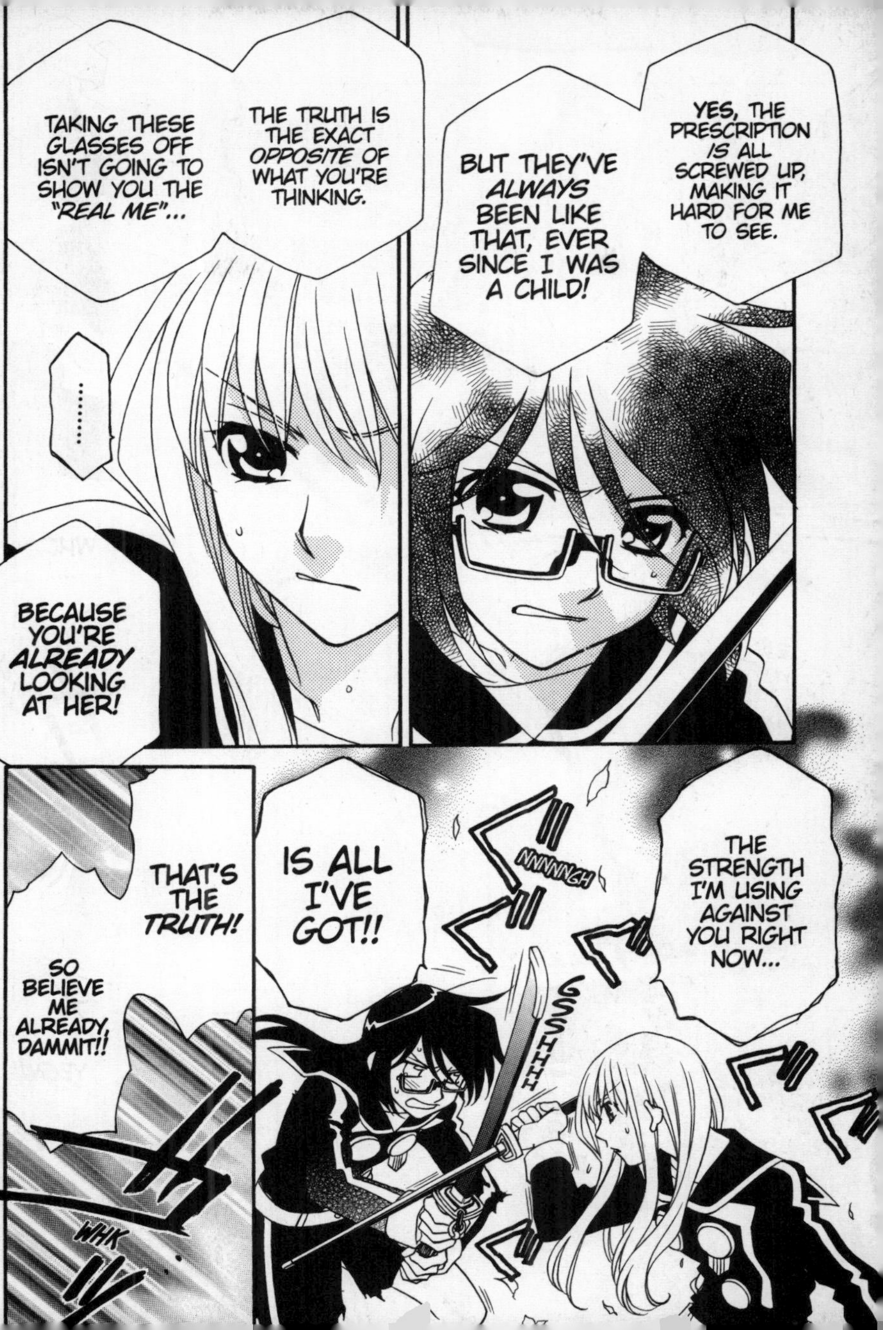
YES, THE PRESCRIPTION *IS* ALL SCREWED UP, MAKING IT HARD FOR ME TO SEE.
BUT THEY'VE *ALWAYS* BEEN LIKE THAT, EVER SINCE I WAS A CHILD!
THE TRUTH IS THE EXACT *OPPOSITE* OF WHAT YOU'RE THINKING.
TAKING THESE GLASSES OFF ISN'T GOING TO SHOW YOU THE *"REAL ME"*...
......
BECAUSE YOU'RE *ALREADY* LOOKING AT HER!
THE STRENGTH I'M USING AGAINST YOU RIGHT NOW...
NNNNNGH
IS ALL I'VE GOT!!
GSSHHHH
THAT'S THE *TRUTH*!
SO BELIEVE ME ALREADY, DAMMIT!!
WHK

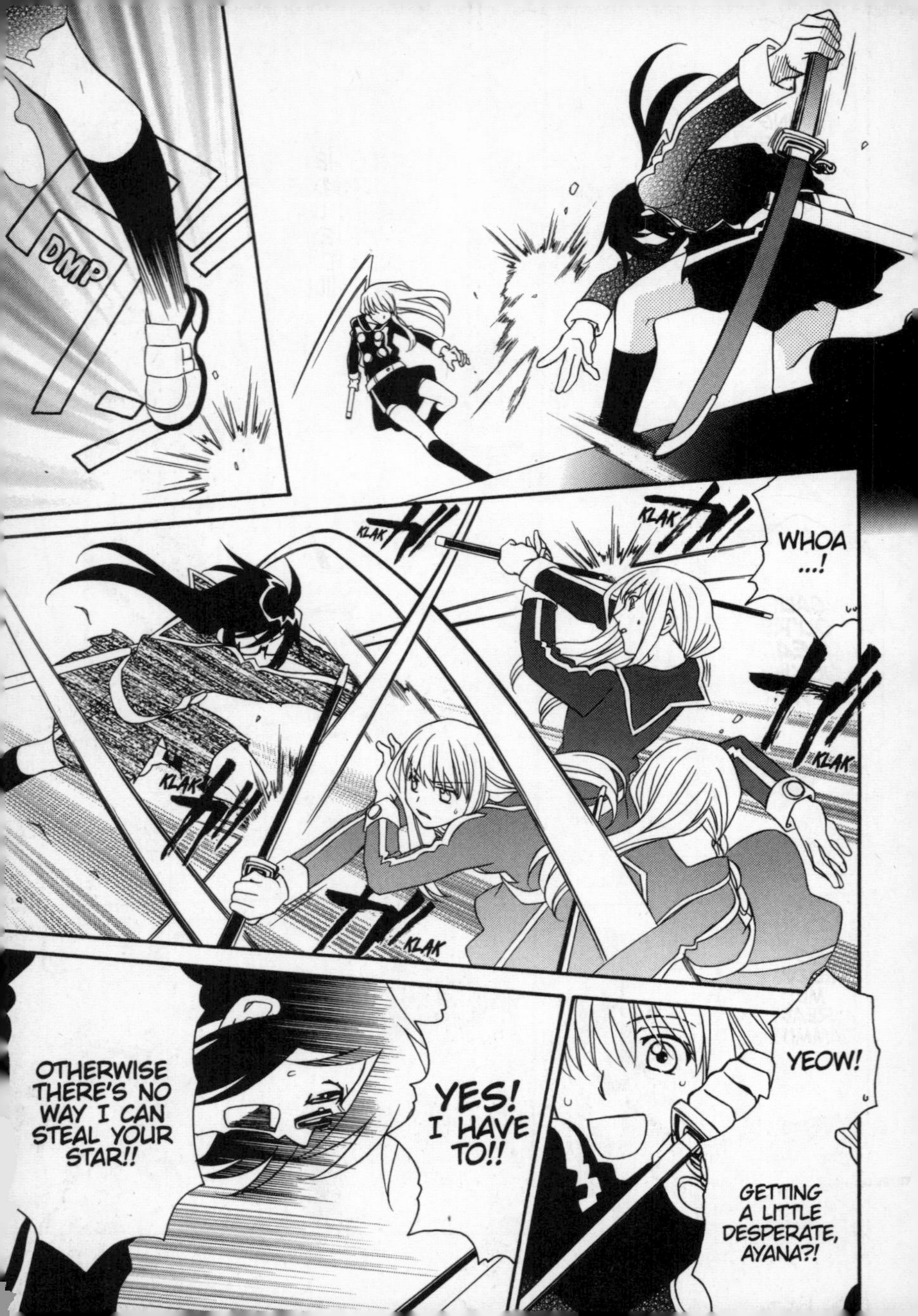
DMP
WHOA ...!
KLAK
KLAK
KLAK
KLAK
KLAK
YEOW!
GETTING A LITTLE DESPERATE, AYANA?!
YES! I HAVE TO!!
OTHERWISE THERE'S NO WAY I CAN STEAL YOUR STAR!!

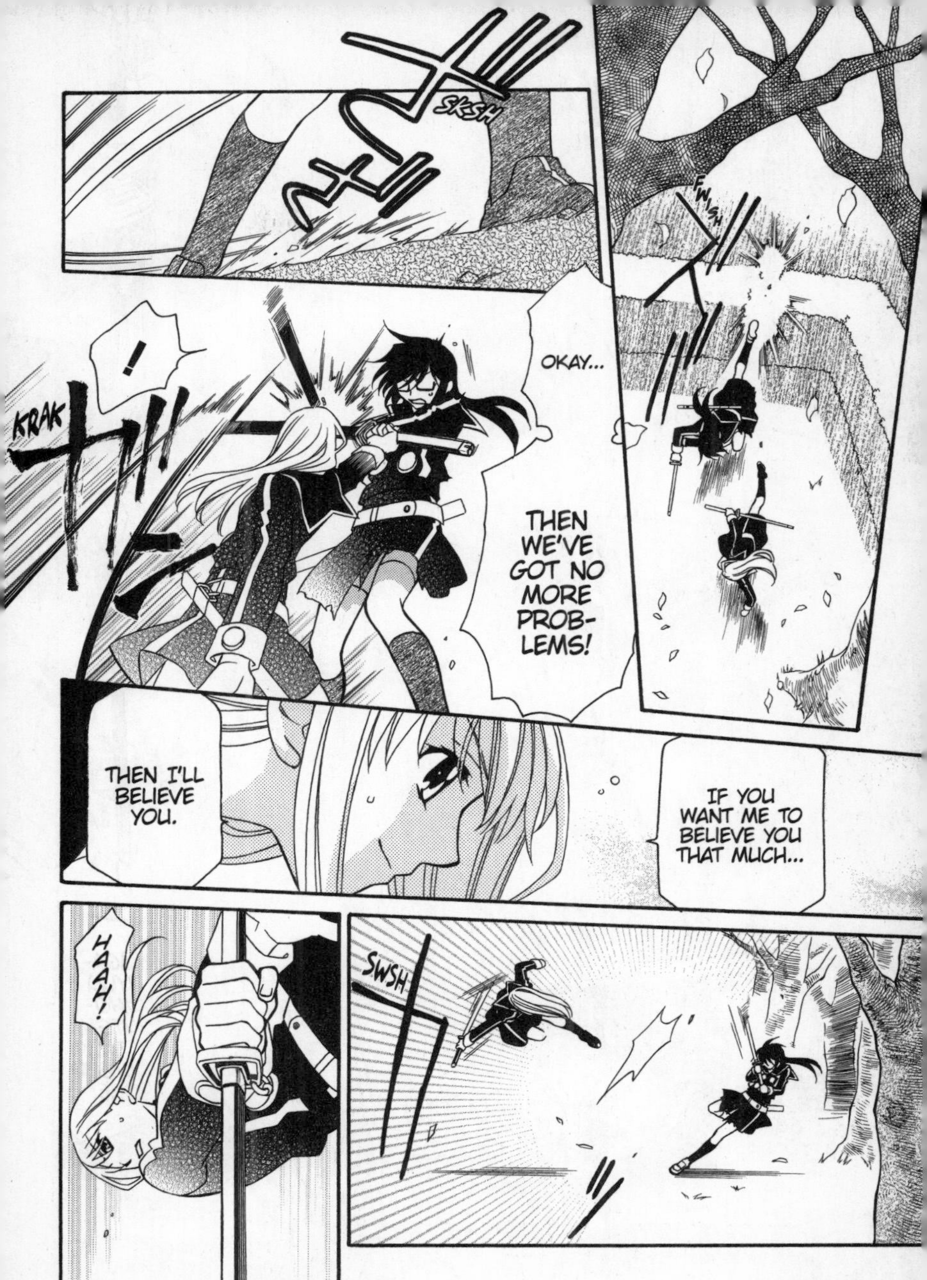
FWISH
SKSH
OKAY...
THEN WE'VE GOT NO MORE PROB-LEMS!
!
KRAK
IF YOU WANT ME TO BELIEVE YOU THAT MUCH...
THEN I'LL BELIEVE YOU.
SWSH
HAAH!

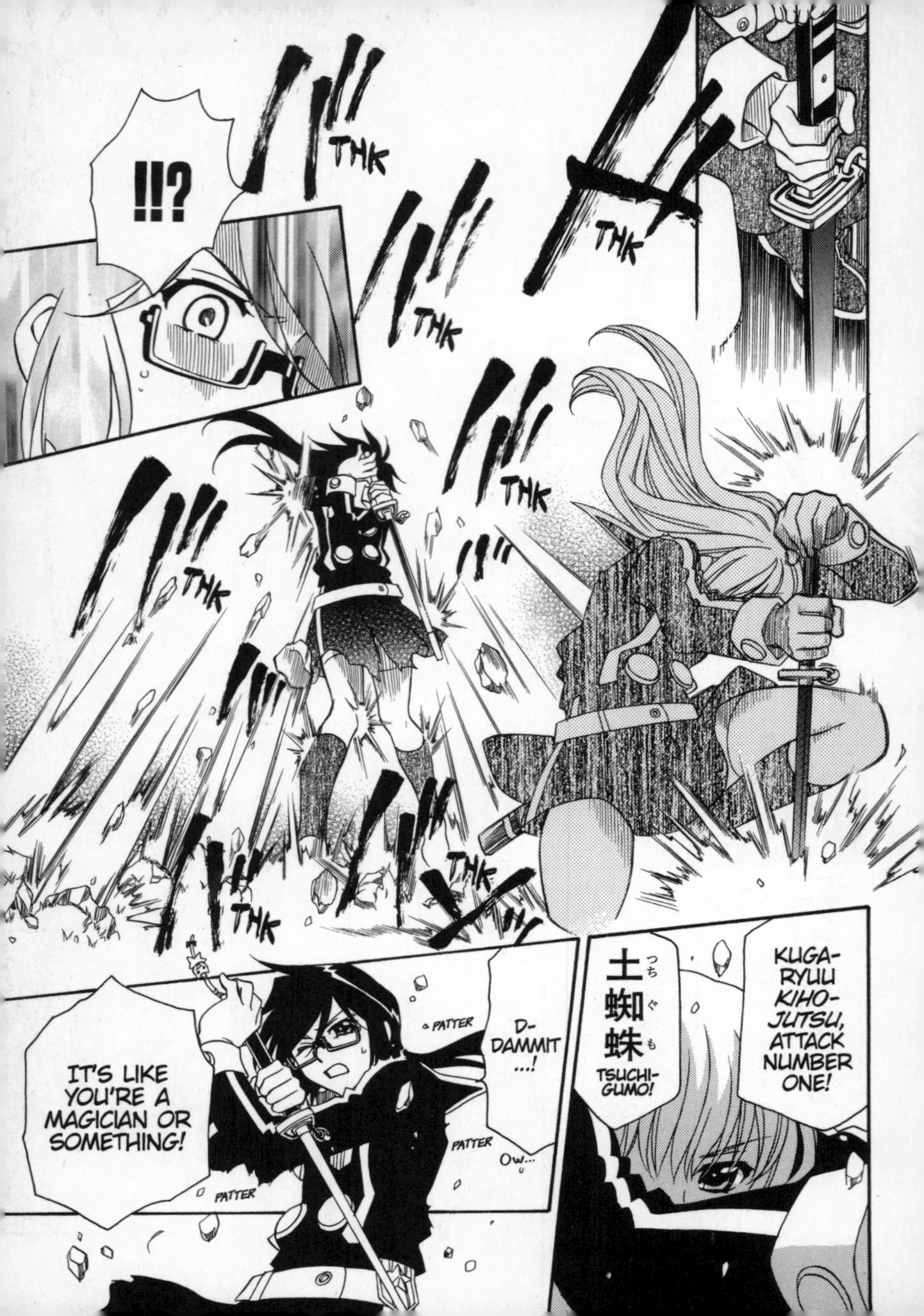
THK
THK
THK
THK
THK
!!?
THK
THK
THK
KUGA-RYUU KIHO-JUTSU, ATTACK NUMBER ONE!
土蜘蛛
つちぐも
TSUCHIGUMO!
PATTER
D-DAMMIT ...!
PATTER
OW...
PATTER
IT'S LIKE YOU'RE A MAGICIAN OR SOMETHING!

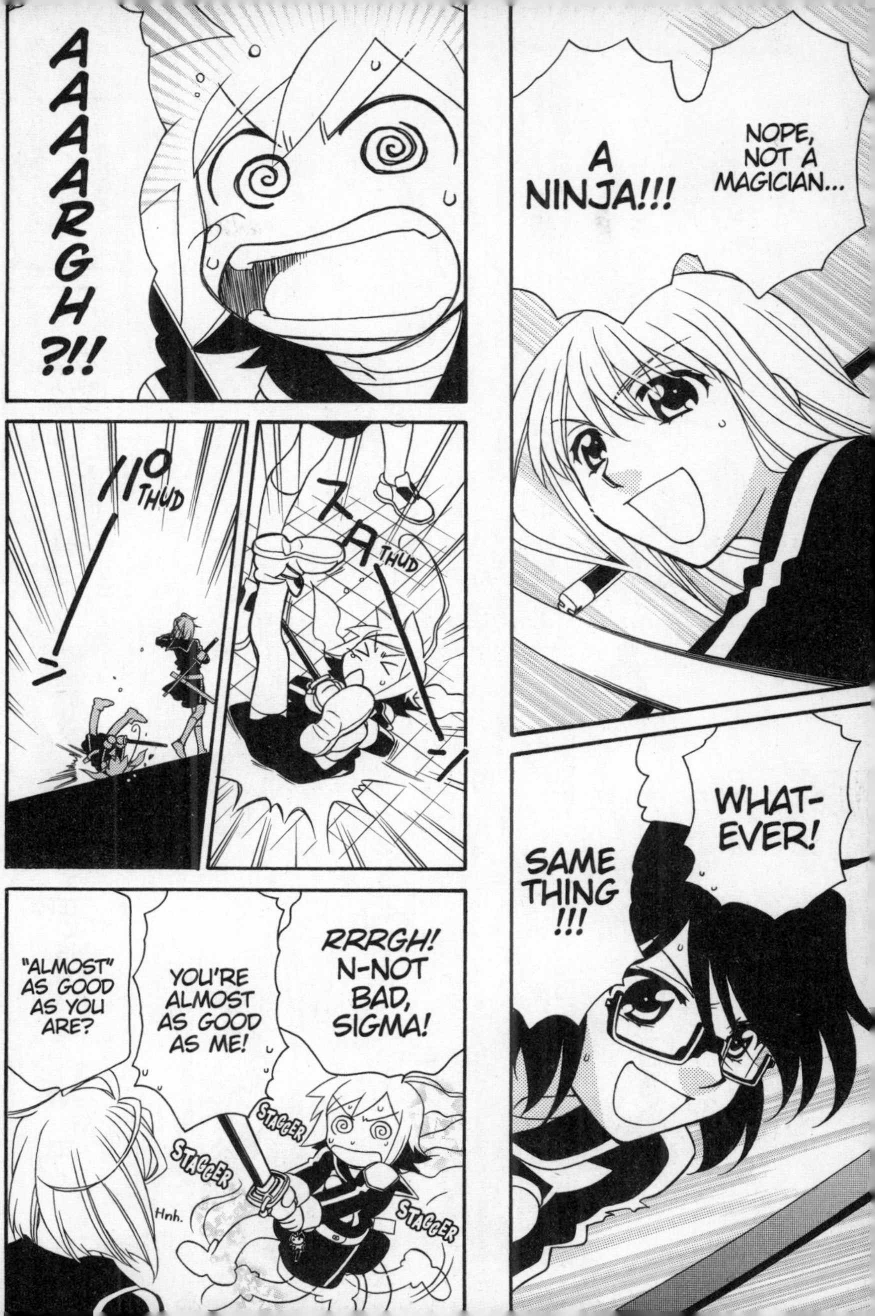
NOPE, NOT A MAGICIAN...
A NINJA!!!
WHAT-EVER!
SAME THING!!!
AAAARGH?!!
THUD
THUD
RRRGH! N-NOT BAD, SIGMA!
YOU'RE ALMOST AS GOOD AS ME!
"ALMOST" AS GOOD AS YOU ARE?
STAGGER
STAGGER
STAGGER
Hnh.

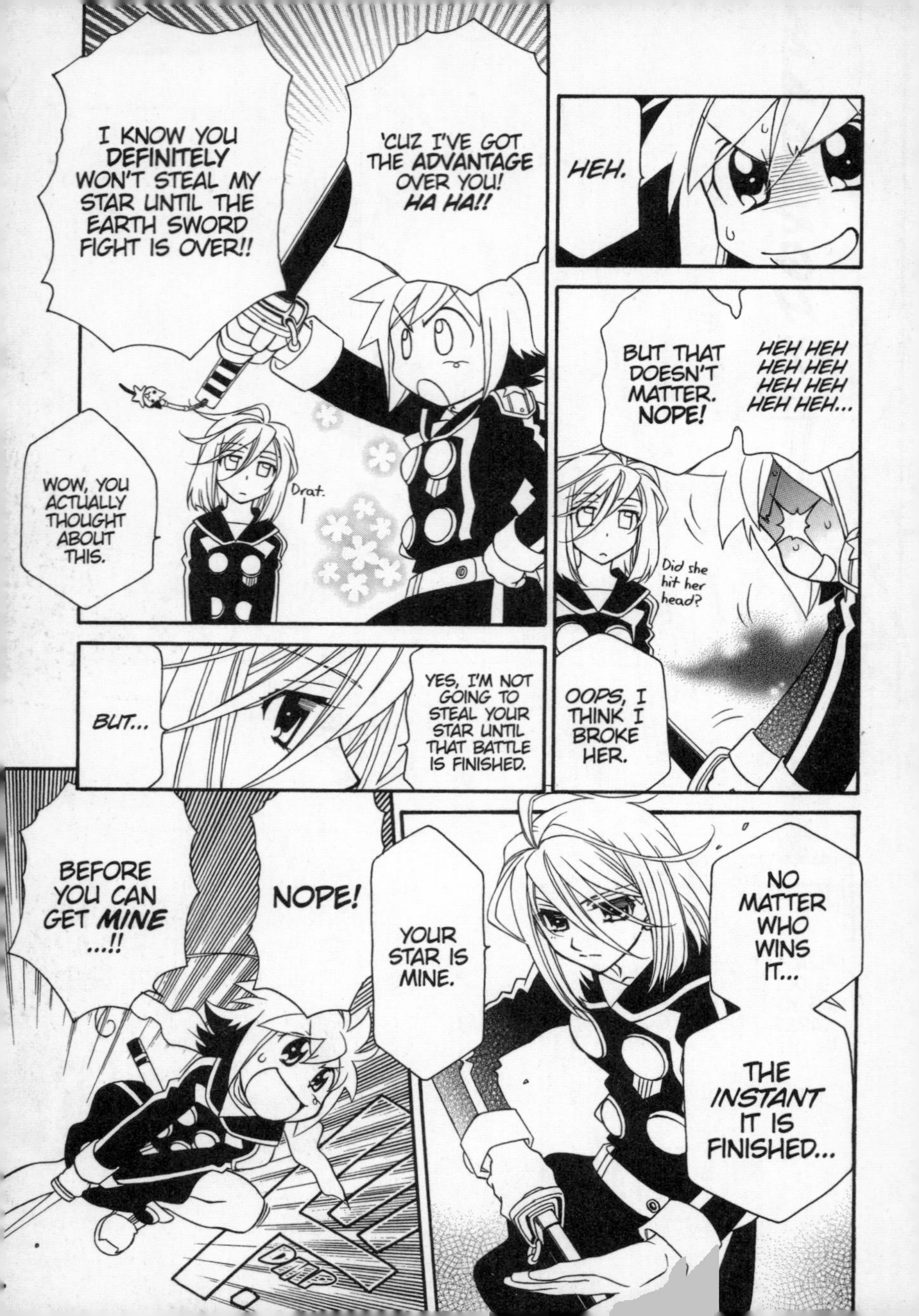
I KNOW YOU DEFINITELY WON'T STEAL MY STAR UNTIL THE EARTH SWORD FIGHT IS OVER!!
'CUZ I'VE GOT THE ADVANTAGE OVER YOU! HA HA!!
WOW, YOU ACTUALLY THOUGHT ABOUT THIS.
Drat.
HEH.
BUT THAT DOESN'T MATTER. NOPE!
HEH HEH HEH HEH HEH HEH HEH HEH...
Did she hit her head?
OOPS, I THINK I BROKE HER.
YES, I'M NOT GOING TO STEAL YOUR STAR UNTIL THAT BATTLE IS FINISHED.
BUT...
NO MATTER WHO WINS IT...
THE INSTANT IT IS FINISHED...
YOUR STAR IS MINE.
NOPE!
BEFORE YOU CAN GET MINE ...!!

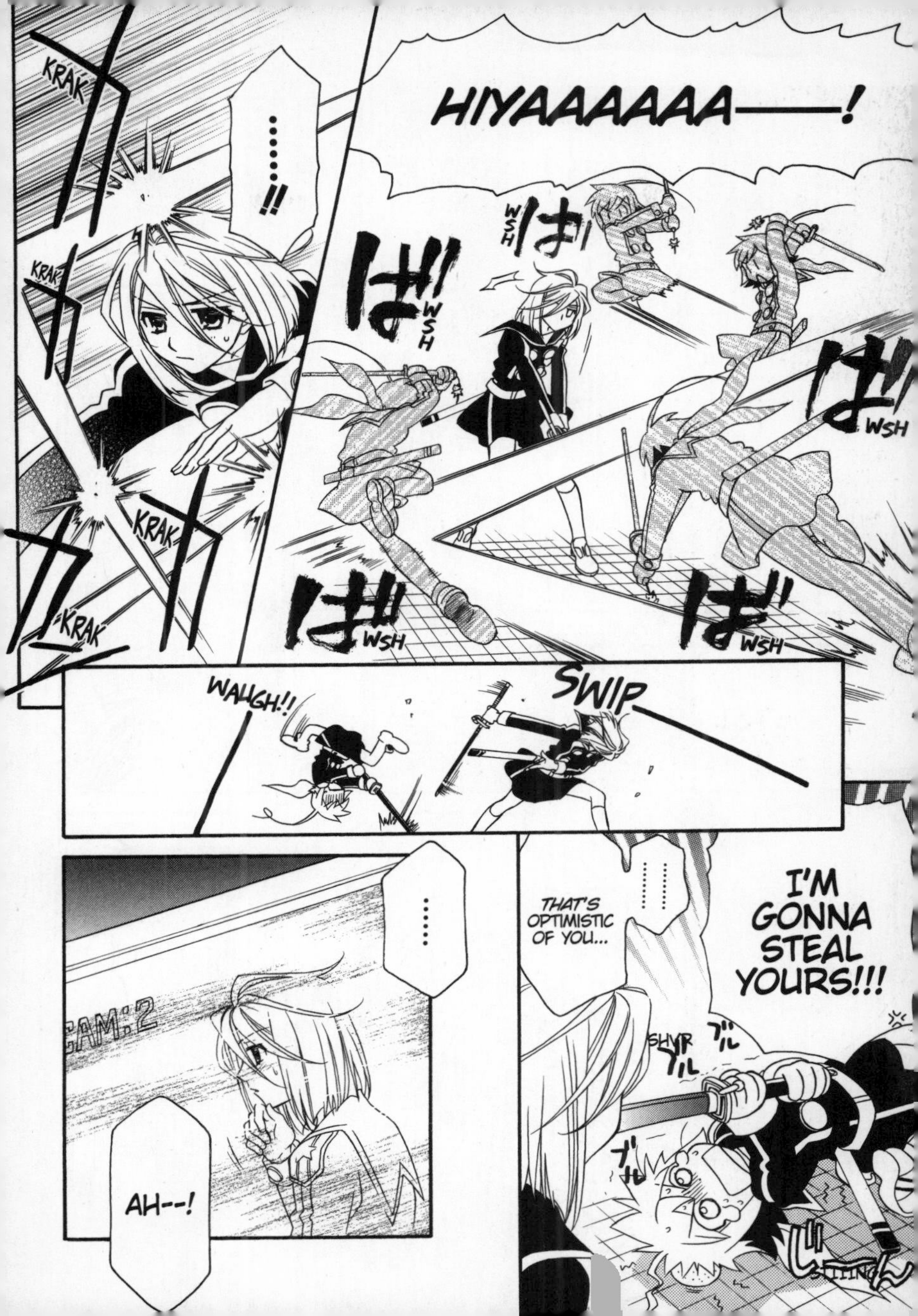
HIYAAAAAAA——!
WSH
WSH
WSH
WSH
WSH
KRAK
KRAK
KRAK
KRAK
......!!
SWIP
WAUGH!!
I'M GONNA STEAL YOURS!!!
......
THAT'S OPTIMISTIC OF YOU...
SHVR
STIIING
......
CAM: 2
AH--!

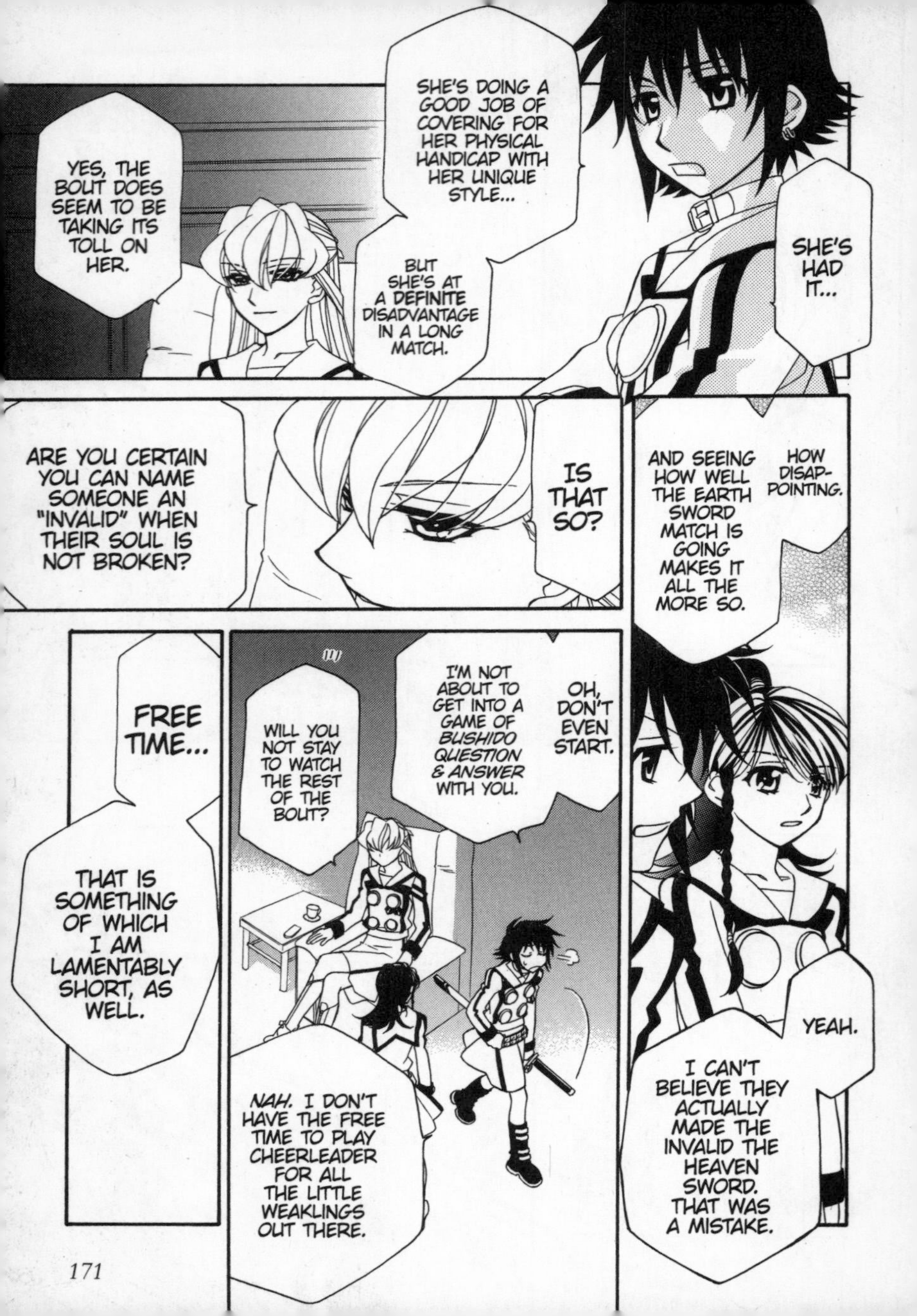
SHE'S HAD IT...
SHE'S DOING A GOOD JOB OF COVERING FOR HER PHYSICAL HANDICAP WITH HER UNIQUE STYLE...
BUT SHE'S AT A DEFINITE DISADVANTAGE IN A LONG MATCH.
YES, THE BOUT DOES SEEM TO BE TAKING ITS TOLL ON HER.
HOW DISAPPOINTING.
AND SEEING HOW WELL THE EARTH SWORD MATCH IS GOING MAKES IT ALL THE MORE SO.
YEAH.
I CAN'T BELIEVE THEY ACTUALLY MADE THE INVALID THE HEAVEN SWORD. THAT WAS A MISTAKE.
IS THAT SO?
ARE YOU CERTAIN YOU CAN NAME SOMEONE AN "INVALID" WHEN THEIR SOUL IS NOT BROKEN?
OH, DON'T EVEN START.
I'M NOT ABOUT TO GET INTO A GAME OF *BUSHIDO* QUESTION & ANSWER WITH YOU.
WILL YOU NOT STAY TO WATCH THE REST OF THE BOUT?
NAH. I DON'T HAVE THE FREE TIME TO PLAY CHEERLEADER FOR ALL THE LITTLE WEAKLINGS OUT THERE.
FREE TIME...
THAT IS SOMETHING OF WHICH I AM LAMENTABLY SHORT, AS WELL.

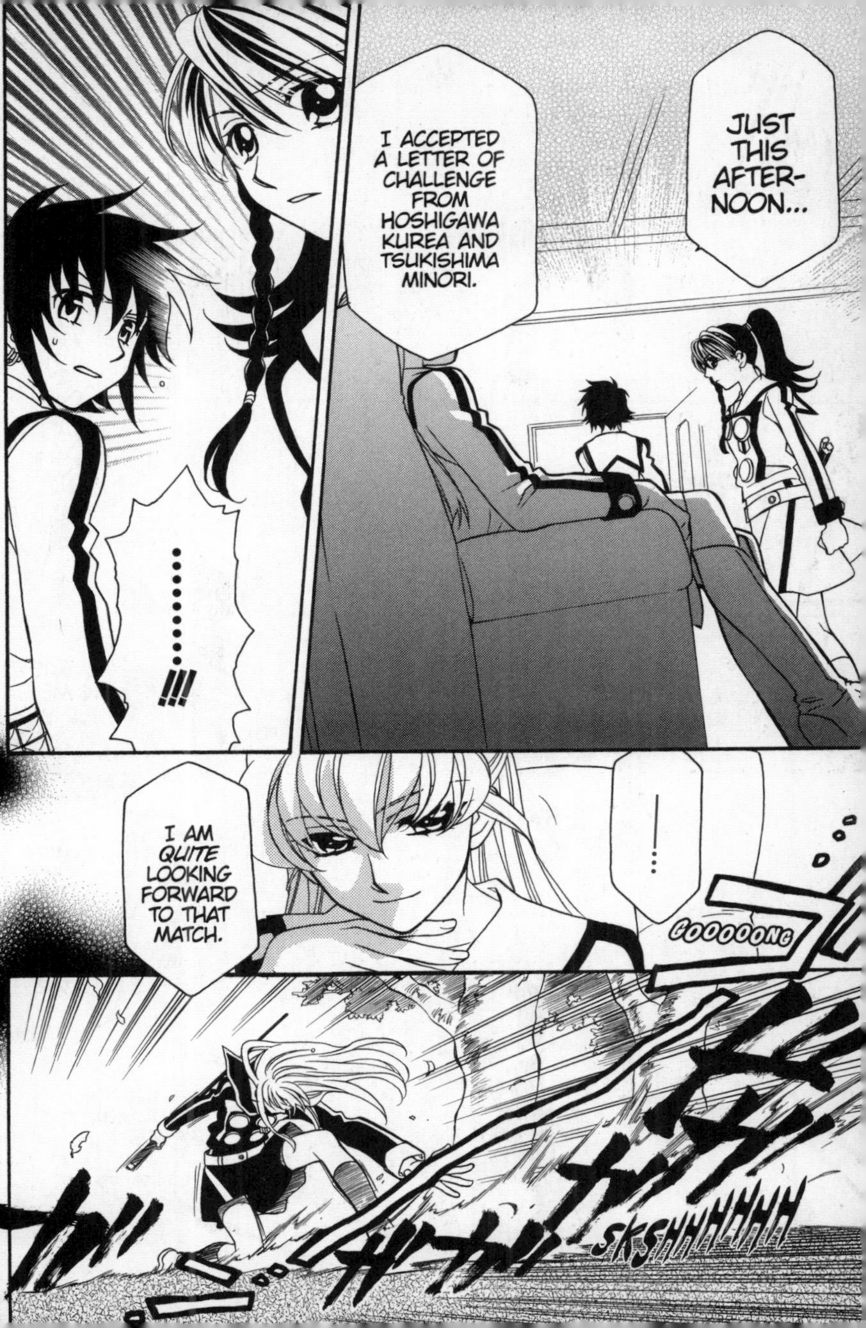
JUST THIS AFTER-NOON...
I ACCEPTED A LETTER OF CHALLENGE FROM HOSHIGAWA KUREA AND TSUKISHIMA MINORI.
........!!!
......
I AM QUITE LOOKING FORWARD TO THAT MATCH.
GOOOOONG
SKSHHHHHH

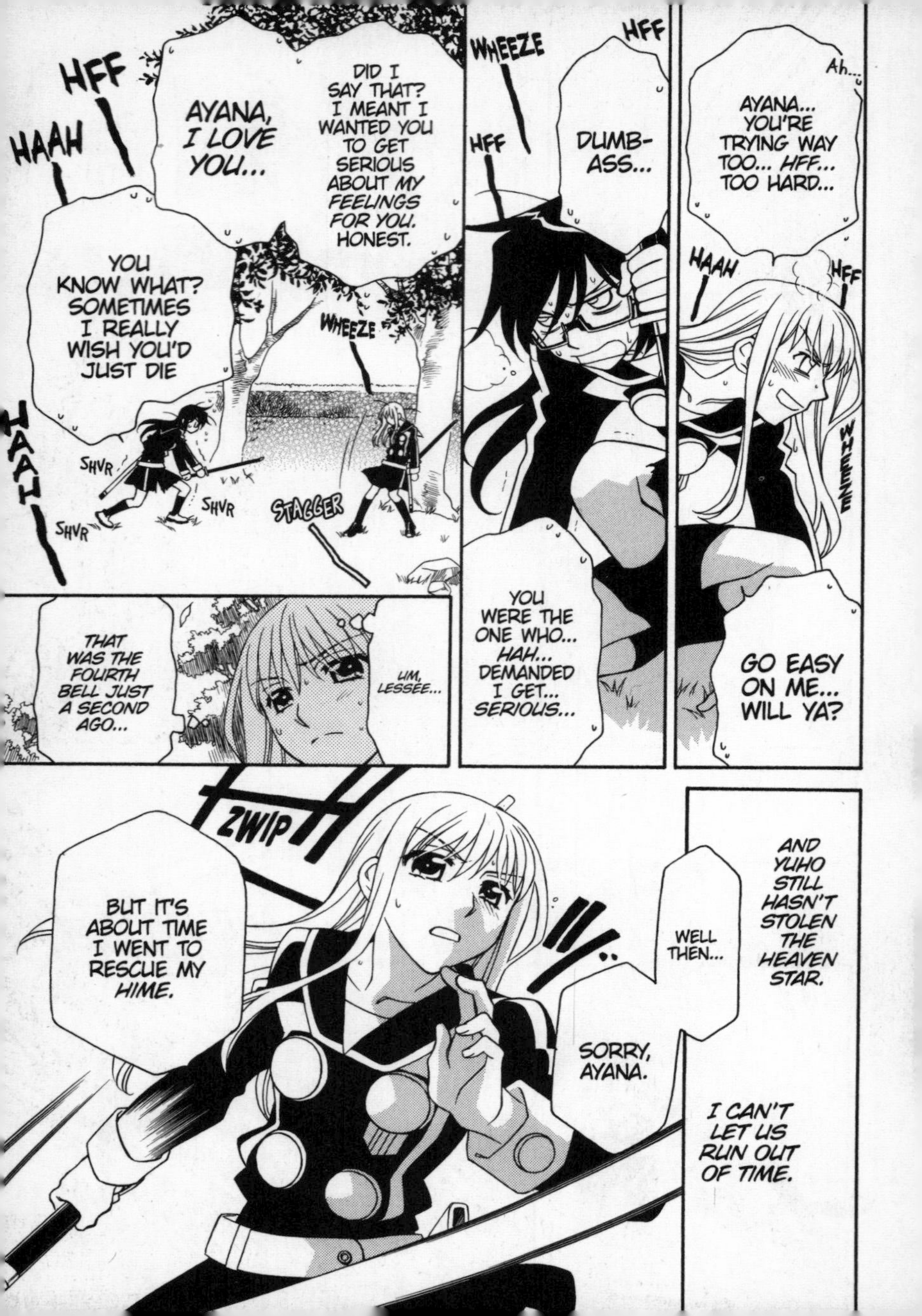
Ah...
AYANA... YOU'RE TRYING WAY TOO... HFF... TOO HARD...
HAAH
HFF
WHEEZE
GO EASY ON ME... WILL YA?
WHEEZE
HFF
HFF
DUMB-ASS...
YOU WERE THE ONE WHO... HAH... DEMANDED I GET... SERIOUS...
DID I SAY THAT? I MEANT I WANTED YOU TO GET SERIOUS ABOUT MY FEELINGS FOR YOU. HONEST.
AYANA, I LOVE YOU...
HFF
HAAH
YOU KNOW WHAT? SOMETIMES I REALLY WISH YOU'D JUST DIE
WHEEZE
HAAH
SHVR
SHVR
SHVR
STAGGER
UM, LESSEE...
THAT WAS THE FOURTH BELL JUST A SECOND AGO...
AND YUHO STILL HASN'T STOLEN THE HEAVEN STAR.
I CAN'T LET US RUN OUT OF TIME.
ZWIP
WELL THEN...
SORRY, AYANA.
BUT IT'S ABOUT TIME I WENT TO RESCUE MY HIME.

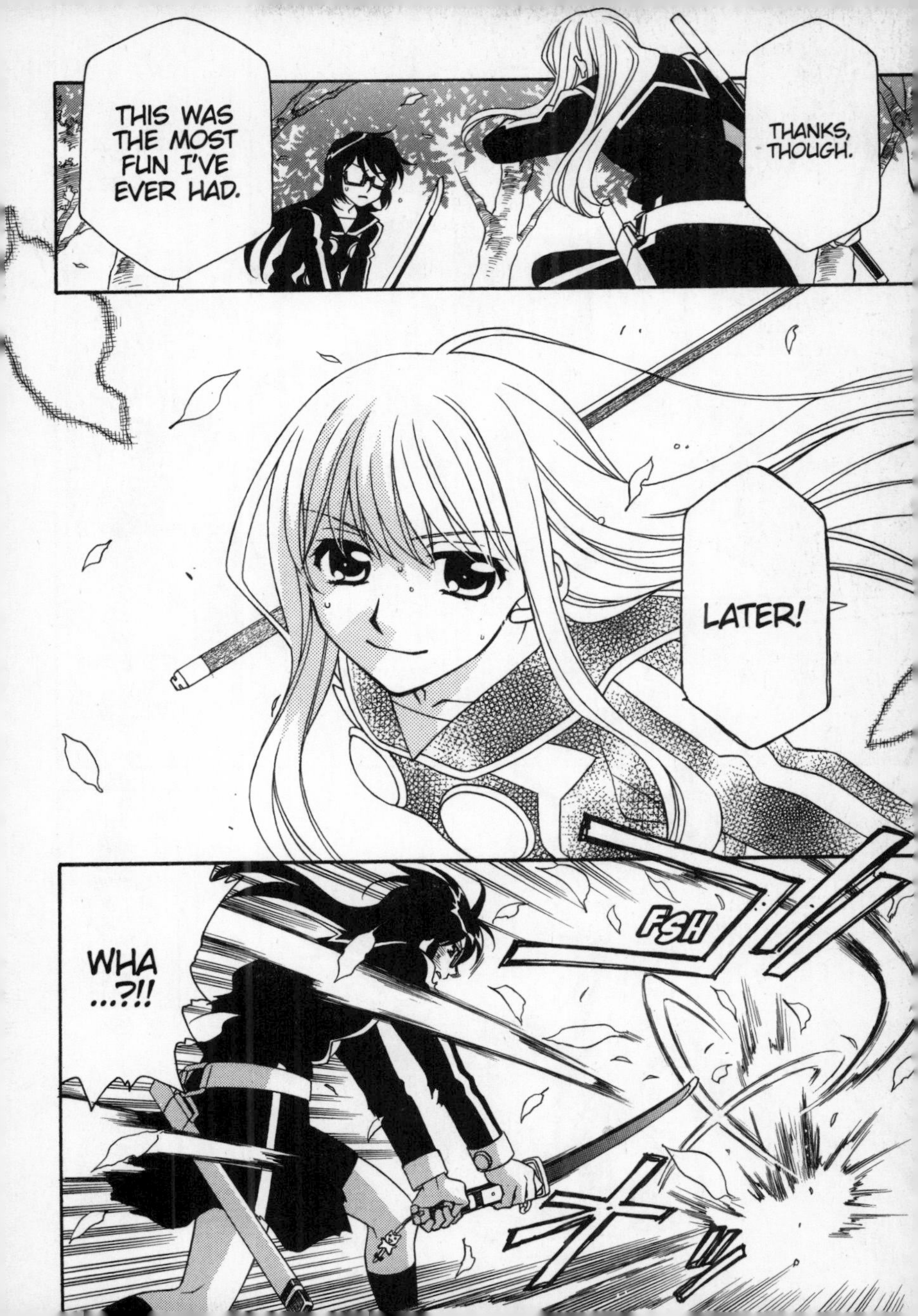
THANKS, THOUGH.
THIS WAS THE MOST FUN I'VE EVER HAD.
LATER!
FSH
WHA ...?!!

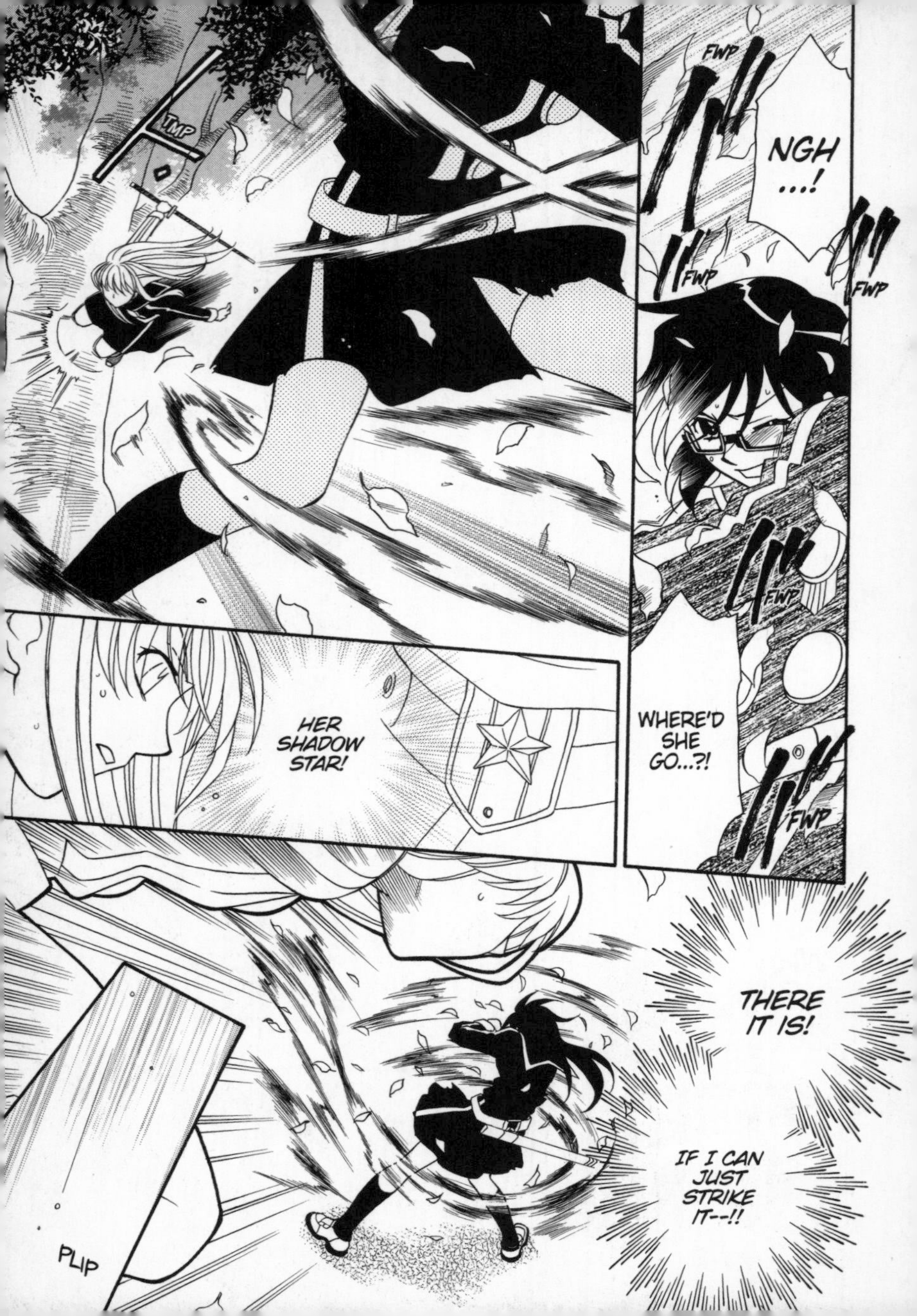
FWP
NGH ...!
FWP
FWP
FWP
WHERE'D SHE GO...?!
FWP
TMP
HER SHADOW STAR!
THERE IT IS!
IF I CAN JUST STRIKE IT--!!
PLIP

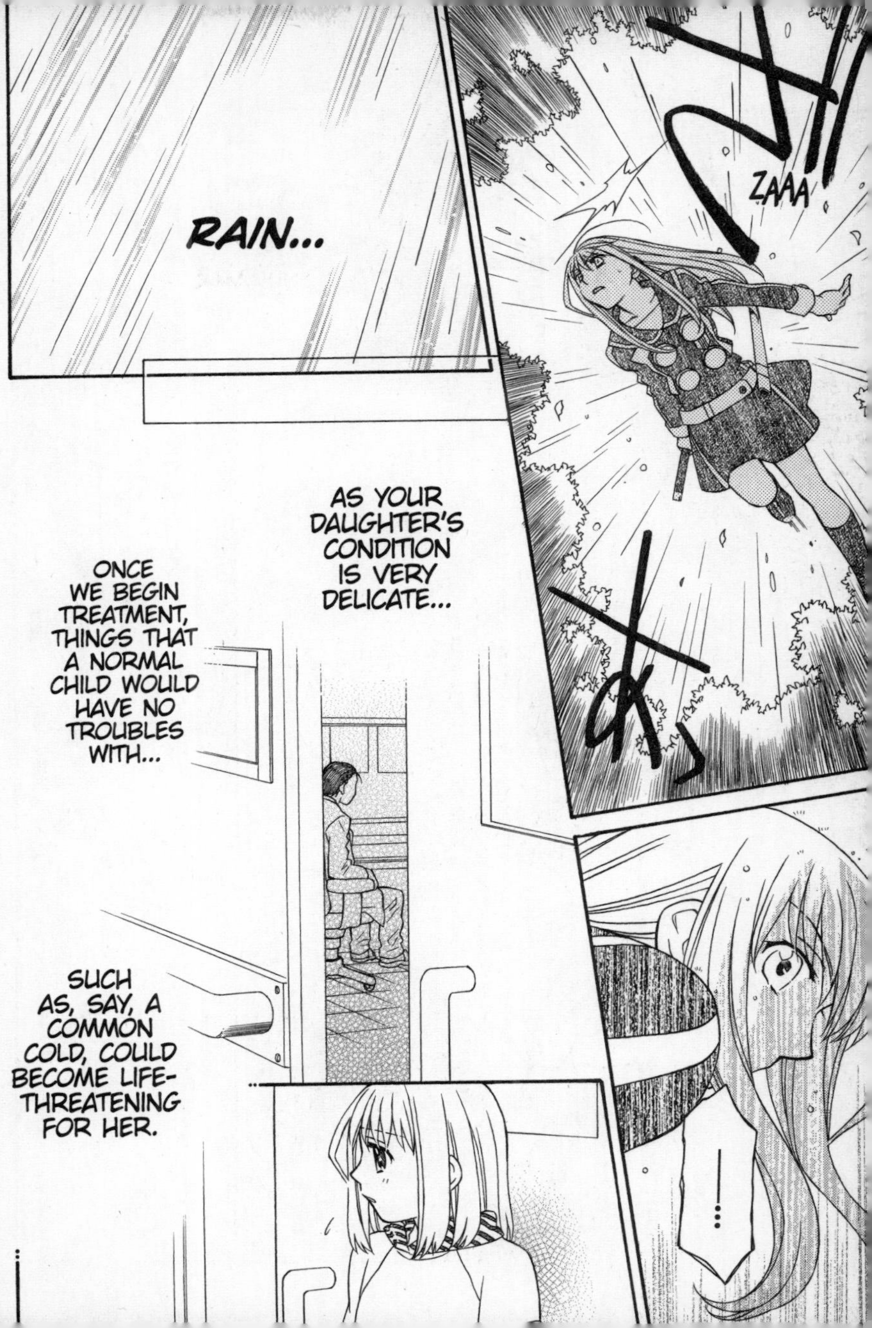
ZAAA
RAIN...
...
AS YOUR DAUGHTER'S CONDITION IS VERY DELICATE...
ONCE WE BEGIN TREATMENT, THINGS THAT A NORMAL CHILD WOULD HAVE NO TROUBLES WITH...
SUCH AS, SAY, A COMMON COLD, COULD BECOME LIFE-THREATENING FOR HER.
...

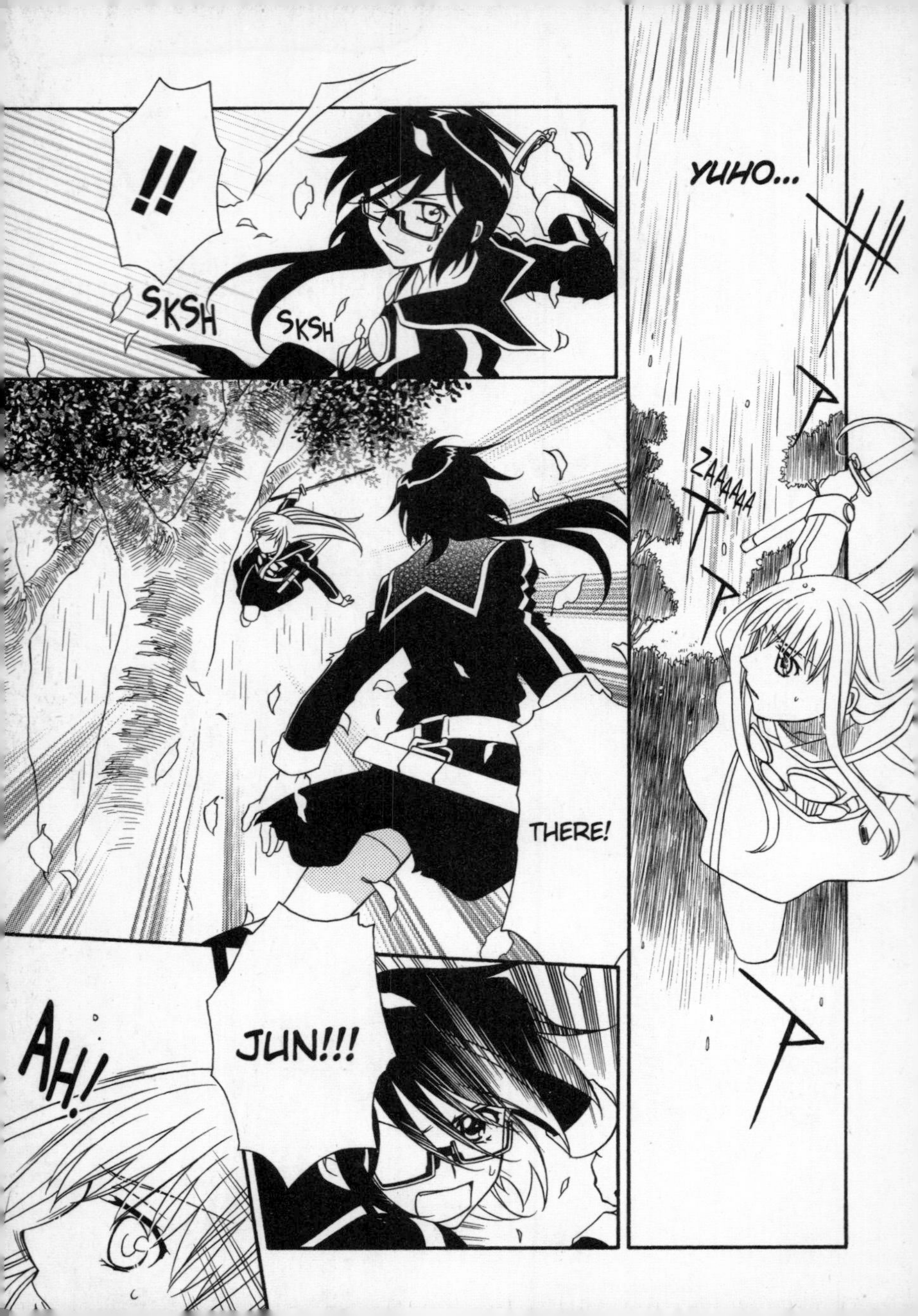
YUHO...
ZAAAAAA
!!
SKSH
SKSH
THERE!
JUN!!!
AH!

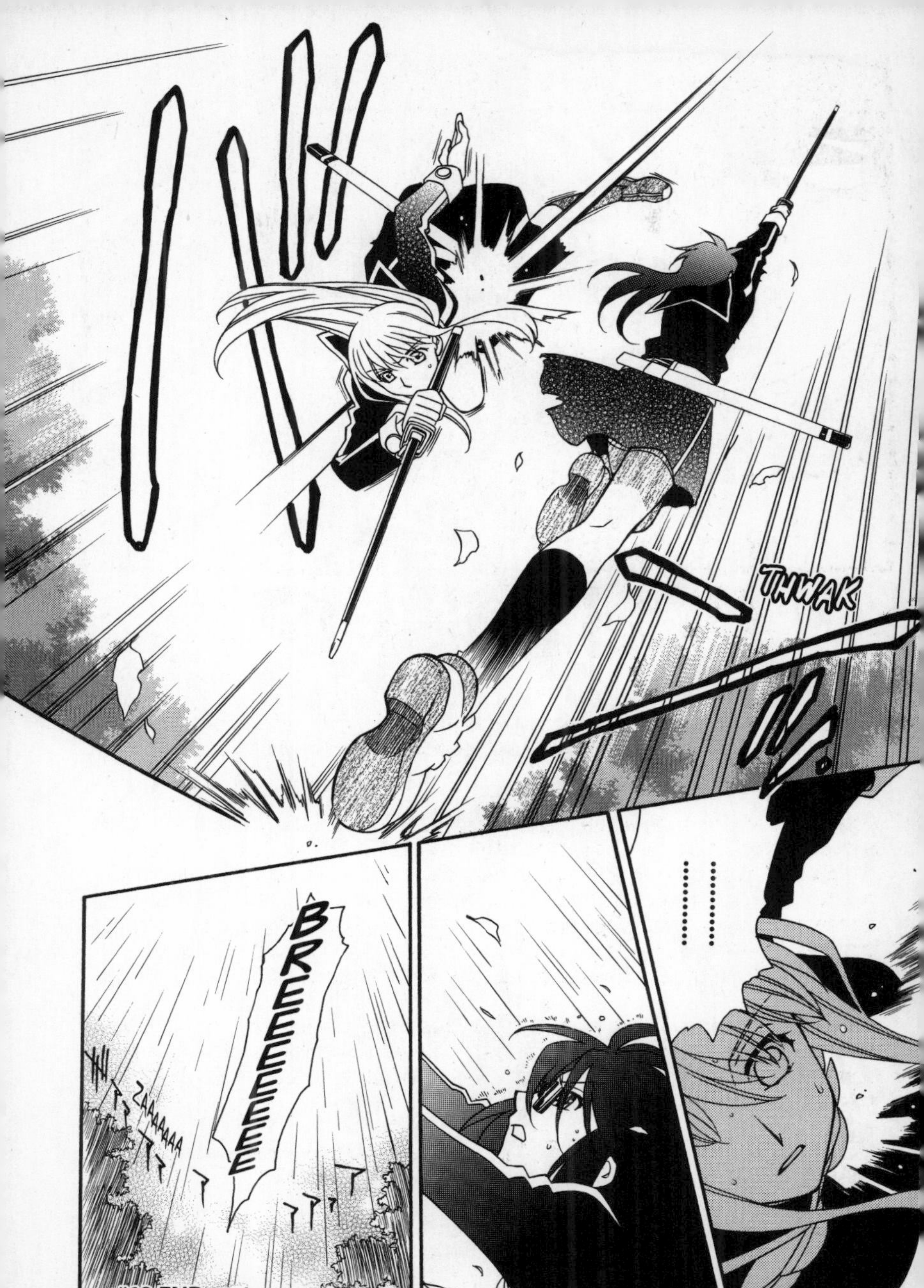
THWAK
......
......
BREEEEEEEEE
ZAAAAAAA

#19 END To be continued...!!

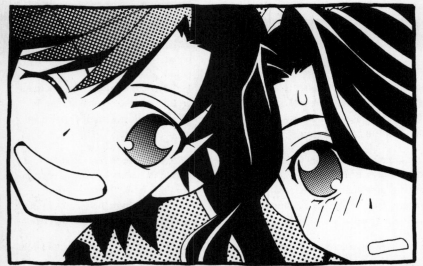

MAYBE I'LL DO AGAKURA/TAKAMI NEXT TIME...

POSTSCRIPT

VOLUME 3!! YESSS!! CONGRATS ME!! THANK YOU!! WOOHOO! THIS IS THE FIRST TIME ONE OF MY VOLUMES WILL EVER COME WITH THE NUMBER '3' ON ITS SPINE! (EXCITED)

AHEM, WELL, ANYWAYS, ON WITH WHAT IS RAPIDLY BECOMING MY REGULARLY SCHEDULED APOLOGY CORNER. ABOUT THE CHARACTER PROFILE PAGES IN [THE JAPANESE EDITION OF] VOLUME TWO, YOU MAY NOTICE THAT THE AGES ARE OFF. WAAAY OFF. SORRY... THE ERROR WAS SPOTTED FAIRLY QUICKLY, BUT THE MANUSCRIPT HAD ALREADY GONE OFF TO PRINT, SO THERE WASN'T ANYTHING WE COULD DO... FURTHER PRINTINGS (IF THERE ARE ANY) AND LATER VOLUMES WILL BE KINDA DIFFERENT, SO I DECIDED TO STOP NOTING AGES*... IT'D GET KINDA CONFUSING IF I DIDN'T, REALLY...

ANYWAYS, I HUMBLY BEG YOUR PARDON FOR MY MANY ERRORS. NOW, ON TO THE NEXT VOLUME! FROM HERE ON OUT, IT'S ALL FIRSTS FOR ME!! THE SERIOUS STORYLINE WILL CONTINUE FOR A BIT YET, BUT PLEASE FIND IT IN YOUR HEART TO CONTINUE LOVING THIS SERIES! IT'LL GET BETTER SOON, I PROMISE!

❀ AS ALWAYS, TO MY PERFECT ASSISTANT & SENSE-SMACKER ⟶ MAKI SEREN **THANK YOU!!** EVERYONE, UNTIL WE MEET NEXT VOLUME, BE WELL!

Hayashiya
LOVE FROM UNDER THE CEILING⟶ 林家 2005. 6

*NOTE: TOR/SEVEN SEAS' RELEASE OF HAYATE X BLADE IS BASED ON LATER PRINTINGS OF THE SERIES WHERE ALL THE AGES WERE REMOVED FROM THE CHARACTER PROFILE PAGES. -EDITOR

HONORIFICS GUIDE

To ensure that all character relationships appear as they were originally intended, all character names have been kept in their original Japanese name order with family name first and given name second. For copyright reasons, creator names appear in standard English name order.

In addition to preserving the original Japanese name order, Seven Seas is committed to ensuring that honorifics—polite speech that indicates a person's status or relationship towards another individual—are retained within this book. Politeness is an integral facet of Japanese culture and we believe that maintaining honorifics in our translations helps bring out the same character nuances as seen in the original work.

The following are some of the more common honorifics you may come across while reading this and other books:

-san – The most common of all honorifics, it is an all-purpose suffix that can be used in any situation where politeness is expected. Generally seen as the equivalent to Mr., Miss, Ms., Mrs., etc.

-sama – This suffix is one level higher than "-san" and is used to confer great respect upon an individual.

-kun – This suffix is commonly used at the end of boys' names to express either familiarity or endearment. It can also be used when addressing someone younger than oneself or of a lower status.

-chan – Another common honorific. This suffix is mainly used to express endearment towards girls, but can also be used when referring to little boys or even pets. Couples are also known to use the term amongst each other to convey a sense of cuteness and intimacy.

Sempai – This title is used towards one's senior or "superior" in a particular group or organization. "Sempai" is most often used in a school setting, where underclassmen refer to upperclassmen as "sempai," though it is also commonly said by employees when addressing fellow employees who hold seniority in the workplace.

Sensei – Literally meaning "one who has come before," this title is used for teachers, doctors, or masters of any profession or art.

Oniisan – This title literally means "big brother." First and foremost, it is used by younger siblings towards older male siblings. It can be used by itself or attached to a person's name as a suffix (niisan). It is often used by a younger person toward an older person unrelated by blood, but as a sign of respect. Other forms include the informal "oniichan" and the more respectful "oniisama."

Oneesan – This title is the opposite of "oniisan" and means "big sister." Other forms include the informal "oneechan" and the more respectful "oneesama."

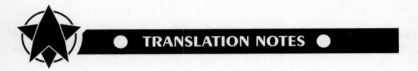

● **TRANSLATION NOTES** ●

22.2
A *"bokken"* is a wooden sword.

32.5
Hayate's actual phrase here was *"Osu,"* a term often used by thugs and blue collar workers. *"Osu,"* in this case, is used as a term of agreement. It can also be used to as a quick greeting.

43.2
In most cases when translating a foreign work, we prefer to leave measurements in their original foreign standards. However, to ensure the original intent of the author comes across when reading, we sometimes make an exception. As many Americans may not be familiar with temperatures measured in Celsius, we have chosen to use the much more familiar readings of Fahrenheit to ensure the fact that Miyamoto having a high fever comes across as it should. The temperature is 39.2°C in the original Japanese edition.

44.3
The Asakusa Samba Carnival is held in August, in Asakusa, Tokyo. Attracting about 500,000 sightseers, the event is the one of the largest of its kind in Japan, filled with dancing, music and comedy. Yes, comedy... Many of the Japanese acts incorporate comedic elements to their performances.

60.4
Jon & Ponch is the Japanese title for the American '70s TV show *CHiPs*.

67.3
"Hime" is the Japanese word for "princess."

79.5

Arale-chan is one of the characters from Akira Toriyama's *Dr. Slump* manga. Her full name is Arale Norimaki and she is a robot designed to look like a little girl. Arale-chan is famous for her excessive energy, strength and naivety.

107.1

"*Obasama*" is the polite form of "*obasan*," which means "aunt."

153.4

Jun's "Kamaitachi" attack literally translates to "cut by a whirlwind."

167.4

"*Kuga-ryuu*" is the school of ninja arts Jun learned. "*Kihou-jutsu*" is a specific technique that projects the user's ki (spirit energy) as a weapon. In the case of the Tsuchigumo, Jun blasts her ki in to the ground to make it shoot projectiles upwards towards her opponent.

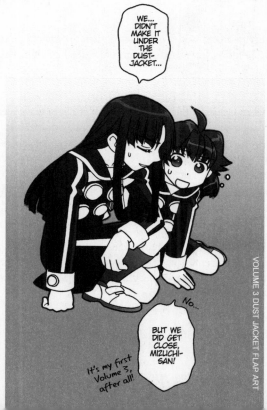

WE... DIDN'T MAKE IT UNDER THE DUST- JACKET...

No...

BUT WE DID GET CLOSE, MIZUCHI- SAN!

It's my first Volume 3, after all!

VOLUME 3 DUST JACKET FLAP ART

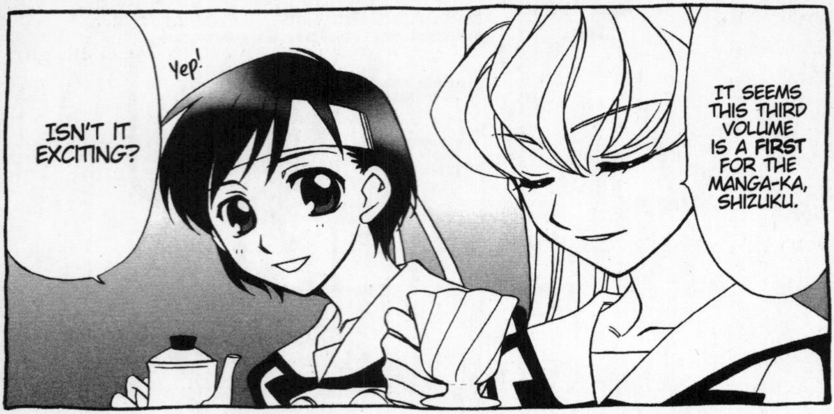
IT SEEMS THIS THIRD VOLUME IS A **FIRST** FOR THE MANGA-KA, SHIZUKU.
ISN'T IT EXCITING?
Yep!

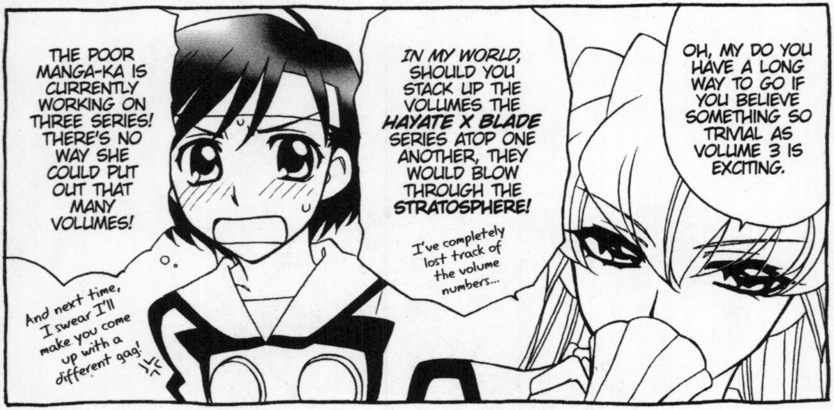
OH, MY DO YOU HAVE A LONG WAY TO GO IF YOU BELIEVE SOMETHING SO TRIVIAL AS VOLUME 3 IS EXCITING.
IN MY WORLD, SHOULD YOU STACK UP THE VOLUMES THE ***HAYATE X BLADE*** SERIES ATOP ONE ANOTHER, THEY WOULD BLOW THROUGH THE **STRATOSPHERE!**
THE POOR MANGA-KA IS CURRENTLY WORKING ON THREE SERIES! THERE'S NO WAY SHE COULD PUT OUT THAT MANY VOLUMES!
I've completely lost track of the volume numbers...
And next time, I swear I'll make you come up with a different gag!

HAYATE CROSS BLADE 3

HAYATE CROSS BLADE
SHIZURU HAYASHIYA

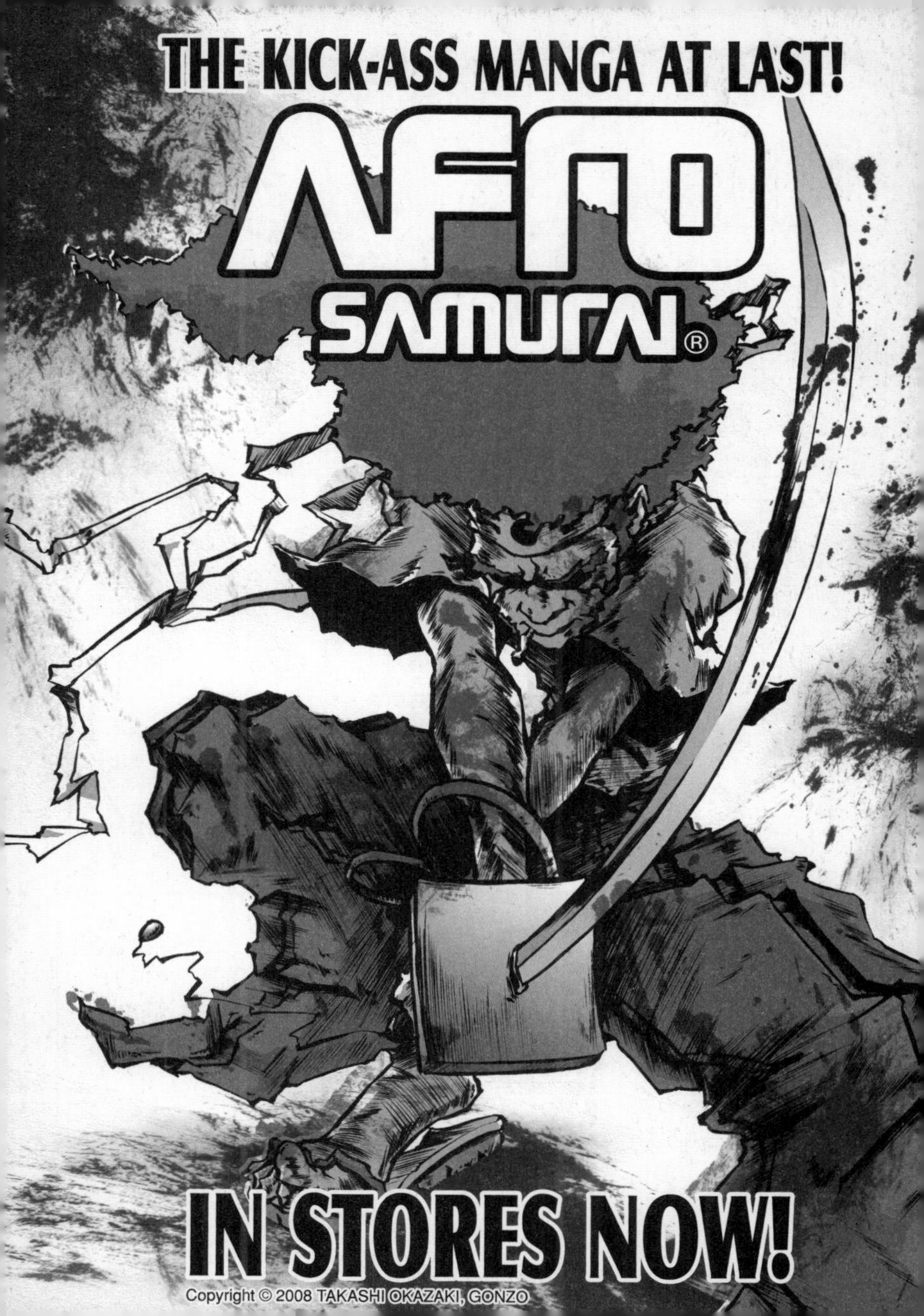

THE KICK-ASS MANGA AT LAST!
AFRO SAMURAI®
IN STORES NOW!
Copyright © 2008 TAKASHI OKAZAKI, GONZO

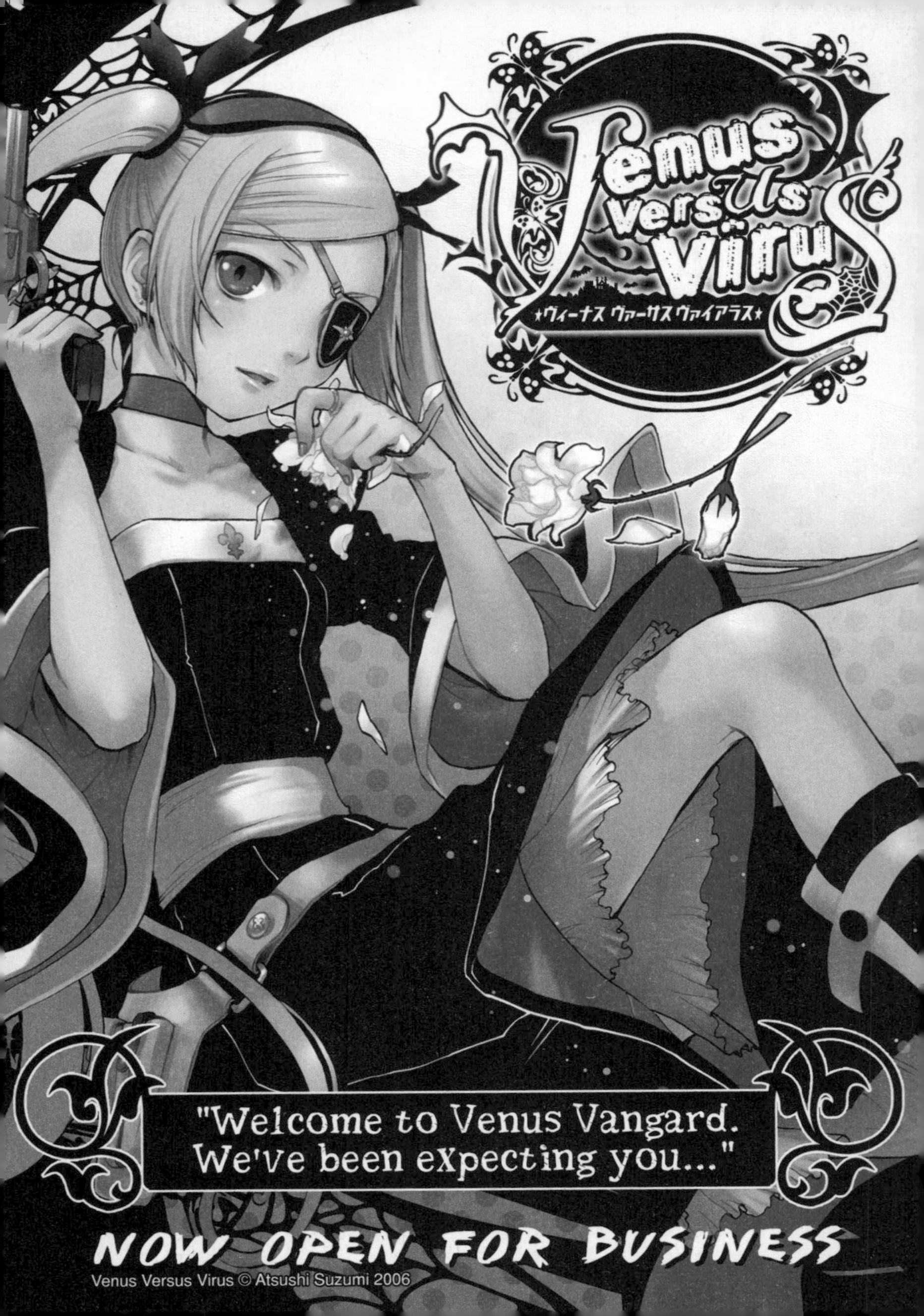
Venus Versus Virus
ヴィーナス ヴァーサス ヴァイアラス
"Welcome to Venus Vangard. We've been expecting you..."
NOW OPEN FOR BUSINESS
Venus Versus Virus © Atsushi Suzumi 2006

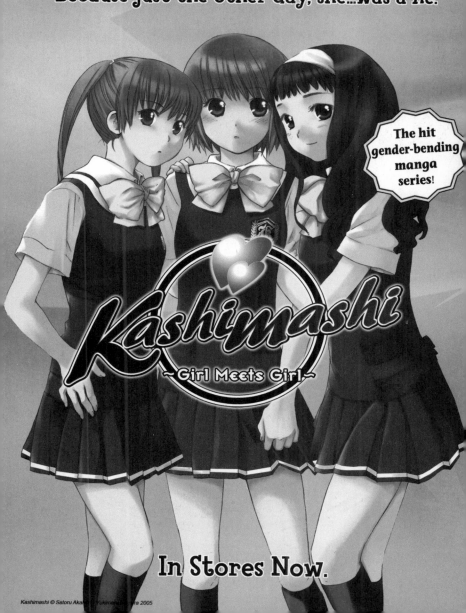

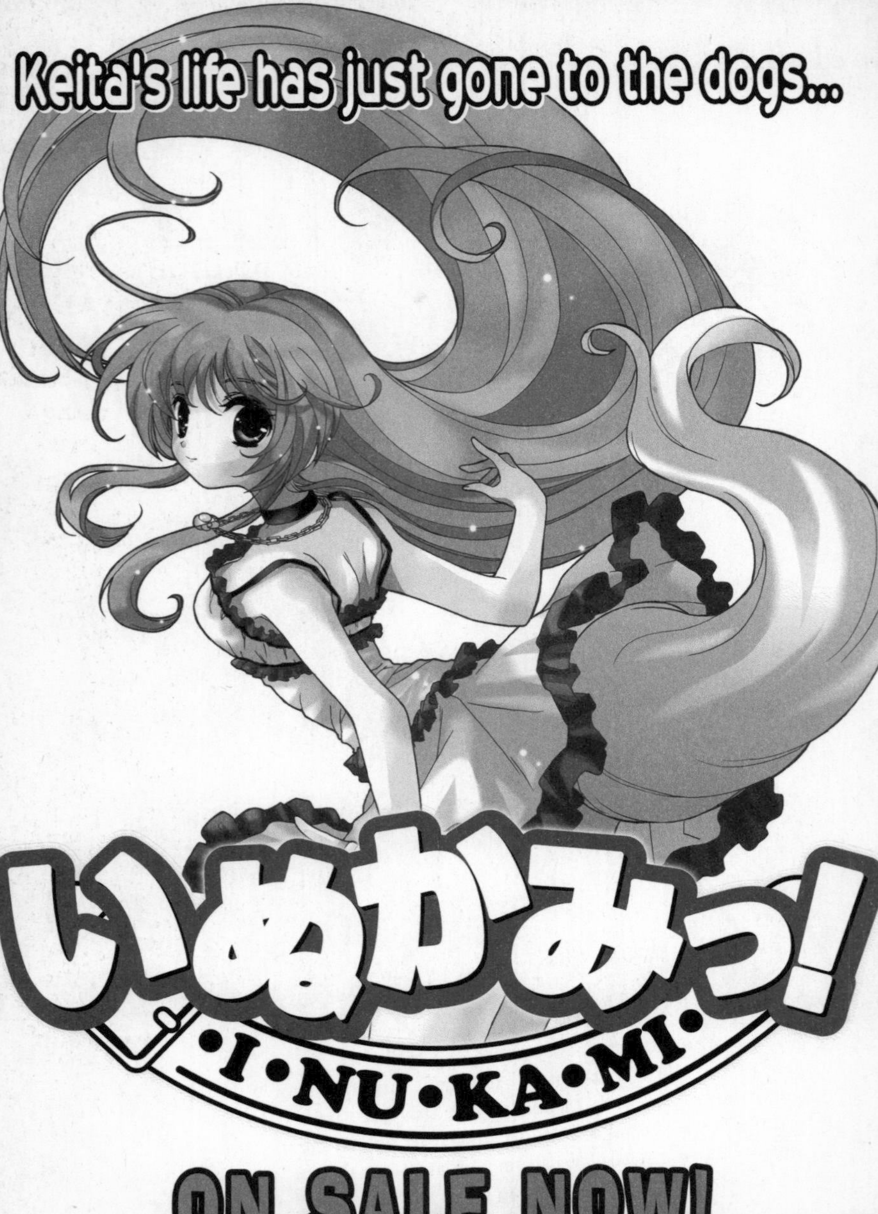
Keita's life has just gone to the dogs...
いぬかみっ!
•I•NU•KA•MI•
ON SALE NOW!

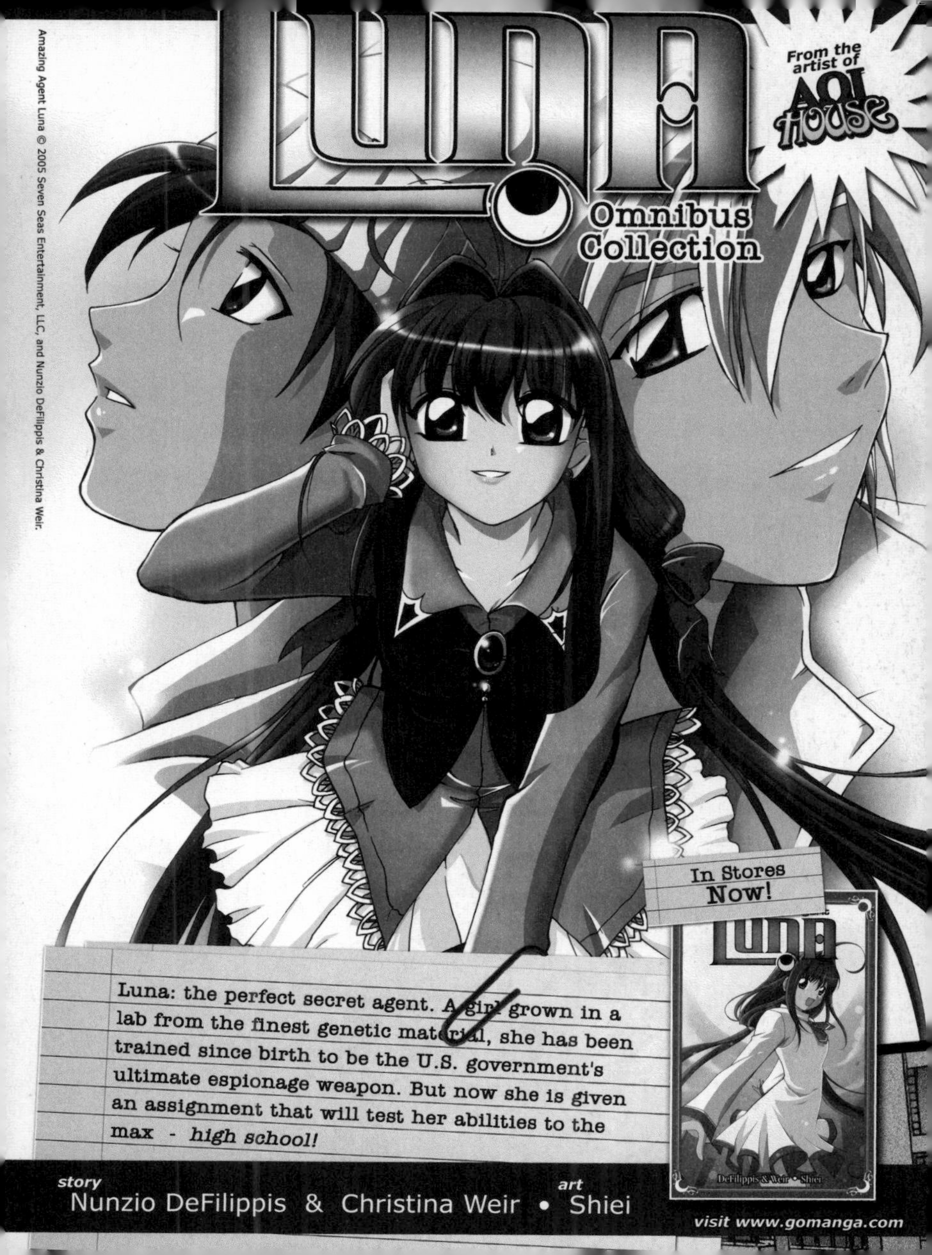
Luna
Omnibus Collection
From the artist of Aoi House
In Stores Now!
Luna: the perfect secret agent. A girl grown in a lab from the finest genetic material, she has been trained since birth to be the U.S. government's ultimate espionage weapon. But now she is given an assignment that will test her abilities to the max - *high school!*
story
Nunzio DeFilippis & Christina Weir • art Shiei
visit www.gomanga.com
Amazing Agent Luna © 2005 Seven Seas Entertainment, LLC, and Nunzio DeFilippis & Christina Weir.

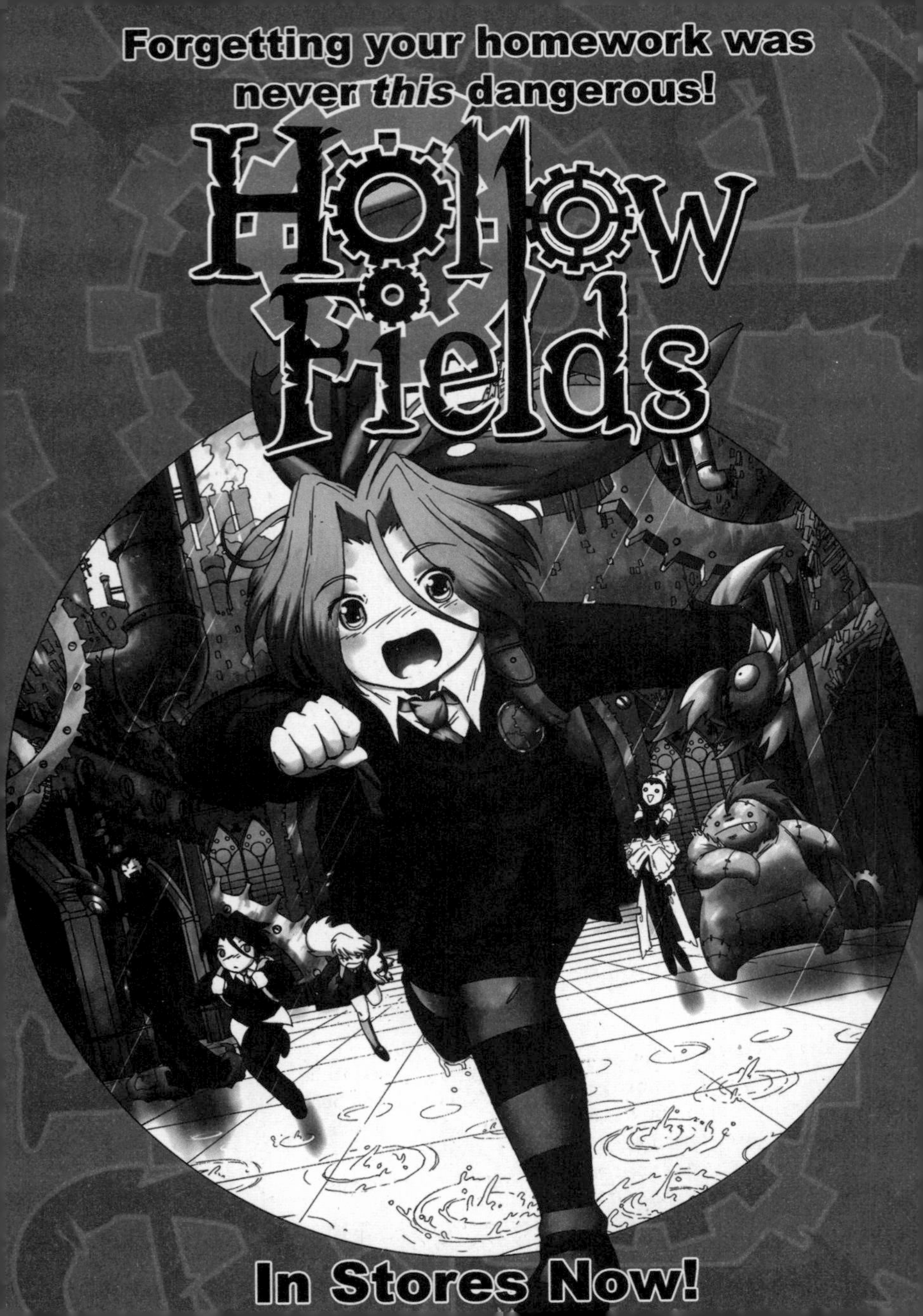
Forgetting your homework was never *this* dangerous!
Hollow Fields
In Stores Now!

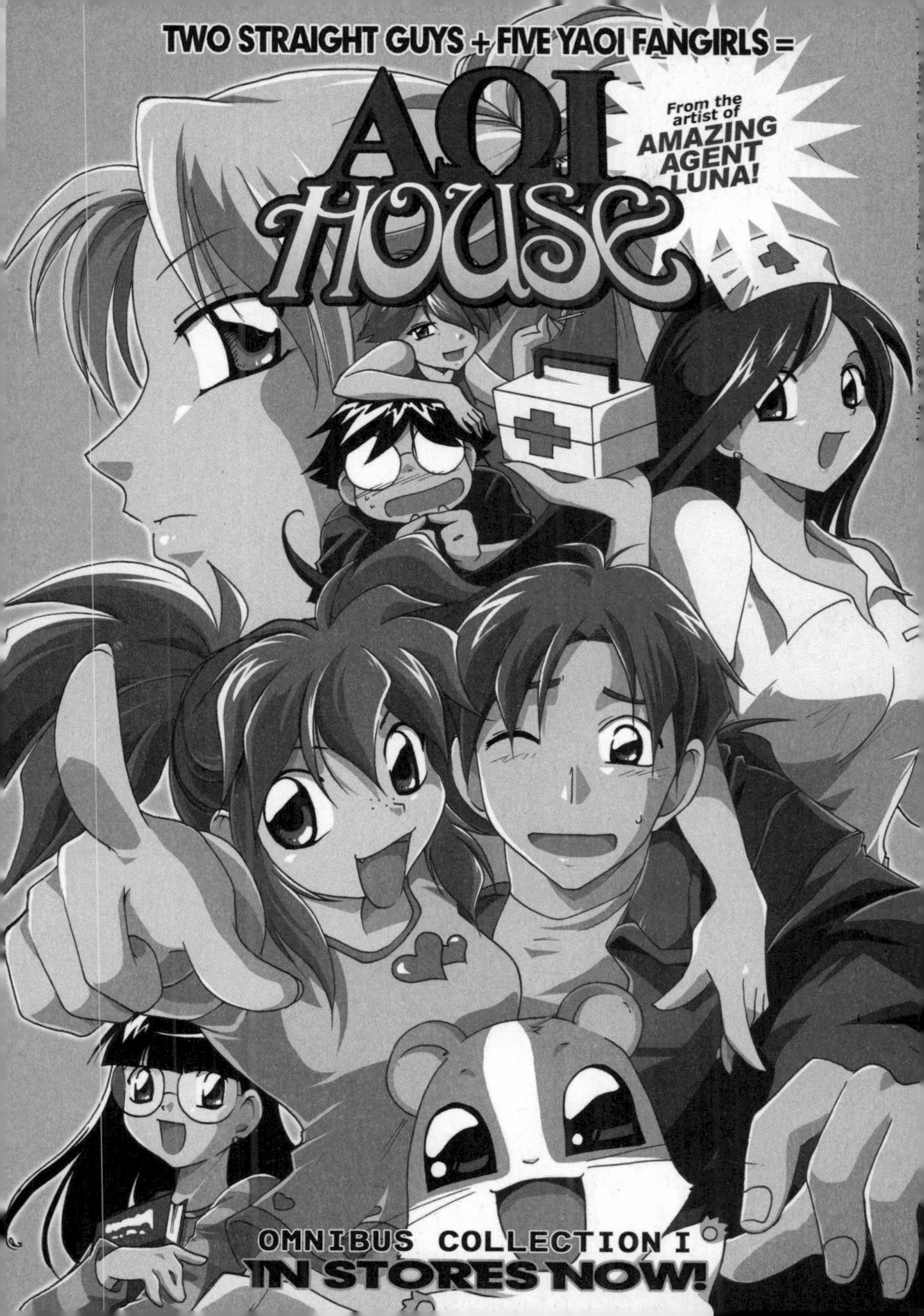
TWO STRAIGHT GUYS + FIVE YAOI FANGIRLS =
AOI HOUSE
From the artist of AMAZING AGENT LUNA!
OMNIBUS COLLECTION I
IN STORES NOW!

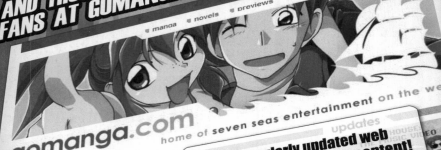

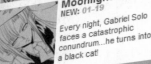
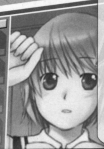

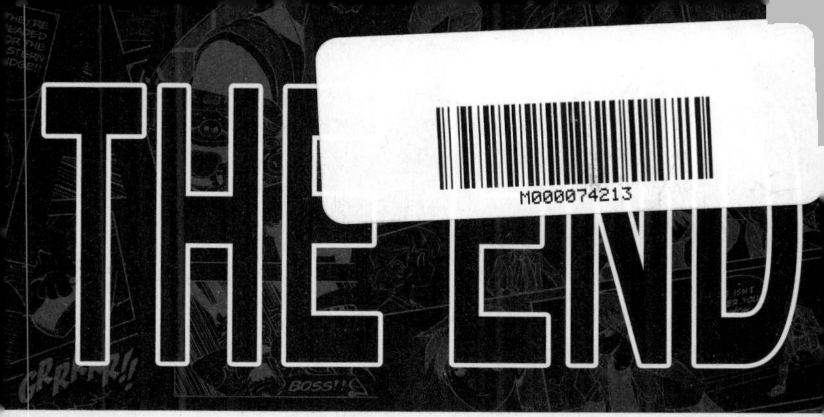
THE END
BOSS!!

YOU'RE READING THE WRONG WAY

This is the last page of
Hayate X Blade Volume 3

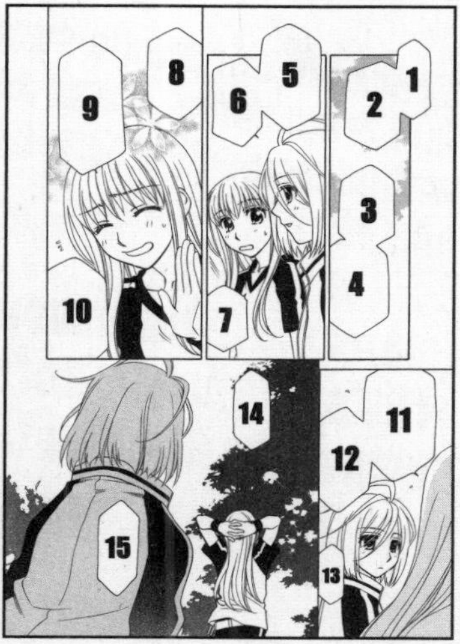
1
2
3
4
5
6
7
8
9
10
11
12
13
14
15

This book reads from right to left, Japanese style. To read from the beginning, flip the book over to the other side, start with the top right panel, and take it from there.

If this is your first time reading manga, just follow the diagram. It may seem backwards at first, but you'll get used to it! Have fun!